SECURITY MANAGEMENT, INTEGRITY, AND INTERNAL CONTROL IN INFORMATION SYSTEMS

IFIP – The International Federation for Information Processing

IFIP was founded in 1960 under the auspices of UNESCO, following the First World Computer Congress held in Paris the previous year. An umbrella organization for societies working in information processing, IFIP's aim is two-fold: to support information processing within its member countries and to encourage technology transfer to developing nations. As its mission statement clearly states,

> *IFIP's mission is to be the leading, truly international, apolitical organization which encourages and assists in the development, exploitation and application of information technology for the benefit of all people.*

IFIP is a non-profitmaking organization, run almost solely by 2500 volunteers. It operates through a number of technical committees, which organize events and publications. IFIP's events range from an international congress to local seminars, but the most important are:

- The IFIP World Computer Congress, held every second year;
- Open conferences;
- Working conferences.

The flagship event is the IFIP World Computer Congress, at which both invited and contributed papers are presented. Contributed papers are rigorously refereed and the rejection rate is high.

As with the Congress, participation in the open conferences is open to all and papers may be invited or submitted. Again, submitted papers are stringently refereed.

The working conferences are structured differently. They are usually run by a working group and attendance is small and by invitation only. Their purpose is to create an atmosphere conducive to innovation and development. Refereeing is less rigorous and papers are subjected to extensive group discussion.

Publications arising from IFIP events vary. The papers presented at the IFIP World Computer Congress and at open conferences are published as conference proceedings, while the results of the working conferences are often published as collections of selected and edited papers.

Any national society whose primary activity is in information may apply to become a full member of IFIP, although full membership is restricted to one society per country. Full members are entitled to vote at the annual General Assembly, National societies preferring a less committed involvement may apply for associate or corresponding membership. Associate members enjoy the same benefits as full members, but without voting rights. Corresponding members are not represented in IFIP bodies. Affiliated membership is open to non-national societies, and individual and honorary membership schemes are also offered.

SECURITY MANAGEMENT, INTEGRITY, AND INTERNAL CONTROL IN INFORMATION SYSTEMS

IFIP TC-11 WG 11.1 & WG 11.5 Joint Working Conference

Edited by

Paul Dowland
University of Plymouth

Steve Furnell
University of Plymouth

Bhavani Thuraisingham
University of Texas at Dallas

X. Sean Wang
The University of Vermont

Library of Congress Control Number: 2005934522

Security Management, Integrity, and Internal Control in Information Systems
Edited by Paul Dowland, Steve Furnell, Bhavani Thuraisingham, and X. Sean Wang

p. cm. (IFIP International Federation for Information Processing, a Springer Series in Computer Science)

ISSN: 1571-5736 / 1861-2288 (Internet)
ISBN-10: 0-387-29826-6
ISBN-13: 9780-387-29826-6
Printed on acid-free paper

9 8 7 6 5 4 3 2 1 SPIN 11577348
springeronline.com

Conference Organizer

General Chairs

Steven Furnell, University of Plymouth
Bhavani Thuraisingham, University of Texas at Dallas

Program Committee Chairs

Paul Dowland, University of Plymouth
X. Sean Wang, University of Vermont

Local Arrangement Chair

Sushil Jajodia, George Mason University

Program Committee

Claudio Bettini, University of Milan, Italy
Andrzej Bialas, Institute of Control Systems, Poland
Jeimy Cano, Universidad de los Andes, Colombia
Gurpreet Dhillon, Virginia Commonwealth University, USA
Neil Doherty, Loughborough University, UK
Jean-Noel Ezingeard, Henley Management College, UK
Csilla Farkas, University of South Carolina, USA
William Hutchinson, Edith Cowan University, Australia
Murray Jennex, San Diego State University, USA
Jorma Kajava, University of Oulu, Finland
Virginia Kleist, West Virginia University, USA
Yingjiu Li, Singapore Management University, Singapore
Peng Liu, Pennsylvania State University, USA
Sean Maynard, University of Melbourne, Australia
Peng Ning, North Carolina State University, USA
Malcolm Pattinson. University of South Australia, Australia
Dalenca Pottas, Nelson Mandela Metropolitan Univ., South Africa
Chris Skalka, University of Vermont, USA
Leon Strous, De Nederlandsche Bank, The Netherlands
Paul Thompson, Dartmouth College, USA
Rossouw von Solms, Nelson Mandela Metro.Univ., South Africa
Jeremy Ward, Symantec, UK
Omar Zakaria, Royal Holloway University of London, UK
Albin Zuccato, Karlstad University, Sweden

Preface

This is the first joint working conference between the IFIP Working Groups 11.1 and 11.5. We hope this joint conference will promote collaboration among researchers who focus on the security management issues and those who are interested in integrity and control of information systems. Indeed, as management at any level may be increasingly held answerable for the reliable and secure operation of the information systems and services in their respective organizations in the same manner as they are for financial aspects of the enterprise, there is an increasing need for ensuring proper standards of integrity and control in information systems in order to ensure that data, software and, ultimately, the business processes are complete, adequate and valid for intended functionality and expectations of the owner (i.e. the user organization).

As organizers, we would like to thank the members of the international program committee for their review work during the paper selection process. We would also like to thank the authors of the invited papers, who added valuable contribution to this first joint working conference.

Paul Dowland
X. Sean Wang
December 2005

Contents

Session 6 – Security Management

Session 7 – Applications

Session 8 – Access Management (II)

SESSION 1 – SECURITY STANDARDS

INFORMATION SECURITY STANDARDS: ADOPTION DRIVERS (INVITED PAPER)

What drives organisations to seek accreditation? The case of BS 7799-2:2002

Jean-Noel Ezingeard and David Birchall
Henley Management College, Greenland, Henley-on-Thames, RG9 3AU, United Kingdom

Abstract: ISO/IEC 17799 is a standard governing Information Security Management. Formalised in the 1990s, it has not seen the take up of accreditations that could be expected from looking at accreditation figures for other standards such as the ISO 9000 series. This paper examines why this may be the case by investigating what has driven the accreditation under the standard in 18 UK companies, representing a fifth of companies accredited at the time of the research. An initial literature review suggests that adoption could be driven by external pressures, or simply an objective of improving operational performance and competitive performance. It points to the need to investigate the influence of Regulators and Legislators, Competitors, Trading Partners and Internal Stakeholders on the decision to seek accreditation.

An inductive analysis of the reasons behind adoption of accreditation and its subsequent benefits suggests that competitive advantage is the primary driver of adoption for many of the companies we interviewed. We also find that an important driver of adoption is that the standard enabled organisations to access best practice in Information Security Management thereby facilitating external relationships and communication with internal stakeholders. Contrary to the accepted orthodoxy and what could be expected from the literature, increased regulation and the need to comply with codes of practice are not seen as significant drivers for companies in our sample.

Key words: Information Security, Adoption, ISO/IEC 17799, ISO/IEC 27001, BS 7799, Best practice

1. INTRODUCTION

BS7799 was initiated in the UK in 1993 as a "Code of Practice" for Information Security Management. It was inspired by a UK ministry (the Department of Trade and Industry – DTI) in co-operation with a number of leading commercial organisations including Shell and a number of major banks, who were perceived as highly developed in security techniques. The Code of Practice became a British Standard in 1995. Globalisation, and the requirement for common security standards encouraged propagation and recognition of BS7799 worldwide, culminating in it becoming the ISO standard ISO/IEC 17799:2000. Further work was done by the British Standards Institution on Management Systems for Information Security, leading to the publication of BS7799 part 2 (BSI, 2002). Although this was not adopted as part of the International Standard, it is used in many countries other than the UK, such as Sweden, Finland, Norway, Japan, China (Hong-Kong), India, Australia, Taiwan and Korea (Waloff, 2002). BS7799 part 2 is expected to be replaced by ISO/IEC 27001:2005 in late 2005 (BSI, 2005). Until then, companies seeking some form of accreditation must do so under BS 7799 Part 2:2002.

Proponents of the standard argue that significant benefits can be gained from its implementation. For instance, the introduction to the Information Security Management Systems (ISMS) part of the standard emphasises the benefits of adoption:

> "The ISMS is designed to ensure adequate and proportionate security controls that adequately protect information assets and give confidence to customers and other interested parties. This can be translated into maintaining and improving competitive edge, cash flow, profitability, legal compliance and commercial image." (BSI, 2002, p3)

From its inception the code received much attention, but as far back as 1996, concerns were raised about its uptake. At the time, a survey of 1452 organisations based in the UK had shown that adoption, or indeed intention to adopt, were very low despite the wide-spread publicity given to the standard at the time (Kearvell-White, 1996). In 2004, awareness of the standard and its detailed content was still thought to be low (DTI, 2004). Perhaps not surprisingly, certification figures for BS 7799 Part 2:2002 themselves are running significantly below 100 organisations in most European countries, as shown in *Table 1*. Some commentators argue that certification figures themselves do not provide an accurate picture of the take-up as many companies choose to use only part of the standard and prefer an incremental approach than full 'all or nothing' certification (von

Solms and von Solms, 2001). In particular, it has been argued that general standards such as ISO 17799 are not always helpful in their entirety because they do not take into consideration the unique circumstances of each company (Baskerville and Siponen, 2002). However, the number of registrations for other standards is strikingly higher than those for BS 7799 Part 2:2002, with over 242,000 accreditations in Europe alone for ISO 9001:2000 (ISO, 2003) and it is legitimate to hypothesise that there is mismatch between what accreditation under BS 7799-2:2002 offers and what companies seek.

Table 1: Number of BS 7799 Part 2:2002 certificates issued in Europe since the creation of the standard. Source: www.xisec.com (31/08/2005)

Country	No. of Certificates	Country	No. of Certificates
Czech Rep	5	Iceland	4
Lithuania	1	Poland	5
Luxembourg	1	Switzerland	8
Macedonia	1	Sweden	7
Romania	1	Norway	10
Slovakia	2	Ireland	11
Slovenia	1	Hungary	13
Belgium	2	Finland	15
Denmark	2	Netherlands	21
Greece	4	Italy	26
Spain	4	Germany	42
Austria	8	UK	212

Despite the low take up of certification for BS 7799 Part 2:2002, the number of calls for greater attention to be paid to Information Security Management have not abated since the inception of the standard. The topic of Information Assurance is now of such concern for governments and international agencies that many have created specialized units to promote the adoption of standards and best practice. For instance the UK government created a specialist division in its Cabinet Office in April 2003 (the Central Sponsor for Information Assurance). At European level this takes the form of the European Network and Information Security Agency (ENISA) created in 2004.

Why then, are there such low certification figures for BS 7799 Part 2:2002 ? This paper attempts to provide a partial answer to the question by investigating what has driven adoption in a sample of companies that are currently accredited. It is organized as follows: Firstly a conceptual framework of adoption drivers is built from the literature. We then describe our research methodology, arguing for an inductive approach based on semi-structured interviews. Lastly, the results of the research are presented in the form of resulting propositions and discussed in a concluding section.

2. LITERATURE REVIEW

We have found little literature directly discussing adoption and certification drivers for BS 7799 Part 2:2002. Consequently we identified three other streams of literature that could help inform our interview questions. Firstly we examined both the practitioner and the academic literature on ISO/IEC 17799 and BS 7799 to identify what *benefits* could be expected or gained from adoption and subsequent accreditation. Secondly, we identified selected references from the literature on technology adoption (including the adoption of security measures) to help us build a picture of general adoption drivers. Thirdly we reviewed the literature on the adoption of other international standards such as ISO 9000 or ISO 9001. Whilst not directly related to the topic of ISO 17799 adoption, the latter two streams offer sufficient theoretical grounding about adoption to help build an interview framework when triangulated with the practitioner literature on ISO/IEC 17799 adoption and BS 7799 certification.

Both practitioner and academic literature on ISO 17799 are quite coy about the potential benefits of adoption and/or certification. There are broadly four categories of benefits that emerge. A summary is given in *Table 2*. Perhaps not surprisingly, given the emphasis placed in the Information Security literature on the need to raise awareness, 'communication' benefits features are often associated with adoption of the standard as the most quoted benefits. The standard is thought of as a good way to demonstrate commitment, demonstrate good practice and reassure. It is also seen as a way to convince or coach both internal and external stakeholders. The second most quoted type of benefit associated with the standard is connected with best practice adoption that the standard should facilitate. Lastly, although more rarely quoted, other business benefits associated with the standard in the literature include operational and competitive benefits.

Table 2: Benefits of ISO 17799 adoption as expressed in practitioner and academic literature

Category	Benefits	Source
Communication with internal stakeholders	Provides an accepted benchmark that facilitates communication with stakeholders	(Pattinson, 2003, Velayudham et al., 2004)
	Helps change staff behaviour	(DTI, 2004)

	Helps Information Security Managers gain senior management recognition	(Li et al., 2000)
Communication with external stakeholders	Enhances trust between business partners	(Barnard and von Solms, 1998)
	Can facilitate trading or procurement of IT services	(von Solms, 1998)
	Useful / requirement to gain cyber-insurance	(Groves, 2003)
Enhanced operational or competitive performance	Helps achieve efficiency and effectiveness	(DTI, 2004) (Note: Efficiency and effectiveness are not clearly defined in the report)
	Helps reduce the costs of security incidents	(Kenning, 2001)
Best practice	Provides guidance in an otherwise complex field, 'useful framework'	(Armstrong et al., 2002, Gossels, 2003, McAdams, 2004)
	Can aid policy development	(Baskerville and Siponen, 2002, Fulford and Doherty, 2003)
	Facilitates the adoption of minimum standards, common security baselines.	(Brooks et al., 2002, Kearvell-White, 1996)

Having identified what benefits were often associated with the adoption of ISO 17799, we also reviewed what triggered other adoption of innovative practices and new technology. A first stream of literature on technology adoption has traditionally focused on the motivation of individual users to adopt IT artefacts or software (for instance research on technology acceptance, such as Venkatesh et al., 2003). A second stream, more relevant in our case, is the literature looking at organisational factors motivating the acceptance of technology at firm level.

In examining this side of the literature we sought to identify groupings of factors that drive adoption. A large proportion of published research of firm level technology adoption decisions is grounded in the strategic positioning school that argues that competitive advantage can be gained from technology if it influences the competitive position of the firm (Ives and Learmonth, 1984). Furthermore, this school of though argues that competitive pressures can act as drivers of implementation.

A good example of such pressures can be found in the literature on the adoption of Electronic Data Interchange (EDI) technology. Here, competitive positioning factors have been found to be particularly relevant in pushing firms to take up the technology. In particular, the bargaining power of trading partners is an important influence in driving the adoption of EDI in small firms (Hart and Saunders 1997; 1998). Earlier, Iacovou *et al.* (1995) had also identified competitive pressure and imposition by trading partners as two types of external pressure that encourage take up. They argued that three key factors that affect drive implementation in this range of organisations are: perceived benefits; organisational readiness; *and* external pressure. Such pressures are not confined to adoption decisions pertaining to technological innovation. Of particular relevance to our general problem area, the coercive effect of powerful trading partners has also been found to play a significant role in the adoption of ISO 9000 (Guler et al., 2002). Interestingly, Guler *et al.*'s study also shows that in the case of ISO 9000, coercive effects also came from Nation States.

Another school of strategy used to examine adoption drivers of technological innovation is that of the Resource Based View of the firm which argues that competitive advantage can be obtained when technology is used to create or exacerbate differences between competitors (Dehning and Stratopoulos, 2003, Feeny and Ives, 1990, Griffiths and Finlay, 2004). Such differences have been found to be a factor playing a role in the sustainability of the advantage (Anderson et al., 1999), particularly where the resources at the source of the difference are not freely mobile (Mata et al., 1995). The idea of *asymmetry*, whether informational, technological or structural, is diametrically opposed to that of *standardisation.* Specifically, the accreditation to any standard is particularly 'mobile' in that standards are widely published. Therefore, the adoption of an international standard and subsequent accreditation, for differentiation purposes may seem paradoxical. However, in the case of ISO 9000 adoption, it has been found that many firms did seek differentiation through take up and subsequent accreditation (Anderson et al., 1999). In such cases the differentiation was sought between firms that were accredited and those that were not. This is akin to Clemons and Row's argument (1991) that there are cases where the first mover advantage is significant in affording an organisation competitive advantage from differentiation and that customer preferences may change to favour the innovator.

In summary, the literature on ISO 17799, the literature on technology adoption and the literature on the adoption of other standards yield to a theoretical classification of adoption and/or certification drivers based on:

- Adoption driven by external pressures, or coercion (such as trading partners or States)
  a) Because certification is a 'licence to trade'
  b) Because certification helps demonstrate superior Information Security performance to potential trading partners

- Adoption driven by the desire to seek competitive or operational advantage through superior Information Security
  a) Because adoption and/or certification will yield, or help achieve, better Information Security practices
  b) Because adoption will help create resource asymmetry that can then be marketed to internal and external stakeholders and customers.

This points to the need to examine the influence of four key contextual aspects of the decision to seek accreditation and its benefits: competitors, trading partners, legislators and regulators and internal stakeholders. This is illustrated in figure 1. Furthermore, because the acquisition of best practice features as a potential motivator, there is a need to examine the accreditation process itself, including the role of consultants and the factors influencing the success of the process.

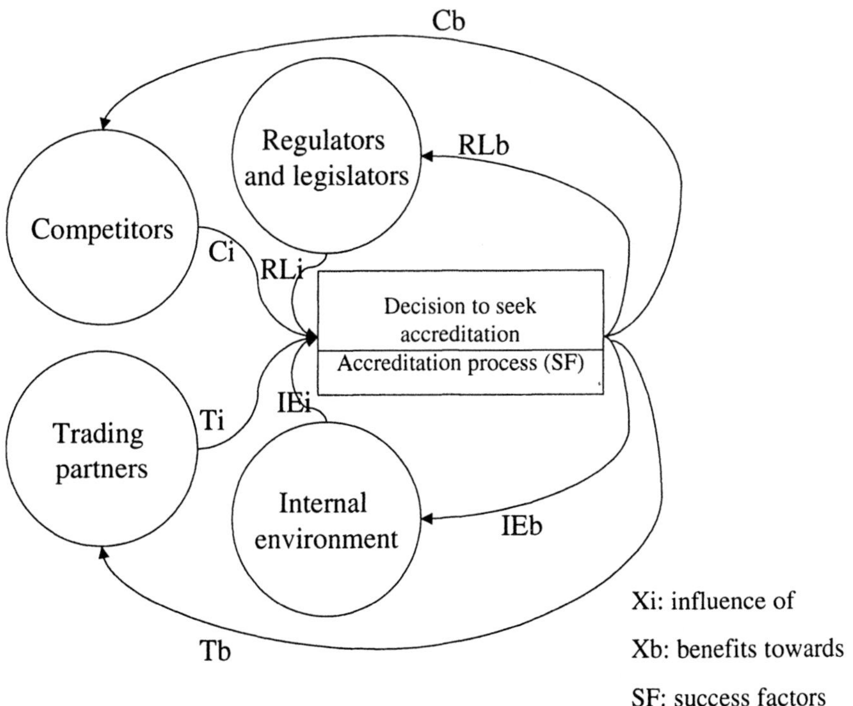

Figure 1. Model of theoretical influences on companies seeking ISO 17799 accreditation and resulting benefits

3. METHODOLOGY

3.1 Research context

The empirical context for the research carried out is complex for two practical reasons. The first is that many organisations are reluctant to discuss their information security arrangements. This lead Kotulic and Clark (2004) to suggest that large scale surveys in the area of information security have a very small chance of attracting a sufficient number of participants to produce worthwhile results. They suggest that "time is better spent focusing on a few selected firms with which the researcher has developed an excellent rapport and trust" (p 605). This potential difficulty was exacerbated by a very pragmatic and simple factor: that the low number of companies accredited (see *Table 1*) would make it very difficult to get statistically meaningful response numbers from a survey.

From an epistemological point of view, the literature review so far has shown that an interpretive approach is needed at this stage of understanding of adoption factors for BS 7799-2:2002 accreditation. Interpretive research in IS is "aimed at producing an understanding of the context of the information system, and the process whereby the information system influences and is influenced by the context" (Walsham, 1993, p4). Although our review of the literature has produced a theoretical classification of adoption drivers which could be used as the basis of a research model and hypothesis, it would be inappropriate to carry on the study relying on what Lee calls "hypothetico-deductive logic" (Lee, 1999). This is because we were interested in gaining further insights under each of the potential drivers identified in the literature review, rather than trying to examine whether they contributed or not to the adoption decision. The literature review has shown that a better understanding of the *context* of the adoption decisions is needed, for instance to understand what external pressures are at play when organisations examine how competitive or operational advantage can be gained through accreditation. Similarly, a better understanding of the *process* by which the context (competitive, legislative or internal) influences the decision to seek accreditation is necessary to explain the true nature of potential external pressures for adoption.

3.2 Research approach

In order to investigate what the adoption drivers behind BS 7799-2:2002 certifications were, we chose an interview-based approach. This was done because of the empirical context explained earlier (difficulties in gaining access and low number of organisations accredited). Because we opted for exploratory, inductive research; we felt that semi-structured interviews would yield greater insights.

We initially developed an interview framework on the basis of the theoretical headings identified in the literature review, although the questions listed in the interview framework (Appendix 1) were used as prompts rather than rigidly followed by the interviewer. Interviews were taped and transcribed by the interviewer. This was done as soon as possible after the interview and ensured that gaps could be bridged from the context. The interviews lasted between 40 and 90 minutes. Our interview base was selected from the published lists of companies that had achieved accreditation under BS 7799-2:2002. Companies were initially approached by phone, either through a 'cold call' or through contacts from the research team. As such, a large amount of convenience sampling is present in our interview pool (shown in appendix 2). As part of this convenience sampling process, we selected two companies we knew (subject 12 and subject 17) that have not actually sought formal 7799 accreditation. However both operate very closely with many of the terms of the certificate. This base represents around a fifth of all UK organisations accredited at the time of the research.

3.3 Analysis procedure

The interpretation of the interview data was based on a simple coding process of the interview transcripts. We used the technique recommended by Miles and Huberman (1994, p58) of a "start-list" of codes (in our case Ci, Cb, Ti, Tb, RLi, RLb, Iei, IEb and SF as shown in figure 1). This was sufficient to allow us to develop the propositions presented in the results section below, and codes were not augmented or revised during the process. Our objective for the analysis was twofold. Firstly we sought to discover regularities, patterns and themes that would deepen our understanding of the theoretical drivers that emerged from the literature review, and the processes through which they influenced the decision to seek accreditation. Secondly we sought to identify new drivers that we had not envisaged from the literature. Again, the process through which they were at play was examined.

4. RESULTING PROPOSITIONS

4.1 Competitive Advantage as a primary motivator

Our model of theoretical influences suggests that competitors and trading partners will influence and benefit from accreditation. In examining the data around Ci, Ti, Cb, and Tb in our interviews we were able to describe theses influences further as they manifested themselves mostly under the heading of 'competitive advantage'. For instance, when asked about their primary motivators for seeking accreditation, a large number of respondents (subjects 3, 4, 5, 7, 10, 13, 14, 15, 17, 18) quoted 'competitive advantage'. Perhaps not surprisingly (most of these companies are providers of IT solutions in one way or another), competitive advantage was described by the interviewee as derived from the improved image that ISO 17799 and accreditation under BS 7799-2:2002 would give the organisation. This improved image could be used as a marketing tool and help generate customer confidence. Many argued that in their sector, accreditation was seen as a primary source of credibility and that customers were increasingly demanding that their suppliers should be accredited. In the words of subject 10, many customers *"asked questions [about Information Security] and sought proof... The external certification clarifies this and grounds it in an independent third party measure"*. For many companies that linked accreditation with improved image, there is no doubt that the 'rubber stamp' provided by the certificate was a motivator. As pointed out by subject 4, the certificate is clearly shown on business cards and email signatures issued by employees of his company.

In addition to improved image with customers or potential customers, subject 10 linked accreditation to competitive advantage because it gave his company the opportunity to *"attract investors by signifying a good quality company with well established procedures"*.

For those companies that did not operate in IT services, competitive advantage through accreditation was seen as much more difficult to obtain. For instance subject 7 suggested that their customers, were influential as an accreditation driver through their security expectations, albeit *"..the majority will have no idea of the meaning and definition of 7799."* Here accreditation is seen as a mechanism for the company to improve its Information Security Management, rather than a 'rubber stamp'. Only one interviewee (subject 3) linked competitive advantage from accreditation as derived from enhanced Intellectual Property protection.

4.2 Increased regulation and the need for compliance are not significant drivers

Increased regulation and the need to comply with codes of practice are often quoted as key drivers of the Information Security efforts of organisations. The standard itself suggests that 17799 compliance should help maintain legislative compliance. Compliance with legislation is the last of its 12 control objectives (ISO, 2000, para 4.1.1) – in other words, a company that does not comply with legislation pertaining to Information Security and Data Protection cannot be accredited as compliant under ISO 17799. In practice, compliance was not seen as a key motivator for implementation in organisations we interviewed. Out of 18 interviewees, only one (subject 14) quoted regulation – the need to comply with the Turnbull report, which sets out Corporate Governance standards in the UK (Turnbull, 1999) – as a motivator of their implementation.

Can this be interpreted as a lack of interest in compliance? Perhaps not so. For instance company 6 has linked its internal auditing procedures with 7799. The interviewee argued that as a result of BS 7799, the audit process was now *"probably tougher"*, indicating that the standard has a role to play in aiding compliance. A similar argument was used by subject 7 who pointed out that *"Ongoing compliance checks [for BS 7799] dovetail effectively with both internal and external audit"*. We also need to take into account that IT auditors and IT risk managers tend to use other frameworks for audit purposes (such as COBIT, see von Solms, 2005). Going back to our model in Figure 1, and more specifically RLi and RLb, our interpretation is that the need for compliance may be a positive moderator of the drive to seek accreditation, but not an influence. It is construed as a nice by-product of accreditation. Any further research should therefore start from this angle.

4.3 Access to, and delivery of, best practice

4.3.1 Best practice for its own sake, or as a lever?

More than half of the interviewees quoted access to best practice in Information Security Management as a motivator for their organisation to achieve compliance and seek accreditation under BS 7799-2:2002. Interestingly, best practice was seen by our interviewees as desirable for two reasons that are different, even though linked. The first reason is access to information and expertise. Some interviewees indicated that accreditation was helpful to their company in its efforts to achieve best practice in Information Security terms. Accreditation was seen as a way to access proven Information Security Management methods. This was the case for subjects 3, 7, 8, 9, 10, 12, 15 and 18. In the words of subject 18, the standard was adopted because it is his company's policy *"that recognized international standards and best practice are incorporated into defining policy and ways of working"*, and as pointed out by subject 10, *"In reality 7799 is purely best practice"*.

The second reason why best practice as embodied by ISO 17799 was seen as desirable by interviewees was in fact connected to the ability, conferred by accreditation, to justify encouraging employees to adhere to 'safe' practices. In the words of subject 2 describing the standard, *"employees can see it is best practice and efficient and it becomes a "standard" way of doing things"*. In a similar vein, other interviewees seemed to take the view that the 'Best Practice' argument could be used as a lever to convince reluctant stakeholders to adopt procedures that might otherwise be seen as cumbersome. For instance subject 6 explained: *"People now accept rules as best practice"*. A similar argument was given by subject 13. In her words: *"Workload has increased slightly due to the adoption of best practice security. However employees generally seem to understand this"*. We also came across evidence in the interviews that this lever was seen as useful to encourage greater attention from top-management to Information Security. As pointed out by subject 3, *"generally 7799 has improved awareness of the importance of security at a Corporate Governance level."*

Looking back at our theoretical model and more specifically the 'IEi' arrow, our interpretation of the interview data so far is therefore that best practice is conceptualised in two ways regarding BS 7799-2:2002 accreditation: as a goal that accreditation can help achieve, but also as a powerful argument to convince (internal) sceptics. Interestingly we also found a third set of views connecting best practice and BS 7799-2:2002 accreditation: that the accreditation process may not actually help. This is discussed next.

4.3.2 Is best practice really achievable through certification?

In looking at the 'IEb' arrow of our original model, we came across, very early in our interview process, mixed views about the value, in best practice terms, of the accreditation process. This was invariably linked to views that more value could have been gained by organisations from the accreditation audit. Firstly, in some cases it appeared that doubts could be raised about the level of expertise and training of the auditors. In the words of subject 3 for instance, *"early audits were the blind leading the blind due to a lack of experience* [of the auditors]". A similar view was echoed by subject 5 as he explained: *"During the initial audits it was clear both auditor and auditee were very much in a learning process due to the recent introduction of the standard"*.

Whilst these two interviewees were the most pessimistic about the opportunities for the accreditation process to be a source of best practice insights, others also expressed unease with the process itself. The auditors' 'style' was quoted by subjects 2, 8, 14 and 16 as being too driven by procedural compliance checks, rather than focussed on providing value. The second aspect of why value from accreditation is not gained, in the form of access to best practice, is therefore that accreditation is sometimes construed as a checking process rather than an enabling one. Only in the eyes of one of our interviewees was the tension between the auditors' role as impartial assessors and their role as sources of knowledge of best practice resolved. This was the case of subject 15 who explained that the BS 7799-2:2002 auditors *"were able to make valid contributions"*.

4.4 The role of senior management

The ISO 17799 standard itself stipulates that management involvement is key. Part 1 states that *"Information security is a business responsibility shared by all members of the management team"* (ISO, 2000, para 4.1.1) , but Part 2 of the British Standard goes further by making evidence of management commitment a requirement. In looking at implementation drivers, it is interesting to go beyond evidence of management commitment at the time when the accreditation is sought, to look at the role of management in *initiating* or *driving* the accreditation process, or if the initiative for accreditation is not originating from top management, what drivers will lead to top management support.

When looking at management commitment to implementation in order to probe the 'SF' construct in our original model, the picture that emerged from our interviews is that all organisations witnessed strong commitment from their senior management *during* implementation. Terms used by our interviewees about their top management's attitudes ranged from *"fully supported"* (subject 6) to *"actively involved"* (subject 18) and *"extremely supportive"* (subject 16). It was clear that those responsible for initiating the accreditation process had managed to gain commitment from senior managers in all the organisations we interviewed. But what led to their support? Here the evidence is more mixed, and our interpretation of the data is that there are two groups of circumstances leading to top management support.

The first set of circumstances occurred in companies where top management was convinced by evidence from the market that accreditation is necessary. We found this was the case in companies represented by subject 3, where top management *"frequently need to be persuaded of the benefits"*. In another organisation *"pressure from customers and the market needs also played an important part in pushing management to support the certification process"* (subject 5). In the case of subject 7, the *"CEO was converted as a result of the competitive advantage and customer security [that accreditation would confer]"*.

The second set of circumstances occurred in organisations where the awareness of technological matters at senior management level is high. This was the case in the companies represented by subjects 2, 10 and 15. Company 2 for instance has a very 'IT oriented' Managing Director who needed little convincing that accreditation was necessary. The company's web-site actually lists her areas of responsibilities as Operations, but also, Field Operations, and IT. Similarly, in the case of company 10 and 15, both respondents suggested that given the markets their companies operated in and their respective cultures, engaging top management and obtaining their support was relatively easy.

5. CONCLUSION

As argued in the introduction, there is a need to understand what motivates organisations to adopt ISO 17799 and seek accreditation under BS 7799-2:2002. This research has contributed to this understanding, firstly at a theoretical level, and secondly by investigating, in some depth, what has driven 18 UK companies to adopt the standard and seek accreditation. We will pick up on two salient findings from our research here. Firstly, it has shown that, in the organisations we interviewed, competitive advantage was often seen as a significant driver of adoption – whereas regulation and encouragement from Information Security bodies, governments and other trade associations very rarely featured in our interviewees' responses. This is contrary to the orthodoxy found amongst many advocates of the 7799 standards as a demonstrably robust control system. This is significant in that it suggests that the message from these third parties perhaps needs to be realigned to emphasise the competitive benefits of adoption and certification.

Here we can speculate that whilst the 'compliance' message may be of interest to auditors, it is likely that the primary initiators of BS 7799-2:2002 accreditation will belong to an Information Systems community of practice where compliance may not be considered as a significant business issue.

The second, paradoxical findings that seems to emerge is about the nature of the intent to adopt best practice through accreditation. Here, we found that the argument of best practice was often used as an internal lever to convince perhaps reluctant employees or senior management to change their behaviour and support changed Information Security practices. At first sight this could be a worrying management practice – and perhaps counter productive in the long term if changes in attitude as well as behaviour are not achieved. It would be beyond the scope of this paper to discuss the organisational politics implications of the practice we unearthed, but is worth asking whether it falls within Information Systems phenomena that and can be used to reduce emancipation by alienating workers (Angell, 1990, p. 173). The main drawback of such an approach, according to Angell is that that managers make the process of security too complex, uncertain and unimaginative. Risk Management actions are, according to Ciborra (2004), *"intertwined in social processes and networks of relationships"*. Many similar observations are grounded in the psychology of risk literature, and the argument that *"risk is what matters to people"* (Renn, 1998). This therefore suggests that accreditation under BS 7799-2:2002 can sometimes act as a pre-requisite to a change towards a culture of best practice, as much as a response to regulatory and competitive pressures to demonstrate that best practice has been achieved.

Finally, we should reflect on the limitations of the work presented here and potential avenues for further research. The fist limitation is largely unavoidable: because there are few organisations accredited worldwide, it is impossible to get a very large sample base for this kind of research. This is compounded by the fact that access to organisations in Information Security research is generally difficult (Kotulic and Clark, 2004). The second limitation is more conceptual. In looking at adoption drivers in those companies that are compliant with the standard and that have sought accreditation, we have left out those companies that have decided *against* accreditation, and instead have chosen partial adoption, or rejected the standard altogether. Whilst knowing why those that have adopted have done so, the picture this provides is by nature partial and can only to some extent help answer the puzzle of why there are so few companies accredited. An interesting line of further enquiry would therefore be to attempt to collect data about what factors influences the decisions of non-adopters of accreditation.

APPENDIX 1: INTERVIEW FRAMEWORK

Heading	Interviewee prompts
Organization Background	What is your: primary activity, target markets sectors, geographic coverage: What (qualified) information security human resources are available within your organisation? Do you outsource any Information Security tasks, if so which, and to what extent? What information security risks exist in the environment in which your business operates?
Adoption and Accreditation process	How wide is the current scope of certification within your organisation? How long did the accreditation process take? What effect did your organisation's size have upon implementation? What were the approximate costs sunk during the implementation process? Were external consultants appointed and how would you rate their effectiveness? What changes to your business processes were necessary during implementation?
Motivation and drivers	What were the primary motivations behind implementation? What effect did certification have upon communication - internal or external?
Benefits	What objectives or benefits were expected as a consequence of accreditation? Have these been achieved? What unforeseen benefits have accrued? How do you assess certification ROI?
Adoption Success Factors	What major barriers did you need to overcome during implementation? What do you consider to be the Critical Success Factors for certification? What lessons were learnt through the implementation process? What advice or guidance was available – i.e. from auditors or BSI?
Internal Stakeholders: Management	How influential was management to gaining accreditation? What management levels were involved and how?

Heading	Interviewee prompts
	How strong is their post implementation involvement?
Internal Stakeholders: Employees	How were employees encouraged to become part of the accreditation program? How critical was employee involvement to the accreditation process? How much training, and what methods were undertaken during accreditation? Has certification had an effect upon employee morale?
External Stakeholders: Governments and regulators	How influential were legal influences to the management's decision making process? What Government influences were apparent during the certification process? What other ISO standards are you certified to?
External Stakeholders: Customers	What are the customer expectations of information security? How do you promote certification as a source of CA in specific customers or markets? What impact has your accreditation had upon customers? Has Customer Satisfaction increased as a consequence of certification?
Other competitive position drivers	How have your competitors reacted to your gaining accreditation? How do you ensure the "security integrity" of third parties to which your systems are linked?
Best practice	How influential was 7799 in guiding process improvements? Do you consider your IT environment more secure as a consequence of implementation?

APPENDIX 2: INTERVIEWEES

Subject	Sector	Title or Department Represented	Type of Interview
1	Logistics	Head of Information Security & Governance	Face to face
2	Energy Metering Service Provider	Quality & Estates Manager	Face to face
3	Information Security Solutions Provider	Director	Telephone
4	Information Security Solutions Provider	Professional Services	Face to face

Subject	Sector	Title or Department Represented	Type of Interview
5	Outsourcing Partner	Quality Assurance Manager	Telephone
6	'big 4' professional services firm	Quality Manager	Face to face
7	Banking IT infrastructure provider	General Manager - Operations	Telephone
8	IT services	Senior Consultant	Telephone
9	Local Government	Head of Information Management	Face to face
10	Outsourcing Partner	Founder	Face to face
11	Insurance and Financial Services	Head of Information Assurance	Face to face
12	Energy	Global Information Security Manager	Telephone
13	Outsourcing Partner – IT services	Quality Manager	Telephone
14	Outsourcing Partner – IT services	Training & Quality Manager	Face to face
15	Information Security Solutions Provider	Technical Director	Face to face
16	Manufacturing	Director of Group Audit	Telephone
17	Publisher	Managing Director	Telephone
18	IT services	Chief Information Officer	Written response

REFERENCES

Anderson, S. W., Daly, J. D. & Johnson, M. F. (1999) Why firms seek ISO 9000 certification: Regulatory compliance or competitive advantage. *Production and Operations Management,* 8(1), 28-43.

Angell, I. O. (1990) Systems Thinking about Information Systems and Strategies. *Journal of Information Technology,* 5(3), 168-74.

Armstrong, J., Rhys-Jones, M. & Rathmell, A. (2002) Corporate Governance & Information Assurance - What Every Director Must Know. Information Assurance Advisory Council, Cambridge - UK.

Barnard, L. & von Solms, R. (1998) The evaluation and certification of information security against BS 7799. *Information Management & Computer Security,* 6(2), 72-77.

Baskerville, R. & Siponen, M. (2002) An information security meta-policy for emergent organizations. *Logistics Information Management,* 15(5/6), 337-46.

Brooks, W. J., Warren, M. J. & Hutchinson, W. (2002) A security evaluation criteria. *Logistics Information Management,* 15(5/6), 377-84.

BSI (2002) BS 7799-2:2002 Information security management systems - Specification with guidance for use. British Standards Institution.

BSI (2005) Frequently Asked Questions for BS 7799-2:2005, British Standards Institution. http://www.bsi-global.com/ICT/Security/27001faq.xalter visited on 31/08/2005

Ciborra, C. (2004) Digital Technologies and the Duality of Risk. *Discussion Paper - Centre for Analysis of Risk and Regulation, London School of Economics,* (27).

Clemons, E. K. & Row, M. C. (1991) Sustaining IT advantage: The role of Structural Differences. *MIS Quarterly,* 15(3), 275-92.

Dehning, B. & Stratopoulos, T. (2003) Determinants of a sustainable competitive advantage due to an IT-enabled strategy. *The Journal of Strategic Information Systems,* 12(1), 7-28.

DTI (2004) Information Security Breaches Survey. Department of Trade and Industry / PriceWaterhouseCoopers, London.

Feeny, D. F. & Ives, B. (1990) In Search of Sustainability: Reaping Long-term advantage from Investments in Information Technology. *Journal of Management Information Systems,* 7(1), 27-46.

Fulford, H. & Doherty, N. F. (2003) The application of information security policies in large UK-based organizations: an exploratory investigation. *Information Management and Computer Security,* 11(3), 106-14.

Gossels, J. (2003) Making Sensible Investments in Security. *Financial Executive,* 19(9), 46.

Griffiths, G. H. & Finlay, P. N. (2004) IS-enabled sustainable competitive advantage in financial services, retailing and manufacturing. *Journal of Strategic Information Systems.,* 13, 29-59.

Groves, S. (2003) The unlikely heroes of cyber security. *Information Management Journal,* 37(3), 34-40.

Guler, I., Guillén, M. F. & Macpherson, J. M. (2002) Global Competition, Institutions, and the Diffusion of Organizational Practices: The International Spread of ISO 9000 Quality Certificates. *Administrative Science Quarterly,* 47, 207-32.

ISO (2000) ISO/IEC 17799:2000 Code of practice for information security management. ISO, Geneva.

ISO (2003) The ISO Survey of ISO 9001:2000 and ISO 14001 Certificates. International Standards Organisation.

Ives, B. & Learmonth, G. P. (1984) The Information System as a competitive weapon. *Communications of the ACM,* 27(12), 1193-201.

Kearvell-White, B. (1996) National (UK) Computer Security Survey 1996. *Information Management & Computer Security,* 4(3), 3-17.

Kenning, M. J. (2001) Security Management Standard - ISO 17799/BS 7799. *BT Technology Journal; London,* 19(3), 132.

Kotulic, A. G. & Clark, J. G. (2004) Why there aren't more information security research studies. *Information & Management,* 41(5), 597-607.

Lee, A. S. (1999) Researching MIS. IN CURRIE, W. & GALLIERS, R. (Eds.) *Rethinking management information systems: an interdisciplinary perspective.* Oxford, Oxford University Press.

Li, H., King, G., Ross, M. & Staples, G. (2000) BS7799: A Suitable Model for Information Security Management. *Americas Conference on Information Systems.*

Mata, F. J., Fuerst, W. L. & Barney, J. B. (1995) Information technology and sustained competitive advantage: A resource-based analysis. *MIS Quarterly,* 19(4), 487-505.

McAdams, A. C. (2004) Security And Risk Management: A Fundamental Business Issue. *Information Management Journal,* 38(4), 36-44.

Miles, M. B. & Huberman, A. M. (1994) *Qualitative data analysis: an expanded sourcebook,* Thousand Oaks, Calif.; London, Sage.

Pattinson, M. R. (2003) Compliance with an Information Security Management Standard: A New Approach. *Ninth Americas Conference on Information Systems,* Tampa.

Renn, O. (1998) Three decades of risk research: accomplishments and new challenges. *Journal of Risk Research,* 1(1), 49-71.

Turnbull, N. (1999) Internal Control: Guidance for Directors on the Combined Code: *The Turnbull Report.* The Institute of Chartered Accountants in England & Wales, London.

Velayudham, C., Shoemaker, D. & Drommi, A. (2004) A Standard Methodology for Embedding Security Functionality Within Formal Specifications of Requirements. *Americas Conference on Information Systems,* New York, August 2004.

Venkatesh, V., Morris, M. G., Davis, G. B. & Davis, F. D. (2003) User acceptance of information technology: Toward a unified view. *MIS Quarterly,* 27(3), 425-78.

von Solms, B. (2005) Information Security governance: COBIT or ISO 17799 or both? *Computers & Security,* 24, 99-104.

von Solms, B. & von Solms, R. (2001) Incremental Information Security Certification. *Computers & Security,* 20(4), 308-10.

von Solms, R. (1998) Information security management (3): the Code of Practice for Information Security Management (BS 7799). *Information Management & Computer Security,* 6(5), 224.

Waloff, I. (2002) Speech by at "7799 Goes Global" conference. *(text available at http://www.bsi-global.com/News/Releases/2002/September/n3f029de8c689a.xalter),* September 5

Walsham, G. (1993) *Interpreting information systems in organizations,* Chichester, Wiley.

DATA QUALITY DIMENSIONS FOR INFORMATION SYSTEMS SECURITY: A THEORETICAL EXPOSITION (INVITED PAPER)

Gurvirender Tejay, Gurpreet Dhillon and Amita Goyal Chin
Department of Information Systems, School of Business, Virginia Commonwealth University, Richmond, Virginia, USA

Abstract: Data is an important asset used for various organizational activities. Poor data quality could have severe implications for information systems security in organizations. In this paper, data is viewed as embodied in the concept of signs. This paper identifies dimensions of data quality by using semiotics as a theoretical basis. We argue that the nature and scope of data quality dimensions changes as we move between different semiotic levels. An understanding of these changes is essential for ensuring information systems security.

Key words: Data quality, information quality, knowledge quality, semiotics, information systems security.

1. INTRODUCTION

Information systems (IS) security has become a core business processes in organizations (Trček, 2003). It not only deals with the computer systems but also the environment in which information is created and used (Armstrong, 1999). As Dhillon (1995) argues, "IS security can be viewed in terms of minimizing risks arising because of inconsistent and incoherent behavior with respect to the information handling activities of organizations." This has led to an increased concern associated with the protection of organizational information assets (Dhillon & Backhouse, 2000). As Feldman & March (1981, pp.177) argue:

> There is no institution more prototypically committed to the systematic application of information to decisions than the modern bureaucratic organization...Information is not simply a basis for action. It is a representation of competence and a reaffirmation of social virtue.

Data is a fundamental information asset. Dhillon & Backhouse (2000) acknowledge that the primary focus of IS security is on data. However, the authors argue for IS security research to also address the changing organizational context in which data is interpreted and used.

Various organizational activities require data in some form or manner. Wang *et al.* (2001) give a grim warning that important corporate initiatives are at a risk of failure unless data quality is seriously considered and improved. Redman (2001) argues that poor data quality would impact setting strategy, its execution, ability to derive value from data, and ability to align the organization. It would also affect decision-making capability, trust between organizations, customer satisfaction, and employee morale. These factors are in fact epidemic to the success of IS security initiatives in an organization. The argument of this research is that we need to understand the inter-dependent nature of data and information to identify the relevant dimensions of data quality. The use of these dimensions would be effective in solving the data quality problems, which in turn would bolster the IS security efforts of an organization.

This paper is organized into five sections. Following a brief introduction, section two presents the notion of signs and discusses the relationship between signs, data and IS security. It provides a basis for the use of semiotics to data quality. This section also explains semiotics and its main branches. Section three presents a semiotic interpretation of data quality dimensions based on the research literature. Section four provides a discussion on the lessons learned from the semiotic analysis of data quality. Finally, section five presents the conclusions.

2. SIGNS, DATA AND IS SECURITY

Peirce (as quoted in Falkenberg *et al.*, 1998, pp.51) defined sign "as something which stands to somebody for something in some respect or capacity." It is comprised of three constituent elements: the symbol (signifying), the referent (signified) and the concept or the idea of significance. Data is considered to be meaningful symbolic constructs, which are a finite "arrangement" of symbols taken from an alphabet (Falkenberg *et al.,* 1998). In other words, the above statements indicate that data is comprised of symbols, which are constituent elements of signs. As suggested by Stamper (1973), signs include the numerical and alphabetical characters, words, sentences, messages and the actions that are interpretable. That is, signs are the basis of data. This allows the use of semiotics as a theory for analyzing data quality dimensions. Semiotics is the process of analyzing signs (Liebenau & Backhouse, 1990). It is concerned with the properties of signs (Stamper, 1973). Semiotics helps in understanding how a sign is created, processed, and used.

The inherent complexity of data calls for using semiotics as a theoretical basis. Data has various explications depending upon the nature of its use. It is utilized at different levels of granularity and frequency. The same data is employed in a large variety of decision tasks and is also shared among multiple stakeholders - data providers, decision-makers, and data custodians. These myriad complexities need to be acknowledged so as to address the problems associated with data quality. Semiotics may be used as a framework to study complex problems where the function and structure of the problem do not lend to an adequate explanation (Nake, 2001).

Semiotics elucidates the intricacies associated with a sign as it moves from the physical world, where it is created, to the social world of norms, where a meaning is attached to it. Semiotic analysis can be used to understand the technical, formal and informal systems of an organization (Liebenau & Backhouse, 1990). Dhillon (1995) conceptualizes IS security in terms of these three sub-systems. Dhillon argues the technical level involves technology and system security measures, while formal rules and procedures address the IS security issues arising at the formal level. At the informal level, pragmatic concerns are paramount towards the development of security culture and environment (Dhillon, 1995).

Table 1. Semiotic levels

Semiotic level	Description
Pragmatics	Concerned with relationship between signs and behavior in context
Semantics	Study of meaning of signs
Syntactics	Study of logic and grammar of sign systems
Empirics	Study of physical properties of sets of signs used to transmit messages

Semiotics analyzes signs at four levels: empirics, syntactics, semantics and pragmatics (Table 1).

2.1 Empirics

Empirics is the study of the physical properties of signs. It is concerned with the signals used to code and transmit the message. It describes the physical characteristics of the medium of communication (Liebenau & Backhouse, 1990). Empirics involves the study of communication channels and their characteristics such as sound and electronic transmission. At an empiric level, signs are viewed as a collection of signals that need to be transmitted from one place to another through the communication channels. At this level, we do not consider what the signals are portraying or what they mean. Data quality at this level is concerned with different data types being generated. Ensuring that the integrity of data at an empirical level is maintained results in good communication and network security.

2.2 Syntactics

Syntactics is the study of logic and grammar of sign systems. It is concerned with the structures rather than the content of signs. Here the focus is on the physical form, regardless of any statistical properties. Syntactics allows for "the constructions of formal rules and the means by which they interrelate" (Liebenau & Backhouse, 1990). It studies the relation of signs to one another and how complex signs originate from simple ones. Syntactics level informs us about how signs signify. Formalism is the key term at this level. At a syntactic level, data quality is ensured through concentrating on the formal and structural aspects. Security at a syntactic level assures a high level of integrity in the formalisms and correctness in system specification.

At a syntactic level, information is viewed only from its material aspect – the structure. A set of signs when formulated together in a structure and governed by certain formal rules, becomes data. In other words, data is the mass of facts that have been created according to a certain structure. As such, we can argue that the type of signs operating at the syntactics level is actually data.

2.3 Semantics

Semantics is the study of the meaning of signs. It deals with the purported relationships between signs and what they signify (Stamper, 1985). Signs become useful only when they indicate certain action. For the interpretation of sign we need to ascertain the meaning of what is expressed in a message. A particular sign would imply different meaning to different individuals in a particular social setting. Semantics is concerned with the explication of various meanings associated with a sign. It deals with "the connections that agents make between the signs that they use and their behavior and actions" (Liebenau & Backhouse, 1990).

Semantics ascribes meaning to the data from the syntactics level. When meaning is attributed to the selected data in a particular context it becomes information. Checkland & Howell (1998) define information as structured data that has contextual meaning. Avison & Fitzgerald (1995) consider information to have meaning that comes from selecting data, summarizing it and presenting it in such a way that it is useful to the recipient. Meaning is appropriated when we draw from our knowledge and apply understanding to information. We deal with only information at the semantics level. Ensuring good quality at a semantic level therefore moves from maintaining quality of data to that of information.

2.4 Pragmatics

Pragmatics is concerned with the relationships between signs and behavior in a given context. It concentrates on the shared assumptions underlying human understanding. The pragmatic structures are the beliefs, expectations, commitments, intentions and communication patterns of people (Dhillon, 1995). The focus of pragmatics is to grasp the intentions of the sender of the message. The emphasis is also on the context of intentional use. At this level, we need to understand the usage of signs by people. This addresses the reason for the signs' signification.

The pragmatic level involves information that has intentional use. At the earlier levels, the concept of signs has been acted upon in terms of providing structure and attributing meaning to make it useful. This matured form is knowledge. Information becomes knowledge at the moment of its interpretation (Miller, 2002). Nonaka & Takeuchi (1995, pp. 58) suggest a relationship to knowledge:

> ...information is a flow of messages, while knowledge is created by that very flow of information anchored in the beliefs and commitment of its holder. This...emphasizes that knowledge is essentially related to human action.

In this section, we have explained the theoretical concepts of semiotics. Semiotics helps us understand and traverse the fine course between the business world and the physical world. The discussion on the four levels of semiotics informs us that the pragmatic level deals with knowledge, semantic level is the information domain, syntactic level is associated with data, and the empiric level involves communication channels. The next section discusses the data quality dimensions at the four semiotic levels.

3. DATA QUALITY DIMENSIONS

In this section, the semiotic analysis of data quality dimensions is presented. The data quality dimension, as defined by Wang & Strong (1996), is a set of data quality attributes that represent a single aspect or construct of data quality. Table 2 summarizes the analysis of dimensions that have been proposed in the research literature.

Table 2. Semiotic analysis of Data Quality dimensions

Semiotic levels	DQ Dimensions	Seminal work
Empirics	Accessibility	Delone et. al. (1992), Goodhue (1995), Miller (1996), Wang et al. (1996)
	Timeliness	Ballou et al. (1985), Caby et al. (1995), Fox et al. (1994), Goodhue (!995), Hilton (!979), Miller (1996), Wang et al. (1996), Zmud (1978)
	Locatability	Goodhue (1995)
	Portability	Caby et al. (1995)
	Security	Miller (1996), Wang et al. (1996)
Syntactics	Accuracy	Ballou et al. (1985), Caby et al. (1995), Delone et al. (1992), Doernberg et al. (1980), Fox et al. (1994), Goodhue (1995), Hilton (1979), Miller (1996), Wang et al. (1996), Zmud (1978)

Semiotic levels	DQ Dimensions	Seminal work
	Appearance, Comparability, Freedom from bias, Precision, Redundancy, Uniqueness, Usable	Delone et al. (1992)
	Arrangement, Readable	Zmud (1978)
	Clarity, Ease of use, Presentation	Goodhue (1995)
	Coherence, Format	Miller (1996)
	Compatibility	Goodhue (1995), Miller (1996)
	Composition, Flexibility, Robustness	Caby et al. (1995)
	Conciseness	Delone et al. (1992), Wang et al. (1996)
	Consistency	Ballou et al. (1985), Caby et al. (1995), Fox et al. (1994), Wang et al. (1996)
	Correctness	Wand et al. (1996)
	Ease of operation, Objectivity	Wang et al. (1996)
	Integrity	Brodie (1980)
	Level-of-detail	Caby et al. (1995), Goodhue (1995)
Semantics	Ambiguity	Doernberg et al. (1980), Wand et al. (1996)
	Believability, Understandability	Wang et al. (1996)
	Content, Informativeness	Delone et al. (1992)
	Factual, Reasonable	Zmud (1978)
	Interpretability	Wang et al. (1996), Caby et al. (1995)
	Meaningful	Goodhue (1995), Wand et al. (1996)
	Reliability	Brodie (1980), Delone et al. (1992), Goodhue (1995), Zmud (1978)
	Validity	Miller (1996)
Pragmatics	Appropriate amount of data, Reputation, value-added	Wang et al. (1996)
	Appropriateness	Caby et al. (1995)
	Completeness	Ballou et al. (1985), Caby et al. (1995), Doernberg et al. (1980), Fox et al. (1994), Miller (1996), Wang et al. (1996), Wand et al. (1996)
	Relevance	Delone et al. (1992), Hilton (1979), Miller (1996), Wang et al. (1996)

Semiotic levels	DQ Dimensions	Seminal work
	Importance, Sufficiency, Usefulness	Delone et al. (1992)

3.1 Empiric dimensions

Empirics deals with the problems in which data is used repeatedly. This level is concerned with establishing means of communication and data handling. The focus is on different data types being generated and their risk of being transmitted erroneously. The dimensions operating at the empiric level include accessibility, timeliness, security, portability and locatability.

Accessibility implies that data should be available, obtainable or retrievable when needed. This view is supported by Delone & McLean (1992), Goodhue (1995), Miller (1996), Wang & Strong (1996) and Chin & Becker (1997). Timeliness is concerned with the age of data, whether data is current. It is achieved if the recorded value is not out of date. Zmud (1978) and Hilton (1979) were the early proponents of timeliness as a dimension. Ballou & Pazer (1985), Caby *et al.* (1995), Fox *et al.* (1994), Goodhue (1995), Miller (1996), and Wang & Strong (1996) also support this dimension. Security as a dimension was proposed by both Miller (1996) and Wang & Strong (1996). Description of this dimension involves keeping data secure and restricting access to it. It involves protecting data from people and natural disasters. Portability and locatability as dimensions were supported by Caby *et al.* (1995) and Goodhue (1995) respectively.

The dimensions operating at the empiric level are associated with the problems of medium of communication rather than data itself. Unavailability of communication channels would lead to the problems of accessibility, timeliness and portability. Unavailable channels would hinder the data from being accessible and updated as per the requirements. On the other hand, unauthorized access to the communication channel would lead to the problems of security. In short, the empiric level deals only with network communication.

3.2 Syntactic dimensions

Syntactics deals with the forms and structures of data. It is concerned with the physical form rather than the content of data. The data quality dimensions operating at the syntactic level include accuracy (Chin & Becker, 1997), appearance (Delone & McLean, 1992), arrangement (Zmud, 1978), clarity (Goodhue, 1995), coherence (Miller, 1996), comparability (Delone & McLean, 1992), compatibility (Goodhue, 1995; Miller, 1996), completeness, composition (Caby *et al.,* 1995), conciseness, consistency, correctness, ease of operation, ease of use (Goodhue, 1995), flexibility, format, freedom from bias (Delone & McLean, 1992), integrity, level-of-detail (Caby *et al.,* 1995; Goodhue, 1995), objectivity, portability, precision (Delone & McLean, 1992), presentation (Goodhue, 1995), readable (Zmud, 1978), redundancy, robustness (Caby *et al.,* 1995), uniqueness (Delone & McLean, 1992), and usable (Delone & McLean, 1992).

Accuracy dimension is concerned with the conformity of the recorded value with the actual value. It is a widely accepted dimension of data quality. Accuracy implies that data is correct, flawless, precise, reliable and certified free of error. Zmud (1978), Hilton (1979), Doernberg & Ziegler (1980), Ballou & Pazer (1985), Delone & McLean (1992), Fox *et al.* (1994), Goodhue (1995), Miller (1996), Wang & Strong (1996) and Caby *et al.* (1995) support accuracy as an important dimension of data quality in their research.

Completeness as a dimension has been supported in the literature, with Doernberg & Ziegler (1980) and Ballou & Pazer (1985) being the earlier advocates. It implies that data must be of sufficient breadth, depth, and scope for the task at hand. Completeness involves recording of all values for a certain variable and is concerned with loss of data. Fox *et al.* (1994), Caby *et al.* (1995), Miller (1996), Wang & Strong (1996), and Wand & Wang (1996) also support this dimension.

Conciseness represents well-presented, succinct, and compact representation of data. This view is advocated by Delone & McLean (1992) and Wang & Strong (1996). Consistency is achieved if the representation of the data value is the same in all cases. It involves continuous representation of data in same format, compatibility with previous data, and consistent representation. Ballou & Pazer (1985), Caby *et al.* (1995), Fox *et al.* (1994) and Wang & Strong (1996) are the proponents of consistency as a dimension of data quality.

Wand & Wang (1996) describe the dimension of correctness as arising from garbling (operational failure), when data derived from the information system, which does not conform to those used to create these data. Ease of operation, as advocated by Wang and Strong (1996), implies that data is maniputable, easily integrated, customized, and usable for multiple purposes. This dimension is similar to the dimension of flexibility as proposed by Caby *et al.* (1995). Flexibility is addressed if data is adaptable, flexible, extendable, and expandable. Miller (1996) describes format as concerned with how the data is presented to the customer.

Integrity as a dimension of data quality was proposed by Brodie (1980). It is a measure of correctness and consists of semantic and physical integrity. Semantic integrity measures consistency and completeness with respect to the rules of the description language. Physical integrity measures the correctness of implementation details. Wang & Strong (1996) identified objectivity as another important dimension. It is concerned with data as being unbiased and impartial.

The dimensions discussed above cover the logic, grammar and structural aspects that compose data. In order to resolve the data quality issues, future research should concentrate specifically on the above discussed dimensions while proposing approaches for improvement.

3.3 Semantic dimensions

The dimensions operating at semantic level are associated with information rather than data. Information is the selected data that has been attributed meaning in a particular context. Semantics is concerned with meaning. It deals with the interpretation of data to get at the meaning of communication. The data quality dimensions from the research literature operating at the semantic level include ambiguity, believability, interpretability, meaningful, reliability, understandability, validity, content, informativeness, factual, and reasonablity. Ambiguity arises as a result of improper representation and is when data can be interpreted in more than one way. This dimension was proposed by Doernberg & Ziegler (1980) and Wand & Wang (1996).

Wang & Strong (1996) considered the dimension of believability as concerned with whether data can be believed or regarded as credible. Interpretability simply means that data should be interpretable, that is, it should be both defined clearly and represented appropriately. This dimension is supported by Caby *et al.* (1995) and Wang & Strong (1996).

Goodhue (1995) and Wand & Wang (1996) consider meaningfulness as an important dimension that is concerned with the interpretation of data. The failure of this dimension results in meaningless data.

Brodie (1980) understood reliability as linked to whether data was dependable, trustworthy and could be relied upon. Agmon & Ahituv (1987) addressed reliability in terms of concepts drawn from the field of quality control. Other researchers who support reliability as a dimension include Zmud (1978), Delone & McLean (1992) and Goodhue (1995). Understandability as a dimension was proposed by Wang & Strong (1996). It is concerned with whether data is clear, readable, unambiguous and easily comprehendible. Data is valid when it can be verified as being true and satisfying appropriate standards related to other dimensions (Miller 1996). The dimensions of content and informativeness were proposed by Delone & McLean, while Zmud (1980) considered factual and reasonablity as the other dimensions.

Ambiguity, interpretability and content as dimensions are concerned with the interpretational aspects of semantics. The issue of credibility is an associative characteristic of meaning. Believability, reliability, validity and factual dimensions strive to capture this issue. Meaning ascribed in semantics is addressed by the meaningful, understandability, informativeness and reasonablity dimensions proposed as part of data quality. The dimensions discussed in this section are actually associated with information. Ascertaining the meaning would lead to appropriate interpretation of data. As such, the issue of interpretation, credibility and meaning are linked to the aspects of information. The dimensions discussed in this section do not form part of data quality and should not be included as such.

3.4 Pragmatic dimensions

Pragmatics deals with the use of information by people. It is concerned with the relation between data, information and behavior, in a given context. The data quality dimensions from the research literature at the pragmatic level[1] include appropriateness, relevance, value added, sufficiency, importance, usefulness, and reputation. These dimensions deal with the pragmatic issues. Intention of use is the underlying focus of these dimensions.

Appropriateness, as a data quality dimension, means that data must be appropriate to the task at hand. Caby *et al.* (1995) and Wang & Strong (1996) are proponents of the appropriateness dimension. Hilton (1979) considered relevancy as an important dimension. This dimension is concerned with the applicability of data to the task at hand. Relevance is a key dimension as if the data does not address its customer needs and when the customer will find the data inadequate. Delone & McLean (1992), Miller (1996) and Wang & Strong (1996) are the other supporters of this view. Wang & Strong (1996) proposed value-added as a dimension that addresses the benefits and advantages of using data. Delone & McLean (1992) also considered sufficiency, importance and usefulness, while Wang & Strong (1996) concentrated on reputation as a valid dimension.

The contextual aspects of pragmatic issues are addressed by appropriateness, relevance and usefulness dimensions. Sufficiency, importance and reputation as dimensions deal with the expectations of the use. Value-added dimension attempts to understand the intention of use. These dimensions are concerned whether data fits the problem task. In doing so, these dimensions are not associated with data quality. That is, these dimensions do not address the issues of data quality. But rather they deal with the issues of knowledge. These dimensions are concerned with the intentional use, that is, how data would be used in relation to the problem at hand. This leads us to the domain of knowledge.

4. DISCUSSION

In the field of data quality, there is a lack of theoretical basis for identifying, classifying and discussing data quality dimensions. The analysis presented in the previous section allows us to develop an in-depth

[1] Although in this paper we argue that at a semantic and pragmatic level, the nature of data changes to information and knowledge, the dominant research literature does not make this distinction.

understanding of the dimensions associated with data quality. Indeed, there are complexities involved with data. Semiotics assists us in this endeavor to unravel and understand the inter-dependent nature of data, information and knowledge. This provides a clear understanding of the dimensions associated with data quality.

Researchers have proposed various solutions and approaches to the problems of data quality by addressing dimensions that actually exist at the pragmatic and semantic levels. A careful analysis of different levels of semiotics would indicate that the pragmatic level is associated with knowledge; semantic level is associated with information, while only the syntactic level is associated with data. In other words, the dimensions operating at the pragmatic, semantic and syntactic levels pertain to knowledge quality, information quality and data quality respectively. In order to improve the quality of data, special attention should be paid to the dimensions operating at the syntactic level. At the same time, dimensions associated with knowledge quality and information quality cannot be ignored. These dimensions should also be acknowledged as part of any equation devised to address the problems of data quality.

Data quality problems range from definition, measurement, analysis and improvement to tools, methods, and processes (Wang *et al.,* 2001). Semiotic interpretation of data quality dimensions addresses the definition, measurement and analysis aspects of data quality, while the improvement aspect is touched indirectly. In terms of measurement, data quality dimensions can also serve as the metrics (Ballou & Pazer, 1985). Wang et al. (2001, pp.12) have used timeliness, security and credibility, among others, as part of data quality metrics. The trouble with such metrics is that it leads us away from the domain of data quality and into the fields of networking, IS security and telecommunications. This problem highlights the need for a sensitive yet deep examination of the dimensions that actually pertain to data quality.

Let us consider the case of a data warehouse. Data warehouse is a repository of data needed for decision making (Ballou & Tayi, 1999). Wang *et al.* (2001), while explaining the European Union Data Warehouse Quality Project, provide the following as data warehouse quality parameters: accessibility, interpretability, usefulness, believability and validation. Given our argument, none of these parameters are related to data (syntactics) quality. These are in fact dimensions of communication (empirics) quality, information (semantics) quality and knowledge (pragmatics) quality. Although, we are concerned with ensuring the quality of data, our current emphasis is on dimensions that do not directly impact data quality. In doing so, we are setting up for disappointment in data quality efforts.

The semiotic analysis of data quality dimensions assists us in solving the measurement issues related with data quality. The dimensions of data quality exist at the syntactic level and may be objectively measured, to an extent, as compared to those of information quality. Information quality dimensions like informativeness, meaningful or believability would be problematic to measure as these are subjective in nature. Their measurement cannot escape the subjective valuation by users.

4.1 Implications for IS Security

Semiotics lends itself as a theoretical framework by which we can understand the nature of data, information and knowledge. It also makes us sensitive to the distinctions among the three. The intricacies involved with data, information and knowledge gives rise to impervious gaps that can be epidemic to the success of an organization. As such, careful thought is required to manage these gaps (see figure 1).

Receptivity gap exists between the empiric and the syntactic level. It arises as a result of problems encountered with transmitting signals through the physical communication channels. As we move from data to information, we would encounter the interpretation gap. Interpretation gap is the interplay between data and information. It arises due to lack of appropriate meaning being attached to data. Usefulness gap is encountered when we derive knowledge from information. It arises when the information is construed with inappropriate intention in a particular context.

Receptivity, interpretation and usefulness gap have implications for IS security and organizational issues. Receptivity gap has technical implications; interpretation gap has an impact on operations, while usefulness gap impacts both decision-making and overall strategy of an organization. In terms of IS security, lack of adequate technical controls would result in a receptivity gap. At this level, the observance of principles of confidentiality, integrity and availability is paramount. The presence of this gap indicates technical IS security failure.

Interpretation gap has an impact on operations. In terms of IS security, it can be addressed in terms of the formal controls. Misinterpretation of IS security policies existing in the form of data would have severe implications for an organization. The non-contextual use of data might lead to incorrect allocation of responsibilities. This would produce an exposure of a weak link. Further, misinterpretation of data would also result in poor predicates for the process of decision-making. It would provide us with incorrect operational information about different processes crucial for IS security. As such, interpretation gap would have severe implications on the effectiveness and efficiency of an economic organization.

Usefulness gap has implications for decision-making capability and affects the strategic function of the organization as well. Inappropriate use of information pertaining to IS security in a particular contextual situation would result in poor decision predicates and in turn, a bad decision. The decision-making capability of an organization would be adversely hampered if the information is used in an inadequate manner. It is also important to understand the context of the information provided. The failure to do so would lead to the establishment of IS security objectives or goals that are based on improper (out-of-context) information. This would result in diverting the focus to a wrong set of priorities. Informal controls of an organization are important to check this gap. The principles of responsibility, integrity, trust and ethics, as advocated by Dhillon & Backhouse (2000), would stand in good stead to overcome this gap.

In terms of strategic function, inappropriate information would influence the policy and strategy formulation. The usefulness gap would also affect the implementation and establishment of corporate security policy and strategy. It would result in failure to align the IS security objectives with those of the organization, subsequently impacting the management's focus. As such, usefulness gap would have implications for the existential thrive of an organization.

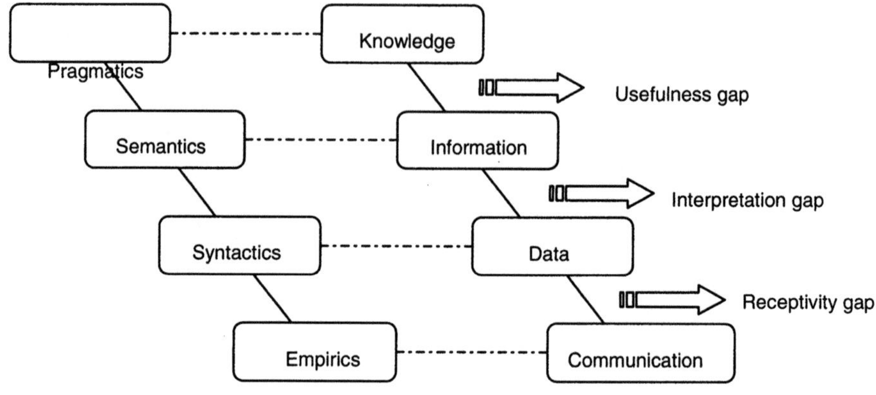

Figure 1. Semiotics, data-information-knowledge and the gaps

5. CONCLUSION

In this paper, data is approached as comprised of signs. We have provided a deeper understanding of data and information. We argue for the need to understand the inter-dependent nature of data, information and knowledge. This would allow us to address the problems of data quality and propose effective approaches towards its improvement. Such an approach would lead to better decision predicates for the process of decision making in modern organizations.

Semiotics is used as a frame of reference to explicate the concepts of data and information to allow critical analysis of dimensions of data quality. This investigation enhances our understanding that the dimensions associated with data quality can only exist at the syntactic level of semiotics. This alleviates the problems of definition and measurement. Further, usefulness and interpretation gaps arise as we attempt to extract knowledge from information and information from data. These gaps have implications for IS security that can be adequately addressed by establishing appropriate formal, as well as, informal controls in an organization.

In terms of future research, it would be valuable to draw implications for organizations based upon the semiotic view of data quality dimensions presented in this research. These implications might address how to measure, assess, manage and improve the quality of data. Limitations of this research arise from the use of semiotics as a frame of reference. We do not state that semiotics is the only theoretical basis from which to look at the concepts of data and information. However, we certainly assert that semiotics as a theory of information is relevant and rewarding in solving the problems with the use of information. Semiotics encompasses all aspects, the mechanical, the abstract, the philosophical and the human (Stamper 1985).

6. REFERENCES

Abate, M.L., Diegert, K.V., and Allen, H.W., 1998, A hierarchical approach to improving data quality, *Data Quality*. 4(1).

Agmon, N., and Ahituv, N., 1987, Assessing data reliability in an information system, *Journal of Management Information Systems*. 4(2): 34-44.

Anderson, James (2003). Why we need a new definition of IS security.

Armstrong, H.L., 1999, *A Soft Approach to Management of IS Security*. Doctoral dissertation, Curtin University of Technology.

Arnold, S.E., 1992, Information manufacturing: The road to data quality, *Data Base*. 15(5): 32-39.

Avison, D.E., and Fitzgerald, G., 1995, The Field of IST, Private communication to Peter Checkland.

Ballou, D.P., and Pazer, H.L., 1985, Modeling data and process quality in multi-input, multi-output information systems, *Management Science*. 31(2): 150-162.

Ballou, D.P., Wang, R., Tayi, G.K., and Pazer, H.L., 1998, Modeling information manufacturing systems to determine information product quality, *Management Science*. 44(4): 462-484.

Baskerville, R., 1989, Logical controls specification: An approach to information systems security, in: *Systems Development for Human Progress,* H.Klein, and K.Kumar, ed., North-Holland, Amsterdam.

Boland, R.J., 1987, The in-formation of information systems, in: *Critical Issues in Information Systems Research*, R.J.Boland, and R.Hirschheim, ed., John Wiley and Sons, Chichester.

Brodie, M.L., 1980, Data quality in information systems, *Information and Management*. 3(6): 245-258.

Caby, E.C., Pautke, R.W., and Redman, T.C., 1995, Strategies for improving data quality, *Data Quality*. 1(1): 4-12.

Checkland, P., and Howell, S., 1998, *Information, Systems, and Information Systems – Making Sense of the Field,* John Wiley and Sons, Chichester.

Chengalur-Smith, I.N., Ballou, D.P., and Pazer, H.L., 1999, The impact of data quality information on decision making: An exploratory analysis, *IEEE Transactions on Knowledge and Data Engineering*. 11(6): 853-864.

Chin, A., and Becker, S., 1997, Improving decision making using confidence scaling for enhanced data quality, AIS Americas Conference, Indianapolis.

Delone, W.H., and McLean, E.R., 1992, Information systems success: The quest for the dependent variable, *Information Systems Research.* 3(1): 60-95.

Dhillon, G., 1995, *Interpreting the Management of Information Systems Security,* Doctoral dissertation. London School of Economics and Political Science.

Dhillon, G. and Backhouse, J., 2000, Information system security management in the new millennium, *Communications of the ACM.* 43(7): 125-128.

Doernberg. D.L., and Ziegler, D.H., 1980, Due process versus data processing: An analysis of computerized criminal history information systems, *New York University Law.* 1: 55.

Falkenberg, E.D., Hesse, W., Lindgreen, P., Nilsson, B.E., Oei, J.L.H., Rolland, C., Stamper, R.K., Assche, F.J.M.V., Verrijn-Stuart, A.A., and Voss, K., 1998, *A Framework of Information Systems Concepts: The FRISCO Report.* University of Leiden, International Federation for Information Processing, The Netherlands.

Feldman, M.S., and March, J.G., 1981, Information in organizations as signal and symbol, *Administrative Science Quarterly.* 26: 171-186.

Fox, C., Levitin, A., and Redman, T., 1994, The notion of data and its quality dimensions, *Information Processing and Management.* 30(1):9-19.

Funk, J., Lee, Y., and Wang, R., 1998, Institutionalizing information quality practice, *Proceedings of Conference on Information Quality, Cambridge, MA*, pp.1-17.

Goodhue, D.L., 1995, Understanding user evaluations of information systems, *Management Science.* 41(12): 1827-1844.

Guynes, C.S., Prybutok, V.R., and Myers, B.L., 1996, Evolving data quality considerations for client/server environments, *Data Quality.* 2(1): 21-27.

Hilton, R.W., 1979, The determinants of information system value: An illustrative analysis, *Journal of Accounting Research.* Autumn: 411-35.

Huh, Y.U., Keller, F.R., Redman, T.C., and Watkins, A.R., 1990, Data quality, *Information and Software Technology.* 32(8): 559-565.

Jarke, M., and Vassiliou, Y., 1997. Data warehouse quality: A review of the DWQ project, *Proceedings of the Conference on Information Quality, Cambridge, MA*, pp. 102-115.

Kahn, B.K., Strong, D., and Wang, R.Y., 2002, Information quality benchmarks: Product and service performance, *Communications of the ACM.* 45(4): 184-192.

Klein, B.D., and Rossin, D.F., 1999, Data errors in neural network and linear regression models: An experimental comparison, *Data Quality.* 5(1).

Lee, Y., Allen, T., and Wang, R.Y., 2001, Information products for remanufacturing: Tracing the repair of an aircraft fuel-pump, *Proceedings of the 6th International conference on Information Quality,* pp. 77-82.

Lee, Y.W., Strong, D.M., Kahn, B.K., and Wang, R.Y., 2002, AIMQ: A methodology for information quality assessment, *Information and Management.* 40: 133-146.

Liebenau, J., and Backhouse, J., 1990, *Understanding Information: An Introduction.* Macmillan, Basingtoke.

Mackay, H., 1998, *The Good Listener*, Pan Macmillan, Sydney.

Miller, F.J., 2002, I = 0 (Information has no meaning), *Information Research.* 8(1).

Miller, H., 1996, The multiple dimensions of information quality, *Information Systems Management.* 13(2): 79-83.

Morris, C., 1946, *Signs, Language and Behavior,* Prentice Hall Braziller, New York.

Nake, F., 2001, Data, information, and knowledge, in: *Organizational Semiotics: Evolving a science of information systems,* K.Liu, R.J.Clarke, P.B.Anderson, R.K.Stamper, and E.Abou-Zeid, ed., Kluwer Academic Publishers, Boston, pp. 41-50.

Nonaka, I., and Takeuchi, H., 1995, *The Knowledge-Creating Company: how Japanese companies create the dynamics of innovation,* Oxford University Press, New York.

O'Leary, D.E., 1993, The impact of data accuracy on system learning, *Journal of Management Information Systems.* 9(4): 83-98.

Pesche, M., 1999, Boundary bath, *Presented at SCOPE1 workshop*, Vienna.

Pipino, L., Lee., Y.W., and Wang, R.Y., 1998, Measuring information quality, *TDQM-97-04, Total Data Quality Management Program*, MIT Sloan School of Management.

Redman, T.C., 1996, *Data Quality for the Information Age,* Artech House, Boston.

Redman, T.C., 1998, The impact of poor data quality on the typical enterprise, *Communications of the ACM.* 41(2): 79-82.

Redman, T.C., 2001, *Data Quality: The field guide*, Digital Press, Boston.

Shankar, G., Wang, R.Y., and Ziad, M., 2000, IP-MAP: Representing the manufacture of an information product, *Proceedings of the 5th International conference on Information Quality,* pp. 1-16.

Shankaranarayan, G., Ziad, M., and Wang, R.Y., 2003, Managing data quality in dynamic decision environments: An information product approach, *Journal of Database Management.* 14(4): 14-32.

Specht, P. H., 1986, Job characteristics as indicants of CBIS data requirements, *MIS Quarterly.* September: 270-286.

Stamper, R.K., 1973, *Information in Business and Administrative Systems,* John Wiley and Sons, New York.

Stamper, R.K., 1985, Towards a theory of information: Mystical fluid or a subject for scientific enquiry? *The Computer Journal.* 28(3): 195-199.

Strong, D.M., 1997, IT process designs for improving information quality and reducing exception handling: A simulation experiment, *Information and Management.* 31: 251-263.

Trček, D., 2003, An integral framework for information systems security management, *Computers & Security.* 22(4):337-360.

Wand, Y., and Wang, R.Y., 1996, Anchoring data quality dimensions in ontological foundations, *Communications of the ACM.* 39(11): 86-95.

Wang, R.Y., 1998, A product perspective on Total Data Quality Management, *Communications of the ACM.* 41(2): 58-65.

Wang, R.Y., Allen, T., Harris, W., and Madnick, S., 2003, An information product approach for total information awareness, *IEEE Aerospace Conference.*

Wang, R.Y., and Strong, D.M., 1996, Beyond accuracy: What data quality means to data consumers, *Journal of Management Information Systems.* 12(4): 5-34.

Wang, R.Y., Lee, Y.L., and Pipino, L., and Strong, D.M., 1998, Manage your information as a product, *Sloan Management Review.* 39(4): 95-105.

Wang, R.Y., Storey, V.C., and Firth, C.P., 1995, A framework for analysis of data quality research, *IEEE Transactions on Knowledge and Data Engineering.* 7(4): 623-640.

Wang, R.Y., Ziad, M., and Lee, Y.W., 2001, *Data Quality,* Kluwer Academic Publishers, Boston.

Zmud, R., 1978, Concepts, theories, and techniques: An empirical investigation of the dimensionality of the concept of information, *Decision Sciences.* 9(2): 187-195.

FROM XML TO RDF: SYNTAX, SEMANTICS, SECURITY, AND INTEGRITY (INVITED PAPER)

C. Farkas, V. Gowadia, A. Jain, and D. Roy
Information Security Lab
Department of Computer Science and Engineering
University of South Carolina
Columbia, SC 29208

Abstract In this paper we evaluate security methods for eXtensible Markup Language (XML) and the Resource Description Framework (RDF). We argue that existing models are insufficient to provide high assurance security for future Web-based applications. We begin with a brief overview of XML access control models, where the protection objects are identified by the XML syntax. However, these approaches are limited to handle updates and structural modifications of the XML documents. We argue that XML security methods must be based on the intended meaning of XML and the semantics of the application using XML. We identify two promising research directions to extend the XML model with semantics. The first approach incorporates traditional database concepts, like key and integrity constraints, in the XML model. The second approach aims to associate XML documents with metadata supporting Web-based applications. We propose the development of security models based on these semantics-oriented approaches to achieve high assurance. Further, we investigate the security needs of Web metadata, like RDF, RDFS, and OWL. In particular, we study the security risks of unwanted inferences and data aggregation, supported by these languages.

1. Introduction

The rapid development of the World Wide Web (WWW) has led to the development of machine understandable, self describing syntax to exchange data. Presently, the eXtensible Markup Language (XML) is the most widely used language to support Web-based applications. To further facilitate these applications, the Semantic Web community has proposed languages, such as the Resource Description Framework

(RDF), and the Web Ontology Language (OWL), for representation of metadata. In addition to the functional requirements, these future applications must also provide data and application security.

During the last five years several access control models have been developed for XML. However, these models target only the simplest interpretation of XML, its purely syntactic form. While this approach might be suitable for some applications, it is unsatisfactory to support general Web application.

In this paper we propose a different approach for XML security, originating from research aiming to extend XML with semantics. We consider two main research directions to extend the XML model with semantics. The first approach extends the XML model with traditional database concepts, like keys and database constraints. The second approach aims to associate XML documents with metadata, supporting Web-based applications. We believe, that security models must be developed based on these semantics-oriented approaches to achieve high-assurance and flexible security.

We start with an overview of XML access control models developed on top of XML syntax. While these models are sufficient to provide secure read accesses to XML, they are limited to handle updates and document restructuring. We show, that these operations may cause violations of confidentiality, integrity, and availability. We present approaches, that seem promising from the perspective of security, to represent the intended meaning of XML. In particular, we present research that extends the XML syntax with RDF, RDFS, and OWL metadata. These metadata facilitate XML restructuring, XML data integration, identification of syntactically different but semantically equivalent XML documents, and to identify security objects.

Although the number of research and development efforts to provide semantics aware security for Web technologies and applications is increasing, these works only target a small fraction of the necessary research. Future work, based on precise formulation of data and application semantics, need to be done. We propose future research directions, including representation of data and applications semantics, development of security models based on these semantics, analysis of the need for metadata security, and study of the inference and aggregation problem in semantic data.

The organization of the paper is as follows. In Section 2 we give an overview of the XML access control research, and its limitations. Section 3 describes research extending the XML model with semantics and developing security models based on these semantics. Section 4 contains our initial evaluation and results on securing metadata. Finally, we conclude and recommend future research directions in Section 5.

2. Extensible Markup Language

The simplest interpretation of an XML document is a tree-structure, composed of properly nested element nodes. In textual representation of XML documents each subtree is delimited by a pair of start and end tags of element name. Each element has zero or more child nodes, which may include other element nodes, text nodes, and attribute nodes. Cardinality constraints and special attributes, like id and idref, allow to express some restrictions on the XML tree.

XML is being increasingly used to support Web-based applications. In addition to the application specific requirements, these applications also require data integrity, confidentiality, and availability. Authorization models, based on syntactic XML trees, identify protection objects as subtrees (collection of nodes) of the XML trees. In this section we give an overview of the existing (syntax-based) XML access control models, point out limitations of these models, and argue that access control should be defined on the intended meaning of XML formatted data, rather than the presentation syntax.

2.1 XML Security

During the last five years, several discretionary access control models [7, 14, 26] have been developed for XML trees. Protection objects correspond to XML nodes, identified by path expressions. These models support authorization propagation, conflict resolution, and expression of obligation and provision at varying degree. They may also support schema-level (i.e., DTD or XML Schema) or data-level (i.e., XML instance) specification of security policies.

The XML Access control model developed by Bertino et al. [8, 9, 6] provides flexible security granularity and considers the case when XML documents do not conform to a predefined Document Type Definition (DTD). The proposed access control model can be used for DTD-based and document-based policies. Security objects are specified by a path expression, identifying one or more nodes in the XML document or DTD. Propagation rules determining access control restrictions for the descendant nodes are also supported.

Damiani et al. [13, 14] defines and enforces access restrictions on the XML document structure and content. The authors propose the construction of partial views of the XML documents, such that the views satisfy the security requirements. Security objects are specified by XPath expressions identifying element or attribute nodes or their collections.

The models proposed by Bertino et al. and Damiani et al. reach a binary decision for granting or denying access to the nodes identified by path expressions. Kudo et al. [25, 26] propose an access control model that provides provisional authorizations [22]. Provisional access control allows to express additional requirements that users must satisfy if their accesses are permitted.

Murata et al. [29] introduce a static analysis technique based on string automata to reduce the overhead of runtime security checking. Given an access control policy, a query expression, and an optional schema, static analysis determines if the query potentially violates the security policy. Static analysis can be performed without evaluating any query expression against an actual database. Run-time (i.e., data level) checking is required only when static analysis is unable to determine whether to grant or deny access requests.

Gowadia and Farkas [18] present an RDF-based access control framework to support context based access control. RDF statements are used to represent meta-data, including security objects and policies. Their aim is to increase data availability while providing security. In [19] the authors address efficient enforcement of their model by using bottom-up tree automata to represent security objects. They support both data and schema level evaluation.

2.2 Limitations of Syntax-Based XML Security Models

Correct enforcement of existing access control models requires that the structure of the document does not change and that the security classifications of the nodes increase downward in the XML tree. Changes in the XML structure or data may result in incomprehensible security policy or data loss. In this section we present two such examples. The first example shows the limitation of handling updates in multilevel secure XML documents. The second example shows the problem of structural rewriting of XML documents.

XML Updates: The focus of access control models developed so far has been on providing read access to the users, without fully considering write access. For instance, when a delete operations is issued, the entire subtree of the deleted nodes is removed [12]. This means that users may delete nodes they are not authorized to read if these nodes are in the subtree of an authorized node. Such blind deletes lead to loss of important information.

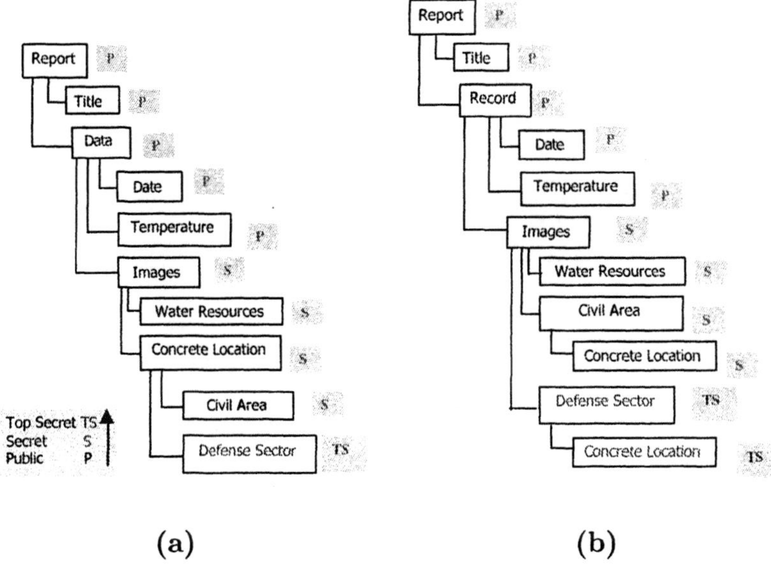

Figure 1. Example MLS XML documents

To illustrate this problem consider the XML document shown in Figure 1(a). The document contains data received from satellite images. The data is classified at three security levels: *TopSecret* > *Secret* > *Public*. If a user with Public clearance deletes the <Data> element, all subtrees of <Data> are also deleted. This includes the Public level <Date> and <Temperature> as well as the Secret level <Images> and its subtrees. This will -incorrectly- reduce the data availability for Secret and Top Secret users.

Finding a secure and correct solution to handle delete is not trivial. Other approaches include:

- Delete only the read authorized (viewable) nodes and allow fragmentation of the XML tree. But then, future querying and policy enforcement will be limited. If the dangling subtrees are connected to the nearest parent nodes then the XML schema would also be violated.

- Refuse to delete any node that has nodes in its subtree that are not authorized for the user. However, this solution would create a covert channel.

Clearly none of the above solutions is acceptable. Further work is needed to evaluate updates in XML documents with different security requirements for the nodes.

Restructuring XML Documents: Another problem with syntax-based access control models is, that it is not possible to have a single access control policy for different XML structures even if they contain the same data. For example, a syntactic policy for XML document in Figure 1(a) cannot be used for securing the XML document shown in Figure 1(b) even if they have the same data values. Observation of the two XML trees show that they only differ in their structure and the tag name <Data> in Figure 1(a) is replaced with tag name <Record> in Figure 1(b).

Such structural variations often arise during merger of two or more organizations, because each organization may already have its own XML data, stored according to local schemas. After merger the organizations still need to enforce local access control policies over the combined data. To ensure correct enforcement, it is necessary to provide conflict resolution strategies and transformation of policies between the different syntactic forms. Performing these transformations by humans is time consuming and may lead to errors. Development of automated tools require that the intended semantics of the XML formatted data is represented in a machine-understandable format.

3. XML and Semantics

Our belief is that security models must be based on semantics rather than syntax. Lack of capabilities to handle data semantics will result in inflexible policies that cannot handle application specific requirements.

Several researchers addressed the problem of extending the current XML model with semantics. We study two of these approaches from the perspective of XML security: 1) database oriented, to support expressiveness required by databases, and 2) Web Services oriented, to support application specific semantics. This section gives an overview of these approaches.

3.1 XML as database

Database researchers attempt to extend the XML model to support database semantics in XML. Although DTDs and XML Schema allow simple constraints for XML, these type of constraints are not sufficient for constraints usually present in databases. Buneman, Davidson, and Fan [10, 16, 15] develop key and integrity constraints for XML. Key constraints are especially important to express semantics of objects identities, thus necessary to identify security protection objects.

Considering XML from the database perspective also led to the development of query languages, like XQuery, XML-QL. The need for efficient query processing led to formal data models and query optimization. Jagadish et al. [21] present a Tree Algebra for XML queries (TAX). TAX is an extension of relational algebra and can express most XML query operations. Hung et al. [20] propose TOSS, an extension of TAX with the semantics of terms stored in TAX databases. The authors incorporate a similarity enhances ontology (SEO) to allow queries over syntactically different by "similar" terms.

Liu et al. [27] propose an XML Semantics Definition Language (XSDL) to express XML author's intended meaning. In XSDL, XML semantics is defined in terms of OWL DL ontology. The mapping between the XML and the ontology is provided using Schema Adjuncts Framework (SAF).

Unfortunately, with the exception of some initial attempts, none of the XML security models incorporate these semantics-aware approaches. We believe that these approaches would be useful to overcome the limitations of current security models. Therefore, we recommend further research to evaluate their applicability for security. The following section will give an overview of the existing, semantic-aware access control models for XML and XML-like languages.

3.2 XML Security and Semantics

Stoica and Farkas [17, 35, 36] propose a method similar to Liu et al. [27]. They manipulate XML documents according to metadata associated to them.

Secure XML Views: In [35] Stoica and Farkas address the restriction that security classifications of the nodes must increase downwards in an XML tree. The authors propose techniques for generating secure and semantic-conflict free XML views from a multilevel secure (MLS) XML. They propose the use of two graphs, a Minimum Semantic Conflict Graph (MSCG) and a Multi-Plane DTD Graph (MPG). MSCG contains all semantic relationships among the XML tags that must be preserved within any partial view. MPG captures the structural relationships among tags and their security classifications.

XML Correlation with Ontologies: In [17] and [36] Stoica and Farkas show that large collections of distributed XML documents are exposed to inference attacks through data correlation and replication. They propose that XML documents to be mapped to ontologies (Fig-

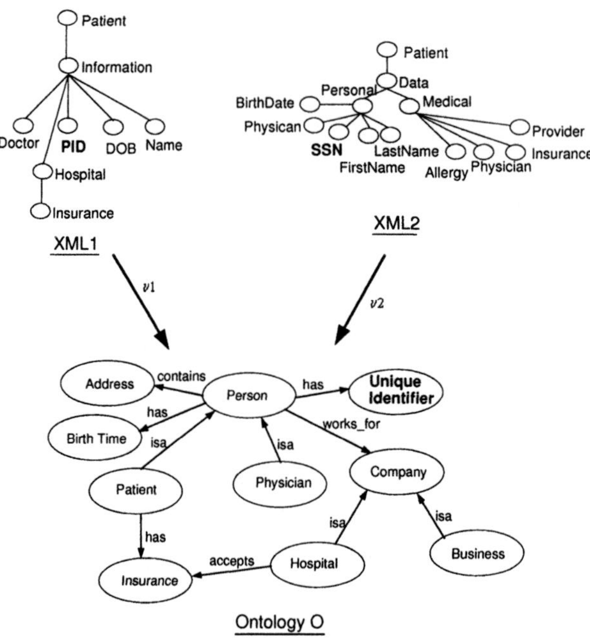

Figure 2. XML mapping to Ontology

ure 2) to convey intended meaning. This mapping is used to identify semantically equivalent XML nodes. Detection of replicated XML data and association among (distributed) XML nodes is aided by generalization of XML terms based on the ontology. For example, the Correlated Inference Procedure detects correlated information under different security classification and syntactic format.

Concept level Access Control: Qin and Atluri [30] propose an access control model to define authorizations on the ontological concepts linked to the semantically annotated Web pages. The access control policies are defined on concept and enforced on the data instances.

XML Updates: Roy [32] addresses the problem of secure and integrity preserving deletes in MLS XML documents. She suggests the use of a unique new domain to relabel nodes that are deleted by a user but the delete would result in document fragmentation or data loss. For example, in Section 2.2 we showed that the deletion of <Data> node would result in disconnecting <Images> from the root. The proposed solution would remove such "deleted" nodes from the view of Public users by relabeling them with the {Deleted} domain. However, these relabeled nodes would still be visible to Secret and Top Secret users, with the indication that they were deleted by a Public user. Clearances

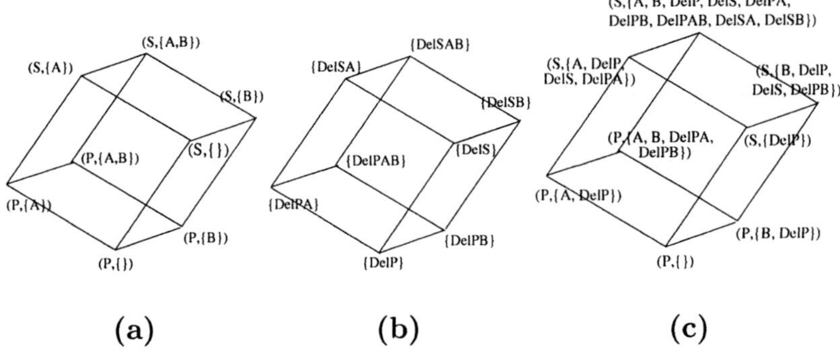

Figure 3. Lattice Structure of Security Levels

of the subjects are assigned such that they can access deleted nodes with strictly dominated labels. Figure 3 shows the original and part of the modified security lattice.

However, work by Roy does not fully solve the problems of XML updates. For example, it preserves minimum nodes required to preserve document structure but does not consider semantics of high-level security data. Can we still use a Top Secret image after its date and location have been deleted? What is the meaning of a Secret value that is calculated from "deleted" Public values? We believe that ontologies play a crucial role to develop semantically correct and secure solutions for the above problems. For example, they would supply data semantics, similar to referential integrity in relational databases. An other area is to evaluate the key constraints in XML documents and their effect on security. Is there a polyinstantiation problem is XML?

XML Normal Form: Finally, machine understandable representation of the intended XML semantics need to be addressed. We propose an approach using ontologies to form equivalence classes of syntactically different but semantically (ontologically) equivalent XML documents. XML Normal Form, a syntactic construct, is used to represent each equivalence class. The proper syntax of XML Normal Form is determined by the ontology representing XML semantics.

Synchronized Multimedia Integration Language Security: Kodali et al. [23, 24] develop security framework for Synchronized Multimedia Integration Language (SMIL) formatted streaming data. SMIL, an XML-like language, supports operational semantics. The authors provide language-based security that respects continuity and synchronization constructs of SMIL. They introduce the concept of SMIL Normal Form, representing the equivalence class of syntactically different but semantically equivalent SMIL document. They develop models for Discretionary (DAC), Mandatory (MAC), and Role-Based (RBAC)Access Control, and address issues like unbreakability of atomic SMIL units.

3.3 Secure XML for Web Services

Web Services (WS) are the Web based ubiquitous applications built on open standards. WS can be advertised, discovered, and invoked over the Web. They are published on the Web using WSDL (Web Services Description Languages) [11]. UDDI [5] is the registry where they are listed in the directory and can be discovered by the requester service. The interacting Web Services exchange all the data and requests in messages format using SOAP (Simple Object Access Protocol) [28]. All of these standards use XML as the underlying data syntax for data discovery, interchange, and processing. All of these interactions occur at the syntactic level where the services are discovered from UDDI by keyword based search. WS-Security specification [4] uses XML digital signature to sign the SOAP messages, XML encryption to encrypt the messages and data, XACML for access control. In addition to this it uses PKI, Kerberos and other conventional security mechanism to provide secure data interchange and processing.

Currently WS use ontologies to improve the performance of automated discovery of registered services. WS security must be able to handle application and business specific requirements.

4. Protecting Metadata

One of the main achievement of the envisioned Semantic Web is the use of complex relationships between entities to support interoperation and data integration. These relationships may also lead to entailments of new facts and relationships. Sheth et al. [2, 3, 34] develop inferencing tools that treat sequence of properties as a new type of relationship. These relationships capture connections and similarities between data resources which are not directly connected. The authors give real life application examples of how to identify useful associations in the domains of businesses and national security. For example, the Passenger Identification, Screening, and Threat Analysis application (PISTA) [33] involves discovering and preventing threats for aviation safety. PISTA demonstrates the use of semantic associations in calculating the possible risk from passengers in a given flight. It extracts relevant metadata from different information resources and channels including government watch-lists, commercial data, flight databases, and historical passenger data. PISTA uses semantic-based knowledge discovery techniques

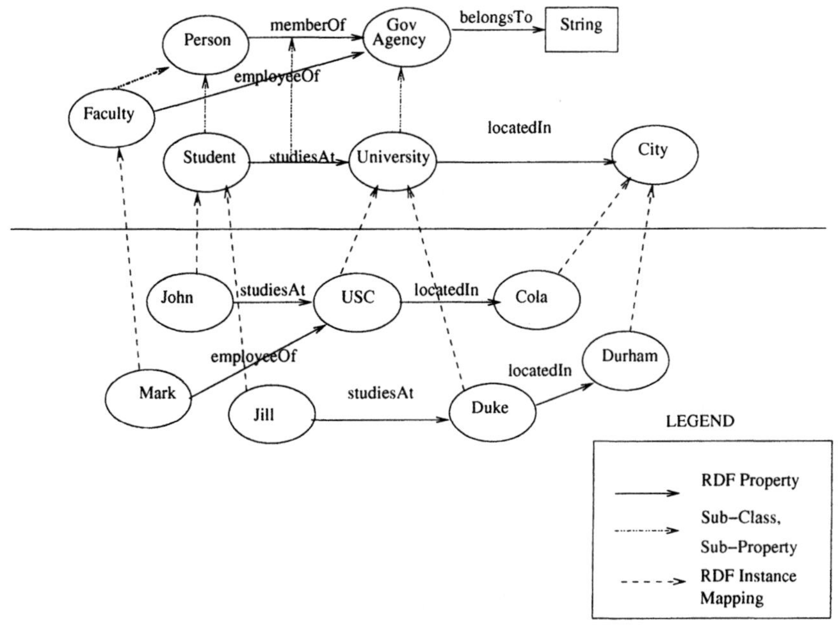

Figure 4. Example RDF Schema and Instance Data

to identify suspicious patterns and categorize passengers into different groups.

Metadata and Security: RDF and RDFS have well defined semantics and entailment capabilities. While these capabilities are needed to improve data integration and interoperation, they may also be used to disclose sensitive data or to disclose a sensitive pattern. Access control models for RDF and RDFS must consider these inferencing capabilities.

Although some of the XML security models utilize metadata to enhance the security, they do not develop security models for metadata. However, the amount of metadata, stored in RDF, RDFS, and OWL format, is increasing; methods and tools are being developed to store, manipulate, and query metadata [1]. Making these metadata publicly available, i.e., for Web applications, raises new security and privacy concerns. Can we use conventional security models, developed for XML and RDBMS, to protect Web data and corresponding metadata? Before answering this question, we need to evaluate the inferencing capabilities of RDF, RDFS, and OWL. For example, RDF and RDFS entailments may generate assertions that are not explicitly stored but could be inferred. From the security perspective this new data should also be secured by the authorization framework and should not violate the security policy.

Jain and Farkas (http://www.cse.sc.edu/research/isl) develop formalism for RDF access control, incorporating RDF and RDF Schema (RDFS) entailments. Security violations occur if a sensitive statement can be entailed from non-sensitive statements. RDF protection objects are represented as RDF-patterns (triples) along with the corresponding security labels. The model has flexible security granularity that allows expressing restrictions on a single resource, property, value, or any combination of these. Conflict resolution strategy addresses the problem of inconsistent classification. The authors also develop techniques to assign security classification to newly generated statements.

For example, consider Figure 4. Assume that the information that USC is a type of GovAgency is confidential. However, releasing the information that <USC rdf:type University> and <University rdfs:subClassOf GovAgency> entails the relationship <USC rdf:type GovAgency>. Even this simple example shows that security models that address entailments must be developed.

A different approach for RDF security is presented by Finin et al. [31]. They propose a policy based access control model for RDF data in an RDF store. The model provides control over the different action modes possible on the RDF store, like inserting a triple, deleting a triple, and querying whether a triple is in the store. The authors define a set of policy rules, enforced by a policy engine to reach the authorization decisions.

We believe that ontologies are crucial for future Semantic Web technologies, providing the basis for representing, acquiring, and utilizing knowledge. Researchers and developers need to consider security aspects of these new technologies and develop appropriate authorization frameworks.

5. Conclusions

This paper presents a brief overview of XML and RDF data and their security models. Our main aim is to indicate the need of precise formulation of data and application semantics and their use to develop security models. We present initial research results aiming to extend the XML paradigm with formal semantics. We give motivating examples and suggest further research directions.

Also, we believe that RDF and ontology languages play a significant role in developing the Semantic Web. However, only a few of the researchers address the need to develop authorization frameworks for metadata. Methods, capable of handling entailments and complex relationships need to be developed. Further, assurance of the security methods need to be established. Finally, enforcement and scalability issues need to be studied to achieve practical solutions. This is especially important when considering the open and dynamic nature of the Semantic Web.

6. Acknowledgment

This work was partially supported by the National Science Foundation under grant number IIS-0237782.

References

[1] Kowari-metastore. http://www.kowari.org.

[2] B. Aleman-Meza, C. Halaschek, J. B. Arpinar, and A. Sheth. Context-aware semantic association ranking. In *Proceedings of the First International Workshop on Semantic Web and Databases*, pages 33–50. LSDIS Lab, University of Georgia, 2003.

[3] K. Anyanwu and A. Sheth. p-Queries: Enabling Querying for Semantic Associations on the Semantic Web. In *WWW '03: Proceedings of the 12th international conference on World Wide Web*, pages 690–699, New York, NY, USA, 2003. ACM Press.

[4] B. Atkinson, G. Della-Libera, S. Hada, and M. Hondo. Web Services Security (WS-Security). http://www-106.ibm.com/developerworks/webservices/library/ws-secure/, April 2002.

[5] T. Bellwood, L. Clment, and C. von Riegen. Universal Description, Discovery and Integration (UDDI) V3.0. http://uddi.org/pubs/uddi-v3.0.1-20031014.pdf, October 2003. OASIS Specification.

[6] E. Bertino, M. Braun, S. Castano, E. Ferrari, and M. Mesiti. Author-X: A Java-based System for XML Data Protection. In *Proc. IFIP WG11.3 Working Conference on Database Security*, The Netherlands, August 2000.

[7] E. Bertino, S. Castano, and E. Ferrari. Securing XML Documents with Author-X. *IEEE Internet Computing*, 5(3):21–31, 2001.

[8] E. Bertino, S. Castano, E. Ferrari, and M. Mesiti. Controlled Access and Dissemination of XML Documents. In *Proc. of 2nd ACM Workshop on Web Information and Data Management*, pages 22–27, Kansas City, 1999.

[9] E. Bertino, S. Castano, E. Ferrari, and M. Mesiti. Specifying and enforcing access control policies for XML document sources. *World Wide Web*, 3(3):139–151, 2000.

[10] P. Buneman, S. Davidson, W. Fan, C. Hara, and W.-C. Tan. Reasoning about keys for XML. *Information Systems*, 28(8):1037–1063, 2003.

[11] E. Christensen, F. Curbera, G. Meredith, and S. Weerawarana. Web Services Description Language (WSDL) 1.1. http://www.w3.org/TR/wsdl, March 2001.

[12] E. Damiani, S. De Capitani di Vimercati, S. Paraboschi, and P. Samarati. A fine-grained Access Control System for XML documents. *ACM Trans. Inf. Syst. Secur.*, 5(2):169–202, 2002.

[13] E. Damiani, S. D. C. di Vimercati, S. Paraboschi, and P. Samarati. Design and Implementation of an Access Control Processor for XML Documents. In *9th World Wide Web Conference*, The Netherlands, 2000.

[14] E. Damiani, S. D. C. di Vimercati, S. Paraboschi, and P. Samarati. Securing XML Documents. In *Conference on Extending Database Technology*, Prague, March 2002.

[15] W. Fan and L. Libkin. On XML integrity constraints in the presence of DTDs. *J. ACM*, 49(3):368–406, 2002.

[16] W. Fan and J. Simeon. Integrity Constraints for XML. In *Symposium on Principles of Database Systems*, pages 23–34, 2000.

[17] C. Farkas and A. Stoica. Correlated Data Inference in Ontology Guided XML Security Engine. In *Proc. of IFIP WG 11.3 Working Group Conference on Data and Application Security*, 2003.

[18] V. Gowadia and C. Farkas. RDF metadata for XML Access Control. In *Proceedings of the 2003 ACM workshop on XML security*, pages 39–48. ACM Press, 2003.

[19] V. Gowadia and C. Farkas. Tree automata for Schema-level Filtering of XML Associations. *Journal of Research and Practice in Information Technology*, page In Press, 2005.

[20] E. Hung, Y. Deng, and V. S. Subrahmanian. TOSS: an extension of TAX with Ontologies and similarity queries. In *SIGMOD '04: Proceedings of the 2004 ACM SIGMOD international conference on Management of data*, pages 719–730, New York, NY, USA, 2004. ACM Press.

[21] H. V. Jagadish, L. V. S. Lakshmanan, D. Srivastava, and K. Thompson. TAX: A Tree Algebra for XML. In *Proceedings of DBPL'01*, pages 149–164, 2001.

[22] S. Jajodia, M. Kudo, and V. S. Subrahmanian. Provisional Authorizations. In *Proc. 1st Workshop on Security and Privacy in E-Commerce*, 2000.

[23] N. Kodali, C. Farkas, and D. Wijesekera. An Authorization Model for Multimedia Digital Libraries. *Journal of Digital Libraries*, 4:139–155, 2004.

[24] N. Kodali, C. Farkas, and D. Wijesekera. Enforcing Semantics Aware Security in Multimedia Surveillance. *Journal on Data Semantics (Springer LNCS)(Invited)*, 2:199–221, 2005.

[25] M. Kudo and S. Hada. XML document security based on provisional authorization. In *CCS '00: Proceedings of the 7th ACM conference on Computer and communications security*, pages 87–96, New York, NY, USA, 2000. ACM Press.

[26] M. Kudo and S. Hada. Access Control Model with Provisional Actions. In *IEICE Trans. Fundamentals*, 2001.

[27] S. Liu, J. Mei, A. Yue, , and Z. Lin. XSDL: Making XML Semantics Explicit. In *Proc. of Semantic Web and Databases, Second International Workshop*, pages 64–83, Toronto, Canada, August 2004.

[28] N. Mitra. SOAP Version 1.2 Part 0: Primer. http://www.w3.org/TR/2003/REC-soap12-part0-20030624/, June 2003.

[29] M. Murata, A. Tozawa, M. Kudo, and S. Hada. XML Access Control using Static Analysis. In *CCS '03: Proceedings of the 10th ACM conference on Computer and communications security*, pages 73–84. ACM Press, 2003.

[30] L. Qin and V. Atluri. Concept-level Access Control for the Semantic Web. In *Proceedings of the 2003 ACM workshop on XML security*, pages 94–103. ACM Press, 2003.

[31] P. Reddivari, T. Finin, and A. Joshi. Policy based Access Control for a RDF Store. In *Proceedings of the Policy Management for the Web Workshop*, A WWW 2005 Workshop, pages 78–83. W3C, May 2005.

[32] D. Roy. Multilevel XML Data Model. Master's thesis, University of South Carolina, Columbia, July 2005.

[33] A. Sheth, B. Aleman-Mezal, I. B. Arpinar, C. Halaschek, C. Ramakrishnan, C. Bertram, Y. Warke, D. Avant, F. S. Arpinar, K. Anyanwu, and K. Kochut. Semantic Association Identification and Knowledge Discovery for National Security Applications. *Special Issue of JOURNAL OF DATABASE MANAGEMENT on Database Technology for Enhancing National Security, Ed. Lina Zhou. (Invited paper).*, August 2003.

[34] A. Sheth, C. Bertram, D. Avant, B. Hammond, K. Kochut, and Y. Warke. Managing semantic content for the web. *IEEE Internet Computing*, 6(4):80–87, 2002.

[35] A. Stoica and C. Farkas. Secure XML Views. In *Proc.of IFIP WG11.3 Working Group Conference on Database and Application Security*, 2002.

[36] A. Stoica and C. Farkas. Ontology guided Security Engine. *Journal of Intelligent Information Systems*, 23:209–223, 2004.

SESSION 2 – SECURITY CULTURE

HOW MUCH SHOULD WE PAY FOR SECURITY? (INVITED PAPER)

Sokratis K. Katsikas[1], Athanasios N. Yannacopoulos[2] , Stefanos Gritzalis[1], Costas Lambrinoudakis[1] and Peter Hatzopoulos[2]

[1]*Dept. of Information and Communication Systems Engineering, University of the Aegean, Karlovassi, Samos, Greece GR-83200;* [2]*Dept. of Statistics and Actuarial – Financial Mathematics, University of the Aegean, Karlovassi, Samos, Greece GR-83200.*

Abstract: Information systems security has become a top priority issue for most organizations worldwide IT managers try to protect their systems through a series of technical security measures. Even though these measures can be determined through risk analysis, the appropriate amount that should be invested in Information Systems security is, by and large, determined empirically. Organizations would also wish to insure their information systems against potential security incidents. In this case both parties, namely the organization and the insurance company would be interested in calculating a fair, mutually beneficial premium. In this paper a probabilistic structure, in the form of a Markov model, is used to provide some insight into these issues.

Key words: Information systems security, security investment, security insurance

1. INTRODUCTION

One of the most crucial steps of any risk analysis exercise, regardless of the method used to carry it out, is the presentation of the findings to the management of the organization whose information systems are the object of the analysis. This is because, in this step, the analysts have to compactly and concisely present their conclusions regarding the risks faced by the organization and the measures that need to be taken to minimize these risks. They have to do so in a language understood by an audience comprising usually high-level and/or mid-level managers, avoiding technical details and focusing on the potential financial impact of the risks (were they to come true) and on the estimated monetary cost of the proposed security countermeasures.

In such presentations, numerous questions, of a very diverse nature, are usually asked. However, there is one issue that is almost invariably brought up: "We appreciate the need for taking security measures and we realize that these will inevitably bear some cost. We are prepared to undertake some cost towards this direction; however, the estimated cost of the overall security package is beyond our allocated budget." According to the theory, the risk analysis exercise has concluded with a *justified* proposal for installing appropriate countermeasures. Moreover, it is well known that security measures are interconnected into a coherent whole; any partial implementation of the *security puzzle* may render the whole effort ineffective, hence useless. Therefore, in theory, the risk analyst must respond to the issue above stating, more or less, "This is what you should do, and you should do all of it. If your budget is inadequate, and prohibits you from implementing all the necessary measures, then there will inevitably be some risks that you will not be countering, but rather implicitly accepting". This approach is technically flawless; however, in terms of management and finances, it is quite unacceptable. By raising the issue above, any competent management team is actually asking whether there is a way of finding out how much the organization *really* needs to invest in security.

Another issue that increasingly comes up in such presentations is related to the management of the residual risk that will remain after having installed the selected security countermeasures. Until the recent past, organizations were implicitly or explicitly accepting this residual risk, as it was conceived as being rather low. Today, successful attacks against information systems can be (and are) launched by teenagers, using software tools that can be acquired at a minimal (or zero) cost. On the other hand, the value of information stored within organizational information systems has tremendously increased in our networked world. The combination of these two factors leads to the conclusion that we can no longer afford to neglect the residual risk, but we should rather try to handle it in the same way we do in other areas of operation: by mitigating it. Recently, several insurance companies have started insuring information systems against security breaches. The main question when we contemplate mitigating risk by insuring against it is how much should we pay for the insurance premium.

In this paper the two questions identified in the paragraphs above are addressed. The paper combines the findings reported in [1] and [2] and presents them in a more technically and managerially oriented (as opposed to mathematically oriented) way. It is organized as follows: In Section 2 a Markov model describing the information system under study is presented.

In Section 3 the question of calculating an actuarially fair premium for insuring the system against security breaches is taken up. Section 4 attempts to answer the question of what is the optimal security investment. Section 5 summarizes our conclusions and highlights our current and future research directions.

2. A MARKOV MODEL FOR DESCRIBING THE SECURITY OF AN INFORMATION SYSTEM

In this section we provide an overview of the continuous time Markov model proposed in [1]. This model was inspired by a general class of actuarial models for disability insurance, proposed in [3]. The model describes the current state of the information system and its possible transitions to different states of non-full operation as a result of occurrence of security incidents, in the course of time.

Let us assume that the system may result into one of N different states after possible security incidents. We will denote these states by i, where i = 1, ..., N. By $i = 0$ we will denote the state where no successful security attack has been made against the system; thus the system is fully operational. We assume that at time $t = 0$ the system is at the fully operational state $i = 0$ and as time passes by it may end up in different states of non-fully operational status, that is it may end up at one of the states $i = 1, ..., N$.

One of the most important steps in the study of various issues related to the function and security of the information system is the determination of the probability of the state of the system at various times. In order to obtain that we propose a Markov model that describes the transition between the various possible states of the system. Let us assume the simplest possible structure in which the only transitions allowed are the transitions $0 \to i$. By $S(t)$ we will denote the state of the system at time t. Clearly, $S(t)$ may take one of the values 0,1, ...,N. In the framework of the Markov model the most important quantities are the transition probabilities between states, i.e. the quantities $P_{ij}(u,t) = P[S(t) = j / S(u) = i]$. By the general theory of Markov processes in continuous time we know that the model may be fully determined by the transition rates, defined, between states $i \neq j$ as

$$\mu_{ij}(u) = \lim_{t \to u} \frac{P_{ij}(u,t)}{t-u}.$$

Observing that only transition rates of the form μ_{0i} are nonzero, and assuming time-invariant transition rates, the transition probabilities are shown in [2] to be given by

$$P_{00}(z,t) = \exp(-\mu_0(t-z)$$

$$P_{0j}(z,t) = \frac{\mu_{0j}}{\mu_0}(1-\exp(-\mu_0(t-z)),$$

where $\mu_0 = \mu_{01} + \mu_{02} + \ldots + \mu_{0N}$.

3. HOW MUCH SHOULD WE PAY FOR INSURANCE?

The question we wish to tackle in this section using the simple model of the previous section is how the insurance company can calculate the fair amount of money it will charge, or, in other words, how one may calculate the net or mathematical premium. There is not a unique way to do this; however we will present here a simple, actuarially fair way of determining the cost of the insurance service.

3.1 Actuarial values of premium and benefits

Having obtained the probabilistic structure of the model which will allow us to characterize the state of the system at different times, we may now calculate the actuarial values of the net premium and the benefits [3]. The benefits, as well as the net premium received depend on the state of the information system, which is a random quantity. Thus, the benefits and the net premium received at time *I* are random variables. The term *actuarial value* denotes the best possible prediction for these random variables, given some information on the system state up to time *t*. Because of the Markov structure of the model, the information from time 0 to time *t* is summed up to the information on the state of the system at time *t*, i.e. it sums up to the information provided by the random variable *S(t)*. As the best possible prediction, we will take the conditional expectation of the random variable given the information provided by *S(t)*. Also note that the benefits and the premium are paid at different times. In order to be able to compare sums of money received or given at different times, we need to evaluate their value at the same time instance. This is done using a properly chosen discounting factor. We will assume (without loss of generality) that there is a constant deterministic interest rate δ. Thus the discounting factor, relating the value of a payment at time t to the value of this payment at time 0 is $e^{-\delta t}$.

Using the above assumptions, the present value at time t of a continuous benefit at rate $c_j(u)$ given by the insurance company to the owner of the information system at time u as long as $S(u)=j$, is the random sum of money

$$Y_t = e^{-\delta(u-t)} \bullet l_{\{S(u)-j\}} \bullet c_j(u) \bullet du$$

where $l_{\{S(u)-j\}}$ is the indicator of the event $\{S(u)=j\}$ and $c_j(u)$ is the benefit amount paid out in the infinitesimal interval $[u, u+du]$.

In a similar manner, one may calculate the premium. Let us assume that the premium paid varies with the state the system is in. The actuarial value of the net premium at time t, paid at time u if the system is in state j and if $S(t)=i$ is given by the formula

$$P_{t,i,j}(u) = e^{-\delta(u-t)} P_{ij}(t,u) c_j(u) du$$

The total benefits and premium paid will result as the sum over all possible states. Thus the actuarial value of the benefits and premium at time t, paid between time t and T, if the system is in the state $S(t)=i$ at time t will be equal to

$$B_i(t,T) = \int_t^T e^{-\delta(u-t)} \sum_{j=0}^{N} P_{ij}(t,u) b_j(u) du$$

$$P_i(t,T) = \int_t^T e^{-\delta(u-t)} \sum_{j=0}^{N} P_{ij}(t,u) p_j(u) du$$

where T is the term of the contract, i.e. the time when the contract expires.

3.2 Calculation of the premium

For the calculation of the premium one may follow several approaches (giving possibly different results). We present here a simple way for obtaining the premium, which does not involve the use of utility functions.

The insurance contract is entered at time $t=0$, when the system is in state

0. A fair way to calculate the premium would be using the *principle of equivalence,* according to which we choose the premium in such a way so that the actuarial value of the benefits at time $t=0$ and in state 0 is equal to the actuarial value of the total premium paid, again calculated at time $t=0$ and state 0. Mathematically this, means that $B_0(0,T) = P_0(0,T)$.

According to this principle the insured expects to pay to the insurer as much as she expects to get (of course in terms of estimates of the random variables involved). In our simple model the insured pays premium only when the system is in state 0. Also recall that in our model only the transition probabilities P_{0i} are non-zero. Using the equivalence principle and the expressions for the transition probabilities obtained in Section 3.1 and assuming that $P_0(u) = P_0$ we can calculate the net premium as [2]

$$P = \frac{\delta + \mu_0}{\mu_0} \bullet \frac{1}{1 - e^{-(\delta+\mu_0)T}} \bullet \int_0^T e^{-\delta u} \sum_{j=0}^{N} \mu_{0j} (1 - e^{-\mu_0 u}) b_j(u) du$$

4. HOW MUCH SHOULD WE INVEST IN SECURITY?

We now assume that the owner of the information system undertakes some security measures that will have an effect on the transition rate from state 0 to the states $j = 1,..., N$. It is reasonable to assume that one may adopt security measures to reduce the risk of transition to particular states. The cost of the security measure related to the transition to state j will be denoted by Z_j. We will further assume, following the work in [4], that there is also another set of relevant parameters, the vulnerabilities of the various information sets. However, departing from the setup of [4], we assume that an expert may define vulnerability parameters for the various states that the system may end up in. Thus we may assume that the transition rates μ_{0j} are functions of the security cost Z_j and of the vulnerability parameter $v(j).\mu_{0j}(z_j, v_j)$. In general, one expects these functions to enjoy the following properties:

P1. $\mu_{0j}(z_j, 0) = 0$, i.e. if the system is completely invulnerable with respect to the risks related to transition to state *j,* there will be no such transition.

P2. $\mu_{0j}(0,v_j) = v_j = \overline{\mu_{0j}}$, i.e. if no security measures are undertaken, then the transition rate to state j will be equal to some constant, which may be defined to be the vulnerability v_j.

P3. $\mu_{0j}(z_j,v_j)$ is a decreasing convex function of Z_j. If we assume that μ_{0j} is twice differentiable with respect to Z_j, then

$$\frac{\vartheta\mu_{0j}}{\vartheta z_j} < 0 \text{ and } \frac{\vartheta^2\mu_{0j}}{\vartheta z_j^2} > 0.$$

This means that the larger the cost of security measures undertaken, the smaller the transition rates become but after a while there is a saturation effect, in the sense that larger security measures have diminishing effect.

Thus, using the above transition rates, we may construct a Markov chain $S^z(t)$, corresponding to the state of the system at time t if the security measures $z = \{z_1,\ldots,z_N\}$ are adopted.

In order to construct a model for determining the optimal security measures, one must first construct a model for the financial losses caused by the transition of the system to one of the states of malfunction. This can be done with the aid of the Markov chain model proposed in Section 2. We will denote by $X^z(t)$ the stochastic process corresponding to the financial losses (measured in terms of some currency) caused by a possible transition of the system to some state of malfunction. The possible losses may be of various types. For instance, one may assume that there is a lump sum loss $d_j(u)$ at fixed time u if $S^z(u) = j$. This is one of the simplest type of possible losses. Other types of losses are possible and can be treated with similar methods as the ones proposed here. For a simpler exposition of our model we will be content here with the treatment of losses of the above type.

The random wealth of the firm at time t will be

$$w - \sum_{i=1}^{N} z_i - X^z(t)$$

where w is the initial wealth of the firm,

$$\sum_{i=1}^{N} z_i$$

is the total value of the security measures adopted by the firm and $X^z(t)$ are the financial losses that the firm faces as a consequence of transitions to certain states of malfunction. We assume that $X^z(0)=0$, i.e the system starts at state 0, which corresponds to the state of perfect working order of the system.

The firm will select security measures so as to maximize the intertemporal expected utility of its random wealth. Therefore, the security measures will be chosen so as to solve the problem

$$\max_{z_1,\dots,z_N} E(U) = E\left[\int_0^T e^{-\delta t} u(w - \sum_{i=1}^N z_i - X^z(t)dt + u(w - \sum_{i=1}^N z_i)\right]$$

possibly subject to the constraint $\sum_{i=1}^N z_i \le K$, where K is a budget constraint corresponding to the maximum amount that may be spent on security. The factor $e^{-\delta t}$ is a discounting factor that models the time impatience properties of the firm and u is a utility function, corresponding to a risk averse agent that is an increasing concave function (see e.g. []). T is the time horizon over which the firm wishes to plan ahead.

We assume that the decision of the security measures adopted is made at time t=0 and is held unchanged throughout the horizon T. A more dynamic model where the decisions are changed over specified time intervals is possible in the above setup, but such a model will not be discussed here.

The Markov structure of the model allows the simplification of the above expectation of the utility function. Assuming losses of the type discussed above and keeping in mind the Markovian nature of the $S^z(t)$ process, one concludes that the optimal security investment program arises as the solution to the set of equations

$$\frac{\vartheta E[u]}{\vartheta z_k} = -\sum_{j=1}^N u'(w - \sum_{i=1}^N z_i - d_j) A_j(z,v) + \sum_{j=1}^N u(w - \sum_{i=1}^N z_i - d_j) \times$$
$$\frac{\vartheta A_j(z,v)}{\vartheta z_k} - u'(w - \sum_{i=1}^N z_i) = 0$$

In the general case, these maximization conditions are nonlinear algebraic equations, which have to be treated numerically. Nowadays, the numerical treatment of such equations is fast, accurate and straightforward with the use of standard commercial numerical packages. The use of such methods may yield quite easily the optimal security investment for the firm, taking into account the characteristics of the firm towards risk (the utility function), the structure of the firm (how much a firm is willing to invest on security) and the structure of the risks the firm is likely to undergo (the probabilistic model for the state of the firm, concerning its security). However, for special cases of utility functions, which are of great practical interest, one may additionally obtain analytic solutions, which help reveal the essential features of our model and allow us to make some observations about possible strategies for optimal security investment. Such types of problems are treated next.

4.1 Some special cases

As a special case of the above general formulation, one may consider the case of the linear utility function. This is equivalent to the criterion of minimization of the expected loss that has been used in related work for the determination of optimal security investment (see e.g. [5].) Further, in order to gain insight into the physical meaning of the mathematical results, consider the case where only two possible states of malfunction exist, one of which is less probable than the other. This can be mathematically modeled by setting $\mu_{01} = \varepsilon\mu_0(z_1)$ and $\mu_{02} = \mu_0(z_2)$ for some function $\mu_0(z_2)$ that enjoys properties P1-P3. In this case, it can be seen [2] that $\mu_0'(z_1) = O\left(\frac{1}{\varepsilon}\right)$ and $\mu_0'(z_2) = O(1)$, implying that $z_1 << z_2$, i.e. the organization should spend a negligible amount of money to counter risk 1 (the less probable one) and should concentrate on risk 2.

Under the same assumptions, if we turn our attention to what happens as $T \to \infty$, we can conclude [2] that, when $d_1 = d_2$, and for $\mu_{0i} = A_i v \exp(-a_i z_i)$ (Class I transition rates), then

$$z_1^* = -\frac{1}{a_1}\ln\left(\frac{\mu_{01}^*}{A_1}\right) + \frac{1}{a_1}\ln(v)$$

Using this result one may discuss the dependence of the optimal security investment as a function of the vulnerability parameter. First of all, this quantity must be positive. This will happen only for large enough values of A_1. For small enough values of A_1, it may well be that below a critical value v^* of the vulnerability parameter the optimal security investment is zero. Otherwise, it is a weakly increasing function of the vulnerability parameter.

On the other hand, if we assume that $\mu_{0i} = A_i v^{a_i z_i + 1}$ (Class II transition rates), then

$$z_1^* = -\frac{1}{a_1} - \frac{1}{a_1}\frac{\ln(A_1)}{\ln(v)} + \frac{1}{a_1}\frac{\ln(\mu_{01}^*(v))}{\ln(v)}.$$

Now the behavior of the optimal investment as the vulnerability parameter changes is different. For this kind of transition functions we observe an abrupt increase of the security investment as the vulnerability parameter approaches values near 1.

The conclusions from this simplified version of the model are that the effectiveness of the security measures plays an important role on the optimal security investment. Specifically, for Class I transition rates we notice that a small increase in the invested amount in security leads to a large decrease of the probability of the system to end-up in a non-fully operational state (effective security measures). In this case the optimal investment curve exhibits saturation properties. On the contrary, for Class Π transition rates, where the security investments are not that effective, the optimal investment curve does not exhibit saturation properties for large values of the vulnerability parameter.

5. CONCLUSIONS

In this paper we have proposed a Markov model describing the transitions of an information system from the fully operational state to states of non-fully operational status, as a result of a security incident that damages an asset of the information system, using the transition intensity approach. This model has been used for estimating the premium of the insurance contract against the expected losses to the organization that will result from potential security incidents. The model is then improved, being now capable of monitoring the effect of security investment on the probability of a security breach to occur. Insight into practical aspects of risk management is shown to be gained by even this, still simple, model.

Our current research work focuses on extending the model so as to waive the assumption that all non-fully operational states of the information system are absorbing states. In other words, the extended model will be capable of handling cases where there is a transition from some state $i, i \neq 0$ to the fully operational state 0. Another extension will be that all the assets of the information system will be modelled, instead of a single asset that is currently supported, thus enabling us to account for interdependencies of security incidents or/and security measures operating on different assets and consequently to obtain a more accurate estimate of the insurance premium.

6. REFERENCES

1. Lambrinoudakis C., Gritzalis S., Hatzopoulos P., Yannacopoulos A.N. and Katsikas, S.K., A formal model for pricing information systems insurance contracts, *Computer Standards & Interfaces* **27**, 521-532 (2005).
2. Yannacopoulos A.N., Lambrinoudakis C., Gritzalis S., Hatzopoulos P., and Katsikas, S.K., A dynamic stochastic model for optimizing information systems security investment, *submitted for publication.*
3. Habennan, S. and Pitacco, E., *Actuarial models for disability insurance*, Chapman and Hall, 1999.
4. Gordon, L.A. and Loeb, P., The economics of information security investment, ACM Transactions on Information and Communication Systems Security, **5**, 438-457, 2002.
5. Varian, H.R., *Microeconomic analysis*, Norton and Co., 1992.

DO NOT SHIP, OR RECEIVE, TROJAN HORSES (*)

Avoiding Network Vulnerabilities Potentially Introduced by Embedded Systems

Corey Hirsch
LeCroy Corporation, 700 Chestnut Ridge Road, Chestnut Ridge, New York, 10977, USA, Corey.Hirsch@LeCroy.Com

Abstract: Academic journals and trade press have explored several likely routes of malware contagion against which information security practitioners need to defend. These include traditional 'tunnels and bridges' that bypass the firewalled corporate perimeter, such as visitor's laptops, VPN tunnels, encrypted & zipped email attachments, unencrypted wireless, and weak authentication. A potential threat that has not been widely documented is embedded Windows ™ based systems and appliances. Corporate networks that are otherwise highly secure often have some tens of nodes that are not generally recognized as 'computers', however run networkable Windows ™ operating systems (OS). These devices range from smart phones to engineering microscopes, from oscilloscopes to print stations, and many others. They may have no single owner, and frequently generic or group user accounts are established on them. They have not been purchased by the IT department and may not appear on IT's lists of machines to patch and monitor. Vendor's practices vary widely, with results for their customers ranging from 'no issue' to 'serious risk'. This paper narrates the embedded appliance infosecurity lifecycle, to provide vendors of such systems with best-in-class precautionary measures they should take on behalf of their customers' security, and to provide purchasers of such appliances with a checklist to enable them to select secure products. LeCroy, a leader in safe and secure Windows ™ appliance engineering, provides the reference case for best-in-class practice. Research in this field is being conducted at LeCroy and elsewhere, in August 2005, by Dr. Julia Kotlarsky of Warwick Business School, and Dr. Ilan Oshri of Erasmus.

(*) Trojan Horse in this context denotes a hidden danger. It escapes detection because it is considered something other than a computer.

Key words: Embedded systems; Windows Network Security; Trojan Horse; Appliances;

1. SCOPE

Digital general-purpose computers have been in use for approximately 60 years. During this period, especially recently, many types of special-purpose machines that had previously been implemented using analog electronics, have been re-designed in digital incarnations, to take advantage of myriad inherent feature and user interface benefits, and design reusability. Numerically controlled machine tools, cameras, television, and scientific equipment are a few examples. Embedded microprocessor is the preponderant design, and therefore Operating System and application software are required, to convert a general-purpose machine to a special purpose one. Embedded system units far outnumber computer units in terms of total annual microprocessor and microcontroller production. Windows ™ based embedded appliance production unit volume is not believed to exceed Windows ™ based computer volume. Windows ™ based appliances in this paper are not limited to those employing Windows ™ CE and Windows ™ XP Embedded operating systems.

Initially, many special-purpose 'programmable appliances' operated with embedded proprietary programming busses, operating systems, and application software. These networks, operating systems and application programs very likely contained vulnerabilities such as buffer overflows and could potentially have been successfully attacked. However given the fragmented nature of the opportunity, few such exploits took place.

In recent years, many vendors have replaced proprietary busses and operating systems with industry standards, and many have offered these appliances as Windows ™ -Networkable machines. A decision to do this may appear to the vendor to offer only upside. The upside is less design investment required by the vendor in areas perceived as low value-add, such as writing hardware drivers and file management systems. Many vendors fail to grasp the corresponding requirement: to become far more sophisticated than the average organization regarding information security, and to provide a comprehensive security regime to protect downstream organizations. Doing one without the other changes the equation to one where the vendor benefits short term but the user assumes a risk over the lifetime of the product.

Today there remain some networkable appliances that still employ proprietary hardware and/or operating systems, as well as non- Windows ™ industry standards such as Linux, and they very likely present network vulnerabilities. In addition, the application programs in such machines, as well as application programs in Windows ™ appliances, likely present vulnerabilities. Anything with a TCP/IP stack may contain a vulnerability. These categories of vulnerability however are outside the scope of this paper.

This paper deals solely with recognizing and mitigating vulnerabilities associated with Microsoft Networking and Windows ™ Operating Systems in embedded systems and appliances (referred to hereafter as 'appliances').

2. CONTEXT

This paper is written with enterprise networks in mind, especially those with several hundred, or more, nodes. Today, myriad tools including anti-spam, anti-virus, anti-spy ware, auto-patching, encryption, firewalls, intrusion detection/prevention, and others often protect such networks. Client computers in such organizations are often purchased, setup, and maintained by an IT group that is trained and equipped to reduce information security vulnerabilities and manage security risks on networks.

In addition to tools, processes are vital in locking down large networks, and many organizations have implemented policies regarding password strength, access control, patching and virus definition updating, and others, that rely on the concept of 'one machine, one owner'.

The tools, and processes, referred to above will probably not encompass network nodes that were purchased, for example, by the facilities department, or the engineering department, or by an individual marketer. The vulnerabilities they introduce are likely to by-pass these defenses, and your perimeter. For example, a shared microscope in an engineering group may offer a soft node in an otherwise hardened network, and a platform from which unauthorized access can be gained, internal reconnaissance conducted, and further damage propagated. A hospital with several medical imagers on its network, a university physics lab with 20 oscilloscope stations, a business with office staff's PDAs in cradles, or a document copy/print station, face the same potential threat.

At this time there is no standard or widely accepted third party certification of vendor's embedded security practices, as there is for example in the quality arena (ISO9000) or financial reporting controls (SAS70), and buyers at this time must therefore make their own enquiries.

This paper narrates the product lifecycle steps in which security should play a role, and implicitly offers vendors suggestions as to how to invest for safety at each, in order to elevate themselves in the vendor maturity model presented below in figure 1. Tests and questions for distinguishing between secure and insecure offerings are included for the consumer community. The text is written grammatically to address consumers as the audience.

3. VENDOR MATURITY MODEL

A tiered vendor classification scheme is introduced:

Best-in-class: Information security practices prominent in every stage of customer interaction and support.

Basic care in product manufacture and delivery: Information security practices prominent in production stage of customer interaction and support, such as AV shipped in package.

Tactical care: Information security practices are prominent if convenient for vendor, such as provision of XP SP2 mods files for customers when appliance's application code requires.

Worst-in-class: Information security not prominent at any stage of customer interaction or support.

4. LIFECYCLE MODEL

The following stages are examined here:

- Product Design
- Shopping; Selling and Demonstration Process
- Production
- Shipment and Receiving
- Deployment
- Service; Calibration or Repair
- End of Life; Disposal, Secure Transfer or Destruction of Data

A discussion of issues, and questions an alert buyer might ask, will be presented for each stage.

5. PRODUCT DESIGN

Design choices as fundamental as motherboard, processor, and chipset will affect the long-term security of the resulting appliance. Vendors may choose a line of commercial components, seeking latest revision processors, memories, busses and peripherals, in support of frequently improved banner spec claims. Or they may choose OEM lines, in support of stable, and more secure, platforms over time. Software will often track HW revision levels, hence the vendor's 'dwell time' on a given OS will be influenced by component choices made early in design. OS's have a security 'sweet spot' as they age; new releases have undiscovered vulnerabilities, while very old OS's are unsupported and without patches when vulnerabilities are found. Best-in-class vendors will have considered their customer's security needs carefully, and their security team will be able to articulate their adoption practices and how those optimize their tradeoff between processor banner specs and overall system security. Hardware security features, such as the Intel disable bit architecture, should play a part in the vendor's chip & chipset selection.

Other design choices reflect the vendor's security culture as well. These include design of ports such as USB, drives, Ethernet connectors, and also design of application software to be compatible with future OS patches. Accessories signal the vendor's thinking; is antivirus (AV) a standard accessory? Are other security options, such as dual factor authentication, or a firewall, available for the product? Are removable drives an option? Has the vendor considered customers' diverse requirements and preferences regarding security, such as sites that may prefer one AV package vs. another? Best-in-class vendors will have covered most bases above. Tactical-care vendors will have mixed coverage, as their strategy will not have been security-aware and hence each decision taken may fall randomly on the security spectrum.

Software licensing for the OS should be undertaken with security in mind. If the vendor's choices limit the user's ability to operate a secure appliance, for example by limiting the number of applications that can be run on the unit, this introduces needless, severe, security risks. The license for example might limit the appliance to two applications, in which case the appliance's application program would utilize at least one, eliminating for example the possibility of running both AV and Site Kiosk, or other risk management packages. The OS license may also impact allowed methodologies for automated OS patching.

The questions below are likely to uncover key indicators of vendor maturity (the salesperson may have to refer these questions to a security team member):

- What is your design-for-security strategy with regards to hardware, mechanical, and OS?
- What product HW and SW options are provided or supported to reduce security risk?
- What EULA (end user license agreement) is provided with this product?
- What steps have been taken to insure the application program will be compatible with future security patches?
- Have any of the standard features of the OS been disabled? (best-in-class answer would be 'yes', or 'optionally')
- Does the application have any back-doors or hard-coded passwords?
- How is the application code tested for bugs?
- Is regression testing performed on new OS and new application updates?
- Are application updates digitally signed?
- What strength encryption, if any, is employed in the appliance? Is NTFS encryption supported?
- Are all unneeded services switched off (such as Telnet)?
- If Internet Explorer is part of the shipped appliance, can it be disabled or replaced by another browser?
- Can the application program be run without Administrator privileges?
- Can the user replace the Windows Firewall with a third party firewall?
- Are performance specifications offered with, and without, AV installed and running? Will running AV (or AntiSpyware) real-time protection interfere with the application program?
- Is the application software compatible with a screensaver?
- Does the application program perform user authentication, and if so does it employ secure methods?
- Does the appliance have potentially insecure access, such as a CD-ROM that will accept a Windows recovery CD?

6. SHOPPING; SELLING AND DEMONSTRATION PROCESS

You may first 'touch' your potential vendor on their website. The odds of a best-in-class vendor having a website that avoids discussing info-security is low, as are the odds of a worst-in-class vendor's site providing comprehensive security information of interest to prospective customers. The shopper in your organization may not be focused on security, for example an engineer looking for a test & measurement tool may not have network security in mind. It is important that CIOs raise awareness of security broadly inside their organizations.

Two critical pages to look for on a vendor's site are the company's privacy policy, and their information security page. These should both be easy to find, normally clickable directly off the home page. They should both be informative and broad, but not deep (truly secure providers do not broadcast technical details of their defenses). If either or both of these pages are not available, this is your first red flag of an immature vendor.

A best-in-class vendor will have trained and equipped its sales-force, such that they will not introduce information security risks during the demonstration or sales process. The appliance they bring along to your site for a demonstration, has presumably been to several other locations recently. Was it connected directly to another prospect's LAN, or to the public Internet? Demonstration or evaluation units should be inspected/evaluated by your IT/security function as well as by end application users.

Questions to ask the salesperson:

- What precautions do you take prior to connecting the appliance to my network, to insure there is no malware contagion?
- What precautions do you take with regard to your laptop PC to insure there is no malware contagion?
- How does your firm guard against spam, malware and spyware on company networks in general, and in particular with regard to demonstration units and salesperson's PC's?
- Ask to see any training documents, brochures or materials on infosecurity that the salesperson has received in the prior year.

7. PRODUCTION

Unless this is a key business partner, you likely are not willing to visit their plant to see first hand what precautions they take during production. However, they should be willing to host such a visit if you wish (and it does not hurt to enquire). You should still be able to find out a good deal, without travel, by asking to be put in touch with the head of the vendor's security team. The questions to ask include:

- Is this product manufactured in your own facilities, or those of a contract manufacturer? If a contract manufacturer is used, how do you insure their production line is secure?
- Are isolated networks in place for production (and for later servicing) of the product?
- Do production and/or service networks contain out of support (old) nodes? Is the equipment used in production certified to be malware-free?
- Is each box externally scanned just prior to shipment? With what tool? (Internal scanning tools introduce difficulties for customers who do not prefer the particular tool which the vendor chose to embed)
- How often are master images updated to reflect most recent patches?
- Do recovery CDs reflect recent images?

For those of you going through Sarbanes-Oxley compliance testing, consider this process parallel to, and as important as, checking the SAS70 of your key infrastructure vendors.

8. SHIPMENT AND RECEIVING

On opening the shipping box there will be several immediate clues as to the security and maintainability of your new asset.

- How long ago was it shipped? If the product was manufactured long ago, and sat in a warehouse or at a distributor for many months, it is more vulnerable when first put onto the internet. Is there a document in the package that gives you the date the unit was last scanned, and packed for shipment?

- Was it shipped with an AV package in the carton? If so, was AV installed on the system drive? (best-in-class answer is, surprisingly, no). AV packages are complex to un-install, so the best-in-class vendor will not pre-judge the user's organizations' preference in AV product, rather they will supply one in the box, and allow the user the choice of installing it or not. This in turn implies the vendor needs a system for scanning the machine from the outside, which is a nontrivial capability.
- Is the Ethernet connector covered with a warning label directing you to a source of detailed security information prior to connection to a LAN? (best-in-class answer is yes)
- If WinXP SP2 or newer, was it shipped with the firewall enabled?
- Is there a restore CD, or hidden partition for emergency recovery? If so, is it at the same level of patching as the disk image? Does the vendor keep this image current (surprisingly, not the best practice)? Best practice is to keep the image current only as of the most recent critical update (defined for embedded appliances as vulnerability to a passive threat).
- What user accounts have been set up by default on embedded Windows system? Does the documentation explain how to alter the default passwords? Are administrator-level access rights easy to protect? Are there instructions for how to reset account access should the unit need to be shipped back for repair? If the answers to these questions are all positive the vendor is probably best-in-class.
- The unit may have been 'off the network' for an extended period, especially if you purchased it from a stocking distributor (see above). Is there provision for safely connecting it to the internet the first time, despite this delay?
- Was it shipped with a certification as to its malware scab results and patch status as of shipment?
- Was it shipped with clear instructions for safe usage over time when networked?
- What choices did the vendor make in the security setup of Windows™? Try running Microsoft's Baseline Security Analyzer for a clear set of security diagnostics.

9. DEPLOYMENT

An 'owner' should be designated for each network node of this type. Often such machines are shared assets, not on the IT team's lists of computers, and if a responsible manager is not identified no one will be aware of its security status.

In settings such as universities, where users will be transitory and difficult to vet, you may need an option to restrain appliance use and/or user access to the underlying Windows ™ OS. Programs such as Site Kiosk, or in-built restriction or access control options can provide this facility. Best in class vendors will have some solution for these settings.

Things to check for:

- Does the product appear to be 'phoning home' to its manufacturer? If so, what information is transferred? If in doubt, ask the vendor and insist on an authoritative response (the salesperson may have no idea).
- How easy is it to get firmware and software updates for the product? Are the source sites for these secured using login credentials? (If this process is insecure, you are at risk every time you download, and just as worrisome this indicates the vendor hasn't thought through the security process for its customers over the whole product lifecycle).
- Does the vendor provide active (such as via email), or passive (such as posting on their website) security updates, such as advice on taking service packs or patches?
- Can disk drives be removed in order to protect data?

10. SERVICE; CALIBRATION OR REPAIR

This stage is the ultimate indicator of best-in-class. Look for these factors:

- What warranty period is offered? How does it compare to industry average?
- What is the long-term support period provided? How does it compare to industry average? The 'sweet spot' is about 7 years; long enough to fully utilize the asset, not so long as to require the

vendor or contract manufacturer to maintain unsupportable OS's on the production or service networks in their factory.
- What is the software support and version update process?
- Does the vendor scan your product prior to connecting it to a network during repair?
- Is the repair network isolated?
- Does the vendor scan your product prior to return shipping it to you?
- If a security problem is discovered, does the vendor contact you to offer a range of possible methods to deal with it?
- How does the vendor insure the privacy of any data you have stored on the appliance during the service process?
- Are instructions provided to facilitate administrator account access during service in a secure manner?

11. END OF LIFE; DISPOSAL, SECURE TRANSFER OR DESTRUCTION OF DATA

If the appliance is one, such as laboratory equipment, that has gathered or stored important data for the customer, then secure disposal is important.

Consider:

- Are storage media removable?
- Are methods for data backup/restore/archive provided?
- Ask the vendor what their WEEE compliance strategy is (**WEEE** is the abbreviation for the Directive on **W**aste **E**lectrical and **E**lectronic **E**quipment being implemented by the European Union. The **WEEE** Directive aims to reduce waste through the re-cycling and reuse of electronic products.)

12. SUMMARY

Vendors opting for standardized networking and OS solutions should consider every step of the customer interaction cycle carefully from a security perspective.

Pending adoption of a third party security certification process, the buyer must beware and make appropriate enquiries to avoid introducing network vulnerabilities into an otherwise hardened corporate network.

EMPLOYEE SECURITY PERCEPTION IN CULTIVATING INFORMATION SECURITY CULTURE

Omar Zakaria[2]
Information Security Group, Royal Holloway, University of London, Egham, Surrey,TW20 0EX England

Abstract: This paper discusses employee security perception perspective. Perception is important as employee behaviour can be influenced by it. The intention is not to attempt an exhaustive literature review, but to understand the perception concept that can be used to cultivate an information security culture within an organisation. The first part highlights some of the concepts of perception. The second part interprets the employee security perception in the case study. Finally, a synthesized perspective on this perception is presented.

Key words: Information security; information security culture; employee; employee security perception; perception; perception analysis; case study.

1. INTRODUCTION

Schlienger and Teufel (2002) argue that information security culture should support all activities in a way that information security becomes a natural aspect in daily activities of every employee (i.e. user). Ward (2002) explains that the development of information security culture must result in change in employee behaviour. Zakaria and Gani (2003) state that information security culture can lead an employee to act as a "human

[2] He has been awarded a scholarship from the University of Malaya, Kuala Lumpur, Malaysia to pursue his PhD at the Royal Holloway, University of London

firewall" in order to safeguard organisational information assets. This means that employees must perceive security practices as part of their daily work routines. Without appropriate employee security perception, an organisation will stay largely exposed to security threats and vulnerabilities, and later will hinder internal security incidents. Thus, the subsequent sections will discuss concepts of perception and describe how the employee security perception can be used to cultivate security culture within an organisation.

2. CONCEPTS OF PERCEPTION

This section discusses the relationship between perception and behaviour. In general, perception may involve conscious awareness (i.e., this awareness is termed a percept or perceive) of objects, groups, symbols and events, which in turn requires some action on the part of the perceiver (Sekuler and Blake, 1994). Whilst behaviour is about what people normally do (i.e. perform an action) that can be objectively measured (Hogg and Vaughan, 2002). Huczynski and Buchanan (2001: 212) elaborate the perception and behaviour relationships in this statement: "to understand each others' behaviour, we need to be able to understand each others perception. We need to be able to understand why we perceive things differently in the first place". We can see that perception can influence behaviour. In terms of information security context, the right perception can help shape positive security behaviour. Positive security behaviour is about recognising how the theoretical security policies and procedures can be applied into practice. Once employees understand this security behaviour, they will practice it. When these practices are common, it will emerge as part of daily work routine. Later, customised security routines will develop, which in turn produces a culture of information security amongst employees within an organisation.

Over many years, researchers have studied perception for several reasons. Some of these reasons are based on practical considerations in order to solve a particular problem (Sekuler and Blake, 1994). Thus, in the following paragraph, we will provide a brief description on practical reasons for studying perception, which in turn can help us to reduce internal security incident problems.

Through the study of perception, one can recognise and rectify possible risky environmental conditions that can endanger the senses and impair the ability to make decisions (Sekuler and Blake, 1994). In relation to aspects of information security, security perception of information risk like avoidance and detection controls can help identify potentially internal security incidents (Peltier, 2001). Perception is able to reveal the actual employee basic assumptions about security within an organisation. Any mismatch between these assumptions with official security policies will influence users' perception on security matters. A wrong users' security perception will discourage them to perform security actions. No security actions amongst users will lead to a likelihood of security incidents happening internally (Egan and Mather, 2005). Therefore, through perception, we can predict possible security behaviour.

Furthermore, studying perception enables one to design devices that ascertain optimal perceptual performance (Sekuler and Blake, 1994). Some of these devices are traffic lights, telephones, alarm clocks and car signals in which people rely on during their daily life routine (e.g., during work, communication, driving, even sleep). In relating to information security, recognition of security perception amongst employees can help to design devices like an effective awareness and training programme, design for daily basic security task, even the way to manifest latent function of security mission explicitly.

Studying perception is also useful for consumer marketing (Sekuler and Blake, 1994). For example, companies in the food and beverage industry can test their products by asking consumers to taste, smell or even look at the appearance before marketing them. Therefore, utilising perception research to any products can help bring those products to the attention of customers. In information security context, we can also apply this marketing style to get employee's perception about the security task to be implemented in the organisation. By utilising this approach, we can get the most appropriate and suitable design of basic security task. Once the design is suitable to everyone, employees would be willing to practice it. This design would then become part of the daily work routine.

Therefore, it is important to make sure that the employee security perception is appropriate or suitable, specifically on information security activities. Appropriate or suitable users' security perception means that everyone assumes security activities are part of their daily work routine. Once appropriate security perception is established amongst employees, security actions will be based on their positive security behaviour, which follows the official security policies. Moreover, we have also discussed several ways to use the perception approach in order to improve security practices within an organisation. In summary, Figure 1 shows one of practical ways to establish an appropriate employee security perception.

In the next two sections, we will discuss the two parts of employee security perception. The beginning part (in section 3) will interpret employee security perception theme in the case study of XYZ Company. Finally (in section 4), we will produce a synthesised perspective on the appropriate employee security perception within a public sector organisation context.

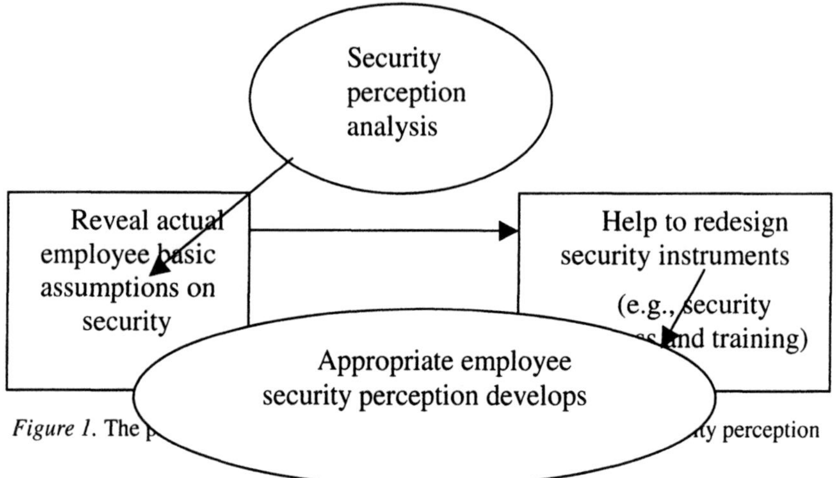

Figure 1. The p … y perception

3. INTERPRETING EMPLOYEE SECURITY PERCEPTION IN THE CASE STUDY

We use the suggested practical way (see Figure 1) for establishing an appropriate employee security perception to interpret the security perception amongst users in the XYZ case study. As discovered in this case study, users in XYZ were already concerned on information security but some of their perception on security tasks was different. Through our analysis of XYZ, employees always claimed that they have a specific Information Communication Technology (ICT) security division within the organisation, which looks after security tasks; their security staff who do the security tasks (e.g., monitor and maintain the security computer system); and their Information Communication Technology Security Officer (ICTSO) person, who does the managing of information security in XYZ. A culture of information security amongst users will not succeed if they are not involved in security activities (Babiak et al., 2005). This is because security activities involve actions which require participation not only from Information Security Officer (ISO) personnel but also from all users. An established security action will produce repeated security work, which in turn can be a part of daily work routines. Later, a security culture environment amongst users will be developed. Without security activities amongst users, there would be no security actions involved, which could lead to inappropriate security perception which derives from statements such as "Security tasks are not a part of my job" or "I am not responsible for any security matters".

Research in XYZ has shown that information security awareness and training programmes do not fully utilised users' security perception analysis in designing its module. There was no survey done in XYZ in order to know the current security perception amongst users. As already mentioned, perception analysis can be used to design an effective security instruments such as design of basic security tasks and security awareness and training programme. Perception analysis can help to structure basic security tasks properly in order to encourage all users to perform them. This is because these security tasks are designed based upon users' requirement (e.g., result from perception analysis). In short, this analysis can help us to design awareness and training programme based upon users' current security problems. In summary, perception analysis is useful to redesign security instruments and help us to understand users' implicit basic assumptions on security matters.

Therefore, highlighting appropriate security perception in users' basic assumptions should be considered as an emergent activity. Thus, the following section will offer a discussion on a synthesised perspective on the development of an appropriate security perception amongst employees.

4. A SYNTHESISED PERSPECTIVE ON APPROPRIATE EMPLOYEE SECURITY PERCEPTION

It becomes clear from the discussion so far that organisations also need to develop a strategic security vision that ties corporate security plans with the result of the users' security perception analysis. As mentioned above, an appropriate security perception amongst users can influence their security behaviour in order to accomplish the pre-determined security goals. Therefore, it is important to change any inappropriate user perception on security matters. It sounds ideal, but can it operate in practice? The following paragraphs in this section will discuss examples on changing user perception on security matters positively. Therefore, this section identifies some key principles for developing an appropriate employee security perception.

Principles

There is a general lack of using employee security perception analysis within an organisation and how it influences employee security behaviour which in turn can help interact with users' daily work routines. Therefore, it is essential to link results from the perception analysis and security practices amongst organisational users. This is because appropriate security perception may produce positive employee security behaviour. As a result, users will perform security tasks and assume it as part of the daily work routine. By adopting an appropriate employee security perception, we tend to highlight its practical applications (e.g., redesign security instruments) that can be used in the development of an information security culture. In short, an appropriate security perception amongst employees will help increase security precautions within an organisation, which in turn, can help reduce internal security incidents from happening. In addition, Sekuler and Blake (1994: 8 and 9) emphasises the rational of studying perception and extending its reasons into the development of an appropriate employee security perception as follows:

> Perception can be thought of as each individual's personal theory of reality, a kind of knowledge-gathering process that defines our view of the world. Because this perceptual outlook guides our activities, both mental and behavioural, we naturally find it fascinating to inquire about the bases of perception.

One can see that Sekuler and Blake's statement shows a clear statement about perception which in turn can help redesign any security programmes and instruments for all employees in an organisation. Underlying these redesigning security programmes and restructuring of security instruments is a set of principles which would give an appropriate security perception and assist analysts to develop a culture of information security amongst employees in an organisation. Moreover, these principles could help to reduce internal security incidents from happening. These principles are:

Principle 1: Manifestation of latent function can increase appropriate security perception amongst employees.

One of the ways to increase appropriate security perception amongst employees is using latent function. A manifestation of the latent function (i.e., from implicit form into explicit form) can be used to make everyone in the organisation aware of security matters. This is because the latent function shows clearly how everyone is responsible in the security precautions within an organisation. The latent function is also like a manifest function that can be used to display a security mission. A simple analogy containing a manifest function and a latent function is the data confidentiality. For example, use of a cryptography mechanism as a mean to protect the data from an unauthorised disclosure during transmission, constitutes a manifest function whereas encouraging users to only practice confidential ways when handling their PC constitutes a latent function. Without highlighting latent function to employees like not practising screen saver on computer monitor while not at the workplace could influence the data confidentiality in the computer system and may cause disclosure of secret information in the organisational computer system. Therefore, once everyone understands the latent function, they may perceive security in a more positive manner, which would encourage them to practice security precautions in their daily work routines. In addition, a security awareness programme can be used to highlight this latent function. Thus, this function can become one of the practical ways to increase appropriate security perception amongst employees and later engender security culture effectively.

Principle 2: Security perception analysis can help to redesign security awareness and training programmes and can also encourage appropriate security perception amongst employees.

As mentioned earlier, perception analysis can reveal the employee implicit basic assumption on security matters. From this analysis, we can find out the problems employees had to deal with any security activities, tasks and precautions in their daily work routines. Once we know the problems, we can redesign security awareness and training programmes to educate them. A redesign programme that includes the latest solution for the current security problems may increase positive security perception amongst staff. This is because security awareness presentation is intended to tell individuals about standards, policies, guidelines, procedures, and encourage them to respond accordingly (McLean, 1992). Security training programme will then develop knowledge and skills, which can assist in their security tasks. At the same time, these programmes can promote security matters, and everyone will be held responsible and requires participation from all staff in security tasks. Once we cope with the latest security problems, we can increase security precautions in the organisation which can lessen internal security incidents from occurring. Thus, figure 2 shows the complete logical hierarchy from Figure 1 to the principles highlighted in section 4 in order to provide a conceptual idea of how an appropriate security perception among staff can be used to develop information security culture.

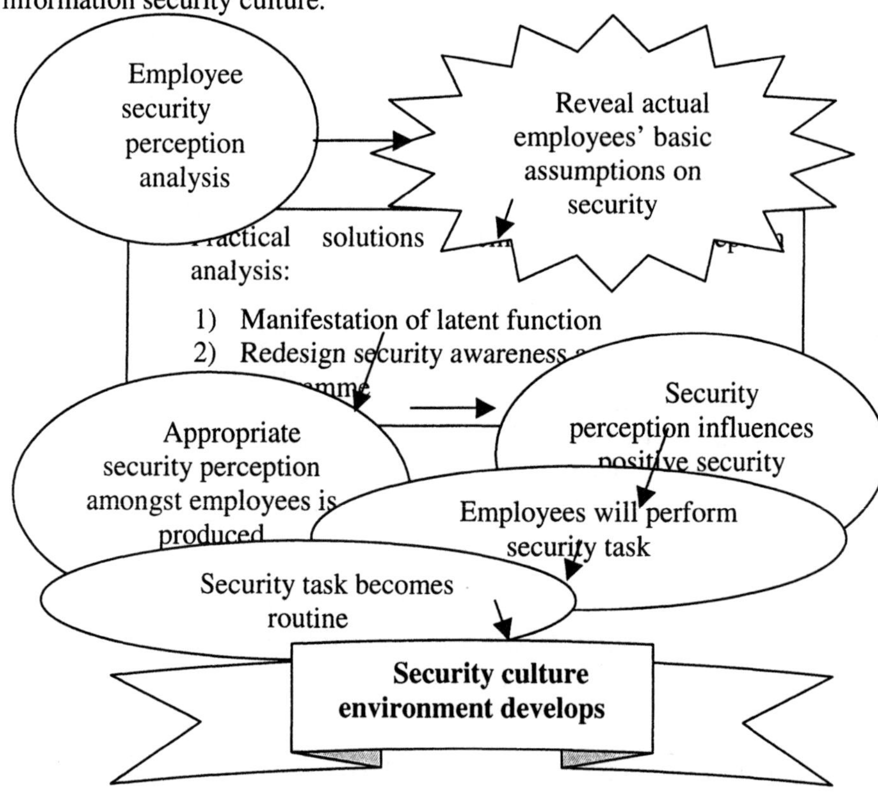

Figure 2. Employee security perception solutions for cultivation of information security culture

5. CONCLUSION

The aim of this section was to highlight the importance of appropriate employee security perception. The basic ideas of perception and its relevant terms are explained in section 1. It seems clear what an appropriate security perception amongst employee's means in the development of a security culture within an organisation. Through security perception analysis, we are promoting practical principle solutions that can be used to increase appropriate security perception amongst users. An appropriate security perception will influence positive security behaviour, which in turn produce employees who are willing to perform all security practices (e.g., security precautions and security tasks) in their daily work routines. Through these proposed principles, we can also change the current nature of security perception from "they are responsible" to "all of us are responsible" in terms of security practices within an organisation. Moreover, performing security practices by everyone in the organisation can help reduce internal security incidents from happening (Babiak et al., 2005). Therefore, we would like to emphasise that an appropriate employee security perception and its analysis can help increase an organisation's ability to meet information security culture challenges.

REFERENCES

Babiak, J., Butters, J., and Doll, M.W., 2005, Defending the Digital Fontier: Practical Security for Management, John Wiley & Sons Inc, Hoboken, NJ.

Egan, M. and Mather, T., 2005, The Executive Guide to Information Security: Threats, Challenges and Solutions, Pearson Education Inc, Upper Saddle River, NJ.

Hogg, M. A. and Vaughan, G. M., 2002, Social Psychology, 3rd Ed, Prentice Hall, Essex, England.

Huczynski, A. and Buchanan, D., 2001, Organizational Behaviour: An Introductory Text, Prentice Hall Europe.

McLean, K., 1992, Information security awareness – selling the cause, *IT Security: The Need for International Cooperation.* Proceedings of the IFIP TC 11 8th International Conference on Information Security IFIP/Sec'92. North-Holland, Singapore, pp. 179-193.

Peltier, T. R., 2001, Information Security Risk Analysis, Auerbach, Boca Raton, Florida.

Schein, E. H., 1992, Organizational Culture and Leadership, 2nd Ed, Jossey-Bass, San Francisco, CA.

Schlienger, T. and Teufel, S., 2002, Information security culture: the socio-cultural dimension in information security management". In Ghonaimy, M. A., El-Hadidi, M. T. and Asian, H. K. (eds), *Security in the Information Society: Vision & Perspectives*, Kluwer Academic, pp. 193-201.

Sekuler, R. and Blake, R., 1994, Perception, McGraw-Hill, Inc. USA.

Ward, J., 2002, Developing a culture of information security, *Proceeding of the 19th World Conference on Computer Security Audit and Control*, London, pp.193-200.

Zakaria, O. and Gani, A., 2003, A Conceptual Checklist of Information Security Culture, *Proceeding of the 2nd European Conference on Information Warfare and Security*, MCIL, Reading, England, pp. 365-371.

SESSION 3 – ACCESS MANAGEMENT

A POLICY FRAMEWORK FOR ACCESS MANAGEMENT IN FEDERATED INFORMATION SHARING

Rafae Bhatti[1], Elisa Bertino[2], Arif Ghafoor[1]
[1]School of Electrical and Computer Engineering, Purdue University, West Lafayette, IN 47907;[2]Department of Computer Sciences and CERIAS, Purdue University, West Lafayette, IN 47907

Abstract: Current mechanisms for distributed access management are limited in their capabilities to provide federated information sharing while ensuring adequate levels of resource protection. This work presents a policy-based framework designed to address these limitations for access management in federated systems. In particular, it supports: (i) decentralized administration while preserving local autonomy, (ii) fine-grained access control while avoiding rule-explosion in the policy,(iii) credential federation through the use of interoperable protocols, with support for single sign on for federated users, (iv) specification and enforcement of semantic and contextual constraints to support integrity requirements and contractual obligations, and (v) usage control in resource provisioning through effective session management. The paper highlights the significance of our policy-based approach in comparison with related mechanisms. It also presents a system architecture of our implementation prototype.

Key words: Federated Systems, Policy-based Management, XML Access Control

1. INTRODUCTION

Federated systems comprise of shared resources belonging to distributed, potentially mutually untrusted, administrative domains. A key property of federated systems is that each participating site retains local autonomy (i.e. administrative control over its resources), which is a main difference between federated and traditional distributed system concepts. Many commercial and government organizations are increasingly adopting the federated approach to online information management, be it for critical infrastructure protection such as the DoD NetCentric Directive [1] or wide dissemination of scholarly work such as the Federated Digital Library initiative [2].

Access management in a federated system includes specification and administration of access control policies of protected information resources belonging to participating sites, and secure federation to allow seamless sharing of those resources. An effective mechanism for access management in such systems must take into consideration the access control requirements as stated in the access control policies of each participating site. However, several challenges arise in developing and enforcing access control policies in a federated paradigm.

The principle of local autonomy impacts the ability of the federation to share and acquire resources [3]. A major problem in this context is policy administration. A centralized administration approach may imply loss of autonomy for participating sites [3], and is ruled out. On the other hand, decentralizing administrative control requires that participating sites specify authorization policies for federated users [3]. This approach preserves local autonomy, but is complicated by the fact that federated systems typically involve a diverse, unseen user pool requiring granular and differentiated access to a diverse set of resources located anywhere across the federation. It, therefore, precludes the use of traditional approaches to distributed authorization (such as X.509 based PKI) that assume knowledge of user identities and resource locations. Even when knowledge of identities is available, the requirement of fine-grained access control would lead to rule-explosion in the access control policy given the size of federated population in open systems. To keep the rule set from becoming prohibitively large calls for a scalable approach.

While decentralizing administrative control requires that participating sites specify authorization policies for federated users in an appropriate format, a related challenge is to transfer the credentials of the federated users across administrative boundaries for them to obtain federated resources according to the applicable authorization policies. We refer to such a mechanism as credential federation. No federated system can achieve its access management goals unless the requirement for credential federation is satisfied. Doing so, however, requires interoperable protocols that can allow participating sites to federate user credentials. Multiple policies may be necessary to evaluate the request of a federated user, which requires the support for combining rules from multiple policies to support composite policy evaluation. A related requirement for credential federation is that of achieving Single Sign On (SSO), which enables persistent authorization support for federated users within a single login session.

The "dual" of credential federation is resource federation, i.e. availability of resources to federated users according to the applicable authorization policies.

Resource federation can occur in two modes, namely resource sharing and resource provisioning. Provisioning may be considered an advanced form of sharing where the resource is actually acquired (rather than just accessed) by the requestor for a specified period of time. It is assumed that the resource will remain within the immediate control of the owner during this time.

While credential federation is aimed at securing the authorization information of federated users, resource federation takes a more usage-oriented view, and is aimed at ensuring effective protection of accessed or acquired resources. For instance, a digital document acquired in a read-only mode by an authorized user for a specified period of time must be protected against any (unauthorized) modifications. In other words, the role of access control should not end after the resource is initially provided, but must persist for the duration of the provisioning session. Traditional access control models do not take a usage-oriented view, and hence are inadequate to capture the protection requirements associated with federated resource sharing.

Lastly, the collaborative nature of a federated system requires the specification of semantic and contextual constraints to ensure adequate protection of federated resources. Semantic constraints include high level integrity principles that need to be captured in the access control policy, such as Separation of Duty (SoD) [4]. For instance, it may be required that no user may acquire the rights to access two design documents from two competing firms. Contextual constraints include temporal or other environmental attributes surrounding an access request that must be evaluated to decide on resource provisioning. For instance, a resource access between two domains may be time-constrained to occur only during business hours. Conditions associated with provisioning and de-provisioning of resources are absolutely critical to the functioning of the federation, especially when resources are provided against some form of obligation (such as service-level agreements, etc.).

Supporting semantic and contextual constraints in the access control policy requires mechanisms for constraint specification, evaluation and enforcement in a decentralized manner. While constraints increase the expressiveness of the policy, enforcing them requires maintaining state information across all user accesses, and is much more complex in a decentralized environment than in a centralized architecture. Reducing the complexity of policy administration, therefore, becomes an immediate concern [19]. Moreover, the integrity requirements and contractual obligations within a federation might change on-demand, and an access management mechanism must be flexible enough to facilitate such adaptation.

All the above cited challenges are unique to the federated paradigm and need to be addressed to ensure effective access management. We believe that a policy-based approach to access management provides a viable solution since it is flexible and adaptable enough to meet these requirements. A key benefit of policies for systems management is that policies are interpreted rather than compiled into program code, so can be changed dynamically without changes to application code [20]. To realize this benefit, however, it is mandated that the policy supports an interoperable and expressive specification that can support these access management needs of a federated system.

1.1 Contributions and organization

The primary objective of this paper is to study the impact of these outlined challenges on the design and administration of an access control policy. In response, we present the design and enforcement architecture of a policy-based framework that addresses them. Our design builds upon the well-known Role Based Access Control (RBAC) model which has been recognized for simplified administration [5] particularly in the context of federated access management [6], and augments it with necessary extensions to support access management in a federated system.

In particular, we support the following key extensions to basic RBAC model:

(i) Delegated administration through the use of trust relationships captured through role hierarchies. Our approach provides scalable decentralization support and preserves local autonomy.

(ii) Credential specification for an unseen, heterogeneous pool of users and resources through a combination of rule-based role assignment and role-based authorization. Our approach allows fine-grained access control while avoiding rule-explosion in the policy.

(iii) Credential federation through the use of interoperable protocols. We support combing rules from multiple policies for composite policy evaluation, and also provide single sign on for federated users.

(iv) Usage control in resource provisioning by employing usage-oriented resource protection policies, and session management mechanism.

(v) Specification and enforcement of semantic and contextual constraints needed to support integrity requirements and contractual obligations in a federated system. Our approach achieves scalability and flexibility through modularized constraint specification and maintains reduced complexity through lazy rule instantiation.

The remaining of the paper is organized as follows. Section 2 introduces design principles of our policy-based approach for access management in federated systems. Section 3 presents the details of the policy framework. Section 4 presents the system architecture of an implementation prototype of our proposed framework. We apply our policy framework in a federated digital library environment (with read-only access), and illustrate design and enforcement of access control policies for secure federation of XML-based digital documents. Section 5 puts our work in perspective with related work, and highlights the particular merits of our work with respect to the outlined challenges. Section 6 concludes the paper.

2. DESIGN APPROACH

Recently, there has been a growing recognition of security problems in federated environments, and several emerging specifications in various stages of standardization have emerged [7-10]. But standards alone won't solve the problem. The answer lies in combining standards with policies that govern how shared information can be used [11]. In this paper, we provide a policy-based solution specific to access management in federated systems with the motivation to address this crucial requirement. Among our design goals is to provide an interoperable specification for expressing access control policies that is compatible with emerging security standards for information federation.

All notable emerging standards for Web-based federation are XML-based; we therefore use an XML-based policy specification language. As a consequence, our policy-based framework facilitates interoperability with complementary security protocols for federated systems. In addition to supporting high-level access control requirements, our language can be used to encode various low-level security policies (such as IPSec) through appropriate XSLT tools, and allow them to be applied in a federated system.

Another design goal is to allow modular specification of authentication and authorization credentials to provide support for pluggable authentication standards to be incorporated. Being neutral to the authentication mechanism, we do not deal with the authentication system needed to generate the authenticator. In other words, we assume that the authentication information supplied to the system is already verified, and is encoded in an authenticating credential usable in our framework.

Our design is focused on specification of policies, and therefore we do not consider certain other auxiliary issues. For example, we do not deal with credential collection and provisioning issues, which include deployment and/or discovery of credentials across multiple applications, typically through the use of directory services (such as LDAP). We also do not deal with identity aggregation issues involving multiple LDAP repositories for manipulating composite credentials. Additionally, we assume that the channels used for network communication are secured by appropriate mechanisms (such as SSL/TLS).

3. X-GTRBAC POLICY FRAMEWORK

This section describes the key features of X-GTRBAC (XML-based Generalized Temporal Role Based Access Control), our XML-based policy specification framework. Our specification language is an extension of the RBAC model suitable for addressing the access management challenges in federated systems discussed in this paper.

3.1 Language Specification

X-GTRBAC language specification is captured through a context-free grammar called X-Grammar, which follows the same notion of terminals and non-terminals as in BNF, but supports the tagging notation of XML which also allows expressing attributes within element tags. The use of attributes helps maintain compatibility with XML schema syntax, which serves as the type definition model for our language. Since it follows BNF convention, X-Grammar can be accepted by a well-defined automaton to allow automatic translation into XML schema documents. This allows automatic creation of strongly typed policy schemas based on the supplied grammar specification. We choose to use X-Grammar syntax instead of directly working with XML schemas for ease of analysis (since existing compiler tools for BNF grammars can be applied) and better readability and presentation. Examples of X-Grammar policies are given in following sections. The complete syntax of X-GTRBAC language specification appears in Appendix A.

3.2 Policy Components

We now describe the main components of our policy language. While doing so, we motivate our design decision by evaluating existing approaches against our stated requirements, and pointing out the merits of our design with respect to our objectives.

3.2.1 Credentials

Credentials are a key component of an access control language. A credential encodes the authentication and authorization information for the users. We have earlier motivated that a heterogeneous and unfamiliar user and resource pool in a federated system complicates credential specification, since it precludes the use of traditional approaches to distributed authorization (such as X.509 based PKI) that assume knowledge of user identities and resource locations.

[12, 13] are well-known examples of distributed schemes that have used identity-based X.509 certificates for user authentication. The authentication information (i.e. public keys) is then used to construct an authorization credential that comprises of a set of resource-specific rules. The credentials are bound to user identities and therefore this approach to credential specification is not scalable. Even when knowledge of identities is available, the requirement of fine-grained access control would lead to rule-explosion in the access control policy given the size of federated population in open systems. Additionally, this approach tightly couples

authentication with authorization, and is therefore inflexible, and violates one of our design principles.

Our policy framework addresses this problem through the use of attribute-based (as opposed to identity-based) credential specification. We adopt a modular approach and allow independent specification of credentials used in authentication and authorization. The authenticating credential comprises of authentication information expressed in terms of user attributes which are used by the access control processor for role assignment. This idea is similar to the one used in [14]. However, unlike in [14], we do not require reliance on X.509 identity-based certificates to encode user authentication information. Instead, the user attributes may be supplied in any mutually agreed format, such as an Attribute Statement in the emerging identity federation standard SAML [7]. This supports the requirement for credential federation (See Section 3.3.3).

An authorization credential comprises of information about role attributes, role hierarchy, and role constraints. Examples of role attributes are time of day, system load, etc. [16]. They are used by the access control processor for controlling assignment of users and permissions to roles. Role hierarchy provides a means of privilege inheritance, and hierarchical role definitions can be applied to extend or specialize existing policies. Role constraints restrict the enabling, activation, and delegation (See Section 3.3.1) of roles to allow fine-grained access management.

The authenticating and authorization credentials used in our framework are included in an XML User Sheet (XUS) and an XML Role Sheet (XRS) respectively. The top-level X-Grammar syntax of XUS and XRS is shown in Figures 1 and 2.

```
<!-- XML User Sheet>                    ::=
<XUS [xus_id = (id) ] >
 <CredType cred_type_id=(id) type_name= (name) >
   [<!—Header>]
   <!-- Credential Expression>
 </CredType>
</XUS>
```

Figure 1. Top-level X-Grammar for XML User Sheet:
Includes definition of authenticating credential

```
<!-- XML Role Sheet>                    ::=
<XRS [xrs_id = (id) ]>
 <Role role_id = (id)
  role_name = (role name)>
  [<!-- Cred Type>]
  [<Junior> (name) </Junior>]
  [<Senior> (name) </Senior>]
  [<!—(En|Dis)abling Constraint>]
  [<!—[De]Activation Constraint>]
  [<!—Delegation Constraint>]
  (<SSDRoleSetID> (id) </SSDRoleSetID>)*
  (<DSDRoleSetID> (id) </DSDRoleSetID>)3*
 </Role>
</XRS>
```

Figure 2. Top-level X-Gramamr for XML Role Sheet:
Includes definition of authorization credential

The credential specification in our framework facilitates a combination of rule-based role assignment and role-based authorization (See Section 3.2.3). Our approach allows fine-grained access control while avoiding rule-explosion in the policy since users are assigned to roles and access rules are specified at per-role rather than per-user level.

3.2.2 Constraints

Constraints are essential to the expressiveness of an access control language. Specification of semantic and contextual constraints is vital to support the enforcement of integrity principles and resource provisioning contracts in a federated system. As motivated earlier, enforcing expressive constraints in a decentralized manner involves maintaining prohibitive amounts of state information and introduces significant complexity. Additionally, adapting the constraints according to on-demand changes in

[3] SSD and DSD refer to static and dynamic SoD respectively.

integrity requirements and contractual obligations within a federation requires a specification format that facilitates such adaptation.

Most well-known distributed authorization schemes [12-15] do not cover the requirements of constraint specification and enforcement as required for access management in federated systems. As mentioned before, [12, 13] tightly couple resource-specific authorization constraints with the identity-information. This method of constraint specification is clearly inflexible to allow on-demand adaptation of constraints; doing so would require issuance of a new credential for the affected users since their identity is bound to the authorization.

Additionally, constraints in [12, 13] are inadequate to capture semantic integrity constraints, such as SoD, in a federated system since doing so at the user level would require prohibitive amount of state information to be maintained. In comparison, enforcing SoD at the granularity of role is more manageable and one has to include in the constraint definition only the roles, as opposed to all permissions, that the user may have access to. The support for contextual constraints based on temporal or other environmental attributes is also limited in [12, 13], since they do not have a formal temporal model, and rely on underlying operating system primitives to enforce temporal constraints. [14, 15] are based on basic RBAC and do not support specification of contextual constraints.

X-GTRBAC supports a variety of constraint categories to adequately capture the access management requirements in federated systems. The constraint specification in X-GTRBAC framework is primarily based on Generalized Temporal Role Based Access Control (GTRBAC) model [17]. GTRBAC is a mechanism using temporal logic to express a diverse set of fine-grained temporal constraints in an RBAC environment. The temporal constraint categories supported by GTRBAC include periodicity, interval, and duration constraints which can be used to constrain the period, interval and duration, respectively, of user-to-role and permission-to-role assignments. Another category is that of trigger-based constraints, which can be thought of as condition-action rules. As the name implies, trigger-based constraints are used to condition the occurrence of an event on another. Moreover, GTRBAC also elegantly captures the SoD constraint among roles to capture integrity requirements. Both static and dynamic SoD constraints are supported. Capturing these constraints at the role level helps reduce state information needed to enforce the constraints.

X-GTRBAC supports modular specification of all the constraints in the GTRBAC model [18]. The modular approach allows independent specification of SoD and temporal constraint definitions which can then be imported into the policy through the use of XML namespaces. Specification of constraints separate from the policy allows reusable constraint definitions that can be used across multiple policies. Additionally, constraint definitions may be changed at one place without requiring change to all dependent policies, facilitating flexible adaptation.

X-GTRBAC additionally supports the specification of contextual constraints based on non-temporal attributes, usually associated with a role [16]. Contextual constraints on role attributes can be used in addition to temporal constraints to support finer granularity of control on user-to-role and permission-to-role assignments.

Top-level X-Grammar syntax of SoD and temporal constraint definitions is shown in Figures 3 and 4. The SoD constraints are included with the role definition in XRS (Figure 2), whereas the temporal constraints are included in assignment policies (Figure 6). An example XML instance of a temporal constraint definition appears in Appendix B.

```
<!-- Separation of Duty Definitions> ::=
  <XSoDDef [xsod_id = (id) ] >
    <!—SoDRoleSets>
 </XSoDDef>
```

Figure 3. Top-level syntax of SoD constraint definition

```
<!-- Definitions of Temporal Constraints>::=
<XTempConstDef [xtcd_id = (id) ] >
   [<!—Interval Expression>]
   [<!-- Periodic Time Expression>]
   [<!-- Duration Expression>]
 </XTempConstDef>
```

Figure 4. Top-level syntax of temporal constraint definition

Temporal constraints are of particular relevance to federated resource provisioning because it requires a set of fine-grained temporal constraints to adequately ensure resource protection while also ensuring its availability per the contractual requirements. This set includes constraints that control the periodicity, interval and duration of resource accesses (i.e. permission assignments) during and across provisioning sessions, in addition to trigger-based constraints that allow provisioning actions to be conditioned on related events. This represents a collection of stateful rules that can be configured in permission-to-role assignment policies. Doing so allows specification of usage-oriented resource protection policies to enforce usage control of federated resources.

3.2.3 Assignment Rules

An integral component of RBAC polices in our framework is the specification of rules for user-to-role and permission-to-role assignments. Rule-based assignment in RBAC policies provides a succinct declarative specification that is both scalable and flexible. It avoids the problem of rule-explosion since rules are specified at per-role (as opposed to per-user or per-resource) level. It is flexible since a declarative syntax allows rules to be modified without changing application code.

As noted earlier, the authenticating credential contains user attributes which are used by the access control processor for role assignment to users, whereas the authorization credential contains role attributes which are used by the access control processor for permission assignment to roles. (Role attributes may be used in user-to-role assignment too.) Additionally, a permission-to-role assignment policy may also include rules on resource attributes to allow specification of usage-oriented protection policy. Resource attributes capture semantic information (or meta-data) about resources, and avoid reliance on fixed resource locations. They also provide a mechanism for fine-grained permission assignment to roles based on precise resource characteristics.

To represent attributes of federated resources, we use application-specific attribute definitions (i.e. ontologies). (Each domain in the federation publishes attribute definitions of its resources to a well-known repository which may be imported for use in an assignment rule using XML namespaces.) The resource attributes are included in the object definition in an XML Permission Sheet (XPS). The top-level X-Grammar syntax of an XPS is shown in Figure 5.

```
<!-- XML Permission Sheet>::=
<XPS [xps_id = (id) ] >
 <Permission perm_id = id [prop= (prop op)] >
    <Object type= (type name) id= (id)>
    [<!-- Attributes>]
    </Object>
    <Operation> (access op) </Operation>
  </Permission>
</XPS>
```

Figure 5. Top-level X-Gramamr for XML Permission Sheet

```
<!-- XML User-Role Assignment Sheet>::=
<XURAS [xuras_id = (id) ] >
 <URA ura_id=(id) role_name=(name)>
  <AssignUsers>
   <AssignUser user_id=(id)>
  <AssignConstraint [op =(AND|OR|NOT|XOR)]>
   // opcode defaults to AND if none specified
  <AssignCondition cred_type=(type name)
  [pt_expr_id=(id) | d_expr_id=(id)] >
  <LogicalExpr [op = (AND|OR|NOT)]>
  // opcode defaults to AND if none specified
   [<!-- Predicate>]+
   </LogicalExpr>
  </AssignCondition>
   </AssignConstraint>
  </AssignUser>
 </AssignUsers>
 </URA>
</XURAS>
```

Figure 6. Top-level syntax of user-to-role assignment policy

Our assignment policy schema specifies a logical expression syntax for rule specification. It does not, however, impose any restriction on the attributes that may be used for composing these rules. The existence and type checking of the queried attribute shall be done in an application-specific manner. For instance, user attributes can be verified through appropriate attribute authorities stated in the authentication credential.

The assignment policies are specified in our framework in an XML User to Role Assignment Sheet (XURAS) and XML Permission to Role Assignment Sheet (XPRAS). The top-level X-Grammar syntax of XURAS is shown in Figure 6 (XPRAS is analogous). Note that these policies include references to temporal constraint definitions. For example, `pt_expr_id` references a periodic time expression. An example XML instance of a role assignment policy appears in Appendix B.

A key feature of our rule specification format is that it allows combing rules from multiple sources to facilitate evaluation of multiple credentials. An assignment rule consists of an assignment constraint, which comprises of multiple assignment conditions. Each assignment condition contains a set of logical expressions to encode rules on a given credential type. Our logical expression syntax allows multiple logical expressions to be combined together in an appropriate rule combining mode using Boolean connectives. The modes supported by the evaluation engine in our prototype are AND (all rules must be true), OR (at least one rule must be true), and NOT (no rule must be true). Several levels of nesting are supported, each under a distinct mode, to allow a fine granularity of rule specification.

An assignment condition is satisfied if all of its included rules encoded using logical expressions are satisfied according to the respective mode. The multiple assignment conditions within an assignment constraint are combined according to a similar set of modes. This effectively allows an assignment constraint to be composed from multiple assignment conditions according to an appropriate combining mode. Role assignment occurs as a consequence of an assignment constraint being satisfied.

We note that the "AND" mode essentially implements "deny-overrides", whereas "OR" mode implements "permit-overrides". The NOT mode allows one to condition a role assignment based on negation. This is useful in instances when it is easier to express exclusion rather than inclusion criterion for membership in a role. Although negation is allowed in the body, it is not allowed in the consequence of a rule. This prevents contradictory rule sets to exist in the specification. This property is helpful when combining rules aimed at a given consequence, since one can always be sure that new rules will not clash with existing rules in the policy.

3.3 Salient Features

In this subsection, we describe the salient features of our policy framework that enables the solution to access management challenges in federated systems outlined in the paper. These features build upon the policy components discussed in the previous subsection.

3.3.1 Delegated Administration

The requirement for local autonomy, and hence decentralization of administrative control, in federated systems poses major challenges in developing access control policies, as has been earlier discussed. The mechanisms for credential and constraint specification in our framework help alleviate part of this problem. The other aspect is related to the policy administration and enforcement mechanism.

Decentralization of policy administration in X-GTRBAC is achieved through the notion of administrative domains. An administrative domain (or domain for short) is a unit of administrative authority. A federated system is then a multi-domain environment where each domain is responsible for managing the users and resources under its administrative control [16].

Delegation of responsibilities is essential to scalable decentralization. Delegation in federated systems is captured through some form of trust relationships [12]. In X-GTRBAC framework, the notion of delegation is elegantly captured through the use of role hierarchies: a junior role inherits all privileges of a senior role. An optional Delegation Constraint may be used in the role definition (See Figure 2) to limit the extent of delegation (in terms of time and associated privileges);

unrestricted delegation is otherwise assumed. This role-based delegation serves as the basis of trust in creating role mappings across multiple domains for federated information sharing. (Each domain in the federation publishes its role definitions to a well-known repository which may be imported for establishing appropriate role mappings using XML namespaces.) For instance, an Employee role from domain B that is mapped as junior to a Manager role in domain A would be allowed to exercise the Manager-level privileges in domain A per its delegation policy, without requiring explicit knowledge of domain B's access control policy.

Delegated administration requires access to a local compliance checker that can compute correspondence between mapped roles with respect to the local domain policies. The use of a compliance checker to ensure compliance of federated requests with local policies is a recognized mechanism for preserving local autonomy in distributed systems [19]. In our X-GTRBAC prototype, the compliance checker is incorporated into an authorization engine residing in each domain. It internally maintains a domain-specific mapping from the foreign (i.e. federated) roles to local roles according to the delegation policies of the local domain.

3.3.2 Lazy Instantiation

Domains, together with delegation, allow scalable decentralization of policy administration. However, the complexity of policy administration remains a concern, since an expressive access control policy would require the local authorization engine to maintain prohibitive amount of state information.

The use of credential-based specification in our policy framework helps mitigate this concern. A credential-based approach allows state information to be reduced since the requestor supplies the credentials relevant to the access request, facilitating lazy instantiation of policy rules. Therefore, the policy does not need to be distributed synchronously to all enforcement points [19]. In our X-GTRBAC prototype, lazy instantiation helps in state-reduction while enforcing the policy, since there is no need on part of the authorization engine to maintain persistent state information, i.e. store the assignment policies for all users and resources.

3.3.3 Credential Federation

The credential specification in a federated system must support federation requirement, as outlined earlier. Many existing distributed authorization schemes [12-15] do not address this requirement due to inherent limitation of their credential specification formats, as discussed in Section 3.2.1.

The modular, attribute-based credential specification in the X-GTRBAC framework allows credential federation through the use of interoperable protocols. In fact, the on-going work on our prototype has assumed a SAML-compliant format for authenticating credentials. SAML standard [7] states that authentication information may be available in various forms, such as X.509 Attribute Certificates, Kerberos tickets or passwords. We employ appropriate translation mechanisms for them to be used with our X-GTRBAC syntax. Since our rule specification supports combing rules from multiple sources, this allows use of our specification in situations when multiple policies are necessary to evaluate the request of a federated user.

For example, consider an extension to the assignment policy in Figure B.2 in Appendix B. This policy requires the user to provide an X.509 Attribute Certificate including certain attributes. Another policy might require the user to also provide a Kerberos ticket. Using our specification, this can be achieved by simply adding another `<AssignCondition>` tag with `cred_type="Kerberos"`, and including the desired rules on credential attributes. The rule combining mechanism discussed earlier can then be used for evaluating this composite policy.

In addition to credential federation, a related requirement is that of providing single sign on (SSO). SSO enables persistent authorization support for federated users within a single login session. Our framework supports SSO through the use of digitally signed SAML statements that capture an authorization decision already issued by a domain corresponding to a user request. This decision statement can subsequently be reused by the user at a domain within the federation without getting re-authenticated, subject to the acceptance of the digital signature.

3.3.4 Usage Control

Persistent protection of federated resources requires effective usage control mechanisms. Traditional access control models do not take this usage-oriented view, and hence are inadequate to capture the protection requirements associated with federated resource sharing.

X-GTRBAC framework allows the specification of usage-oriented resource protection policies as discussed in Section 3.2.2. However, enforcement of these policies requires effective session management mechanism. In our X-GTRBAC prototype, this session management support is provided through the implementation of periodicity, interval and duration constraints associated with resource provisioning and de-provisioning. In addition, it also implements trigger-based constraints that allow provisioning and de-provisioning actions to be conditioned on related events. For example, the provisioning of a resource may be automatically discontinued when the associated duration constraint expires. This set of constraints represents a collection of stateful rules that are configured in permission-to-role assignment policies, and enforced by the session management mechanism. Stateful rules help keep the complexity of maintaining the policy low.

3.4 Policy Composition

An overall X-GTRBAC policy is composed[4] from these individual policy components as shown in Figure 7. The complete X-Grammar policy syntax is provided in Appendix A.

```
<!-- Policy Definition>    ::=
<Policy policy_id =(id) >
    <PolicyName> (name) </PolicyName>
    <!-- XML User Sheet>
    <!-- XML Role Sheet>
    <!-- XML Permission Sheet>
    <!-- XML User-Role Assignment Sheet>
    <!-- XML Permission-Role Assignment Sheet>
</Policy>
```

Figure 7. The overall X-GTRBAC policy

4. SYSTEM ARCHITECTURE

In this section, we present the system architecture of our X-GTRBAC prototype designed for access management in a federated environment. In particular, we apply our policy framework in a federated digital library environment (with read-only access). The use of this prototype illustrates the design and enforcement of access control policies for secure federation of XML-based digital documents. XML is increasingly being used as the preferred digital format on the Web; therefore we work with XML documents.

[4] Policy composition as used here refers to combining multiple distinct components of a policy together into a single document. This should not be confused with composing a single policy from multiple, potentially overlapping, policies through formal analysis.

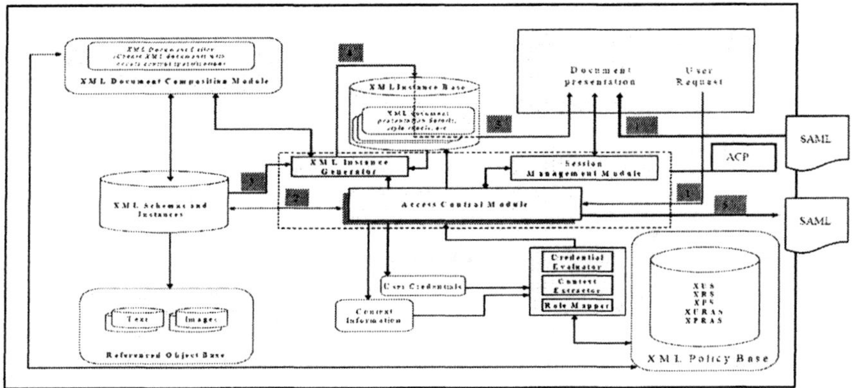

Figure 8. The system architecture for federated digital library prototype

The system architecture is shown in Figure 8. This architecture is implemented at each participating site in the federation. We now highlight the role of the key components of the prototype.

4.1 Policy specification

XML Document Composition Module (XDCM) is used by each participating site to compose policy documents. Each site first encodes its X-Grammar policy definitions which are then translated into XML schemas using a custom translator and exported to XDCM. The policy documents are then composed in XML inside the XDCM, and verified against the imported schema definitions.

XML Policy Base (XPB) contains all policy related XML documents composed by XDCM. These include XML User Sheet (XUS), XML Role Sheet (XRS), XML Permission Sheet (XPS), XML User to Role Assignment Sheet (XURAS), and XML Permission to Role Assignment Sheet (XPRAS). Also stored in XPB are the constraint definitions, including XSoDDef (Figure 3) and XTempConstDef (Figure 4).

XML Schemas and Instances contains actual XML documents at a participating site to which the users of the federated library will be requesting access. Each site also includes a list of objects that may not be available locally but are known to exist in the federation, so that the users can request access to them through their local site. *Referenced Object Base* constitutes the physical objects present in the local system that are referenced from within the XML documents. Note that binary encoding allows objects to be embedded within XML documents, and those objects may themselves be protected resources.

As is the usual case, the default policy of the federation is no authorization, i.e. no user is authorized to access any document unless there exists an explicit rule granting him/her an authorization.

4.2 Policy enforcement

Upon receiving an access request, the *Access Control Module (ACM)* extracts the policy information from the policy base and works closely with the XPB to enforce the authorization constraints on the release of the request resource. The access request may either be from a local or a federated user. The request includes the requesting subject, the requested resource and the requested permissions on the resource. It may optionally include an authenticating or authorization credential to assist in authorization decision[5]. We use a SAML-compliant format for all access requests. If the requested resource is not available within the system, the ACM simply returns (or appropriately redirects) the request. Otherwise, it proceeds as follows.

As a first step, the ACM forwards the access request (expressed as a SAML Authorization Decision Query) to the *Credential Evaluator (CrE)*. It simultaneously forwards the currently available contextual information to the *Context Evaluator (CoE)*. CrE first translates the credential included in the request from the SAML format to X-GTRBAC format. Based on the kind of credential, CrE does the following.

If it is an authenticating credential (expressed as a SAML Attribute Statement included in the query), the CrE assigns the user to an appropriate role within the system according to the user-to-role assignment policy after consulting the XPB. This process requires input from the CoE regarding (successful) evaluation of temporal and non-temporal contextual constraints before the role assignment takes place. The non-temporal constraints not only involve rules on user attributes but may also involve rules on attributes of the role for a fine-grained access control. Following a successful role assignment, the user is issued an authorization credential by the system.

If it is an authorization credential (expressed as a previously issued SAML Authorization Decision Statement included in the query), CrE inspects if the role information in the credential corresponds to a local role. If it doesn't, it means that it is an SSO request and includes the role of the federated user in his/her original domain. In this case, CrE invokes the *Role Mapper (RM)* to map the user to a local

[5] In our current prototype, the supporting credentials are explicitly included in the access request. The support for credential collection (using mechanisms as SAML Authentication Request protocol) is explicitly stated earlier to be outside the scope of this work.

role according to the delegation policy of the system. After this step, the user acquires the privileges of the assigned or mapped role in the local system.

After establishing the role of the user, the next step is to determine the authorization of the user to obtain the requested permission on the requested resource. At this stage, the CrE evaluates the authorization credential of the user according to the permission-to-role assignment policy after consulting the XPB. This process requires input from the CoE regarding (successful) evaluation of temporal and non-temporal contextual constraints before the permission assignment takes place. The non-temporal constraints not only involve rules on role attributes but may also involve rules on attributes of the resource for a fine-grained access control. The result of the evaluation is returned to ACM (expressed as a SAML Authorization Decision Statement), together with any applicable resource provisioning constraints retrieved from XPB, as discussed in Section 3.2.2.

As a final step, the ACM forwards the authorization information for the user to the XIG. XIG consults the access rights of the requesting user on the requested XML document, and accordingly generates XML views in response to the request. Such XML views are cached in *XML Instance Base (XIB). Session Management Module (SMM)* is responsible for monitoring the provisioning and de-provisioning constraints associated with the requested document, as described in Section 3.3.4. The ACM, SMM, and XIG together constitute the *XML Access Control Processor (ACP).*

5. RELATED WORK

While using policies for management of systems is not an entirely novel concept, and has been applied previously in the context of network systems management [20], the policy-based approach for access management in federated systems has not been deeply investigated.

One notable example of policy-based language for systems management is Ponder [21]. Ponder is a declarative policy language with the ability to support authorization and delegation policies, as well as obligation policies (which are condition-action rules, much like trigger-based constraints in our framework). However, authorization policies in Ponder are primarily aimed at allowing network users to manage network objects, with known user groups and object locations, and are therefore inadequate for a federated environment where users and resources are not identified in advance. It therefore does not support credential specification and federation requirements for access management in federated systems discussed in the paper.

Ponder supports specification of contextual constraints, based on temporal and non-temporal parameters. However, contextual constraint specification is tied into the authorization policies, which reduces their modularity, and hence flexibility. Ponder also supports specification of SoD constraints through the use of meta-policies. However, the specification is at user-level, and is more complicated to maintain in a federated environment as opposed to a role-based SoD constraint. On the other hand, Ponder is well suited to the task that it is designed for, i.e. network services management. It has a well-developed management toolkit that allows policy specification, deployment, and dynamic adaptation suitable for a network environment.

The access control model for federated systems presented in [3] is based on a tightly coupled architecture. It concerns with defining principles for designing access control policies in federated systems, and does not deal with policy-based management issues. It therefore does not address the particular issues related to credential specification, credential federation, usage control or session management highlighted in this paper.

[22] presents an RBAC model for federated information systems. This system supports credential federation and SSO. However, it does not support all of our design requirements, including specification of semantic or contextual constraints, and usage-oriented resource protection policies.

Various policy models have earlier been used for access control in centralized and traditional distributed systems, but not many approaches have been designed to meet the requirements for policy-based access management in federated systems as described in this paper. Akenti [23] and Permis [24] are access control systems which use policies encoded in X.509 attribute certificates. Both assume authenticating credentials to be used for issuance of authorization certificates, much like our approach. Akenti supports discretionary access control (i.e. identity based), leading to rule explosion in policy rule set. Permis uses role-based access control; it, however, does not provide support for specification and enforcement of user-to-role and role-to-permission assignment policies. Both these schemes also provide no support for specification of semantic or contextual constraints, and usage-oriented resource protection policies.

Shibboleth [25] and Liberty Alliance [26] define protocols for attribute-based authentication in support of SSO in Web-based environments. The attributes in Shibboleth are always acquired from his/her home site by the resource provider, whereas those in Liberty Alliance protocol can be provided by any identity provider on the Internet. Liberty Alliance protocol therefore establishes a circle of trust between identity provider and resource providers. Both schemes provide particular emphasis on user privacy, and the identity of the user is not known to the resource provider. However, the role of these schemes is limited to distributed authentication, and providing attribute information for a user to be used in authorization decisions. They do not include mechanisms for specifying and enforcing authorization policies.

With reference to our emphasis on usage control, a relevant work appears in [27]. It presents a usage control specification to extend the capabilities of traditional access control models to support resource protection policies. They provide a logic defining states, authorizations, and actions relevant to resource usage, and use the notion of mutable attributes to allow state transitions and enforce usage control. The significant contribution of the model is that it provides logic-based semantics of usage control. However, it does not provide an enforcement mechanism.

SAML [7] and XACML [8] are emerging specifications aimed at addressing different aspects of distributed access management. As noted earlier, SAML primarily provides a mechanism for credential federation, but does not provide any policies for use of those credentials. Also, SAML does not incorporate a way to establish trust between business partners exchanging credentials. XACML provides support for policy specification for expressing access control policies. XACML can also combine multiple rules and multiple policies under various modes (deny -overrides, permit-overrides), which is similar to the rule and condition combining feature, respectively, in our language. XACML can be configured to support role-based access control and usage-oriented resource protection policies. It, however, primarily acts only as a PDP (Policy Decision Point) and lacks the temporal infrastructure to enforce the access control policy, such as the session management mechanism to enforce usage control in our framework. Our framework can therefore provide the functionality of both a PDP and a PEP (Policy Enforcement Point).

6. CONCLUSION

In this paper, we have presented the salient features of our X-GTRBAC policy framework for access management in federated systems. Our framework has been designed to address the key challenges for developing access control policies for federated information sharing. In particular, it supports: (i) decentralized administration while preserving local autonomy through the use of trust relationships captured through role-base delegation, (ii) fine-grained access control while avoiding rule-explosion in the policy through a succinct declarative credential specification, (iii) credential federation through the use of interoperable protocols, with support for single sign on for federated users, (iv) specification and enforcement of semantic and contextual constraints to support integrity requirements and contractual obligations, and (v) usage control in resource provisioning through effective session management.

The resource protection requirements in our framework are related to the Digital Rights Management (DRM) approach [28]. DRM, however, is a much broad notion, and also includes mechanisms for protection of resources while outside the administrative control of the owner. This usually requires self-protection mechanisms, i.e. the use of embedded features (such as watermarks). We only deal with policies for resource protection under administrative control of the owner, and do not make assumptions about physical protection of resources.

There are other aspects of access management that need to be incorporated in our policy framework. Our current approach for role mapping abides by the local autonomy principle, and hence no form of external access mediation is necessitated. In a more general case, this may on one hand be overly-restrictive, and on the other hand lead to security breaches due to transitive establishment of undesirable delegation links. Therefore, a mediation mechanism is necessary to fairly regulate federated information sharing while ensuring security of federated resources. Composing an access mediation policy in a federated system poses considerable challenge since participating sites do not have a-priori knowledge of each other's access control polices. These challenges are likely to be addressed as part of future work.

ACKNOWLEDGEMENTS

Portions of this work have been supported by the sponsors of the Center for Education and Research in Information Assurance and Security (CERIAS) at Purdue University, and the National Science Foundation under NSF Grant# IIS-0242419.

REFERENCES

[1] http://www.fas.org/irp/doddir/dod/d8320_2.pdf
[2] http://www.educause.edu/ir/library/pdf/erm0348.pdf
[3] S. D. C. di Vimercati, P. Samarati, "Access control in federated systems", In proceedings of ACM New Security Paradigm Workshop, pages 87-99, Lake Arrowhead, CA, USA, 1996.
[4] D. D. Clark, D. R. Wilson, "A comparison of commercial and military computer security policies," In IEEE Symposium on Security and Privacy, pages 184-194, Oakland, April 1987.
[5] R. S. Sandhu, E.J. Coyne, H.L. Feinstein, C.E. Youman, "Role-Based Access Control Models", IEEE Computer 29(2): 38-47, IEEE Press, 1996.
[6] http://www.enterprisenetworksandservers.com/monthly/art.php/1117
[7] http://xml.coverpages.org/saml.html
[8] http://www.oasis-open.org/committees/tc_home.php?wg_abbrev=xacml
[9] http://www-106.ibm.com/developerworks/webservices/library/ws-secure/
[10] http://www-128.ibm.com/developerworks/library/specification/ws-polfram/

[11] http://www.nwfusion.com/news/2002/0715saml.html

[12] M. Blaze, J. Feigenbaum, and A. D. Keromytis, "KeyNote: Trust management for public-key infrastructures," in Security Protocols International Workshop, Springer LNCS, no. 1550, pp. 59-63, 1998.

[13] C. M. Ellison, "SPKI requirements," RFC 2692, Internet Engineering Task Force Draft IETF, Sept. 1999. See http://www.ietf.org/rfc/rfc2692.txt.

[14] A. Herzberg, Y. Mass, J. Mihaeli, D. Naor, and Y. Ravid, "Access control meets public key infrastructure, or: Assigning roles to strangers", In Proceedings of the 2000 IEEE Symposium on Security and Privacy, pp. 2–14, 2000. IEEE Press.

[15] N. Li, J. C. Mitchell, W. H. Winsborough, "Design of a role-based trust management framework", In Proceedings of the 2002 IEEE Symposium on Security and Privacy. IEEE Computer Society Press, May 2002.

[16] J. B. D. Joshi, R. Bhatti, E. Bertino, A. Ghafoor, "An Access Control Language for Multi-Domain Environments", IEEE Internet Computing, vol. 8, no. 6, pp. 40-50, November/December 2004.

[17] J. B. D. Joshi, E. Bertino, U. Latif, A. Ghafoor, "Generalized Temporal Role Based Access Control Model (GTRBAC) ", IEEE Transaction on Knowledge and Data Engineering, vol. 17, no. 1, January 2005.

[18] R. Bhatti, J. B. D. Joshi, E. Bertino, A. Ghafoor, "X-GTRBAC: An XML-based Policy Specification Framework and Architecture for Enterprise-Wide Access Control", ACM Transactions on Information and System Security (TISSEC), Vol. 8, No. 2.

[19] A. Keromytis, S. Ioannidis, M. Greenwald, J. Smith, "The STRONGMAN Architecture", In Proceedings of the Third DARPA Information Survivability Conference and Exposition (DISCEX III), Washington, D.C. April 22-24, 2003.

[20] L. Lymberopoulos, E. Lupu, M. Sloman, "An Adaptive Policy Based Management Framework for Network Services Management", In Special Issue on Policy Based Management of Networks and Services, Journal of Networks and Systems Management, Vol. 11, No. 3, Sep. 2003.

[21] N. Damianou, N. Dulay, E. Lupu, M Sloman, "The Ponder Specification Language", Workshop on Policies for Distributed Systems and Networks (Policy2001), HP Labs Bristol, 29-31 Jan 2001.

[22] K. Taylor, J. Murty, "Implementing role based access control for federated information systems on the web", Proceedings of the Australasian information security workshop conference on ACSW frontiers 2003, p.87-95, February 01, 2003, Adelaide, Australia.

[23] M.Thompson, A. Essiari, S. Mudumbai, "Certificate-based Authorization Policy in a PKI Environment", ACM Transactions on Information and System Security, (TISSEC), Volume 6, Issue 4 (November 2003) pp: 566-588.

[24] D.W. Chadwick, A. Otenko, "The PERMIS X.509 role based privilege management infrastructure", In proceedings of the seventh ACM Symposium on Access Control Models and Technologies, Monterey, California, USA.

[25] http://shibboleth.internet2.edu/docs/draft-mace-shibboleth-arch-protocols-latest.pdf

[26] http://www.projectliberty.org/resources/specifications.php

[27] X. Zhang, J. Park, F. Parisi-Presicce, R. Sandhu, "A Logical Specification for Usage Control", In proceedings of the ninth ACM Symposium on Access Control Models and Technologies, Monterey, California, USA .

[28] B. Rosenblatt, B. Trippe, S. Mooney, "Digital Rights Management: Business and Technology", New York: Hungry Minds/John Wiley and Sons, 2001.

Appendix A:

X-GTRBAC Grammar

[Basic Definitions]

```
<!-- Policy Definition> ::=
<Policy policy_id =(id)>
 <PolicyName> (name) </PolicyName>
 <!-- XML User Sheet>
 <!-- XML Role Sheet>
 <!-- XML Permission Sheet>
 <!-- XML User-Role Assignment Sheet>
 <!-- XML Permission-Role Assignment Sheet>
 [<!-- Local Policy Definitions>]
 [<!-- Policy Relationship Definitions>]
</Policy>
<!-- XML User Sheet>                    ::=
<XUS [xus_id = (id) ]>
 [<!-- Definitions of Credential Types>]
 <!-- User Definitions>
</XUS>
<!-- Definitions of Credential Types>        ::=
<XCredType [xctd_id = (id) ] >
 [<!-- Credential Type Definition>]+
</XCredType>
<!-- Credential Type Definition>
::=     <CredType cred_type_id = (id)
              type_name= (type name) >
 <!-- Attribute List>
</CredType >
<!-- Attribute List> ::= <AttributeList>
   [<!-- Attribute Definition>]+
</AttributeList>
<!-- Attribute Definition>                ::
 <Attribute name= (name) usage = "mand | opt"
   type = (type) />
<!-- User Definitions >                 ::=<Users>
   [<!-- User Definition>]+
</Users>
<!-- User Definition> ::=       <User user_id = (id)>
   <UserName>[(name)]</UserName>
   <!—CredType>
   <MaxRoles>(number)</MaxRoles>
</User>
<!—CredType   > ::=
<CredType cred_type_id = (id)
   type_name= (type name) >
 [<!—Header>]
 <!-- Credential Expression>
</CredType>
<!-- Credential Expression > ::= <CredExpr>
  <!-- AttributeValuePairs>
  <!-- DomainSet>
</CredExpr>
<!-- AttributeValuePairs> ::=
[<Attribute name= (name)> (value) </Attribute>] +
<!-- XML Role Sheet>                   ::=
<XRS [xrs_id = (id) ]>
  [<!-- Role Definition>]+
</XRS>
<!-- Role Definition>                  ::=
<Role role_id = (id)
        role_name = (role name)>
 [<!-- Cred Type>]
 [<!—(En|Dis)abling Constraint>]
 [<!—[De]Activation Constraint>]
 (<SSDRoleSetID> (id) </SSDRoleSetID>)*
 (<DSDRoleSetID> (id) </DSDRoleSetID>)*
   [<Junior> (name) </Junior>]
   [<Senior> (name) </Senior>]
   [<LinkedRole type= (delegator |
      delegatee) >(name)</LinkedRole>]
   [<!—Delegation Constraint>]
   [<Cardinality> (number) </Cardinality>]
  </Role>
  <!-- Separation of Duty Definitions>
  ::=    <XSoDDef [xsod_id = (id) ]>
        <!—SoDRoleSets>
         </XSoDDef>
  <!-- SoDRoleSets >::=
        [<!—SSDRoleSets>] [<!—DSDRoleSets>]
  <!-- SSDRoleSets > ::=      <SSDRoleSets>
        [<!—SSDRoleSet>]+
      </SSDRoleSets>
  <!—SSDRoleSet> ::=     <SSDRoleSet>
        [<SSDRole ssd_role_set_id =(id)
          ssd_cardinality = (number)>
          (role name)
        </SSDRole>]+
</SSDRoleSet>
  <!-- DomainSet>   ::=     <DomainSet>
     [<!—DomainID>]+
  </DomainSet>
  <!-- DomainID>::=     <DomainID>(id)</DomainID>
  <!-- DSDRoleSets >   ::=     <DSDRoleSets>
   [<!—DSDRoleSet>]+
</DSDRoleSets>
  <!—DSDRoleSet>::=     <DSDRoleSet>
   [<DSDRole dsd_role_set_id =(id)
          dsd_cardinality = (number)>
          (role name)
</DSDRole>]+
</DSDRoleSet>
  <!-- XML Permission Sheet>::=
  <XPS [xps_id = (id) ]>
   [<!-- Permission Definition>]+
  </XPS>
  <!-- Permission Definition>            ::=
  <Permission perm_id = id [prop= (prop op)] >
  <Object type= (type name) id= (id)>
   [<!-- Attributes>]
  </Object>
  <Operation  context=  (name)>   (access  op)
</Operation>
  <!-- DomainSet>
  </Permission>
  <!-- XML User-Role Assignment Sheet>::=
  <XURAS [xuras_id = (id) ]>
   [<!-- User-role Assignment>]+
  </XURAS>
  <!-- User-role Assignment>::=
  <URA       ura_id=(id)       role_name=(name)>
 <AssignUsers>
     [< !—Assign User>]+
 </AssignUsers>
  </URA>
  <!—[De]Assign User >               ::=
 <[De]AssignUser user_id=(id)>
   <!—[De]Assign Constraint >
 </[De]AssignUser>
  <!-- XML Permission-Role Assignment Sheet>::=
```

```
<XPRAS [xpras_id = (id) ]>
 [<!-- Permission-Role Assignment>]+
</XPRAS>
<!-- Permission-Role Assignment>::=
 <PRA pra_id=(id) role_name=(name)>
 <AssignPermissions>
     [<!—Assign Permission>]+
</AssignPermissions>
 </PRA>
<  !—[De]Assign  Permission>          ::=
<[De]AssignPermission perm_id=(id)>        <!—
[De]Assign Constraint >
 </[De]AssignPermission>
 <!—[De]Assign Constraint>        ::=
<[De]AssignConstraint [op =(AND|OR|NOT|XOR)]>
   // opcode defaults to AND if none specified
 [<!—[De] Assign Condition>]+
 </[De]AssignConstraint>
<!—[De]Assign Condition>         ::=
<[De]AssignCondition cred_type=(type name)
    [pt_expr_id=(id) | d_expr_id=(id)]  >
   [<!-- Logical Expression>]
</[De]AssignCondition>
 <!—(En|Dis)abling Constraint>      ::=
<(En|Dis)abConstraint[op = (AND|OR|NOT)]>
   // opcode defaults to AND if none specified
   [<!-- (En|Dis)abling Condition>]+
</(En|Dis)abConstraint>
 <!—(En|Dis)abling Condition>      ::=
<(En|Dis)abCondition [pt_expr_id=(id) |
                 d_expr_id=(id)]  >
  [<!-- Logical Expression>]
</(En|Dis)abCondition>
 <!—[De]Activation Constraint> ::=
 <[De] ActivConstraint[op = (AND|OR|NOT)]>
  // opcode defaults to AND if none specified
   [<!—[De]ActivationCondition>]+
</[De]ActivConstraint>
 <!—[De]Activation Condition>      ::=
<[De]ActivCondition [d_expr_id=(id)]>
  <!-- Logical Expression>]
</[De]ActivCondition >
 <!-- Logical Expression>          ::=
 <LogicalExpr [op = (AND|OR|NOT)]>
 // opcode defaults to AND if none specified
 [<!-- Predicate>]+
 </LogicalExpr>
 <!-- Predicate>              ::= <Predicate>
  { <Operator> (gt|lt|eq|neq) </Operator>
    [<FuncName>(name)</FuncName>]
    [<ParamName>(name)</ParamName>]+
    <RetValue>(value)</RetValue> }
  | <!--LogicalExpression>
 </Predicate>
```

[Temporal Definitions]

```
 <!--   Definitions   of   Temporal   Constraints>::=
<XTempConstDef [xtcd_id = (id) ]>
   [<!—Interval Expression>]
   [<!-- Periodic Time Expression>]
   [<!-- Duration Expression>]
 </XTempConstDef>
 <!-- Periodic Time Expression>      ::=
<PeriodicTimeExpr pt_expr_id = (id)
  <!-- Start Time Expression>
 </PeriodicTimeExpr>
 <!—Interval Expression>          ::=
 <IntervalExpr i_expr_id = (id)>
 <begin> (date)</begin>
  <end>(date)</end>
 </IntervalExpr>
 <!-- Start Time Expression>  ::= <StartTimeExpr
 [pt_id_ref = (pt_id)]>
  [<Year> (all|odd|even) </Year>]
  [<!--MonthSet>]
  [<!--WeekSet>]
  [<!--DaySet>]
 </StartTimeExpr>
 <!--MonthSet>
::=<MonthSet>
  (<Month>(1|..|12)</Month>)1-12
  (represents # of months from the start of current Year)
 </MonthSet >
 <!--WeekSet>                          ::=
<WeekSet>
  (<Week>(1|..|5)</Week>)1-5
   (represents # of weeks from the start of current Month)
 </WeekSet >
 <!--DaySet>                           ::=
<DaySet>
  (<Day>(1|..|7)</Day>)1-7
  (represents # of days from the start of current Week)
 </DaySet >
 <!-- Duration Expression>          ::=
 <DurationExpr d_expr_id = (id)>
  <cal> (Years|Months|Weeks|Days)</cal>
  <len> (number)</len>
 </DurationExpr>
```

[TM Credential Definitions]

```
 <!--Header>       ::=  <Header>
   <!--  Principal >
   <!--  Issuer >
   <!--  Validity>
   [<!--  Digital Signature >]
   </Header>
 <!-- Issuer>          ::=          <Issuer>
  <!-- Principal>
  </Issuer>
 <!-- Principal>::=  <Principal>
<NameID mode=(saml:NameID@format)>
       (String) </NameID>
 </Principal>
 <!-- Validity>         ::= <Validity>
  <IssueTime>(xs:dateTime)</IssueTime>
  [<NotBefore>(xs:dateTime)</NotBefore>]
  [<NotOnOrAfter>(xs:dateTime)
    </NotOnOrAfter>]
 </Validity>
 <!--  Digital Signature >  ::= <DSig>
 (ds:Signature) </DSig>
 <!—Delegation Constraint>   ::=
 <DelegationConstraint [op = (AND|OR|NOT)]>
  // opcode defaults to AND if none specified
 [<!-- Delegation Condition>]+
 <!—Delegation Condition>        ::=
 <DelegationCondition [pt_expr_id=(id) |
                   d_expr_id=(id)]  >
   [<!-- Logical Expression>]
 </DelegationCondition>
 [d_expr_id = (id)] [i_expr_id = (id)]>
```

Appendix B

```
<?xml version="1.0" encoding="UTF-8"?>

<XTempConstDef xtcd_id="IFIP_XTCD">
  <IntervalExpr i_expr_id="Year2005">
        <begin>2005:01:01</begin>
        <end>2005:12:31</end>
  </IntervalExpr>
  <DurationExpr d_expr_id="SixWeeks">
        <cal>Weeks</cal>
        <len>6</len>
  </DurationExpr>
  <DurationExpr d_expr_id="OneWeek">
        <cal>Weeks</cal>
        <len>1</len>
  </DurationExpr>
  <PeriodicTimeExpr
pt_expr_id="PTQuarterWeekSeven"
i_expr_id="Year2005"
d_expr_id="SixWeeks">
    <StartTimeExpr>
        <Year>all</Year>
        <MonthSet>
            <Month>1</Month>
            <Month>4</Month>
            <Month>7</Month>
            <Month>10</Month>
        </MonthSet>
        <WeekSet>
            <Week>7</Week>
        </WeekSet>
    </StartTimeExpr>
  </PeriodicTimeExpr>
</XTempConstDef>
```

Figure B.1: This temporal constraint definition includes a periodic time expression (PTE) which states that the access is allowed beginning the seventh week of every quarter of year 2005, and is allowed for a duration of six weeks. Note that duration expression and interval expression are referenced inside a PTE.

```
<?xml version="1.0" encoding="UTF-8"?>

<XURAS xuras_id="IFIP_XURAS">
 <URA ura_id="uraBorrow" role_name="Borrower">
  <AssignUsers>
   <AssignUser user_id="any">
    <AssignConstraint>
      <AssignCondition cred_type="X.509 AC"
          pt_expr_id="PTQuarterWeekSeven">
       <LogicalExpr op="AND">
        <Predicate>
         <LogicalExpr op="OR">
           <Predicate>
             <Operator>neq</Operator>
             <FuncName>hasValue</FuncName>
             <ParamName>DLN</ParamName>
             <RetValue>null</RetValue>
           </Predicate>
           <Predicate>
             <Operator>neq</Operator>
             <FuncName>hasValue</FuncName>
             <ParamName>SSN</ParamName>
             <RetValue>null</RetValue>
           </Predicate>
         </LogicalExpr>
        </Predicate>
        <Predicate>
         <Operator>gt</Operator>
         <FuncName>hasValue</FuncName>
         <ParamName>valid_date</ParamName>
         <RetValue>2005:12:31</RetValue>
        </Predicate>
       </LogicalExpr>
      </AssignCondition>
    </AssignConstraint>
   </AssignUser>
  </AssignUsers>
 </URA>
</XURAS>
```

Figure B.2: This is a role assignment policy for the `Borrower` role in the federated digital library system. It states that any user (`any` is a keyword) can be assigned to this role if he/she supplies a SAML authentication credential supporting the following conditions: (i) credential has a non-null DLN *or* SSN attribute for the user, *and* (ii) the credential is valid beyond the year 2005. Additionally, the PTE of Figure B.1 is referenced in the assignment policy to constrain the applicable time period of the policy.

A HIERARCHICAL RELEASE CONTROL POLICY FRAMEWORK

Chao Yao[1], William H. Winsborough[1] and Sushil Jajodia[1,2]
[1] *Center for Secure Information Systems, George Mason University, Fairfax, VA 22030-4444;* [2] *The MITRE Corporation, 7515 Colshire Dr. Mclean, VA 22102-7508*
cyao@gmu.edu, wwinsborough@acm.org and jajodia@mitre.org

Abstract With increasing information exchange within and between organizations, it becomes increasingly unsatisfactory to depend solely on access control to meet confidentiality and other security needs. To better support the regulation of information flow, this paper presents a release control framework founded on a logical language. Release policies can be specified in a hierarchical manner, in the sense that each user, group, division and organization can specify their own policies, and these are combined by the framework in a manner that enables flexibility within the context of management oversight and regulation. In addition, the language can be used naturally to specify associated provisions (actions that must be undertaken before the release is permitted) and obligations (actions that are agreed will be taken after the release).

This paper also addresses issues arising due to the fact that a data object can be released from one entity to another in sequence, along a release path. We show how to test whether a given release specification satisfies given constraints on the release paths it authorizes. We also show how to find the best release paths from release specifications, based on weights specified by users. The factors affecting weights include the subjects through which a path passes, as well as the provisions and obligations that must be met to authorize each step in the path.

Keywords: Policy; Release Control; Access Control

Introduction

There are increasing needs for collaboration between organizations. In order to cooperate on common tasks, organizations need to release data that are not normally made available externally. For example, a hospital needs to release individual medical records to another institute to facilitate medical research. Such data release might compromise organizational confidentiality or personal privacy. Release control systems offer a means to regulate such data release.

The principle of release control is already in common use. When an organization publishes documents, its security officers may manually verify it does not contain sensitive information. The process is automated in some network firewalls. By including application-level inspection, a network firewall can use a "dirty-word" list to identify and intercept sensitive objects. No matter which release control mechanisms organizations use, they need to specify release policies.

Release control can often better manage information-flow than can access control. Once data is retrieved from a controlled data source, access control no longer assists in regulating its further dissemination. By contrast, as long as the data remains within a release-controlled environment, its further propagation can be regulated through release control.

This paper is concerned with how to specify release policies. We borrow some techniques introduced for use in access control, which regulates the direct access of users to data. However, we adapt those techniques and introduce new ones for use in release control. This is necessary because of the following three characteristics of data release that distinguish it from access control.

First, the role of the *sender* is instrumental. Different senders should have different privileges. Many senders may be permitted to release objects that are routinely made available to the receiver; however, it may be important to permit certain subjects to release objects to receivers that are normally not permitted to receive them. For example, a project leader may be permitted to send a project report to a customer, while ordinary project team members may not.

Second, while a policy may not allow a data object to be passed directly from one user s to another r, there could nevertheless exist a path composed of legal releases though which the object could be passed from s to r. A release control policy should be able to regulate such release paths; this would not be a meaningful objective for an access control policy.

Third, subjects and sensitive data typically belong to units within an organization. Thus, each unit has its own domain comprising data and users over which it should have some control. For example, an accounting department may own sensitive financial data and should be able to control to whom those data can be released. On the other hand, higher authorities within the organization should be able to override or otherwise compose the policies of lower authorities, although they are not concerned about most of the details of policies of the lower authorities.

For example, the accounting department could have policies that permit expense reports to be sent to all employees within the organization, while the organization director's policy stipulates that certain reports can be sent only to a few members of upper management; obviously, the policies of the organization should be able to override those of the accounting department.

Based on the above observations, this paper presents a hierarchical release control policy framework. We introduce a logical language that allows users to specify release policies in a flexible and hierarchical manner.

A novel feature of our framework is that it combines subpolicies defined by various authorities within an organization. That is, each unit defines its own subpolicies and these are then combined in a hierarchical manner. For instance, the policies of an organization can be formed by composing the policies of the departments in the organization in a specified way. We show that this hierarchical composition of policies can easily be expressed with our logical language.

When users specify release policies, they should be able to use not only positive authorizations, but also negative authorizations (prohibitions). For example, a dirty-word list in a firewall is a kind of negative authorization. Release control systems should be able to support both negative and positive authorizations, and to resolve any conflicts that arise between them. They should also be able to define flexibly whether or not to release when no specific authorizations or prohibitions apply (called the *decision policy*). By borrowing techniques introduced by Jajodia et al. [JSSS01] for access control, our framework allows specifying both positive and negative release authorizations and incorporates notions of authorization derivation, conflict resolution, and decision policy.

Often certain actions must be performed as a condition of release. Such actions are called *provisions* if they must be performed before release and *obligations* if they must be performed at some time after release. *Sender provisions* and *sender obligations* must be undertaken by the sender and *receiver provisions* and *receiver obligations*, by the receiver. Example sender provisions could include generating a log entry and attaching a copyright notice, a disclaimer, or a watermark to the released data; a sender obligation might be to transmit a follow-up customer-satisfaction survey form in 3 days; a receiver provision could be to present certain (additional) credentials; a receiver obligation could be to delete released data after 3 days. Our extended framework allows users to specify provisions and obligations in association with release control policy.

When an object is released to one receiver, one of the things that the receiver can potentially do with it is to release it further. We solve two problems related to such release paths. Sometimes confidentiality requires that certain release paths not be authorized. In this case, we need a way to detect them so that they can be blocked. On the other hand, a user may wish to discover legal paths that could be used to achieve a desired release. For the former purpose, our language allows defining policies to block undesired release paths. We show how to check whether such paths exist, enabling policy administrators to ensure they do not commit policy changes that permit illegal paths. For the latter purpose, we allow users to define weight functions associated with release paths based on various factors, and we show how to find the best release paths based on the assigned weights.

The paper is organized as follows. Section 1 gives an overview of our framework. Section 2 introduces the basic framework and language, and then extends them to support propagations and obligations. Section 3 presents technique for efficiently evaluating our policies. Section 4 discusses related work and Section 5 concludes.

1. System Architecture and Framework Overview

In this section, we first present system architectures for release control to understand the context in which release policies are applied. Then we overview the important components of the policy framework.

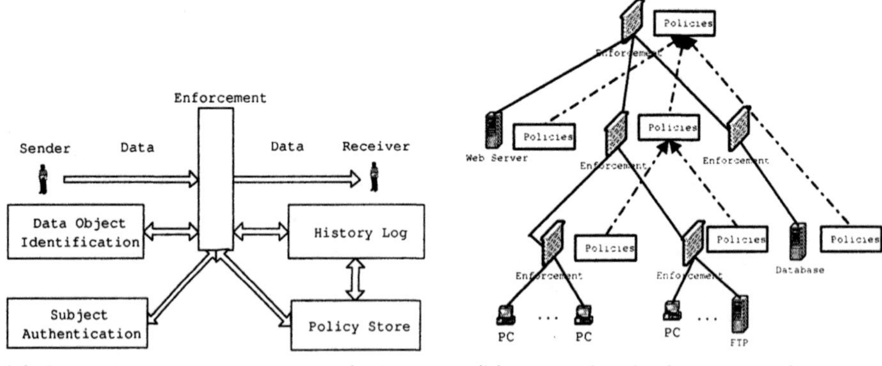

(a) General system architecture of release control

(b) Hierarchical release control system

Figure 1. System Architecture

1.1 System architecture

One general system architecture for release control is as shown in Figure 1(a). There is a filter-like enforcement point that intercepts each message that a sender attempts to release to a receiver. It invokes object-identification and subject-authentication components, and queries the policy store to determine whether the release is authorized. In an alternative architecture (not shown), the enforcement point does not actively intercept the messages, but passively responds to release queries and issues a permit token when the data release is authorized.

In some environments, sensitive data are distributed over an organization that consists of hierarchically organized units. A release control system in such an organization could be composed of smaller release control subsystems that correspond to the organizational units, as shown in Figure 1(b). Similarly, each unit may have a stake in the definition of policy. Thus, whether or not actual enforcement is distributed, it may be necessary to gather policy components that are defined in a distributed manner, so as to assemble the complete policy of the organization that is to be enforced consistently throughout.

1.2 Subjects and objects

Subjects in our framework can act as senders and as receivers. Subjects can be users, groups, or roles. In most applications, subjects and objects are organized into hierarchies. Policies are specified to explicitly authorize the release of an object o from sender s to receiver r. Implicit authorizations can be derived from these explicit authorizations in the usual manner by propagating them down the hierarchies. Such propagation enables higher entities in the hierarchy to generalize lower entities. Since we allow negative authorizations, conflicts may occur between derived authorizations. The policies used to resolve such conflicts can be specified using our language.

1.3 Policy authority

Policies in our framework consist of logic programs that define certain predicates used by the release control system. Many policy authorities contribute clauses. There are two kinds of predicate symbols in our language, *authority predicates* and *global predicates*. Each authority predicate belongs to a specified authority, and is denoted by an authority name followed by a predicate name, separated by a dot. Thus, our framework deviates from standard logic in that authority predicate symbols are structured (pairs). Authority can be looked upon as an administrator role that has the privileges to manage the policies of the corresponding organizational unit. Each release control system has its authorities organized in a hierarchy that has a single topmost authority, denoted a^T. This hierarchy usually resembles the structure of the organization. Only administrators associated with authority a can contribute or modify clauses that define the predicates of a. The body of such a clause can contain predicates of other authorities that are lower in the authority hierarchy than a, as well as global predicates, which are discussed in the following paragraph. The release decisions are determined by predicates of the topmost authority. This gives the topmost authority ultimate control over release decisions.

Global predicates are used to represent the object and subject hierarchies, as well as the association of subjects and objects with certain authorities. They are defined globally by the organization, rather than being associated with a particular authority. By contrast with authority predicates, global predicates are standard predicate symbols in the sense of being unstructured individuals.

Acct Authority

$acct.canrls(expenseDoc, manager, org2, +) \leftarrow .$

$acct.dercanrls(O, S, R, +) \leftarrow in(O, O'),\ acct.canrls(O', S, R, +)$

$acct.rls(O, S, R, +) \leftarrow acct.dercanrls(O, S, R, +)$

$acct.error \leftarrow path(O, S, org3), in(O, expenseDoc)$

Tech Authority

$tech.canrls(doc1, manager, org2, +) \leftarrow .$

$tech.rls(O, S, R, +) \leftarrow tech.canrls(O, S, R, +)$

Org Authority

$org.rls(O, S, R, +) \leftarrow\ acct.rls(O, S, R, +),\ tech.rls(O, S, R, +),\ in(O, expenseDoc)$

$org.rls(O, S, R, -) \leftarrow\ \neg org.rls(O, S, R, +)$

Figure 2. An example for release policy specifications

EXAMPLE 1 *Consider the clauses in Figure 2. There are three authorities in an organization, acct (the accounting department), tech (the IT department), and org (the whole organization). The topmost authority is $a^T = org$. The first group of clauses are contributed by acct. The first of these clauses says that manager can send the document type expenseDoc to another organization org2. The second indicates that positive authorizations propagate down the object hierarchy. The third makes acct's final release decision from the derived authorizations. This will be inte-*

grated below into the final decision for the system as a whole. The fourth expresses an integrity constraint that no sender can transmit to org3 *any object dominated by expenseDoc via any sequence of release. (Valid release specifications dom not make a.error true for any authority a.) The second group of clauses are contributed by tech:* doc1 *can be sent from manager to org2. The third group of clauses are contributed by org, the topmost authority. The first says that if a document is dominated in the object hierarchy by expenseDoc, then release of the document is permitted as long as both acct and tech authorize the release. The second clause contributed by org says that if a release is not authorized, then it is prohibited. This ensures that the policy defines a complete decision, meaning that all releases are either permitted or denied. (See Section 2.) In our context, for every o, s, r, exactly one of the atoms* $org.rls(o, s, r, +)$ *and* $org.rls(o, s, r, -)$ *is true. It determines the final release decision. From the clauses that make up this policy, it follows that if* doc1 *is an expenseDoc, then the release of* doc1 *from manager to* org2 *is authorized.*

1.4 PO actions

As discussed in Section , certain actions, called provisions and obligations, must be taken as a condition of release. We refer to them in general as PO-actions. Following Bettini et al. [BJWW02], PO-actions are represented using a special class of predicates and positive Boolean combinations of PO-actions are represented by PO-formulas, as introduced formally below in section 2.4. For example, the PO-formula $(Watermark \wedge Log) \vee SignContract$ expresses that to permit the release we must either embed a watermark into the data and record the release into log, or sign a contract. Although we defer the details to a later section, the basic idea is that we associate a PO-expression with each clause. This PO-expression is then used to define PO-formulas for atoms inferred by using the clause.

EXAMPLE 2 *From the following clauses, we can infer that* $acct.rls(doc1, manager, org2, +)$ *is true. Let us consider the PO-formula associated with this atomic formula. The PO-expression* $\top$*, which is associated with the first clause (see table below), represents that the PO-formula associated with* $in(doc1, expenseDoc)$ *is trivially true: no PO-actions are required. From the second clause, we associate* $acct.canrls(expenseDoc, manager, org2, +)$ *with* $Watermark$*. For the third clause, the formula variable* f_2 *in the PO-expression represents the PO-formula associated with (an instance of)* $acct.canrls(o', s, r, +)$*. Consider the instance of clause 3 obtained by substituting o by* doc1*,* o' *by expenseDoc, s by* *manager, and r by org2. In this case, f_2 is substituted by Watermark, because it is the PO-formula associated with the second positive atom in the body, acct.canrls(expenseDoc, manager, org2, +). Replacing f_2 in the PO-expression $Log \wedge f_2$ accordingly, we obtain the PO-formula associated with acct.rls(doc1, manager, org2, +),* viz., *$Log \wedge Watermark$. From the fourth clause, we find that SignContract is associated with acct.rls(doc1, manager, org2, +). So acct.rls(doc1, manager, org2, +) is associated with the PO-formula $(Log \wedge Watermark) \vee SignContract$, which represents the required PO-actions for the release authorization for doc1 from manager to org2.*

Clause	**PO-expression**
$in(doc1, expenseDoc) \leftarrow$	$\top$
$acct.canrls(expenseDoc, manager, org2, +) \leftarrow$	$Watermark$
$acct.rls(O, S, R, +) \leftarrow in(O, O'),\ acct.canrls(O', S, R, +)$	$Log \wedge f_2$
$acct.rls(doc1, manager, org2, +) \leftarrow$	$SignContract$

2. Release Control Framework

We formalize the basic elements in our framework as follows.

DEFINITION 3 (DATA RELEASE DOMAIN) *A* data release domain *consists of a 4-tuple $(Obj, Sub, PO, Auth)$ in which:*

1 Obj is a partially ordered set whose elements $o \in Obj$ are called objects;

2 Sub is a partially ordered set whose elements $r, s \in Sub$ are called subjects;

3 PO is a partially ordered set whose elements $p \in PO$ are called PO-actions;

4 Auth is a partially ordered set whose elements $a \in Auth$ are called authorities and which has a maximal element, $a^T \in Auth$.

We use $\sqsubseteq$ to denote the order relation over each of these sets.

In the remainder of this section, we present the language for basic authorization policies and then extend it to support policies with PO-actions.

2.1 Basic release specification language

We introduce a basic specification language to specify release authorization policies. We assume familiarity with the basic concepts of logic programming. (See for instance [Llo87].) The language contains the following symbols and constructs:

1 **Constant Symbols**: There is a constant for each $o \in Obj$, $s \in Sub$, and $a \in Auth$. In addition, $+$ and $-$ are also constants.

2 **Variable Symbols**: There are *subject/object* variables ranging over the sets *Obj* and *Sub*. We use O for variables range over *Obj* and S and R for variables ranging over *Sub*, often with subscripts or primes.

3 **Subject/Object Terms**: A *subject* (respectively, *object*) *term* is a subject (respectively, object) constant or variable. We use σ for sender subject terms, ρ for receiver subject terms, and ω for object terms.

4 **Predicate Symbols**: The set of predicate symbols is partitioned into predicates that have special roles in the release control policy and auxiliary predicates.

(a) A 4-ary predicate symbol, **a.canrls**, with the arguments $(\omega, \sigma, \rho, sign)$. It represents authorizations explicitly specified by the authority a.

(b) A 4-ary ternary predicate symbol, **a.dercanrls**, with the same arguments as **a.canrls**. It represents authorizations derived by the system from explicit authorizations, typically by propagating authorizations down the subject and object hierarchies.

(c) A 4-ary predicate symbol, **a.rls**, with the same arguments as **a.canrls**. It represents the final authorization decision made by the authority A.

(d) A 4-ary predicate symbol, **a.path**, taking the form $a.path(\omega, \sigma, \rho)$. It represents that there is a release path for the object ω from the sender σ to the receiver ρ. Such a path is a sequence of linked release authorizations from the authority a.

(e) A predicate symbol, **a.error**, used to detect certain integrity violations within the policy itself.

(f) A binary predicate symbol, **in**, with the form $in(\omega_1, \omega_2)$ or $in(\sigma_1, \sigma_2)$. It represents the domination relationship in a hierarchy.

(g) A binary predicate symbol, **dirin**, with the form $dirin(\omega_1, \omega_2)$ or $dirin(\sigma_1, \sigma_2)$. It represents the direct domination relationship in a hierarchy.

(h) A binary predicate symbol, **auth**, with the form $auth(\omega, a)$, $auth(\sigma, a)$, or $auth(\rho, a)$. It represents that the object or subject belongs to the authority.

(i) Other **user-defined** predicates to describe the properties of subject or objects.

We next define the core of our release policies. Later we extend this core so as to support provisions and obligations.

DEFINITION 4 (BASIC RELEASE SPECIFICATION) *A basic release specification RS is a set of Horn clauses over the language presented above. These clauses may include negated*[1] *literals in their bodies, and must satisfy the restriction that every variable that appears in the head of a clause also appears in the body. In addition, clauses must satisfy the restrictions presented in Figure 3, and RS must contain* $a^T.error \leftarrow a^T.rls(O,S,R,+), a^T.rls(O,S,R,-)$ *and* $a^T.rls(O,S,R,-) \leftarrow \neg a^T.rls(O,S,R,+)$. *If* $RS \models a^T.rls(o,s,r,+)$, *then the release for o from s to r is* authorized*; if* $RS \models a^T.rls(o,s,r,-)$, *then the release is* blocked.

Including $a^T.error \leftarrow a^T.rls(O,S,R,+)\ ,\ a^T.rls(O,S,R,-)$ in the release specification makes that there don't exist conflicts. Including $a^T.rls(O,S,R,-) \leftarrow \neg a^T.rls(O,S,R,+)$ in the release specification makes it complete, as shown in [JSSS01]. This means that any specification RS makes one and only one of $a^T.rls(o,s,r,+)$ and $a^T.rls(o,s,r,-)$ true for each triple of constants (o,s,r).

Integrity rules. A clause with the head of $a.error$ is called an *integrity rule.* An integrity rule derives an error every time the conditions in the body of the clause are satisfied. It imposes an constraint on the release specification. A valid release specification cannot make $error$ true.

DEFINITION 5 (RELEASE PATH) *Given a set of release clauses, a* Release Path *from s to r for o is a sequence of subjects* $s_0, s_1, \ldots, s_n$ *such that* $s_0 = s$, $s_n = r$, *and* $a.rls(o,s,s_1,+)$, $a.rls(o,s_1,s_2,+)$, $\ldots$, $a.rls(o,s_{n-1},r,+)$.

Clauses that specify the *path* predicate are straightforward:

$$a.path(O,S,R) \leftarrow a.rls(O,S,R,+)$$
$$a.path(O,S,R) \leftarrow a.path(O,S,S')\ ,\ a.path(O,S',R)$$

EXAMPLE 6 *The following integrity rule prohibits there being a release path from staff to org1 for doc1:*

$$a^T.error \leftarrow org.path(doc1, staff, org1, +)$$

[1] As we discuss in Section 3.1, each permitted set of clauses is stratified, so all of the standard semantics of negation as failure coincide.

Predicate	Clauses defining predicate
rel-preds	Facts only (no clause body).
$a.canrls$	Body may contain rel-preds and arbitrary preds of a', $a' \sqsubseteq a$.
$a.over$	Body may contain $a.canrls$, rel-preds and arbitrary preds of a', $a' \sqsubseteq a$.
$a.dercanrls$	Body may contain $a.over$, $a.canrls$, rel-preds and arbitrary preds of a', $a' \sqsubseteq a$. Occurrences of $a.dercanrls$ must be in positive literals.
$a.rls$ +	When head is of the form $a.rls(\omega, \sigma, \rho, +)$, body may contain $a.dercanrls$, $a.canrls$, rel-preds and arbitrary preds of a', $a' \sqsubseteq a$.
$a.rls$ −	When head is of the form $a.rls(\omega, \sigma, \rho, -)$, body contains just one literal, *viz.*, $\neg rls(\omega, \sigma, \rho, +)$, and ω, σ, and ρ are all variables.
$a.path$	Body may contain positive uses of $a.rls$ and $a.path$ only.
$a.error$	Body may contain positive uses of $a.path$, $a.rls$, $a.dercanrls$, $a.canrls$, rel-preds and arbitrary predcates of a', $a' \sqsubseteq a$.

Figure 3. Restrictions on the form of clauses defining the various predicates in our language. The predicates *in*, *dirin*, *auth* and user-defined predicates are called rel-preds. Predicates and literals associated with the authority a are called predicates and literals of a, respectively.

Disjunction of the authorizations of authorities:

$$org.rls(O, S, R, +) \leftarrow acct.canrls(O, S, R, +)$$
$$org.rls(O, S, R, +) \leftarrow tech.canrls(O, S, R, +)$$

Conjunction of the decisions of authorities:

$$org.rls(O, S, R, +) \leftarrow acct.rls(O, S, R, +),\ tech.rls(O, S, R, +)$$

Sender authority takes precedence:

$$org.rls(O, S, R, +) \leftarrow acct.rls(O, S, R, +),\ auth(S, acct)$$
$$org.rls(O, S, R, +) \leftarrow tech.rls(O, S, R, +),\ auth(S, tech)$$

Figure 4. Rules enforcing various composition policies.

DEFINITION 7 (VALID BASIC RELEASE SPECIFICATION) *A basic release specification RS is* valid *if RS* $\not\models$ *a.error for all authorities* $a \in Auth$.

2.2 Composition policies

Here we want to show that there are various ways in which a higher authority can compose authorizations defined by lower authorities. Figure 4 presents several possible composition policies in the context of our running example. As the topmost authority is *org*, truth values assumed by *org.rls* determine the final release decisions.

2.3 Legal release paths

Sometimes users may want the evaluation of release specifications to return not only release authorizations, but also release paths. Users may want to send o from s to r via other subjects in the case where direct release is not authorized. Given (o, s, r) and a set of subjects I as intermediate nodes of release paths, the problem is to find one or more legal release paths from s to r. Sometimes we may want to find an optimal path based on costs assigned to edges through which the path passes. We discuss algorithms to compute such paths in Section 3.2.

2.4 PO extension

We follow Bettini et al. [BJWW02] in associating PO-formulas with atoms entailed by the clauses in our policies. However, we take a slightly different approach: because we aim to enable higher authorities to override policy decisions made by their underlings, we provide a similar capability with respect to PO-actions. So while in the prior work each clause used in the proof of an atom could contribute PO-requirements to the PO-formula associated with the atom, in our framework, the decision whether to include PO-requirements associated with a given subtree in the proof is made by the PO-expression associated with the clause at which the subtree is rooted. PO-expressions generalize PO-formulas by allowing the use of *formula variables* whose values range over PO-formulas. Formula variables are disjoint from the standard subject/object variables, whose values range over the domain of interpretation.

PO-actions are represented by PO-atoms, which are constructed using special PO-predicate symbols, constants, and variables. The special symbol $\top$ is also a PO-atom, signifying that no PO-action is required. A PO-formula is either a PO-atom, a disjunction of PO-formulas, or a conjunction of PO-formulas. We next explain how we associate a PO-formula with each ground atom in the least Herbrand model of a release specification.

The policy author associates a PO-expression with each clause he authors. A PO-expression is either a PO-atom, a formula variable, a disjunction of PO-expressions, or a conjunction of PO-expressions.

DEFINITION 8 (RELEASE SPECIFICATION) *A* release specification *consists of a basic release specification and a mapping associating a PO-expression with each clause in the former. Each formula variable occurring in a PO-expression must correspond to a positive literal occurring in the body of the clause with which the PO-expression is associated. (Neg-*

ative literals are not associated with PO-formulas.) This correspondence is established by numbering the formula variables and positive literals, and associating with one another the variables and literals that have the same number. For instance, the variable f_2 in Example 2 represents the PO-formulas associated with the ground instances of the second positive literal, $acct.canrls(o', s, r, +)$. Each object variable occurring in a PO-expression must occur in the clause with which the PO-expression is associated. This ensures that PO-formulas associated with ground atoms are also ground.

During policy evaluation, each ground instance of a clause defines a PO-formula by substituting for each formula variable in the clause's PO-expression the PO-formula associated with the corresponding atom in the body. The PO-formulas defined by all ground clause instances having the same head are then combined by disjunction to obtain the PO-formula associated with the ground atom that is that common clause head.

3. Evaluation of Release Specifications

This section discussed methods for the evaluation of release specifications. We first consider individual releases, and then turn to sequences of releases of a data object from one subject to another.

3.1 Materializing release specifications

The materialized authorizations of the highest authority are the evaluation results of a release specification. Recall that authority predicate symbols are pairs in our system. For example, $acct.canrls$ is a different predicate from $tech.canrls$. Predicates with lower authority can appear in the body of clauses defining predicates with higher authority, whereas the reverse is prohibited. This, and the other restrictions presented in Figure 3, ensure the set of clauses given by a release specification is locally stratified. Therefore, the data complexity of its evaluation is quadratic time in the number of ground instances of the clauses in the specification, as illustrated in [Gel89]. As the number of variables in each clause is typically bounded by a small constant, the number of ground instances of each clause is bounded by a polynomial in the size of the specification (including the definitions of predicates representing the hierarchy). Thus, the complexity of evaluation is also bounded by such a polynomial.

For the extended framework, note that all PO-formulas are positive and hence consistent. Consequently, if a release specification's underlying basic release specification is RS, then if $RS \models a^T.rls(o, s, r, +)$, the corresponding release can be permitted, provided some combination of PO-actions is undertaken. The evaluation of the least Herbrand model of *RS* is not affected by the PO-expressions in the policy. We can evaluate the PO-formulas for each atom in the least Herbrand model in a bottom-up fashion, as illustrated in [BJWW02].

3.2 Computation of release path

Given a release specification *RS*, a triple (o, s, r), and a (possibly empty) set of subjects I, a basic path evaluation algorithm returns a possibly empty set of paths. Each path consists of a sequence of subjects, $s_0, s_1, \ldots, s_n$, such that $s_0 = s$, $s_n = r$, for each i, $0 \leq i < n$, $RS \models a^T.rls(o, s_i, s_{i+1}, +)$. Letting the PO-formula associated with $a^T.rls(o, s_i, s_{i+1}, +)$ be p_i, the PO-formula associated with the path $s_0, s_1, \ldots, s_n$ is $p = p_0 \wedge \ldots \wedge p_{n-1}$.

A basic path evaluation algorithm determines whether a release specification *RS* is valid and identifies all integrity violations within it. Such an algorithm can be obtained as follows. Given an object o, we compute all atoms $a^T.rls(o, s, r, +)$ entailed by *RS*, and find the PO-formula p associated with each such atom. Then we construct a directed graph whose nodes are given by *Sub* and which has edge (s, r) just in case $RS \models a^T.rls(o, s, r, +)$. We associate with this edge the PO-action associated with $a^T.rls(o, s, r, +)$. A release path corresponds to a path in this directed graph. There are well-known algorithms to check whether there exists a path between two nodes and to find all paths between two nodes.

When a user seeks a legitimate release path for getting a data object from a given sender to a given receiver, the user does not want a set of paths, but rather an optimal path based on certain assigned weights. The factors that affect such weights could be, for instance, the subjects through which the path passes and the PO-formulas associated with the edges in the path.

We now consider how to find an optimal path. We first assign weights to edges based on PO-actions and nodes (senders and receivers). We can still use the well-known algorithms for the shortest path. However, calculation of path weights is more complicated when basing them on PO-formulas associated with edges. A PO-formula expresses that one of a collection of sets of PO-actions needs to be executed, where each set corresponds to a disjunct in the DNF (disjunction normal form) of the PO-formula. So the weight assigned to a PO-formula is the minimum weight among the disjuncts of the DNF of the PO-formula. For example, given a PO-formula $(Log \wedge Watermark) \vee Sign$, if the weights of *Log*,

Watermark, and *Sign* are 1, 2 and 3, respectively, then the weight of the disjunctive clause $Log \wedge Watermark$ is $1 + 2 = 3$ and the weight of the disjunctive clause *Sign* is 2; hence the weight of the PO-formula is the minimum value 2.

To calculate a path's weight, we need to first find the PO-formula of the path. This is the conjunction of PO-formulas associated with edges in the path. Thus, the weight of a path is not simply the sum of the weights of its edges. The calculation of the weight of the PO-formula associated with a path can take advantage of pruning. For example, suppose there are two PO-actions *Log* and *Watermark*, where the weight of *Log* is less than that of *Watermark*. If one edge has a PO-formula $Watermark \vee Log$, and an adjacent edge has a PO-formula *Log*, then the PO-formula associated with the path consisting of these two edges is $(Log \wedge Watermark) \vee Log$. $Log \wedge Watermark$ certainly cannot have less weight than *Log*, so the formula can be pruned to be *Log*. This example also illustrates that, if the formula associated with an edge is $Log \vee Watermark$, even though the weight of *Log* is less than *Watermark*, we still need to keep track of both during the computation because we may subsequently encounter another edge in the path that has a PO-formula *Watermark*.

4. Related Work

Much of the extensive prior research in access control is highly relevant to release control. For instance, Jajodia et al. present an access control framework, FAF [JSSS01], that uses Horn clauses to express multiple access control policies (*e.g.*, open or closed, and positive or negative). They show that FAF specifications are locally stratified and can be evaluated in polynomial time. Our work is based on FAF. However, FAF does not address data release, nor does it allow policies to be composed of components specified by multiple authorities. It also does not allow provisions and obligations to be required as a condition of authorization.

Another important line of work in access control concerns the RBAC model[SCFY96, SBM99]. In RBAC, there is an administrator hierarchy [SBM99], where different administrators have different administrative privileges. However, in RBAC, even when multiple administrative roles have authority over various portions of the authorization specification, these portions are disjoint and the manner in which these portions are composed is somewhat trivial. Again, release is not addressed, nor typically are provisions and obligations.

Bettini et al. [BJWW02] study provisions and obligations in policy management. They introduce a framework for augmenting logical programs which associates a PO-formula with each policy clause. Our framework regarding provisions and obligations is quite similar, though PO-expressions we associate with clauses generalize PO-formulas in manner that makes our approach better in the context of multiple policy authors whose authorities are organized hierarchically. There are also related works [BdVS00, WJ02] that introduce policy algebras to combine authorization specifications for access control. Bonatti et al. [BdVS00] model policy as a set of ground terms over an alphabet for (subject, object, action) terms whereas Wijesekera and Jajodia [WJ02] model policies as non-deterministic transformers (relations) over a collection of subjects, objects, and action terms. Operands are policies, which are combined by operators such as addition, conjunction, and negation. Our framework language can be used to implement most policy algebra operators. Furthermore, we organize the specification of distributed policies in a hierarchical manner, which captures structural features of organizations, and hence is simple and manageable.

Another research area related to release control is flow control [Den76, Fol89, MMN90, ML97, SBCJ97]. This line of work focuses mainly on the context of multi-level security, concentrating on information flow between objects in programs. It seeks to control not only data release, but also the further propagation of any information derived from that data. In this sense it is much more ambitious than release control, which does not trace information flow through computations.

5. Conclusions

We have observed that the world's increasing reliance on information sharing heightens the need for mechanisms and models that protect confidentiality, and that access control alone is inadequate to modern requirements. We present a release control framework to better satisfy these needs. By providing for distributed, hierarchical specification of policy throughout an organization, and by allowing release policy clauses to include provisions and obligations that must be satisfied for release to be permitted, we create a framework that is both powerful and flexible. We have extended prior work associating provisions and obligations with authorizations in a manner that reflects our goal of enabling senior authorities to override policy authored by their juniors.

This paper concentrates on the specification of release control policies, rather than on their enforcement. Enforcement mechanisms of release control are more complicated than those of access control. This is because it is difficult to detect reliably when data transmission is occurring, and identify senders, receivers, and data objects on the fly, as data objects are transmitted. Further research in release control enforcement is clearly needed.

Acknowledgments

This work was partially supported by the NSF grants CCR-0113515, IIS-0242237, and IIS-0430402.

References

[BdVS00] Piero A. Bonatti, Sabrina De Capitani di Vimercati, and Pierangela Samarati. A modular approach to composing access control policies. In *ACM Conference on Computer and Communications Security*, pages 164–173, 2000.

[BJWW02] Claudio Bettini, Sushil Jajodia, Xiaoyang Sean Wang, and Duminda Wijesekera. Provisions and obligations in policy management and security applications. In *VLDB*, pages 502–513, 2002.

[Den76] Dorothy E. Denning. A lattice model of secure information flow. *Commun. ACM*, 19(5):236–243, 1976.

[Fol89] Simon N. Foley. A model for secure information flow. In *IEEE Symposium on Security and Privacy*, pages 248–258, 1989.

[Gel89] Allen Van Gelder. The alternating fixpoint of logic programs with negation. In *Proceedings of the Eighth ACM SIGACT-SIGMOD-SIGART Symposium on Principles of Database Systems, March 29-31, 1989, Philadelphia, Pennsylvania*, pages 1–10. ACM Press, 1989.

[JSSS01] Sushil Jajodia, Pierangela Samarati, Maria Luisa Sapino, and V. S. Subrahmanian. Flexible support for multiple access control policies. *ACM Trans. Database Syst.*, 26(2):214–260, 2001.

[Llo87] John W. Lloyd. *Foundations of Logic Programming, Second Edition.* Springer, 1987.

[ML97] Andrew C. Myers and Barbara Liskov. A decentralized model for information flow control. In *SOSP*, pages 129–142, 1997.

[MMN90] Catherine D. McCollum, J. R. Messing, and LouAnna Notargiacomo. Beyond the pale of mac and dac-defining new forms of access control. In *IEEE Symposium on Security and Privacy*, pages 190–200, 1990.

[SBCJ97] Pierangela Samarati, Elisa Bertino, Alessandro Ciampichetti, and Sushil Jajodia. Information flow control in object-oriented systems. *IEEE Trans. Knowl. Data Eng.*, 9(4):524–538, 1997.

[SBM99] Ravi S. Sandhu, Venkata Bhamidipati, and Qamar Munawer. The arbac97 model for role-based administration of roles. *ACM Trans. Inf. Syst. Secur.*, 2(1):105–135, 1999.

[SCFY96] Ravi S. Sandhu, Edward J. Coyne, Hal L. Feinstein, and Charles E. Youman. Role-based access control models. *IEEE Computer*, 29(2):38–47, 1996.

[WJ02] Duminda Wijesekera and Sushil Jajodia. Policy algebras for access control the predicate case. In *ACM Conference on Computer and Communications Security*, pages 171–180, 2002.

SESSION 4 – RISK MANAGEMENT

MANAGING UNCERTAINTY IN SECURITY RISK MODEL FORECASTS WITH RAPSA/MC

James R. Conrad,[1] Paul Oman,[2] and Carol Taylor[3]
Department of Computer Science, University of Idaho, Moscow, ID 83844-1010
[1]conr2286@uidaho.edu, [2]oman@uidaho.edu, [3]ctaylor@uidaho.edu

Abstract This report describes an information security risk assessment process that accommodates uncertainty and can be applied to deployed systems as well as systems under development. An example is given for a critical infrastructure but the technique is applicable to other networks. RAPSA/MC extends the Risk Analysis and Probabilistic Survivability Assessment (RAPSA) systems-level process model with a Monte-Carlo (MC) technique capturing the uncertainty in expert estimates and illustrating its resulting impact on the model's forecast. The forecast is presented as a probability density function enabling the security analyst to more effectively communicate security risks to financial decision makers. This approach may be particularly useful for visualizing the risk of an extreme event such as an unlikely but catastrophic exploit.

Keywords: Security risk analysis and management, Methods for dealing with incomplete or inconsistent information, Critical infrastructure protection.

1. Introduction

RAPSA/MC is a Monte-Carlo technique for capturing and expressing security risks in a computer network. Taylor et al. developed the Risk Analysis and Probabilistic Survivability Assessment (RAPSA) process [Taylor et al., 2002] which combines the quantification of Probability Risk Assessment (PRA) with Survivable Systems Analysis (SSA) [Ellison et al., 1999] to focus resources on the mission critical services of a system. The goal was to use SSA to tame the complexity of a large network and thereby permit quantification of critical threats. The RAPSA process captured each expert's estimate as an expected value, a single fixed quantity representing the average of the possibilities. But a security analyst needs a method to capture the uncertainty in an expert's estimate and to visualize its resulting impact on the model's forecasts; the Risk Analysis and Probabilistic Survivability Assessment Monte-Carlo (RAPSA/MC) process extends RAPSA with a Monte-Carlo simulation that provides that capability.

Decisions about new security technologies become investment decisions when, for example, an urgently needed intrusion detection system competes for resources with the other needs of an organization. The security analyst may be called to help position the value of the proposed investment with other contenders, to explain to the decision makers why this security investment is needed and to quantify the risks facing the organization if it is or is not implemented. Quantifying security risks as financial exposures simplifies their evaluation with the organization's other needs. Charting uncertainty in the forecast guides the financial decision makers to focus on what they do best, managing risks and opportunities.

2. Modeling Information Security Risks

Information security models often take one of two approaches, a low-level approach that models the detailed topology of a network and the specific vulnerabilities of its objects, or a systems-level approach that abstracts the details into high-level risks. A well-known example of the low-level approach includes the Take-Grant model [Lipton and Snyder, 1977] addressing the question as to whether a particular system with a given initial state is safe with respect to some specific access right [Bishop, 2003]. An advantage of the Take-Grant model is its ability to answer this important question in linear time.

As the size of a network increases, the application of low-level approaches becomes increasingly challenging for the analyst. In a complex enterprise, an analyst may become responsible for the security of hundreds or even thousands of network nodes, each with a myriad of unknown and known vulnerabilities. When human intervention is required to analyze the vulnerabilities of each node, even linear-time models may become unbearably expensive. To make matters worse, the security analyst's best intentions may be thwarted by an organization's limited budget that precludes a low-level detailed analysis of every vulnerability. Problems of this nature are often addressed with systems-level models.

Several systems-level security models express threats or opportunities as financial variables that quantify information security risks in terms of their financial impact. This approach can be traced back at least as far as the U.S. Government's pioneering FIPS guideline on information security in large data centers that proposed the use of the Average Loss Expectancy (ALE) metric [Soo Hoo, 2000]. Given a set of harmful outcomes, O_i, the frequencies of those outcomes, F_i, and the economic impacts of those outcomes, $I(O_i)$, the ALE metric is defined as:

$$ALE = \sum_{i=1}^{n} I(O_i)F_i \tag{1}$$

Soo Hoo cautions [Soo Hoo, 2000] that ALE, an *expected value*, equates high-probability but low-impact events with *extreme events* (those that though unlikely are catastrophic when they do occur). This critique can be important for financial decision makers because the reliance upon expected values obfuscates the consequences of a decision with the potential to kill the "cash cow on their watch." Financial decision makers should be made aware of which decisions ask them to "bet the farm." Haimes notes that the Partitioned Multi-objective Risk Method (PMRM) [Haimes, 1998] offers an alternative to the expected value approach and warns that when "...expected value is used as the sole risk measure, risk is likely to be grossly misinterpreted" with the potential for bad management decisions. Haimes continues, "...incorporating the risk of extreme events into the total risk management framework enhances the realism and the representation of risks." In short, the use of expected values alone misleads the financial decision makers with oversimplification. The analyst needs a straightforward mechanism to help the financial decision makers visualize the information security risks to the organization's assets and services.

A second critique of ALE is the potential for ALE-based models to auger into complexity [Soo Hoo, 2000] as they attempt to enumerate and address all known threats, assets and vulnerabilities in a large enterprise network. This path leads back to the pitfall of the low-level models: many organizations simply cannot afford to manually review every known detail of their operating network. This fundamental issue, how to analyze the security of a complex network within the constraints of a limited budget, likely underlies the motivation for many systems-level models.

Other approaches for quantifying security in systems-level models have been proposed. Geer urges [Geer, 2001] the use of Return-on-Investment (ROI) to guide information risk management decisions. Magnusson argues [Magnusson, 2005] for Net Present Value (NPV). Likewise, Butler champions the use of portfolio analysis methods [Butler et al., 1999] to guide software investment decisions. Schechter introduces a novel market-based approach [Schechter, 2004] to quantify the strength of a secured system as the market price to discover its next new vulnerability. Within this context, Schechter asserts that the strength of a system having a known vulnerability is negligible. Soo Hoo suggests a stochastic approach [Soo Hoo, 2000] to evaluate the role of uncertainty in information security decisions, and Conrad champions using Monte-Carlo methods [Conrad, 2005] for this endeavor.

3. Survivable Systems Analysis

Each of the above security risk models offers an approach to quantify a set of known threats to an information system. But how can we discover the threats to a complex system? Survivable Systems Analysis (SSA) defines a qualitative methodology that focuses the search on just those threats to the most critical features [Software Engineering Institute, 2005] of an information system. The SSA method emerged from the study of Survivable Network Analysis [Ellison et al., 1999] at Carnegie Mellon. SSA offers several useful features:

- SSA focuses resources on the most critical functions of a software system found to be essential for its survival. This addresses Soo Hoo's second critique of ALE above.
- SSA methodology can be applied to an existing (already deployed) software system.
- SSA can also be applied to a new software system under development. Executable code is not required to support the SSA methodology.

The SSA methodology emphasizes survivability defined as a "system's capability to fulfill its mission (in a timely manner) in the presence of attacks, failures or accidents" and focuses on the "delivery of essential services and preservation of essential assets with timely recovery of full services and assets following the attack" [Ellison et al., 1999]. SSA approaches this goal by bolstering three characteristics of a survivable system: resistance, recognition and recovery. Resistance refers to the system's capability to repel an attack. Recognition refers to its ability to detect an attack in progress as well as assess the resulting damages. And recovery denotes the system's ability to fulfill its mission (albeit in a reduced capacity) during the attack, limit the extent of damages during the attack, and restore full service following the attack. The SSA methodology consists of four steps:

1 The System Definition step reviews both the system's responsibilities as defined in its Use-Cases as well as the components of the system's architecture.

2 The Essential Capability Definition step identifies those services and assets that are essential to the system's mission. This step identifies the essential components of the architecture that must survive an attack.

3 The Compromisable Capability Definition step enumerates the threats to the system and maps them onto the architecture's compromisable components, those whose security (confidentiality, integrity or availability) would be damaged by intrusion.

4 The Survivability Analysis identifies the soft-spot components of the architecture and constructs and analyzes a survivability map for opportunities to enhance the components' resistance, recognition and recovery characteristics.

4. Adding Monte-Carlo Simulation to RAPSA

Taylor et al. formed RAPSA by merging the SSA process with Probabilistic Risk Assessment (PRA) in order to simplify the quantification of security risks by focusing on just the mission-critical threats [Taylor et al., 2002]. The four steps of the RAPSA approach are:

1 The System Self-Assessment step identifies the mission objectives and partitions the system into essential and non-essential services.

2 The Threat Identification step enumerates the system's vulnerabilities, threats to those vulnerabilities and captures the attack stages for the essential services.

3 The Risk Quantification step quantifies the threats for each intrusion scenario and proposes mitigations. RAPSA considers the use of event or fault trees that are championed in some detail by threat modeling processes [Swiderski and Snyder, 2004].

4 The Risk Mitigation Trade-off constructs a survivability map augmented to quantify the mitigated risks and the costs of the proposed information security investments.

RAPSA addresses the expected value problem of risk analysis calculations by manually partitioning the random variable distributions into a few segments known as fractiles. However, the tedious nature of the calculations and the subjectivity of the partitioning process can frustrate its application in large, complex networks. The Monte-Carlo technique automates the partitioning and the manipulation of random variable distributions. A Monte-Carlo tool partitions the probability axis into hundreds or even thousands of fractiles, evaluating the model at each and collecting the resulting forecast. In each *iteration* of the simulation, the Monte-Carlo tool samples the chosen distributions and repeatedly executes the risk analysis model for each set of sampled values.

With the Monte-Carlo approach, RAPSA becomes RAPSA/MC and its application is very straightforward for the security analyst to apply. Because no executable code is required to support the methodology, RAPSA/MC can be applied before as well as after a system is placed in production. Thus, RAPSA/MC can be proactively incorporated into a software life-cycle to address security requirements during a system's development as opposed to waiting for the maintenance phase. The proactive application of security methodologies early in the life-cycle might lead to efficiency improvements over the reactive maintenance approach of securing a released product.

5. A RAPSA/MC Example

The data presented here are derived from Taylor et al. [Taylor et al., 2002] to enable comparison and validation with the RAPSA/MC approach. The example discusses a security assessment of the Supervisory Control And Data Acquisition (SCADA) equipment within a hypothetical electric utility's distribution substation. Because of the substation's unattended and often remote nature, considerable attention has been directed towards its physical security [Luo and Tu, 2005]. However, SCADA systems are increasingly networked [Brown, 2000] and are vulnerable to an electronic cyber attack that could be launched from a great distance with little risk to an intruder [Oman et al., 2002].

The electric power grid is a very large, complex real-time control system with hundreds of operators and thousands of real-time control actuators. High voltage optimizes efficient power transmission over long distance lines. However, local distribution requirements call for substantially lower voltages. An electrical substation often contains transformers to "step-down" high transmission voltage to lower voltage for local distribution as well as remotely accessed switch-gear, protection, phase-adjustment and metering equipment. Remote operation can be achieved through standard information system networking protocols augmented with protocols that are unique to the electric power industry [Woodward, 2001]. In some cases, the substation may even have an IP address or an 802.11 transceiver.

RAPSA/MC Step 1 leverages methodologies of RAPSA [Taylor et al., 2002] and SSA [Ellison et al., 1999] to identify the system's mission and partition its architecture, essential components and services into those that must survive an attack from those that are non-essential. The objective is to reduce the complexity of the security assessment by focusing the analyst's resources on the system's critical mission. Within the context of the electric power example, Taylor notes that the substation's mission is clear: deliver power to customers. While the details are omitted here for brevity, the analysis concludes that the example's essential services include remote monitoring and controls that are necessary for protection and changing loads.

RAPSA/MC Step 2 leverages from RAPSA and SSA to enumerate threats to the essential services and their supporting components. Table 1 identifies three example threats (drawn from Taylor [Taylor et al., 2002]) and their compromised essential (soft-spot) components. Note that example threats two and three use the same trojan exploit that becomes more disruptive in the hands of a knowledgeable attacker who uses the substation's SCADA equipment to attack the capital intensive assets of the utility's distribution system. Alternative methodologies for discovering these threats include Hierarchical Holographic Modeling [Haimes, 1998] [Longstaff et al., 2000] and Threat Modeling [Swiderski and Snyder, 2004].

Table 1. Example Threats and Compromised Components

Threats	*Compromised Components*
1. Hacker discovers the phone number of a modem on the substation's computer, successfully penetrates its authentication system and logs in.	Real-time control system device data altered/destroyed, devices reset, communication blocked or re-routed.
2. Utility employee is tricked into installing a trojan on a computer with access to the substation. The trojan installs a root-kit and "phones" home to the remotely located hacker.	Real-time control system device data altered/destroyed, devices reset, communication blocked or re-routed.
3. Similar to #2 only the attack is launched by a skilled attacker with power distribution knowledge who has deliberately targeted electric power utilities for sabotage.	Similar to the above plus damage to the electrical power distribution equipment.

RAPSA/MC Step 3 quantifies the threats. Like RAPSA, the RAPSA/MC process relies upon expert estimates for modeling parameters such as the number of intrusion events and the extent of damages. But the RAPSA/MC process captures the uncertainty of the experts' estimates with probability distributions (similar to Figure 1) in a Monte-Carlo simulation of the model's random variables.

Table 2 illustrates example values for each of the identified threats from Table 1 using hypothetical expert estimates to illustrate the process. All three threats compromise the SCADA equipment and could potentially lead to power outages (failure of the critical mission) or even damage to the electrical distribution equipment.

The variables $\{r_1, r_2, r_3\}$ capture the expected value of the expert's estimates for the annual intrusion rates. This particular example assumes that while the experts can predict the long-term intrusion rate, the year-to-year intrusion count is a random process. The example simulates the variability in the intrusion count in any given year using the Poisson random number generators in column three of Table 2.

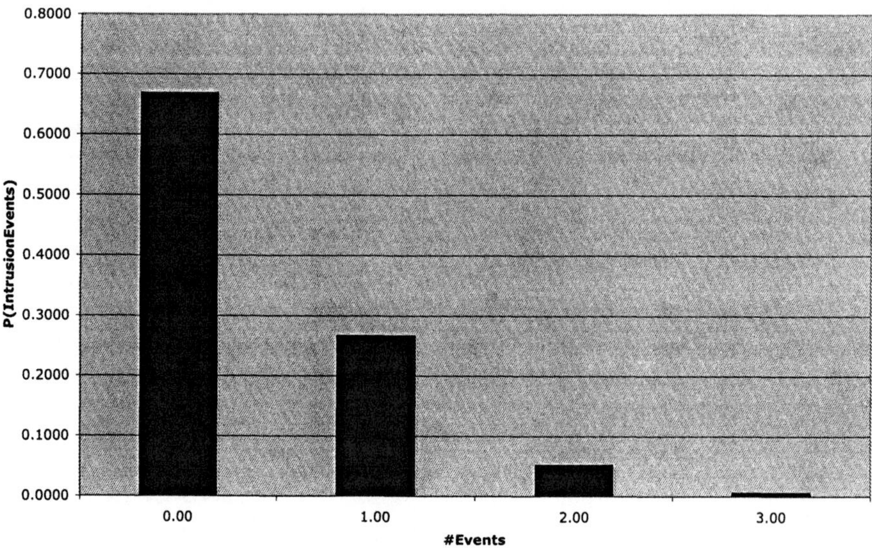

Figure 1. Probability of Intrusion Events for Threat-1

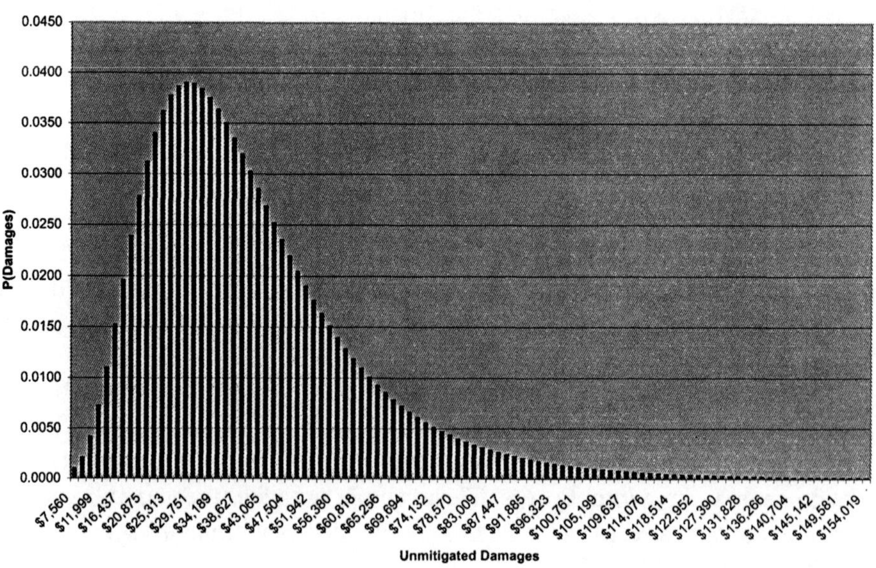

Figure 2. Prob. of Annual Unmitigated Damages from Threat-1

Table 2. Quantified Example Threats Against Unmitigated Targets

Threat	*Estimated Annual Intrusion Rate*	*Simulated Annual Intrusion Count*	*Estimated Unmitigated Damages*	*Estimated Stdev of Unmitigated Damages*	*Simulated Unmitigated Damages*	*Annual Unmitigated Damages*
1	$r_1 = 0.4$	$c_1 = \text{RPoisson}(r_1)$	$e_1 = \$100,000$	$s_1 = \$250,000$	$d_1 = \text{RLognormal}(e_1, s_1)$	$u_1 = c_1 * d_1$
2	$r_2 = 0.5$	$c_2 = \text{RPoisson}(r_2)$	$e_2 = \$150,000$	$s_2 = \$250,000$	$d_2 = \text{RLognormal}(e_2, s_2)$	$u_2 = c_2 * d_2$
3	$r_3 = 0.1$	$c_3 = \text{RPoisson}(r_3)$	$e_3 = \$1,000,000$	$s_3 = \$1,100,000$	$d_3 = \text{RLognormal}(e_3, s_3)$	$u_3 = c_3 * d_3$

Table 3. Example Survivability Map for Threat-1

Threat	*Mitigation*	*Resistance Strategy*	*Recognition Strategy*	*Recovery Strategy*
1	0	Current: Regular modem, weak password, no logging.	Current: Analysis of substation fault	Current: Locate damage, reset devices and restore from backups.
1	1	Dial-back modem, policy requires individual passwords and forbids single system password.	Logging. Weekly review of logs for intrusion evidence.	Reset devices and restore from backups.
1	2	Restrict dial-in user actions, restrict user access by time-of-day.	Logging + Intrusion Detection System (IDS) transmits alert	Reset devices and restore from backups.

The variables $\{e_1, e_2, e_3\}$ and $\{s_1, s_2, s_3\}$ capture the expert's estimates for the mean and standard deviation (stdev) of damages arising from successful unmitigated intrusions. The variables $\{d_1, d_2, d_3\}$ simulate the lognormal uncertainty in the expected damages arising from a single intrusion of each threat using the mean and extreme values of the previous two columns. Column seven calculates the annual damages in $\{u_1, u_2, u_3\}$ as the product of the simulated intrusion count $\{c_1, c_2, c_3\}$ and the simulated unmitigated damages $\{d_1, d_2, d_3\}$. Figure 2 illustrates the probability density function from a simulation of the annual unmitigated damages arising from Threat-1 (u_1).

Some details behind Table 2 deserve a closer examination.

- The choice of a Poisson distribution (e.g., Figure 1) to simulate the annual intrusion count reflects a desire to model unique successful intrusions (as opposed to clusters of identical unsuccessful attempts or even repeated successful exploits of the same target). In this particular example, the analyst has great confidence in the estimates for the $\{r_1, r_2, r_3\}$ rates and is concerned only with simulating the *variability* (randomness) of the Poisson process.

- The example's choice of the Lognormal distribution for damages (e.g., Figure 2) reflects a potential for extremely high (unbounded) damages, positively skewed with a minimum of zero and a strong mode below the mean. The $\{d_1, d_2, d_3\}$ variables simulate the expert's *uncertainty* (lack of knowledge) in the damage estimate.

- This example equates the expert's *uncertainty* (lack of knowledge) about the damages (e.g., Figure 2) with the *variability* of the successful intrusion events (e.g., Figure 1). When a distinction must be made between *uncertainty* and *variability*, alternative approaches [Vose, 2000] are available.

- RPoisson() and RLognormal() are representative of functions that are typically available in a Monte-Carlo tool for generating random numbers in Poisson and Lognormal distributions.

RAPSA/MC Step 4 summarizes the qualitative aspects of the proposed mitigations in a survivability map, quantifies the mitigations and finally selects an optimal investment. Table 3 presents the survivability map for just the first threat identified in Table 1. The mitigation strategies in Table 3 originated from RAPSA's application of SSA [Taylor et al., 2002].

Table 4. Quantified Mitigations for the Example Threats

Threat	*Mitigation*	*Estimated Minimal Effectiveness*	*Estimated Typical Effectiveness*	*Estimated Maximal Effectiveness*	*Simulated Effectiveness*	*Annual Mitigated Damages*
1	0	$me_{10} = 0.000$	$te_{10} = 0.000$	$xe_{10} = 0.000$	$se_{10} = 0.000$	$sd_{10} = u_1 - u_1 * se_{10}$
1	1	$me_{11} = 0.495$	$te_{11} = 0.550$	$xe_{11} = 0.605$	$se_{11} = \text{RTriangle}(me_{11}, te_{11}, xe_{11})$	$sd_{11} = u_1 - u_1 * se_{11}$
1	2	$me_{12} = 0.788$	$te_{12} = 0.875$	$xe_{12} = 0.963$	$se_{12} = \text{RTriangle}(me_{12}, te_{12}, xe_{12})$	$sd_{12} = u_1 - u_1 * se_{12}$
2	0	$me_{20} = 0.000$	$te_{20} = 0.000$	$xe_{20} = 0.000$	$se_{20} = 0.000$	$sd_{20} = u_2 - u_2 * se_{20}$
2	1	$me_{21} = 0.540$	$te_{21} = 0.600$	$xe_{21} = 0.660$	$se_{21} = \text{RTriangle}(me_{21}, te_{21}, xe_{21})$	$sd_{21} = u_2 - u_2 * se_{21}$
2	2	$me_{22} = 0.780$	$te_{22} = 0.867$	$xe_{22} = 0.953$	$se_{22} = \text{RTriangle}(me_{22}, te_{22}, xe_{22})$	$sd_{22} = u_2 - u_2 * se_{22}$
3	0	$me_{30} = 0.000$	$te_{30} = 0.000$	$xe_{30} = 0.000$	$se_{30} = 0.000$	$sd_{30} = u_3 - u_3 * se_{30}$
3	1	$me_{31} = 0.558$	$te_{31} = 0.620$	$xe_{31} = 0.682$	$se_{31} = \text{RTriangle}(me_{31}, te_{31}, xe_{31})$	$sd_{31} = u_3 - u_3 * se_{31}$
3	2	$me_{32} = 0.720$	$te_{32} = 0.800$	$xe_{32} = 0.880$	$se_{32} = \text{RTriangle}(me_{32}, te_{32}, xe_{32})$	$sd_{32} = u_3 - u_3 * se_{32}$

Table 5. Forecasted Total Annual Costs

Mitigation	*Annual Mitigated Damages*	*Estimated Annual Investment Expenses*	*Total Annual Cost*	*Forecasted Mean Cost (From Simulation)*	*Forecasted 90th Percentile Cost (From Simulation)*
0	$amd_0 = sd_{10} + sd_{20} + sd_{30}$	$ie_0 = \$0$	$tac_0 = amd_0 + ie_0$	\$64,000	\$160,000
1	$amd_1 = sd_{11} + sd_{21} + sd_{31}$	$ie_1 = \$6,000$	$tac_1 = amd_1 + ie_1$	\$38,000	\$87,000
2	$amd_2 = sd_{12} + sd_{22} + sd_{32}$	$ie_2 = \$20,000$	$tac_2 = amd_2 + ie_2$	\$49,000	\$94,000

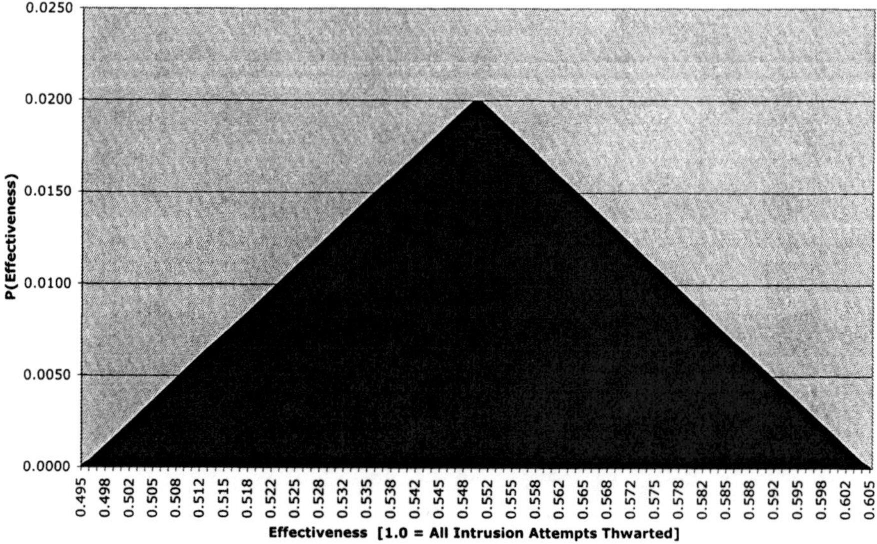

Figure 3. Effectiveness of Mitigation-1 Against Threat-1

Table 4 introduces the quantitative behaviors of the three mitigations discussed above. Each row of the table addresses one proposed mitigation for a single threat. Estimates are solicited from the experts for the minimum effectiveness (me_{ij}), the typical effectiveness (te_{ij}) and the maximum effectiveness (xe_{ij}) for each mitigation (j) of each threat (i). The effectiveness estimates define the fraction of intrusion attempts of a particular threat that will be deterred by this mitigation. In each iteration (year) of the simulation, these three effectiveness estimates are used as parameters in column six to calculate a simulated (random) effectiveness value using a rough triangle distribution (e.g. Figure 3). Column seven calculates the simulated annual mitigated damages for each iteration.

Table 5 forecasts the Total Annual Costs (tac_j) arising from both the annual mitigated damages (amd_j) and the annual investment expenses (ie_i). The total annual costs are calculated as the sum of the annual mitigated damages and the annual investment expense for each mitigation.

6. Analyzing the Example RAPSA/MC Simulation

The RAPSA/MC example illustrates a tremendous potential for uncertainty in the unmitigated damage estimates. It highlights the expert's struggle to estimate the potential damages that might be inflicted by the casual intrusion of

Threat-1 (Figure 2). In this case, the expert selected a lognormal distribution with a mean value at $40,000 and the 90th percentile at $66,000, there exists a remote possibility for very much larger damages. The uncertainty in this estimate reflects the hypothetical expert's lack of knowledge as to whether a "casual" intruder's damages will be confined to the information systems, extend to power outages, or further extend to the power distribution equipment. The RAPSA/MC process captures this uncertainty rather than oversimplify it into an *expected value*.

The Monte-Carlo tool runs the simulation by executing the model through hundreds or even thousands of iterations, each modeling the events of one potential year. It begins by "throwing" random numbers into the distributions (c_i, d_i and se_{ij}) and recalculating the forecasted Total Annual Costs (tac_j) and capturing those results. The example employs 10,000 iterations with Latin Hypercube Sampling to simulate the variability and uncertainty in the random variables. Following the simulation run, the Monte-Carlo tool charts the captured results as forecasts (Figures 4, 5 and 6) for each mitigation. Please note that the very large P($0), P($6,000) and P($20,000) columns are omitted from the left-hand side of the three forecast charts. This is done to facilitate readability of the distributions as the probability of no damages (just mitigation investment expenses) in this particular example is quite high (about 0.38 which is nearly an order of magnitude larger than any other single column).

Table 5 also documents the forecasted mean and 90th percentile values for the three proposed mitigations in Figures 4, 5 and 6. These and other statistics are available from the Monte-Carlo tool following a simulation run.

The forecast chart for Mitigation-0 (Figure 4) illustrates the risks of doing nothing (no investment). The mean annual loss due to damages is $64,000 and there exists a 10% probability of an annual loss in excess of $160,000.

When the annual investment expenses are included as they are in this version of the example, the decision makers are likely to choose Mitigation-1. The statistics for Mitigation-1 suggests that an annual investment of $6,000 will limit the mean costs to $38,000 but there still remains a 10% exposure to annual costs exceeding $87,000.

We might contemplate alternative scenarios that would lead to a different investment choice. If, for example, the investment expenses for Mitigation-2 ($20,000) could be reduced, it would become far more attractive. Or if the 90th percentile figure for Mitigation-1 had been extremely high (say... $500,000 vs $87,000) then the decision makers might choose Mitigation-2 simply to buy down their exposure to an extreme event. Likewise, if the investment costs had been significantly higher for both Mitigation-1 and 2, then the decision makers might choose to do nothing at all (e.g. choose Mitigation-0) unless the 90th percentile figures were extremely high for doing nothing in which case they might again choose a "real" mitigation investment to buy down their

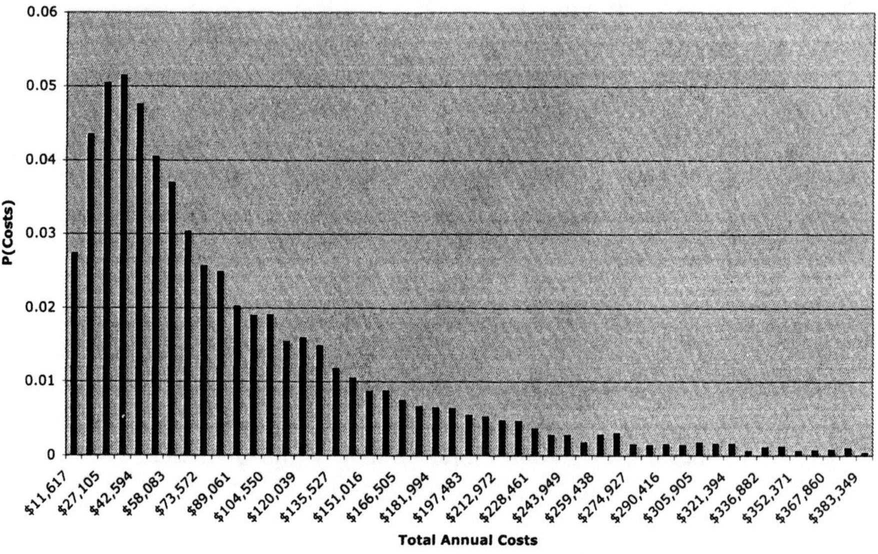

Figure 4. Forecasted Annual Costs for Proposed Mitigation-0

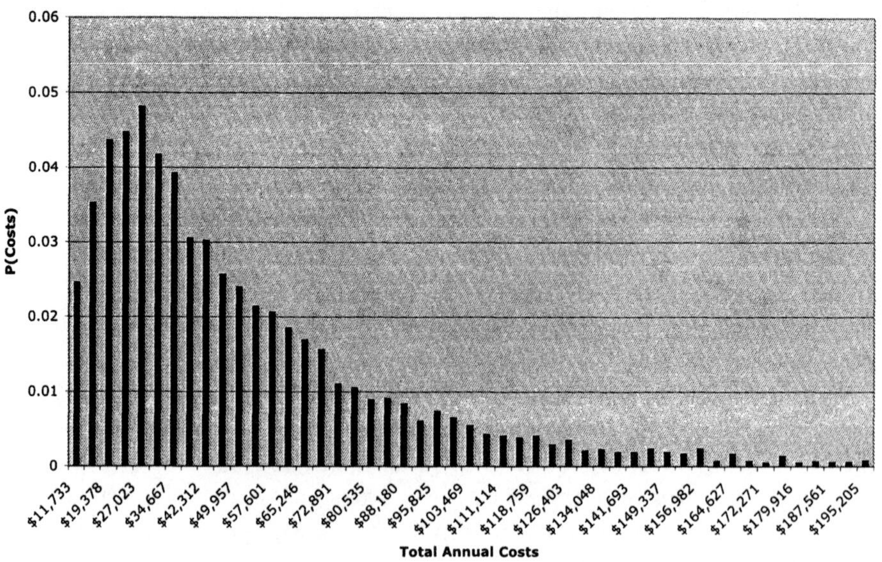

Figure 5. Forecasted Annual Costs for Proposed Mitigation-1

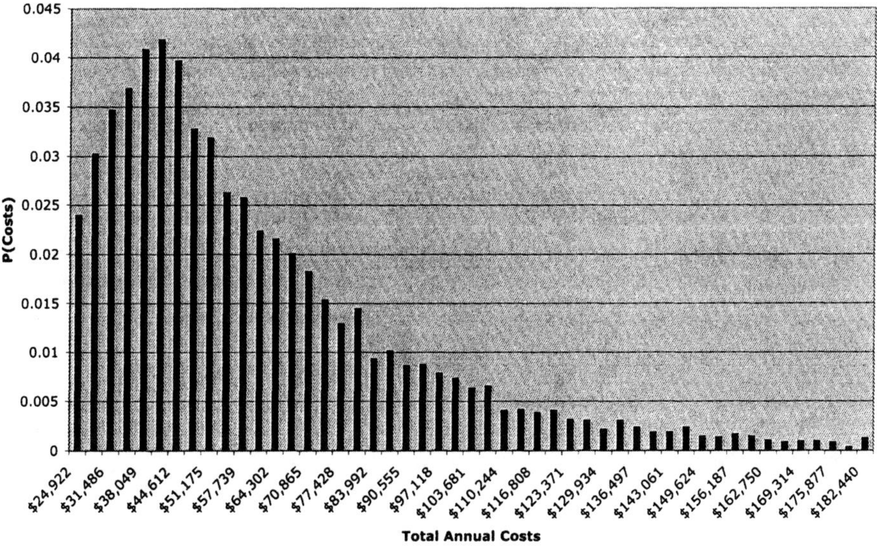

Figure 6. Forecasted Annual Costs for Proposed Mitigation-2

exposure to an extreme event. Tradeoffs between an attractive expected return and catastrophic risk potential are common in financial decisions.

7. Conclusions

RAPSA/MC quantifies information security risks as financial variables facilitating the comparison of security mitigations with an organization's other opportunities. RAPSA/MC combines qualitative methodologies for identifying threats with Monte-Carlo quantitative methodologies for simulating uncertainty in security parameters. While the Monte-Carlo technique cannot alone break the dependency of the systems-level models on expert estimates, it does enable these models to express uncertainty in their forecasts. The RAPSA/MC forecasts are probability density functions (Figures 4, 5 and 6) that provide financial decision makers with the opportunity to consider the potential for extreme events as well as the mean value of the proposed mitigation. Even though a proposed mitigation might offer the optimal mean value, the decision makers may choose an alternative that offers a lower risk of a catastrophic extreme event. The process is usable both for evaluating released systems and systems under development as no executable code is required for the risk assessment.

References

Bishop, Matt (2003). *Computer Security: Art and Science.* Addison-Wesley, Boston, MA.

Brown, Steven M. (2000). Applying internet technology to utility scada systems. *Utility Automation*, 5(5):25–26.

Butler, S., Chalasani, P., Jha, S., Raz, O., and Shaw, M. (1999). The potential of portfolio analysis in guiding software decisions. First Workshop on Economics-Driven Software Engineering Research.

Conrad, James R. (2005). Analyzing the risks of security investments with monte-carlo simulations. In *Fourth Workshop on the Economics of Information Security (WEIS05)*, Harvard University (USA).

Ellison, Robert J., Linger, Richard C., Longstaff, Thomas, and Mead, Nancy R. (1999). Survivable network system analysis: A case study. *IEEE Software*, 16(4):70–77.

Geer, Daniel E. (2001). Making choices to show ROI. *Secure Business Quarterly*, 1(2).

Haimes, Yacov Y. (1998). *Risk Modeling, Assessment, and Management.* John Wiley and Sons, New York, NY.

Lipton, R. J. and Snyder, L. (1977). A linear time algorithm for deciding subject security. *J. ACM*, 24(3):455–464.

Longstaff, Thomas A., Chittister, Clyde, Pethia, Rich, and Haimes, Yacov Y. (2000). Are we forgetting the risks of information technology? *IEEE Computer*, 33(12):43–51.

Luo, Yi and Tu, Guangyu (2005). Who's watching the unattended substation. *IEEE Power and Energy Magazine*, 3(1):59–66.

Magnusson, Christer (2005). Shareholder value and security investments. *IEEE Communications Magazine*, 43(1):3–4.

Oman, Paul, Schweitzer III, Edmund O., and Frincke, Deborah (2002). Concerns about intrusions into remotely accessible substation controllers and scada systems. In *Proc. 27th Annual Western Protective Relay Conferences.*

Schechter, Stuart Edward (2004). *Computer Security Strength and Risk: A Quantitative Approach.* PhD thesis, Harvard University, Cambridge, Massachusetts.

Software Engineering Institute (2005). Survivable systems analysis.

Soo Hoo, Kevin J. (2000). How much is enough? A risk-management approach to computer security. Technical report, Stanford Consortium for Research on Information Security and Policy.

Swiderski, Frank and Snyder, Window (2004). *Threat Modeling.* Microsoft Press, Redmond, WA.

Taylor, Carol, Krings, Axel, and Alves-Foss, Jim (2002). Risk analysis and probabilistic survivability assessment (RAPSA): An assessment approach for power substation hardening. In *ACM Workshop on the Scientific Aspects of Cyber Terrorism*, Washington, D.C. ACM.

Vose, David (2000). *Risk Analysis: A Quantitative Guide.* John Wiley and Sons, West Sussex, England, 2nd edition.

Woodward, D. (2001). The hows and whys of ethernet networks in substations. Technical report, Schweitzer Engineering Labs.

THE MITIGATION OF ICT RISKS USING EMITL TOOL: AN EMPIRICAL STUDY

Jabiri Kuwe Bakari[1], Christer Magnusson[2], Charles N. Tarimo[3] and Louise Yngström[4]

Department of Computer and System Sciences, Stockholm University/Royal Institute of Technology, Forum 100, SE-164 40 Kista, Sweden, Tel: +46 (0)8 16 1697, Fax: +46 (0)8 703 90 25, E-mails: {si-jba[1], christer[2] si-cnt[3], louise[4]}@dsv.su.se

Abstract: As the dependence on ICT in running organisations' core services is increasing, so is the exposure to the associated risks due to ICT use. In order to meet organisational objectives in ICT dependent organisations, risks due to ICT insecurity need to be addressed effectively and adequately. To achieve this, organisations must have effective means for the management of ICT risks. This involves assessment of the actual exposure to ICT risks relevant to their environment and implementation of relevant countermeasures based on the assessment results. On the contrary, in most organisations, ICT security (or ICT risk management) is perceived by the top management as a technical problem. As a result, measures for ICT risk mitigation that are ultimately put in place in such organisations tend to be inadequate. Furthermore, the traditional way of managing risks by transferring them to the insurance companies is not yet working, as it is difficult to estimate the financial consequences due to ICT-related risks. There is, therefore, a need to have methods or ways which can assist in interpreting ICT risks into a financial context (senior management language) thereby creating a common understanding of ICT risks among technical people and the management within ICT-dependent organisations. With a common understanding, it would be possible to realise a coordinated approach towards ICT risk mitigation.

This paper is an attempt to investigate whether ICT risk mitigation can be enhanced using a customised software tool. A software tool for converting financial terminologies (financial risk exposure) to corresponding ICT security terminologies (countermeasures) is presented. The Estimated Maximum Information Technology Loss (EMitL) tool is investigated for its suitability as an operational tool for the above-mentioned purpose. EMitL is a tool utilised in a framework (Business Requirements on Information Technology Security - BRITS) to bridge the understanding gap between senior management and the technical personnel (when it comes to ICT risk management). This work is based on an empirical study which involved interviews and observations conducted in five non-commercial organisations in Tanzania. The study was designed to establish the state of ICT security management practice in the studied organisations.

The results of the study are being used here to investigate the applicability of the EMitL tool to address the observed state. The results from this study show that it is possible to customise EMitL into a usefully operational tool for interpreting risk exposure due to ICT into corresponding countermeasures. These results underline the need to further improve EMitL for wider use.

Key words: ICT Risk management, EMitL tool, Countermeasures

1. INTRODUCTION

The demand for adequate ICT security in ICT-dependent organisations continues to grow as the types and patterns of threat change. ICT security forms an important component of modern business strategic planning processes as well as the operational environment. Risks due to ICT insecurity need to be addressed effectively and adequately if an ICT-dependent organisation is to meet its business objectives. ICT security risks are threats that can have an impact on the availability, confidentially and integrity of information, as well as communications and services. Thus, organisations must have effective means for management of ICT-related risks specific to their environments (Frisinger, 2001).While this can be viewed as a common business-risk problem which calls for traditional risk management methods, the existing traditional methods for handling traditional business risks in organisations (conventional notions of risks and available styles and methods such as insurance coverage) tend to be difficult to employ directly for ICT risks (risks pertaining to computerised information systems). Uncertainties in quantifying ICT- related risk, make it a special kind of risk. Often, as a consequence, ICT-related risks are either left out in the overall risk-assessment process or addressed by ad-hoc technical controls, which make it hard to ensure whether the pertaining risks have indeed been adequately hedged to meet the business objectives. To avoid duplication of effort, it is appropriate and desirable to combine information security risk assessments with other business-related risk assessments.

ICT security should be a component of the overall risk management process within an organisation. ICT security is risk management with a focus on ICT (Blakley, B., McDermott, E., and Geer, D., 2001). Risk management is part of management's responsibility. However, there is often a tendency by the management to neglect or omit ICT security problems from the general organisational risk management process. This is due to inadequate understanding of ICT security issues and (as noted earlier) difficulties in having reliable estimations of the financial consequences caused by ICT security problems. Hence, application of traditional ways for managing risks by having them transferred to the insurance companies is not straightforward. Further, ICT security is perceived by top management to be a technical problem. There is, therefore, a need to have tools which can assist in interpreting ICT risks into a financial context (senior management language) and thereby creating a common understanding of ICT risks among technical people and the management within ICT-dependent organisations. With a common understanding, it would be possible to attain a coordinated approach towards ICT risk mitigation.

Approaches such as OCTAVE, COBIT, ITIL, ISO 17799 etc., (ISACA, 2005; ITIL, 2005; ISO 17799) have been developed to address the problem. Each of these addresses the problem from a specific perspective, based on certain philosophical assumptions. All of these various forms of approaches are aimed at providing the means for ICT risk management.

ICT risk management in an organisation begins with identification of what needs protection and why. It also involves being able to have a notion of the extent of the pertaining risks either qualitatively, quantitatively or both. After risk assessment, the organisation must take appropriate steps to mitigate the identified risks. Specific items in such identified risk elements could be aspects such as: ICT security, Physical security risks, Deficiencies in personnel knowledge, training and practices, Security documentation practices, etc. It is not our intention to review or analyse existing ICT risk management approaches in any detail, as that has been addressed in various literature such as in (Frisinger, 2001, Magnusson, 1999, Baskerville, 1993, Anderson, A., et al, 1991, Alberts & Dorofee, 2003). Instead, the intention here is to investigate whether ICT risk mitigation can be enhanced using a customised software tool. Thus, a software tool for converting financial terminologies (financial risk exposure) to corresponding ICT security terminologies (countermeasures) is presented and evaluated. The Estimated Maximum Information Technology Loss (EMitL) tool is investigated for its suitability as an operational tool for the above-mentioned purpose. EMitL is a tool utilised in the Business Requirements on Information Technology Security (BRITS) framework to bridge the understanding and perception gap between the senior management and the technical expertise as regards to

ICT risk management. The tool was developed for and tested in commercial organisations. An attempt is made here to utilise the tool in non-commercial organisations.

2. METHODOLOGY

This study employs data from a previous study which had to do with investigation of the state of ICT security management as being practised in five non-commercial organisations (X, Y, Z, U and V) (Bakari, 2005; Bakari et al., 2005). Hence, the results from the study are used here as input to investigate the applicability of the EMitL tool in addressing the observed state. By putting the collected data into the tool, the tool generates a set of corresponding countermeasures that would have been in place given the observed state. The generated countermeasures for each organisation are then analysed to see their relevance to the observed state. Figure 1, below shows a pictorial representation of the process.

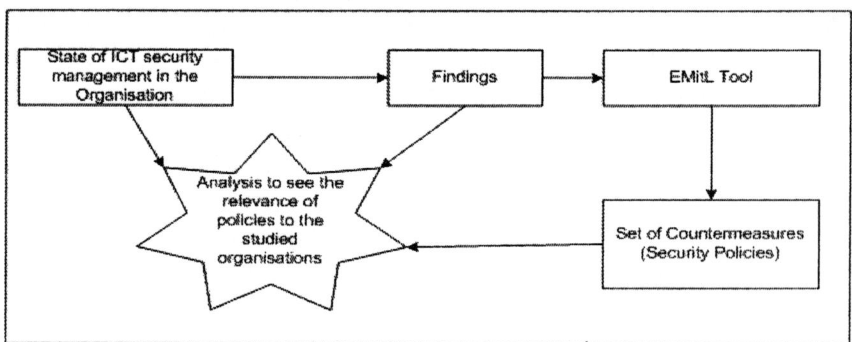

Figure 1. Summarising input and output to EmitL tool

In the next section we briefly describe the EMitL tool.

3. EMITL TOOL

EMitL is an interactive database-based tool designed to generate security countermeasures based on an organisation's exposure to ICT-related risks. EMitL is utilised as a component of the BRITS framework, which is a Systemic-Holistic framework, combining finance, risk transfer, ICT and security in a coherent system. The framework can be viewed as consisting of the top management and the technical personnel regimes with EMitL acting as a bridge between them, as shown in figure 2 below. The resulting conceptual structure is known as the BRITS framework. BRITS was developed to address the communication discontinuity existing due to the lack of common terminologies between the organisation's top management (potential risk exposure—financial) and technical people (ICT security experts—technical). Thus in the framework, the EMitL tool converts financial terminology into ICT security terminology and vice versa.

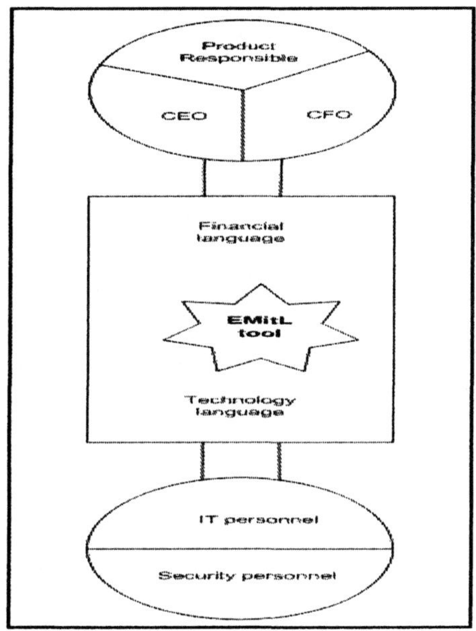

Figure 2. Function of EmitL tool: Source (Magnusson, 1999)

By bridging the two components, the vulnerabilities in ICT can be explained in financial terms, as well as in technical terms. The tool is conceptually structured into three groups; logical, physical, and organisational. It consists of approximately 1,000 security requirements in total. These include: authentication mechanisms; protection of accountability or non-repudiation; access control measures; protection of routing patterns; prevention against denial of service attacks; measures against data and program modification, insertion or destruction. Physical security countermeasures include: power supply and spare parts, fire protection, prevention of water damages, access and mechanical protection. Organisational security countermeasures include: roles and responsibilities, installation, configuration and operation of software and hardware and protection of intellectual property. In addressing these measures, the tool has considered four levels of security which comprise the following ICT areas: user workstation, a server, network applications, local area networks, remote connections and common ICT. Common ICT areas include organisational issues such as, user identities and user management, general access control and accountability principles (Magnusson, 1999, P. 165-168).

EMitL maps potential damage exposure against security properties and then generates the corresponding countermeasures. The countermeasures are grouped into four security levels, starting with security level 1 (low security) to level 4 (highest security). Figure 3 below shows the snapshot of the EMitL tool interface. In the figure, for example, the hedge policies 'Liability' for 'service interruption', 'Defamation', 'Infringement of Privacy' and Infringement of trademark' were the input.

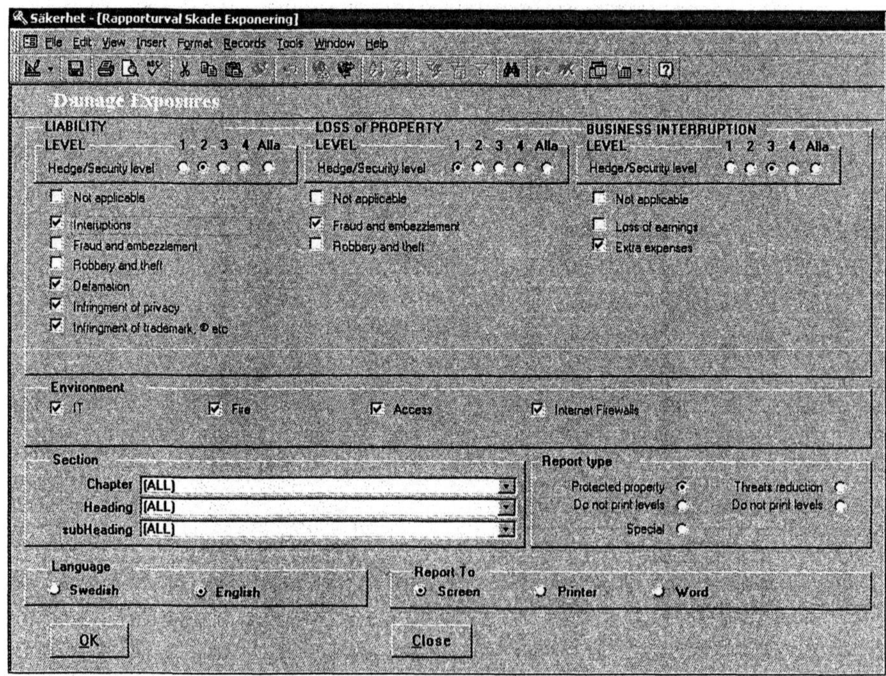

Figure 3. Snapshot of the EmitL tool interface

The level of protection required in this particular example is equivalent to hedge level 2. Consequently, the output are countermeasures against ('service interruption', 'defamation', 'infringement of privacy' and 'infringement of trademark') based on the adequate countermeasures at security level 2. In the framework, the damage exposure is divided into Liability, Loss of property and Service interruption.

Table 1 maps damage exposure against affected ICT security properties. The outcome of running the interactive database with the obtained parameters from an organisation is a set of countermeasures which should have been in place given the input parameters provided in the tool. This set of countermeasures is produced as a report.

Table 1. Damage exposure and ICT security properties

	ICT security Properties		
Damage exposure	Integrity	Availability	Confidentiality
Liability			
Service Interruption		X	
Fraud & Embezzlement	X		
Robbery & Theft			X
Defamation	X		
Infringement of Privacy			X
Infringement of Trademark, © etc.	X		
Loss of Property			
Fraud & Embezzlement	X		
Robbery & Theft			X
Service Interruption		X	

Source: (Magnusson, 1999, P. 143)

The report is compared with the current organisation's ICT practices in order to estimate the security awareness and control in the organisation. This could further assist in sorting out among the generated countermeasures which ones are being practised by the organisation and which are not. The result of comparisons is a state of security documented in the form of a survey report that gives an overview of the security awareness and vulnerabilities in the organisation. This report can further be used to estimate the Expected Maximum Loss (EML) if the identified risks are not mitigated.

4. BRIEF STATE OF ICT SECURITY IN THE STUDIED ORGANISATIONS

Following the earlier study on the subject (Bakari, 2005), the following are (in brief) the findings. The dependency on ICT to run core services has been observed to be substantial and is continually growing in the studied organisations. Analysis of relevant ICT security issues pertaining to the studied environment yielded different results at different levels. For example, at the strategic level there is no defined budget for ICT security, while at the operational level, the complex problem of ICT security is perceived to belong to the IT departments or rather treated as a technical problem. Organisation-wide ICT security policy is non-existent in the studied organisations. Table 2 indicates the state of ICT security as regards to budgets apportioned to ICT and the presence of ICT security policy.

Table 2. ICT Security budget and status of ICT security Policy

ORGANISATION	ICT BUDGET	ICT Security Budget	ICT Security Policy
X	3.2%	No	Non-existing
Y	5%	No	Outdated /Directed to IT staff, but not aware of its existence
Z	0.5%	No	Non-existing
U	1.6%	No	Non-existing
V	2%	No	In preparation

In the study, to establish the status of countermeasures in place, a separate interview with IT managers and system administrators was conducted. A typical example of the questions was "Are there any documented policies and procedures for physical access control of hardware and software?" The results of responses on whether or not the countermeasures are being practised show that most of the countermeasures are not practised as indicated in figure 4. The few practised countermeasures are mostly on an ad-hoc basis. The interpretation of the results was according to (Alberts and Dorofee, 2003) wherefrom the questionnaires were originally adopted. For example, looking at the issues related to contingency and disaster recovery, none of the organisations was found to be practising. The responses for the state of basic ICT security issues and practices indicate the existence of uncoordinated low level ICT security activities and these are mainly based on individual initiatives within departments. Service interruption has been observed to be a major potential problem, which could result in unavailability of the services and consequently cause extra expenses. Finally, we would like to highlight here that, while the state of ICT security is not good enough, the perceived low insecurity incidences reported should not mean that there are no potential threats. Actually, the observed situation poses the greatest threat! Simply put it means that there is a big problem in place but its existence and magnitude is not known.

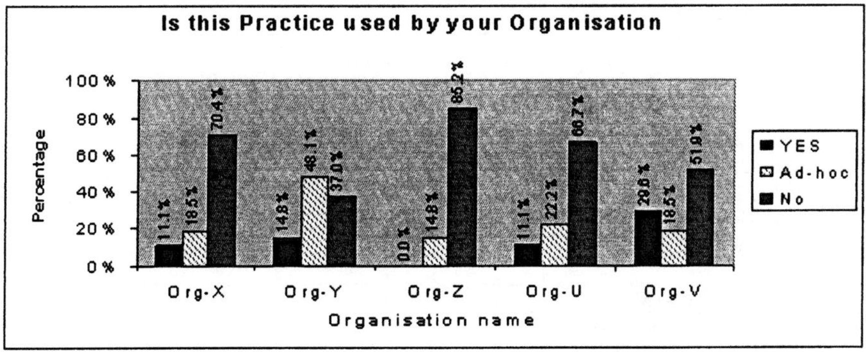

Figure 4. Responses on the countermeasures being practised by organisation

Note:

YES - If the practice is always or nearly always used. In the situation where there were many respondents, 75% or more respondents was considered YES.

Ad-hoc - If the practice does exist but not used very much, not documented and not communicated to staff, or used by some departments or individuals only

No - If the practice is not used or not used very much. In the situation where there were many respondents, 75% or more respondents was considered as No.

5. FINDINGS AND DISCUSSION

5.1 Results of subjecting the findings from the organisations to the EMitL tool

Using data gathered in responses from the top management and operational management, analysis of the same was performed for each organisation. The results are summarised in table 3. 4 represents the highest level of potential risk, 3 indicates medium—high, 2 indicates medium, 1 indicates low and 0 (zero) means not applicable. The EMitL tool interface has only one hedge policy level/security level for each set of damage exposures. Therefore an assumption had to be made where more than one security level is indicated, in order to increase the overall security level. This means one has to consider a higher security level where more than one security level exists. Results from each column were summarised first and then fed into the EMitL tool (See figure 3 in section 3 above). Table 4 shows how the security levels (columns –ARL) had been assumed to reflect the level that appears with the highest frequency.

Table 3. Damage exposure levels (Security levels)

Damage exposures	Damage exposure levels (Security level)				
	Organ. X	Organ. Y	Organ. Z	Organ. U	Organ. V
Liability					
Service Interruption	1	0	0	4	0
Fraud & Embezzlement	0	2	0	2	0
Robbery & Theft	0	0	4	2	0
Defamation	3	2	3	1	2
Infringement of Privacy	2	2	2	2	2
Infringement of trademark,© etc.	2	0	3	0	2
Loss of Property					
Fraud & Embezzlement	1	4	4	3	1
Robbery & Theft	0	0	2	2	0
Service Interruption					
Loss of sales	0	0	0	4	0
Extra expense	3	4	3	4	3

In case the same frequency is observed, a higher security level is assumed in order to increase the level of assurance. In the table organisation **X** had ARL 2, 1 and 3 respectively as shown also in the interface in figure 3 (section 3 of this paper).

Table 4. Showing different input parameters to database EmitL

Organisation	Liability						A.R.L	L/Property		A.R.L	B/Interrp		A.R.L	Output
	BI	FE	RT	DE	IP	IT		FE	RT		LS	EE		Countermeasures
X	√	×	×	√	√	√	2	√	×	1	×	√	3	847
Y	×	√	×	√	√	×	2	√	×	4	×	√	4	802
Z	×	√	√	√	√	√	3	√	√	3	×	√	3	880
U	√	√	√	√	√	×	2	√	√	3	√	√	4	803
V	×	×	×	√	√	√	2	√	×	1	×	√	3	847

Key:
BI – Business Interruption
FE - Fraud and Embezzlement
RT – Robbery and Theft
DE – Defamation
IP – Infringement of Privacy
IT – Infringement of Trademark
A.R.L – Assumed Running Level (EMitL – database)
× - Not applicable
√ - Applicable

The outcome generated after running the EMitL tool with the supplied parameters from table 4 is a report consisting of various security countermeasures. The report can be viewed on screen or exported to a Word file and printed. Depending on the parameters supplied for a particular organisation, the length of the generated reports typically ranged from 90 to 108 pages with countermeasures ranging from 802-880 (see last column – table 4). The output countermeasures consist of logical security measures structured into four security levels (security level 1, 2, 3, and 4). These measures are mapped to IT security properties, confidentiality (C), Availability (A) and Integrity (I). Some measures protect only one security property (referred to as unique measures), some protect two security properties (referred to as dual measures) and some protect all three security properties (referred to as generic measures).

An analysis was then made to find out to what extent a given type of security countermeasure addresses the security property and at what security level. In the next section we present the results of the analysis.

5.1.1 Unique measures

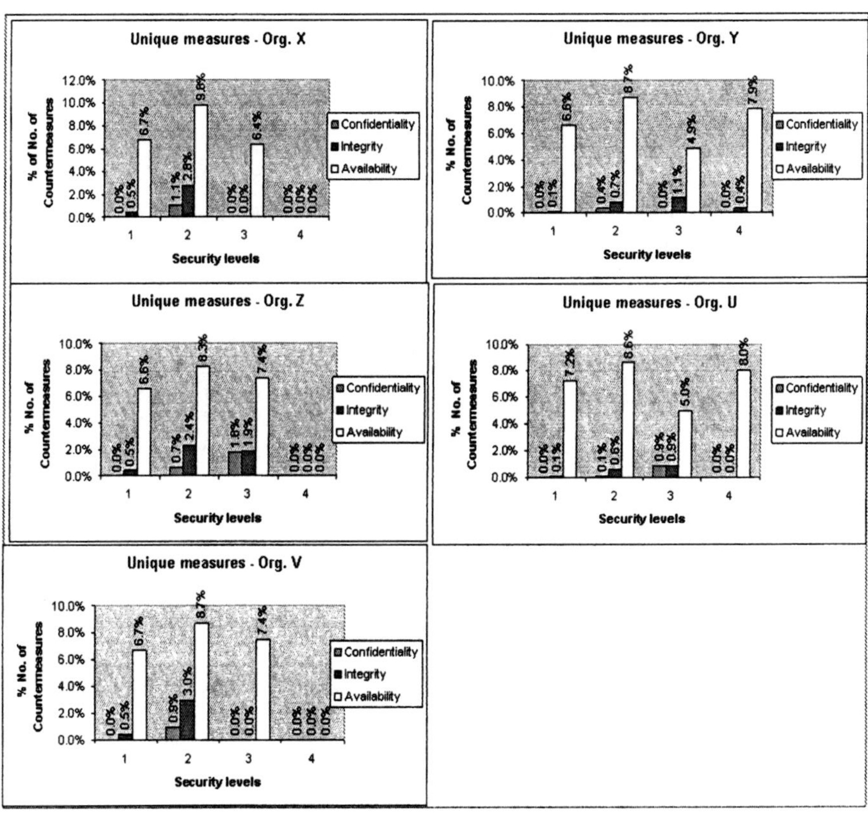

Figure 5. Percentage No. of Unique countermeasures vs. Security levels- Org. (X,Y, Z, U, V)

The focus of unique measures from the reports produced was found to be mainly on availability measures. Figure 5 presents the % number of unique measures plotted against security levels. By looking at the outcome of unique measures in all five organisations, we can observe that the focus was mainly on availability measures.

The analysis indicates that most of the countermeasures address fire evacuation route, storage, fire plan, how to handle fire-fighting equipment, automatic extinguisher systems, training and drills. The availability measure is used to benchmark ICT systems belonging to products that are exposed to service interruption and liability claims due to service interruption. An example of unique measure output from the database EMitL is given in example box 1.

Example box 1

Information

Security Level 1

2040 The target group for all fire prevention information shall be all personnel.

Property protected: Availability

5.1.2 Dual measures

Dual measures address two security properties. The dual countermeasures (Availability and Confidentiality) which carry more than 30% of the measures were found to be about "Mechanical access control" where most of the proposed measures could be at a very advance level as compared with the status of the organisations studied. Figure 6 presents the percentage number of dual countermeasures vs security levels. Example box 2 shows a sample of dual countermeasures.

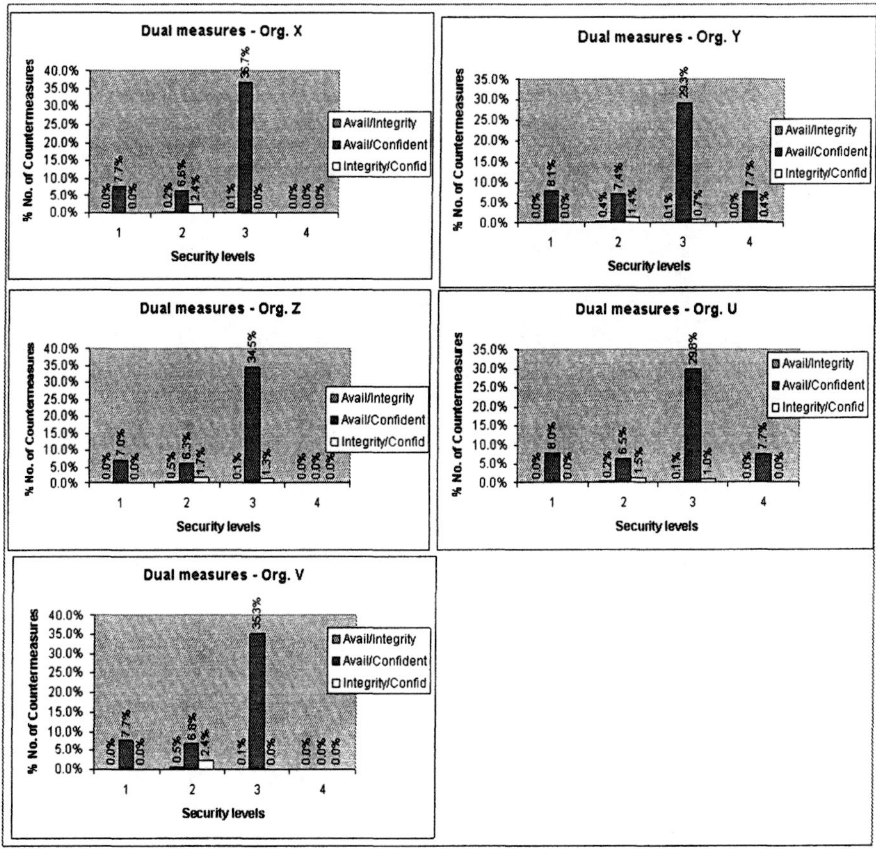

Figure 6. Percentage No. of Dual countermeasures vs security levels – Org. (X, Y, U, V, Z)

Example box 2:

Motorised pedestrian gates

Security Level 1

1810 All equipment, products and/or constructions for lock and armature units shall be of suitable design for their function, in good working order and be installed in the correct fashion.

Property protected: Confidentiality, Availability

Security Level 2

1820 If the gate is equipped with a pull handle, the locking mechanism shall consist of a single latchbolt lock with interlocking striking plate. If a trigger handle is installed, locking shall be carried out with a double latchbolt lock with an interlocking striking plate. A retaining mechanism in the form of a lock cylinder ring shall be installed on both inner and outer sides of the door. Electric striking plates shall be of extra strength construction. The automatic swing door function shall be conditioned on the status of the electric striking plate (locked/unlocked).

Property protected: Confidentiality, Availability

5.1.3 Generic measures

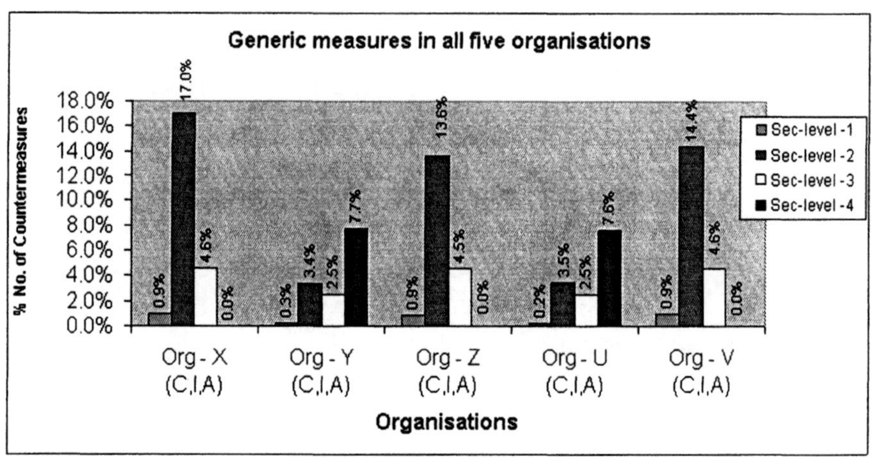

Figure 7. Percentage No. of Countermeasures vs. security levels – Org. (X, Y, Z, U, V)

Generic measures address all three security properties (figure 7). 13.6%, 14.4% and 17% of the total countermeasures for organisations X, Z and V respectively are at level two which was found mainly to addresses organisational and procedural measures. These included roles and responsibilities (See example box 3).

Example box 3:

Organisation and Procedures

Roles and Responsibilities

Security Level 2

1520 Security incidents or violations observed by system administrators, operators, or any user shall be reported to the security officer in charge.

Property protected: Confidentiality, Integrity, Availability

The requirement (see example box 3) could be seen as a measure to primarily protect confidentiality. However, this measure also protects (though indirectly) integrity and availability. For example, if an intruder manages to get the system administrator's password (which means violating confidentiality) and use it to gain access to core systems, it means the intruder can gain access to critical systems and thereby perform unauthorised modification of the systems or data (in this case violating integrity). Finally the intruder can cause operational breakdown (system malfunction) and thereby (violating availability) (Magnusson, 1999).

5.2 Discussion

An analysis of the state of ICT security in the studied organisations indicates that no ICT security policy existed in any of the organisations and the few existing technical procedures were on an ad-hoc basis. The results from the EMitL tool in the form of countermeasures that should have been in place seem to address most of the identified gaps at the operational and technical level when the implementation is customised to the environment. For example, in the dual countermeasure, the generated countermeasure from the tool about mechanical access control was suggesting automatic gates which are on the advanced side with respect to the current situation of the studied environment. Hence, customisation of the tool in that respect could lead to the relevant results. With reference to figures 5, 6 and 7 above, we could see that the countermeasures addressing security property "Availability" feature with a high frequency of occurrence for unique measures and the same is true when we look at dual measures "Availability and confidentiality" countermeasures which also have a high frequency of occurrence (from 29.3% to 36.7%). This security property is against the damage exposure "Service interruption" (See table 1 in section 3 above) and appears to be the major concern in the studied organisations by causing more extra expenses.

The study has indicated that the tool could enhance ICT risk mitigation in some ways. As noted earlier, there was a communication gap between the top management and the technical personnel with respect to ICT risks and their controls. The top management is expected to understand that ICT security is a business problem rather than a technical one and on the other hand the technical people need to understand that ICT security is more than a technical problem (it is more than firewalls, IDS and antivirus!). Using the tool, it was possible to bridge the understanding gap due to differences in perspectives and the language used between the top management and the technical people in an organisation. Using risk information from the top management, the tool generates relevant countermeasures for the environment which would need customisation. However this depends very much on accuracy in getting the organisation's actual risk exposure at the stage of establishing potential risk exposure pertaining to that particular organisation. Also, at a higher level, the tool helps in giving a rough direction of what needs to be done in order to manage ICT-related risks. This comes out in the form of a Survey Report as described in this paper. According to the previous analysis and discussion above, there is relevance between the observed ICT security state and the proposed countermeasure from the tool, although some of the suggested countermeasures need customisation to match the actual environment. This proves its usefulness and suitability for the purpose.

The downside of the tool is as follows. It needs customisation for each organisation as different organisations have different security requirements and hence it is not something that can be used directly. The database engine that contains the countermeasures needs to be updated continuously to reflect the changes in ICT risks profiles. Thus, it suffers the same limitations as the ones suffered by anti-virus tools.

When comparing EMitL/BRITS with other ICT security methods such as ISO 17799, OCTAVE, ITIL, COBIT etc., we came to the conclusion that each of these other methods addresses a portion of the overall ICT risk management problem while EMitL provides a means of combining them all together. For example, OCTAVE serves as the first step when approaching ICT risk management problems; COBIT is used mainly for auditing; ISO 17799 is mainly used to address HOW issues, etc. On the other hand, the idea behind BRITS-EMitL is to make it possible to provide a framework that makes use of all of these in a coherent system to address the organisation's ICT risk management problem.

6. CONCLUSION

This paper has attempted to investigate the applicability of the EMitL tool in mitigating ICT risks using the empirical data collected from five non-commercial organisations in Tanzania. The information captured from the top management in their language (financial), which was later entered into the tool, resulted in countermeasures which would have been in place in the respective organisations. On analysis, the generated countermeasures were seen to mitigate potential risk exposures which were pointed out by the management as discussed in the paper. This implies that the EMitL tool could be a useful tool in bridging the identified communication gap between the management and technical departments when it comes to managing ICT-related risks.

However, the usefulness of the tool needs to be kept current with respect to the changes in ICT security threats, organisation needs, and technologies. Ongoing improvements to the database (security measures, practices, and technology) are necessary to keep up to date with potential attackers and to keep abreast of the organisation's service needs.

REFERENCES

Alberts, C., and Dorofee, A., 2003, "Managing Information Security Risks", the OCTAVE Approach, Addison Wesley, USA.

Anderson, A., and Shain, S., 1991, "Risk management in Information Security hand book, Macmillan publishers Ltd.

Bakari, J. K., 2005, "Towards A Holistic Approach for Managing ICT Security in Developing Countries: A Case Study Of Tanzania", Ph.L thesis, Department of Computer and Systems Science, SU-KTH, Stockholm.

Bakari, J., Yngström, L., Magnusson, C., and Tarimo, C. N., 2005, "State of ICT Security Management in the Institutions of Higher Learning in Developing Countries: Tanzania Case study", The 5th IEEE (ICALT 2005), Kaohsiung, Taiwan. Pp. 1007-1011

Baskerville, R., 1993, "Information Systems Security Design Methods: Implication for Information System Development", ACM Computing Surveys, Vol.25, No.4.

Blakley, B., McDermott, E., and Geer, D., 2001 "Information Security is Information Risk Management" ACM Press, New York, USA.

Frisinger, A., 2001, 'A Generic Security Evaluation Method for Open Distributed Systems' Ph.D Thesis, Department of Teleinformatics, Royal Institute of Technology, Sweden.

ISACA, 2005, (April 15, 2005) http://www.isaca.org

ISO 17799, Information technology – Code of practice for information security management

ITIL, 2005, (April 15, 2005); http://www.itil.org.uk/

Magnusson, C., 1999 "Hedging Shareholders Value in an IT dependent Business Society" THE FRAMEWORK BRITS, Ph.D Thesis, Department of Computer and Systems Science, University of Stockholm and the Royal Institute of Technology, Stockholm.

RISK COMMUNICATION, RISK PERCEPTION AND INFORMATION SECURITY

Malcolm Pattinson[1] and Grantley Anderson[2]
[1]University of South Australia, malcolm.pattinson@unisa.edu.au; [2]Anderson Analyses, grantley.anderson@bigpond.com.au

Abstract: This paper puts forward the view that an individual's perception of the risks associated with information systems determines the likelihood and extent to which she or he will engage in risk taking behaviour when using a computer. It is suggested that this behavior can be manipulated by 'framing' a communication concerning information system risk in a particular manner. In order to achieve major effectiveness in getting an information security message across to a computer user, this paper discusses and demonstrates how his or her individual cognitive style should be considered when framing the risk message. It then follows that if the risk taking behaviour of computer users becomes less risky due to an increase in the level of perceived risk, then the level of information security increases.

Keywords: Information Security, Risk Perception, Risk Communication, Field-Dependent (FD), Field-Independent (FI), Framing.

1. INTRODUCTION

For too long now, the information security fraternity, and indeed management, have focused their attention on hardware and software solutions in their attempt to mitigate against risks to their information systems. We are now starting to see this focus change slightly with the realisation that people issues are equally important. Backhouse et al, (2004) and Jackson, et al, (2004) are two such papers that draw attention to the social aspects of information systems and the security surrounding them. It is a universally accepted fact that IT/IS people are an important component of any information system. One only has to look at the relevant textbooks for a definition of 'information system' to realise that people are one of the five components that comprise an information system. The other components are hardware, software, data and procedures.

This paper is concerned with the perception that computer users have of the risks to the information systems. For example, when someone asks "What is the risk of your computer getting a virus - is it high, medium or low?" What do you say? What they are really asking you is "What is your individual perception of the risk?" (Note that 'actual' information systems risks can never be measured - risks are intangible and subjective and can only be estimated). What influences your answer - past experience, knowledge about viruses, recent media reports or your mood on that day?

It is suggested that, although these factors and others have a bearing on your response (that is, your perception), so does the way that the question is phrased. If the question was rephrased as "What is the risk of your computer getting a virus and causing havoc for many colleagues - is it high, medium or low?". Does this 'reframing' and provision of additional information influence your answer and therefore your perception of the risk? The answer to this question is the crux of this paper.

2. RISK PERCEPTION

The manner in which people see the risks associated with information security determines what decisions they will make regarding the actions they will take (or not take) in conjunction with whatever risk security measures their particular organisation has put in place. Unfortunately, to date, not much is known about the perceptions that computer users hold concerning information systems risk.

However, research into risk perception in general has identified some important factors. The influence these factors have on risk perception is considered to be a function of the extent to which the risk is viewed as (a) voluntary, (b) under control, (c) representing a threat or catastrophe, or (d) having potential for a reduction in gains, or an increase in losses (Heimer, 1988).

The literature on risk perception seems to be devoid of research into its prevalence in the information security domain. However, in terms of general risk perception research, there is an abundance of articles and studies that look at factors that influence risk perception. For example, Bener (2000) claims that there is a range of social, cultural and psychological factors that contribute to risk perception. Furthermore, Otway (1980) lists other factors that shape risk perception such as the information people have been exposed to, the information they have chosen to believe and the social experiences they have had, to name a few.

One of the factors that is purported to have an influence on risk perception is the way in which the risk message is communicated to computer users and IT management. Bener, (2000) is one such author that supports this view, and he claims that risk is communicated within an organisation that contributes to the risk perception of the different individuals within that organisation. It then follows that if people's perception of risk is changed, there is the likelihood that their risk-taking behaviour will change. If this behaviour changes for the better, then it can be argued that the actual risk is lessened.

3. RISK COMMUNICATION

Risk communication has been defined by numerous authors. For example, (O'Neill, 2004) defines it as"...an interactive process of exchanging information and opinions between stakeholders regarding the nature and associated risks of a hazard on the individual or community and the appropriate responses to minimise the risks. The key behavioural change lies in risk communication designed to change people's perception of the risk and to increase their willingness to manage the risk." (p. 14).

Similarly, the US National Research Council, (1989) defines it as "an interactive process of exchange of information and opinion among individuals, groups and institutions. It involves multiple messages about the nature of risk and other messages, not strictly about risk, that express concerns, opinions and reactions to risk messages or to legal and institutional arrangements for risk management" (p. 21 as cited in Bener, 2000 & Backhouse et al, 2004).

The media plays a significant role in influencing people's perception of information system risk. One only has to look at the impact of the terrorist attack on the world trade centre twin towers on September 11, 2001. Another example is the reporting of the phishing software that logs keystrokes and subsequently gains banking information including user name and password.

The challenge with any form of risk communication is how to target a specific audience. For example, computer users, the subjects of this proposed research, range from executives through to general users through to IT experts, all of which have a different understanding and appreciation of information system risks. One approach, as described by O'Neill, (2004), is to divide the world's population into four types, namely, those who are risk averse, those who are risk tolerant, people who deny risk and people who seek out risk and then target each of these groups with different messages.

Alternatively, one could target individuals rather than groups, as put forward in this paper, by phrasing information security 'messages' to suit the individual. This internationally accepted approach is called 'message framing' or just 'framing'.

4. FRAMING

Framing is a concept that relates to the way a set of facts or a situation is described by a communicator. It also relates to a type of cognitive set that the receiver of a communication may use in order to interpret and make sense of any communication that he or she receives. From the point of view of the receiver, the way in which a message is framed as it is received will have an impact upon the course of action that he or she will choose to undertake.

In terms of risk communication effectiveness, the way a message is framed by a sender has significant potential to set decision boundaries in that it may determine what is included and what is left out of consideration by the receiver. Of even greater significance is the fact that not all the "in" elements will receive the same attention. A receiver's framed message tends to focus the individual on certain elements in a situation, while leaving other elements either unexamined, or at best, relatively obscured (Russo & Schoemaker, 1989).

Consider a risk communication written (or framed) in two different ways in two different messages. In the first message the aim is to provide an explanation of a potential event that threatens the security of an organisation's computer systems, such as a computer virus that has the potential to wipe out critical data files stored on hard disk. For example, one approach might be to phrase the message such that the emphasis is on how such an event will cause the organisation's technical competence to come into question as well as causing substantial costs to be incurred.

In the second message of the communication, information is provided as to what each individual computer user must do in order to ensure that the organisation's information security protocols have been properly implemented and observed. For example, the communication would be phrased in such a way that the emphasis is on how the prevention of such a security breach can be achieved by individual computer users exerting some effort in following a set of laid down procedures designed for that purpose.

Numerous studies (Tversky & Kahneman (1981), McNeill et al (1982), Meyerowitz & Chaiken (1987) on framing support the view that the way a situation is framed can have a substantial impact on people's risk taking behaviour. However, it is our belief that what should be of particular interest to information security managers and supervisors relates to more than just the general finding that people are more inclined to take risks in order to avoid losses than they are to take risks in order to make gains. Rather, it is the finding, derived mainly from the educational literature, that the importance placed on a particular message by an individual may be as much influenced by that person's cognitive style, as it is influenced by the core content of the message (Chinien, 1990).

We believe this distinction to be an important one. Principally because one of the surprising findings of this proposed research into human factor problems associated with information security procedures, is that very little has been written about individual differences in the way that individual computer users process information that has been presented to them, be that by hard copy written communications or by computer interface methods. Consequently, it would not be surprising to find that few information security managers and supervisors are aware that human information processing factors are predominately a consequence of an individual computer user's personal cognitive style.

5. COGNITIVE STYLE

As a personality dimension, an individual's cognitive style has a significant impact on the way that she or he collects and interprets information that is presented to her or him. Cognitive style is not considered to be a fixed personality trait, rather it is viewed as the preferred and habitual approach that an individual adopts when organising and presenting information. A number of such styles are described in the literature. However, since it describes how effectively an individual is able to restructure information using salient cues and field arrangements, for our purposes the dimension of Field Dependence versus Field Independence seems the most appropriate one to discuss and examine.

FD/FI has been researched extensively (Witkin et al, 1997; Ausburn & Ausburn, 1978) and is an established construct in the domain of psychology.

Why is this personal characteristic important? The focus of this paper is on the perception of risk and although the way that people perceive risks is a complex sociological and psychological phenomenon, the authors of this paper are suggesting that one way of changing individual risk perceptions is to communicate in a way that is aligned to each individual's FD/FI cognitive style. The aim of this proposed research is to determine whether the framing of potential threat scenarios has an effect on computer user risk perception, particularly if the threat scenarios are framed in an FD sense for FD people and an FI sense for FI people.

Much of the literature on framing refers to wording a situation in terms of potential gains and potential losses. In particular, a substantial amount of this literature relates to the medical profession, such as the Meyerowitz & Chaiken (1987) research into the effect of a negatively worded (or gain-frame) pamphlet versus a positively worded (loss-frame) pamphlet about breast self-examination.

But framing doesn't only relate to wording a situation in terms of potential gains and losses. It can also refer to elements such as:

- how it affects the subject
- self justification or previous action
- support investment already made
- social benefits and costs
- self image
- organisational image
- reputation
- face saving

Table 1. Summary of the FD/FI cognitive style construct

Individuals classified as FD	**Individuals classified as FI**
Drawn to people	Enjoys own company
Like to have people around them	Not sensitive to others around them
More non-verbal behaviours	Less non-verbal behaviour
Prefer occupations which require involvement with others	Prefer occupations with less interaction
Take a longer time to solve problems	Solve problems rapidly
Alert to social cues	More aloof, theoretical
Highly developed social skills	More abstract & analytical
Sensitive to social criticism	Initially thought to be males but inconclusive
Extremely influenced by others	Less inclined to be influenced
Teachers	Prefer maths & physical sciences
Global way of perceiving	Analytic way of perceiving

So, how might we frame the explanation of a potential threat and its impact to the two different types of cognitive styles, field-independent and field-dependent so that their level of perceived risk is raised?

6. FRAMING MESSAGES IN TERMS OF FD/FI

The aim of this research is to show that when the explanation of a potential threat scenario is couched in a way that is in line with an individual's cognitive style, then that individual is likely to perceive the risk to be higher than if the explanation was framed differently.

Therefore, for FD types, the potential threat scenario should be framed in a way that highlights:

- the global impact,
- the social implications,
- the impact it would have on people/individuals,
- what individuals can do to mitigate against the risk,
- the benefits to individuals
- how we might be viewed by others or
- how our image might suffer.

Conversely, for FI types, the potential threat scenario should be framed to emphasise:

- physical effects
- a practical/pragmatic solution to the problem with little regard to the impact on people
- a quick fix solution
- hardware and/or software solutions

The following three threat scenarios have been framed according to the FD/FI cognitive style.

Table 2. Threat Scenario No. 1 - Theft of desktop computer

Written for FD's	**Written for FI's**
Your office was broken into and a desktop computer was stolen by an unknown external person. Sensitive information could be leaked to unauthorised people that could be embarrassing for the organisation. Depending on your backup procedures, this could be costly for the IT department to recover.	Your office was broken into and a desktop computer was stolen by an unknown external person. You will be without a computer until a replacement çan be purchased. You may have to use one of the office laptops in the meantime. Recovery of all data could be difficult if you did not backup everything.

Table 3. Threat Scenario No. 2 - A virus infection

Written for FD's	Written for FI's
Your office desktop computer has been infected with a virus. If not addressed immediately, it might spread through the whole organisation, causing inconvenience and loss of productivity. It may damage people's hard drives, causing valuable & sensitive information to be lost. This would be embarrassing for the organisation.	Your office desktop computer has been infected with a virus. If not addressed immediately, it could damage your computer files preventing you from doing your work. This could be embarrassing for you because you obviously did not run anti-virus software properly.

Table 4. Threat Scenario No. 3 – A software bug

Written for FD's	Written for FI's
An accidental software bug in one of our application programs could cause our computer system to crash. This, in turn, could cause a delay in processing the fortnightly pays, or prevent invoices from being processed on time. Futhermore, employee confidence in the computer system could be impacted.	An accidental software bug in one of our application programs could cause our computer system to crash. To prevent this breach from occurring in the future, we have to tighten up our testing procedures to ensure that all programs are thoroughly tested before they are put into production.

7. CONCLUSION

The primary aims of this paper were, firstly, to emphasise the importance of human factors/behaviour as management strive for an acceptable level of information security within their organisations. The second aim was to present a risk communication approach, namely cognitive style framing, that management might consider in an attempt to change user risk-taking behaviour of computer users at all levels. It is suggested that a positive change of this nature can reduce the level of risk.

This paper supports the view that an acceptable level of information security is best achieved by addressing all components of an information system, particularly issues relating to the people component. It also attempts to contribute to an ever-increasing amount of research into the sociological aspects of risk as it relates to the domain of information security. Also examined is the concept that better risk communication, by deploying the concept of framing, will mitigate against the actual information risks as depicted in Figure 1 below.

This is essentially a theory paper. However, the authors expect to present some preliminary findings of a pilot study to sample test a range of threat scenarios at the IFIP WG11.1 conference in December 2005.

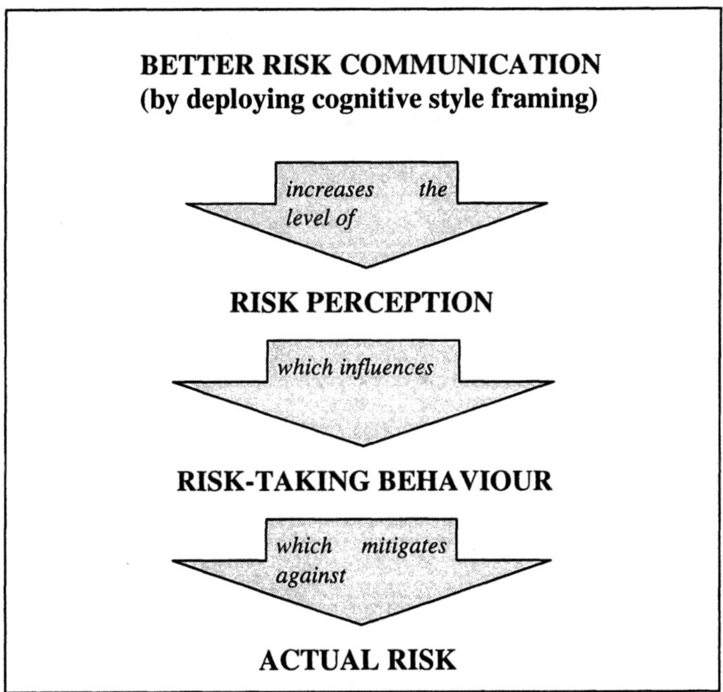

Figure 1.

8. REFERENCES:

Backhouse J., Bener A., Chauvidul N., Wamala F. & Willison R., 2004, "Risk Management in Cyberspace", Available at http://www.foresight.gov.uk/Previous_Projects/Cyber_Trust_and_Crime_Prevention/Reports_and_Publications/, viewed 27 April 2005.

Bener, A. B., 2000, "Risk Perception, Trust and Credibility: A Case in Internet Banking", PhD thesis, London School of Economics and Political Sciences, Available at http://is.lse.ac.uk/research/theses/default.htm, viewed 27 April 2005.

Chinien, C. A., 1990, "Examination of Cognitive Style FD/FI as a Learner Selection Criterion in Formative Evaluation", *Canadian Journal of Educational Communication*, Vol 19, pp. 19-39.

Fischhoff B., Bostrom A. & Quadrel M. J., 1993, "Risk Perception and Communication", *Annual Review of Public Health*, Vol. 14, pp. 183-203.

Heimer, C. A., 1988, "Social Structure, Psychology, and the Estimation of Risk", *Annual Review of Sociology*, Vol 14, pp. 491-519.

Jackson J., Allum, N. & Gaskell, G., 2004, "Perceptions of Risk in Cyberspace", Available at http://www.foresight.gov.uk/Previous_Projects/Cyber_Trust_and_Crime_Prevention/Reports_and_Publications/, viewed 27 April 2005.

Johnson C., 2002, Available at http://www.dcs.gla.ac.uk/~johnson/teaching/safety/open_assessments/assess2002.html, viewed 28 July 2004.

McNeil B. J., Pauker S. G., Sox H. C. & Tversky A., 1982, "On the Elicitation of Preferences for Alternative Therapies", *New England Journal of Medicine*, Vol 306, pp 1259-1262.

Meyerowitz B. E. & Chaiken S., 1987, "The Effect of Message Framing on Breast Self-examination Attitudes, Intentions and Behaviour", *Journal of Personality and Social Psychology*, Vol. 52, No. 3, pp 500-510.

O'Neill P., 2004, "Developing A Risk Communication Model to Encourage Community Safety from Natural Hazards", paper presented at the Fourth NSW Safe Communities Symposium, Sydney, NSW.

Otway H. J., 1980, "Risk Perception: A Psychological Perspective", *Technological Risk: Its Perspective and Handling in Europe*, M. Dierkes, S. Edwards & R. Coppock.

Russo J. & Schoemaker, P. J. H., 1989, *Confident Decision Making*, London, Piaktus Press.

Tan F.B., 1999, "Exploring Business-IT Alignment Using the Repertory Grid", *Proceedings of the 10th Australasian Conference on Information Systems.*

Tversky A. & Kahneman D., 1981, "The Framing of Decisions and the Psychology of Choice", *Science*, Vol. 211, pp 243-248.

Wilson R. M. S., 2001, "The Framing of Financial Decisions: A pilot study", *Research Series Paper 2001:3*, ISBN 1859011713, Loughborough University.

A HOLISTIC RISK ANALYSIS METHOD FOR IDENTIFYING INFORMATION SECURITY RISKS

Janine L. Spears
The Pennsylvania State University, Smeal College of Business, University Park, PA 16802

Abstract: Risk analysis is used during the planning of information security to identify security requirements, and is also often used to determine the economic feasibility of security safeguards. The traditional method of conducting a risk analysis is technology-driven and has several shortcomings. First, its focus on technology is at the detriment of considering people and processes as significant sources of security risk. Second, an analysis driven by technical assets can be overly time-consuming and costly. Third, the traditional risk analysis method employs calculations based largely on guesswork to estimate probability and financial loss of a security breach. Finally, an IT-centric approach to security risk analysis does not involve business users to the extent necessary to identify a comprehensive set of risks, or to promote security-awareness throughout an organization. This paper proposes an alternative, holistic method to conducting risk analysis. A holistic risk analysis, as defined in this paper, is one that attempts to identify a comprehensive set of risks by focusing equally on technology, information, people, and processes. The method is driven by critical business processes, which provides focus and relevance to the analysis. Key aspects of the method include a business-driven analysis, user participation in the analysis, architecture and data flow diagrams as a means to identify relevant IT assets, risk scenarios to capture procedural and security details, and qualitative estimation. The mixture of people and tools involved in the analysis is expected to result in a more comprehensive set of identified risks and a significant increase in security awareness throughout the organization.

Keywords: risk analysis, information security, risk management, business process, data flow diagram, risk scenario.

1. INTRODUCTION

Managing information security is essentially managing a form of risk. The management of risk generally involves conducting a risk analysis to identify and evaluate risks, and then employing risk management techniques to mitigate or reduce risks where deemed appropriate. Likewise, the standard approach to managing information security involves conducting a risk analysis to identify risks to confidentiality, integrity, and availability of information systems, which is followed by risk management where safeguards are employed to mitigate those risks.

Traditional risk analysis methods applied to information systems focus foremost on technology with limited attention to people and processes. However, an information system is comprised of technology, people, processes, and data. Therefore, an effective security risk analysis must examine each of these aspects. As such, traditional risk analysis methods are seen as inadequate (e.g., Halliday et al., 1996; e.g., Gerber and von Solms, 2005). This paper examines the traditional risk analysis method, along with its strengths and limitations, and then proposes an alternative holistic method that addresses these limitations.

The paper is organized as follows. The next section defines risk and describes the purpose of a risk analysis. §3 describes the traditional risk analysis method, along with its strengths and limitations. Next, a holistic risk analysis method is proposed in §4, followed by an example and the method's benefits. §5 describes evaluation criteria for a risk analysis and how it applies to the proposed method. §6 suggests future areas of research, followed by a conclusion in §7.

2. RISK ANALYSIS

Risk is defined as (a) the possibility of loss or injury, and (b) the liability for loss or injury if it occurs (Merriam-Webster Inc., 1996). *Risk analysis*, in the context of information security, "is the process of examining a system and its operational context to determine possible exposures and the potential harm they can cause" (Pfleeger and Pfleeger, 2003). *Risk management* involves using the output from risk analysis to determine the selection and implementation of controls (safeguards) to reduce risk (Gerber and von Solms, 2005).

Risk analysis has traditionally been used in business for analyzing financial instruments and insurance products (e.g., Baskerville, 1991; Barrese and Scordis, 2003; Gerber and von Solms, 2005). In both cases, risk analysis is driven by quantitative analysis of asset value to determine the feasibility of investing in the financial instrument or insurance product. Likewise in information security, (Alberts and Dorofee, 2001) risk analysis is often used to determine the feasibility of investing in security safeguards that reduce risks to information security (Baskerville, 1991). The other key reason for conducting risk analysis, which is the focus of this paper, is to identify security requirements (ISO/IEC 17799).

3. TRADITIONAL RISK ANALYSIS OF INFORMATION SECURITY

The traditional method for conducting information security risk analysis is technology-driven (e.g., Halliday et al., 1996; Humphreys et al., 1998 p. 49; Gerber and von Solms, 2005) because it focuses primarily on known threats to types of computing assets employed by an organization. This is due in large part to the historical origin of widely-used computer security guidelines (NIST, Common Criteria, RAND Corp, ISO 17799, SSE-CMM) that were initially developed for securing governmental and military computing infrastructures. Given that these leading security guidelines were not initially developed for information systems within a business environment, methods for identifying risks related to people (internal and external to the organization) and business processes are lacking.

For the purposes of this paper, the word *traditional* is used to denote risk analysis practices generally cited in the literature as being the conventional or common approach (e.g., Halliday et al., 1996; Kolokotronis et al., 2002; Suh and Han, 2003; Tan, 2003). Steps in a traditional risk analysis are summarized in Figure 1.

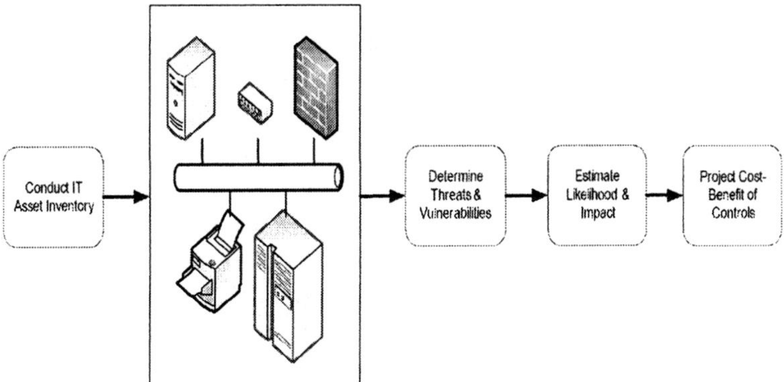

Figure 1. Traditional risk analysis for information security

The first step when conducting a risk analysis is to identify the IT assets to be protected. IT assets generally include hardware, software, data, people, documentation, and applicable facilities (Suh and Han, 2003). Note that although *people* is typically included as a type of IT asset, traditional risk analysis places minimal emphasis on people and is typically concerned solely with user identification and authentication. However, risk may be incurred by the procedures that people use to handle information. Next, for each identified asset, threats (undesired events that may occur) and vulnerabilities (existing weaknesses) related to confidentiality, integrity, and availability are identified. This is typically determined by using standard checklists (NIST, 2005) and the expertise of the security analyst. Risk is then quantified as the likelihood (i.e., probability) that a security event will occur (i.e., that a vulnerability will be exploited) multiplied by the expected monetary loss of such an event (risk = probability * expected loss). This output is used to compute a cost-benefit analysis of implementing security safeguards that will reduce risk to an acceptable level (e.g., Pfleeger and Pfleeger, 2003; Tan, 2003; Gerber and von Solms, 2005).

3.1 Strengths of Traditional Risk Analysis

The traditional risk analysis method for information security has several advantages. First, the method is widely known as the de facto standard taught in textbooks and endorsed by industry-accepted security guidelines (e.g., NIST, 2002; Pfleeger and Pfleeger, 2003).

Second, given that traditional risk analysis has focused primarily on technology, this aspect of security has been richly developed. For example, extensive lists of known threats and vulnerabilities to various technical assets are publicly available. These lists provide valuable guidance when conducting a risk analysis.

Third, automated software packages are available that perform the detailed calculations and manage the risk analysis data. These software packages are based on the traditional method of risk analysis.

Fourth, quantitative measures used in the traditional method can be used to support a cost-benefit analysis of investments in security safeguards. This is, of course, provided the calculations are reasonably accurate.

Finally, the traditional method of conducting a risk analysis for information security is closely related to risk analysis techniques employed in the financial and insurance sectors. This point, along with the mathematical foundation of the method, may add credibility.

3.2 Limitations of Traditional Risk Analysis

The traditional risk analysis method for information security has several key limitations. First, this technology-driven method places very limited emphasis on the people and process aspects of information systems. This is a major oversight, given that people and processes are widely considered to be the leading causes of security breaches (e.g., Siponen, 2000; Dhillon, 2001; Wade, 2004). In addition, there is no common approach to identifying which IT assets are to be included in the analysis. An IT professional developing a list of technical assets may not be aware of important user-developed spreadsheets and applications that contain significant security risks. Specific confidential information that warrants safeguarding may also be omitted.

Second, estimates of expected losses are based on the value of assets, and are widely inaccurate for a variety of reasons. Determining the value of intangible assets, such as information, is considered difficult, if not impossible, to estimate (Gerber and von Solms, 2005). Yet, information is one of the most important assets of an organization and is the focal point of information security. Estimates for the value of tangible assets may be inaccurate because in many cases only replacement costs are considered, which does not include the financial loss due to disruption of operations (Suh and Han, 2003). In cases where cost of disruption of operations is included in the asset value, the estimate is highly subjective. Finally, expected financial losses based on asset value typically do not include the social impact of a potential breach, such as loss of customer confidence (Bennett and Kailay, 1992).

Third, probability estimates of the likelihood of an identified vulnerability being exploited are commonly considered to be wild guesswork. One reason for this is that likelihood is determined by past history of security breaches, and this is largely underreported (e.g., Strang, 2001; Yazar, 2002; Keeney et al., 2005). Another reason that estimates of likelihood of occurrence are inaccurate is because making a more accurate estimate requires a high level of expertise by the estimator (e.g., Gerber and von Solms, 2005), which an organization may not possess. See Baskerville (1991) for additional discussion on weak quantitative estimates inherent in traditional risk analysis, which continue to exist.

A fourth limitation of the traditional method to risk analysis is the time and cost involved in conducting such an analysis. The bottom-up nature of the traditional method (i.e., driven from a micro, technology assets perspective) tends to be time-consuming, especially in medium to large organizations (Halliday et al., 1996). Significant amounts of time may be spent analyzing assets of low importance to critical business processes.

A fifth limitation to a technology-focused analysis is that it is often solely conducted by IT professionals. This is problematic because business users are not involved, which only contributes to a lack of security awareness across an organization. Equally important, risks inherent in business processes that may be identifiable by a business user may go undetected by an IT professional.

In summary, the traditional method of conducting risk analysis for information security employs calculations based largely on guesswork to estimate probability and financial loss of a security breach. Secondly, its focus on technology is at the detriment of considering people and processes as significant sources of security risk. Finally, an IT-centric approach to security risk analysis does not involve business users to the extent necessary to identify a comprehensive set of risks, or to promote security-awareness throughout an organization.

4. A PROPOSED HOLISTIC RISK ANALYSIS METHOD

A holistic risk analysis, as defined in this paper, is one that attempts to identify a comprehensive set of risks by focusing equally on technology, information, people, and processes. The method is also holistic in nature by receiving input from a variety of participants within the organization, coupled with input from (security) industry-accepted guidelines. *The focus of this holistic method is on the identification of information security risks within critical business processes.* Key aspects of the method include user participation in the analysis, business-driven analyses, system diagrams as a means to extract relevant IT assets, and qualitative analysis.

Identifying risks that impact business processes provides a top-down analysis that defines the focus, scope, and relevance of the analysis. The proposed method, by its very nature, requires the involvement of a variety of senior management, business users and IT professionals. Once IT assets are identified and analyzed by participants, the method makes use of publicly available security checklists and guidelines (e.g., CERT, NIST) in order to capture known threats and vulnerabilities. Qualitative measures are used to estimate the impact of identified risks. These features counter the limitations of the traditional method of risk analysis identified in §3.

4.1 The Holistic Risk Analysis Method Described

In a holistic risk analysis, senior management identifies core business functions within the organization. Core business functions may be major departments within a firm, such as finance, marketing, human resources, procurement, etc. Senior management of each identified business function identifies critical business processes within their respective business function. Critical business processes are those that are vital to the financial stability and operation of an organization, of which there may be one or more. Examples include: process sales orders, procure raw materials, generate financial statements, process payroll, etc. Information security risks are identified by analyzing the associated technology, people, information, and processes that have the greatest impact on the operation of these business processes. The proposed holistic risk analysis method contains the following steps (see Figure 2):

1. Identify core business functions within the organization and their critical business processes
2. For each business process, identify the critical information system
3. Obtain an updated architecture diagram of the critical information system that includes its supporting infrastructure, and develop a list of IT assets
4. Obtain updated data flow diagrams (DFD) to identify user groups, sub-processes, external (including subordinate) systems, and information flows through the system
5. Identify confidential information from the DFDs
6. Update the list of IT assets based on information obtained from the DFDs
7. Determine the relative necessity (or importance) of each IT asset to the business process
8. Develop a risk scenario for each technical asset of high importance, each type of confidential information, and each user group with access to confidential information
9. Identify threats and vulnerabilities for each IT asset being analyzed
10. Estimate the impact of a security breach to the asset

An initial list of relevant technical assets is developed from architecture diagrams. This list of IT assets is later appended with assets identified in DFDs. Technological assets involved in handling confidential data are ranked as high in importance, even in cases where a technological asset is determined to be of low or medium necessity to the business process. For example, imagine a home healthcare products firm that occasionally transmits customer medical information by email to varying insurance companies. A paper copy is also mailed to the insurance company, so the email is not considered critical to the process of communicating medical information. However, this data is confidential. Therefore, the email template and the security features employed are ranked as high importance due to the confidential nature of the data being transmitted.

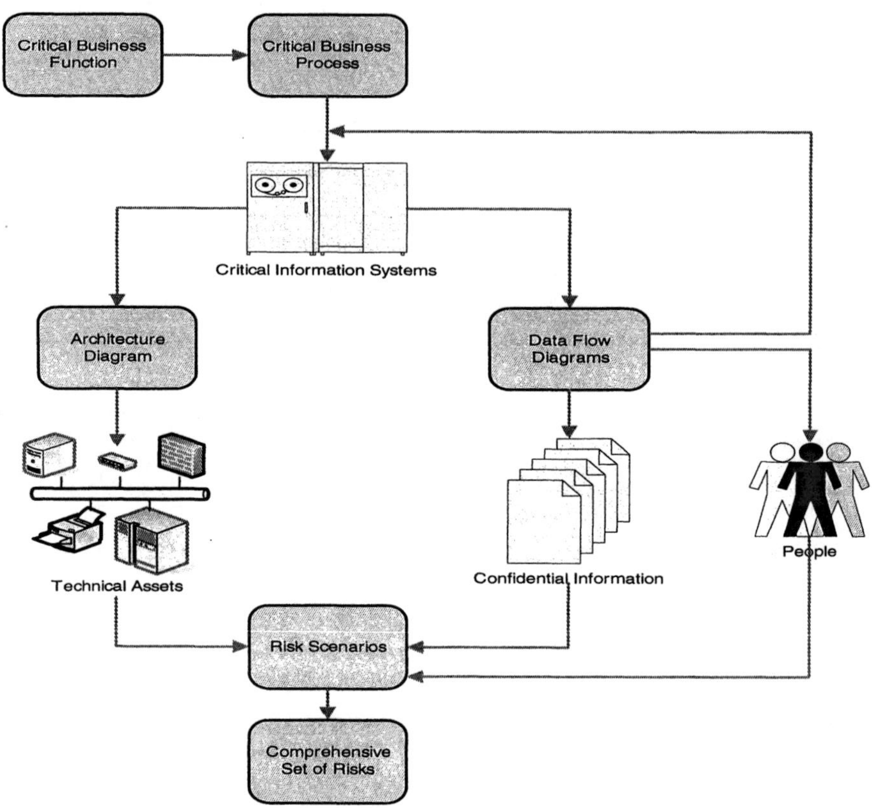

Figure 2. Holistic risk analysis for information security

Data flow diagrams are chosen because they illustrate how information flows to, from, and within a system. This is important information in a security risk analysis given that information is the essential asset to be protected. DFDs reveal information, people, and external (or subordinate) information systems. An initial (context) DFD is iteratively decomposed to lower levels of detail until all major processes within a system have been identified, along with the information flows to and from those processes.

Risk scenarios are narrative descriptions of situations that could result in a security event, either intentional or unintentional, within a targeted system (Freeman et al., 1997). In the holistic method, a risk scenario is created for each technological asset of high importance to the critical business process, each type of confidential information, and each user group with access to confidential information. As shown in Figure 3, a risk scenario includes the asset; a list of existing security safeguards; threats and vulnerabilities; influences (e.g., conditions, events) that increase the likelihood that a vulnerability will be exploited; a history of known security breaches associated with the asset. The categories of *existing safeguards* and *influences on the likelihood of a breach* in the risk scenarios were borrowed from de Ru and Eloff (1996). The format varies slightly, depending upon the type of asset. Risk scenarios for technical assets and information types indicate who/what/where/how the asset is created, modified, deleted, and archived. Scenarios for user groups identify the contact manager, when/how security policies were communicated to the user group, types of confidential information accessed, and the purpose of that access.

As indicated in Figure 3, threats and vulnerabilities associated with an asset are contained in its risk scenario. Threats and vulnerabilities are identified from three sources: a) security industry-accepted guidelines and checklists, such as ISO17799, CERT, and NIST, b) expertise of participating IT staff, and c) information from the risk scenario that further stimulates thinking of participants who are knowledgeable of local practices.

Participants involved in developing a risk scenario for a given asset estimate the potential impact of a breach in the asset's confidentiality, integrity, and availability. Impact is estimated using a nominal scale and is determined for each vulnerability identified.

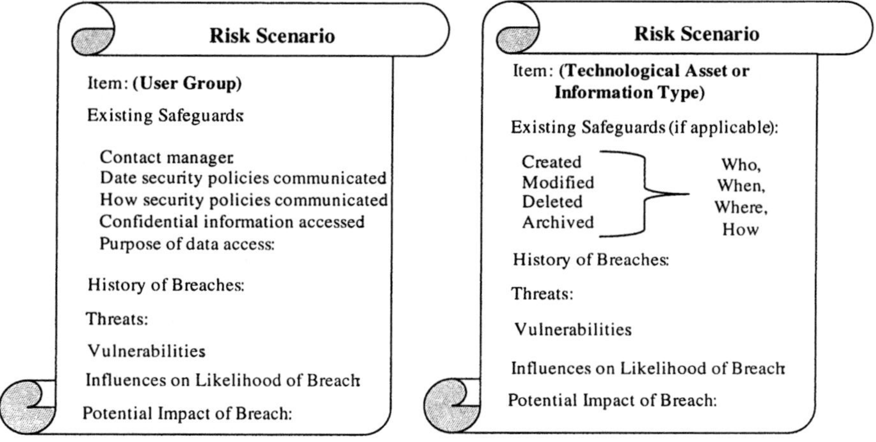

Figure 3. Risk scenarios

4.2 Example of a Holistic Risk Analysis

Finance is identified as a core business function. Senior management in the Finance department identify the *generation of financial statements* as a critical business process that is essential to the financial stability of the firm. An internally developed *financial reporting system* is used to generate the financial reports, and is identified as a critical information system for this business process. An existing architecture diagram depicts the network infrastructure supporting the financial reporting system. This diagram is updated to reflect any infrastructural changes. (If no architecture diagram previously existed, one would be created.) Using the architecture diagram, an IT professional from the network/infrastructure group develops a list of IT assets. This list contains servers, gateways, operating systems, etc.

A systems analyst and business user liaison work together to update existing data flow diagrams (DFDs) previously created during the analysis and design of the financial reporting system. (If no DFDs previously existed, they would be created.) DFDs indicate information flows to, from, and within a system. DFDs also indicate external entities (e.g., people, systems) that exchange data with the system and its sub-processes.

This example illustrates how a DFD and user input can reveal IT assets that may otherwise be overlooked in an analysis conducted solely by IT technical staff. As shown in Figure 4, a DFD indicates that press releases are sent to external press agencies. This information flow was not captured in the architecture diagram, or known by the IT technical staff, because the information is sent manually by fax. The DFD also indicates that Excel spreadsheets provide critical, confidential input to the financial reporting system. This detail is also unknown to IT technical staff because the spreadsheets are user-developed.

The high-level DFD in Figure 4 would be decomposed, such that sub-processes within the reporting system are identified, along with their information flows. Examples of sub-processes within the reporting system include *obtain current performance data*, *compute performance variances*, *compute historical comparisons*, etc. By analyzing sub-processes, information flows within a system are revealed at a greater level of detail, which in turn may identify areas of potential threat or vulnerability with regard to how information is handled. Upon completing an analysis of the DFD in this example, the list of IT assets is updated with the following assets:

- fax technologies used to send the press releases,
- the Excel spreadsheets,

- information types (e.g., actual and projected earnings, performance ratios, etc.),
- user groups (finance department, corporate executives, and press agencies),
- and other relevant assets identified in subordinate DFDs

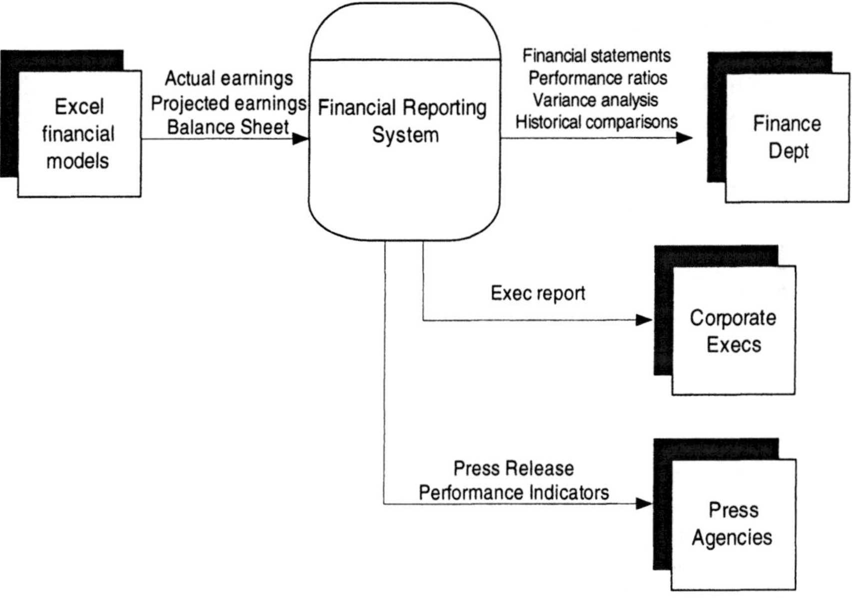

Figure 4. Contextual data flow diagram. (Squares indicate user groups and external systems. Arrows indicate information flows. A rounded rectangle represents a process.)

The teams that updated the architecture and data flow diagrams collaborate to rank the importance of the technological assets, user groups, and information to the business process of generating financial reports. The Excel spreadsheets that provide critical input to the financial reporting system are ranked of high importance, and a holistic risk analysis is subsequently conducted for this subordinate information system.

A risk scenario is created for each technological asset ranked as highly important, each type of confidential information, and each user group with access to confidential information. In this example, scenarios are developed for two types of information (actual and projected earnings), two user groups (finance department and corporate executives), and relevant technical assets identified in the architecture diagram. Data sent to press agencies are no longer confidential, so a risk scenario is not created for this user group. Note that the Excel spreadsheets are treated as a subordinate system due to their detailed financial models, and a separate risk analysis is conducted.

Information contained in a risk scenario for *actual earnings* indicates the data is created from weekly files imported from Excel by a financial analyst. The only existing safeguard is control of user access to the financial reporting system that is authorized by a senior finance manager. A confidentiality breach had occurred the previous quarter when actual earnings were leaked to stock analysts and the press prior to the press release. On a scale of high, medium, low, the impact of such a breach is ranked high given its potential impact on stock market reaction. Other threats and vulnerabilities are identified using publicly available security checklists, the expertise of IT staff, and business users involved in creating the risk scenario. Scenario participants estimate the impact of each vulnerability should it be exploited.

4.3 Benefits of the Holistic Risk Analysis

A holistic risk analysis has several benefits over a traditional risk analysis. First, the risk analysis is driven by critical business processes – that is, those processes that are deemed essential to the financial stability and operation of the organization. In doing so, the risk analysis has a clear focus with relevant boundaries, and has a greater chance of obtaining participation from business management. Participation from business management is likely to result in a more comprehensive (holistic) set of identified risks than would be the case from a risk analysis conducted primarily by IT professionals. For example, risks to confidential information are more likely to be identified with input from business users. This is because business users are better suited to identify confidential data, which may be internal or external to the larger information system known to IT staff (e.g., could be contained in spreadsheets, etc.). Business users are also better suited to identify the procedures used in handling the data, as well identify the user groups (both internal and external to the firm) that have access to such data (either manually or electronically).

Second, the proposed model uses structured diagrams developed during the design of critical information systems. Using structured diagrams for security risk analysis further leverages the resources invested in developing such diagrams during the analysis and design of information systems. In addition, developing data flow (DFD) and architecture diagrams are techniques commonly employed within organizations and do not require security expertise. Using DFDs will likely result in additional IT staff being involved in security initiatives. For example, business and systems analysts responsible for developing DFDs are not typically involved in the traditional risk analysis method. DFDs are used because they identify information flows in a system, and the related processes, people, and external (or sub) systems.

Third, risk scenarios capture the security history of an asset, as well as procedural information that may expose asset vulnerabilities that were not previously considered. For example, vulnerability checklists identify known technical vulnerabilities for an asset type. However, an organization's local operating environment contains additional vulnerabilities that must be uncovered. Many of these vulnerabilities are due to the existence or absence of procedures. The information contained in the risk scenarios stimulates thinking and are a third source of input for identifying threats and vulnerabilities (the other two sources being checklists and IT expertise).

Fourth, a qualitative estimate of the impact of a security breach has several advantages over calculating quantitative estimates. Qualitative measures simplify the risk estimation, are more useful when the asset value is irrelevant or unknown, and are less time-consuming (Bennett and Kailay, 1992; Suh and Han, 2003).

Finally, the proposed holistic risk analysis method requires the involvement of a multitude of roles, such as senior management, business users, systems analysts, database administrators, networking/infrastructure professionals, and security staff. Involving such a mixture of people in the process used to identify security risks will likely result in a significant increase in security awareness throughout the organization. This is a major benefit given that employees are said to typically not know their responsibilities in dealing with information security (Wade, 2004) and are responsible for an estimated 61% - 81% of violations to existing security safeguards (Bennett and Kailay, 1992; Dhillon, 2001).

5. EVALUATING THE HOLISTIC RISK ANALYSIS METHOD

Criteria for evaluating "an effective risk assessment," identified in Freeman, Darr, and Neely (1997), may be applied to a holistic risk analysis. As indicated in Table 1, an effective holistic risk analysis is *timely*, *cost-effective*, *complete*, *consistent*, and *understandable*.

Table 1. Evaluation criteria for an effective risk analysis (Freeman et al. 1997).

Evaluation Criteria	Description	Applied to the Holistic Method
Timely	The process provides the best available data in a timely manner.	A top-down risk analysis that is driven by critical business processes will have a clear focus with relevant boundaries, which is expected to result in a more timely analysis. Secondly, a qualitative analysis is expected to be less time-consuming because time is not spent gathering data for specific monetary or probabilistic values.
Cost-effective	The effort to accomplish the risk analysis is commensurate with the value of the results.	This holistic method leverages investments in existing architecture and data flow diagrams from system design. Secondly, this method is expected to uncover a greater number of procedural risks than the traditional method. It is anticipated that many of theses risks may lead to valuable, yet inexpensive, procedural safeguards.
Complete	The process is comprehensive with respect to some underlying structure, to reduce the likelihood of being "blind-sided" by an unanticipated security event.	A comprehensive analysis is conducted by involving both business users and various IT professionals. Secondly, the method places an equal focus on technology, information, people and processes.
Consistent	The rationale and methods for evaluating and reporting threats, vulnerabilities, and risks within the	Subsystems are identified via architecture diagrams, data flow diagrams, and system users and designers. Subsystems then follow the same analysis as the initial information system under analysis.

Evaluation Criteria	Description	Applied to the Holistic Method
	system are consistently applied and interpreted within and among all subsystems.	
Understandable	The rationale for the process and supporting techniques used to conduct the risk analysis have as *structured* a basis as possible and are understandable to customers without jargon. (This description replaces the word *technical* as specified by Freeman, Darr, and Neely with *structured* so that it applies to the entire holistic method.)	The holistic method involves business users and various IT professionals much in the same manner as that of the system design process. Similarly, the holistic method is performed in a structured manner with each participant, to include senior management, understanding the process and techniques as related to his/her role.

6. FUTURE RESEARCH

As previously mentioned, the traditional risk analysis method is often used to determine the economic feasibility of implementing security safeguards. Given that the traditional risk analysis method focuses on technological assets, attempts to manage information security have been skewed towards implementing increasingly complex technological safeguards (Dhillon, 2001). The holistic method requires participation from a greater variety of roles within the business and IT communities, and as such, a more comprehensive set of risks is expected to be identified than would be the case with the traditional method. A more comprehensive set of risks would likely result in a higher number of low-cost, important, procedural safeguards. A future study would be useful to test these propositions.

The output of a risk analysis serves as input to risk management. This paper proposes a holistic method for conducting risk analysis that involves a variety of participants and parallels system analysis and design practices. Additional research is needed to develop a risk management method that effectively parallels the remainder of the SDLC (system development lifecycle) with the end goal of reducing security risks. Establishing a theoretical foundation for why information security practices can benefit from applying information systems development practices is also an important task for future research.

According to Cerullo and Cerullo (2004), there is a current trend to integrate business continuity planning with IT security planning. Business continuity planning involves identifying critical business functions and major risks that could result in their interruption. Future research could study how the holistic risk analysis method proposed in this paper could be used to facilitate business continuity planning and vice versa.

7. CONCLUSION

This paper examined the role of a risk analysis in information security planning and critiqued the traditional method for conducting risk analysis. An alternative holistic method for conducting risk analysis was proposed. The holistic method has several benefits. First, the risk analysis is driven by critical business processes, which provides focus and relevance to the analysis. Second, structured data flow and architecture diagrams developed during analysis and design of information systems are used during the security risk analysis, which further leverages the resources invested in developing such diagrams. Third, information contained in the risk scenarios stimulates thinking and are a third source of input for identifying threats and vulnerabilities (the other two sources being checklists and IT expertise). Finally, the proposed holistic risk analysis method requires participation from a variety of roles, such as senior management, business users, systems analysts, database administrators, networking/infrastructure professionals, and security staff. Involving such a mixture of people in the process used to identify security risks will likely result in a more comprehensive set of identified risks, and will likely result in a significant increase in security awareness throughout the organization.

REFERENCES

Barrese, J. and Scordis, N., 2003, "Corporate risk management." Review of Business 24(3):26.

Baskerville, R., 1991, "Risk analysis as a source of professional knowledge." Computers & Security 10(8):749-764.

Bennett, S. P. and Kailay, M. P., 1992. An application of qualitative risk analysis to computer security for the commercial sector. Computer Security Applications Conference, Eighth Annual, San Antonio, TX, IEEE.

CERT, 2001, Alberts, C. and Dorofee, A., (January 30, 2001), "An introduction to the OCTAVE method." from http://www.cert.org/octave/methodintro.html.

CERT, 2005, Keeney, M., Kowalski, E., Cappelli, D., Moore, A, Shimeall, T. and Rogers, S., (May 11, 2005),. Insider threat study: computer system sabotage in critical infrastructure sectors, http://www.cert.org.

Cerullo, V. and Cerullo, M. J., 2004, "Business continuity planning: a comprehensive approach." Information Systems Management 21(3):70-78.

de Ru, W. G. and Eloff, J. H. P., 1996, "Risk analysis modelling with the use of fuzzy logic." Computers & Security 15(3):239-248.

Dhillon, G., 2001, "Violation of safeguards by trusted personnel and understanding related information security concerns." Computers & Security 20(2):165-172.

Freeman, J. W., Darr, T. C. and Neely, R. B., 1997, Risk assessment for large heterogeneous systems. Computer Security Applications Conference, 1997, San Diego, CA, IEEE.

Gerber, M. and von Solms, R., 2005, "Management of risk in the information age." Computers & Security 24:16-30.

Halliday, S., Badenhorst, K. and von Solms, R., 1996, "A business approach to effective information technology risk analysis and management." Information Management & Computer Security 4(1):19.

Humphreys, E. J., Moses, R. H. and Plate, H. E., 1998, Guide to Risk Assessment and Risk Management. London, British Standards Institute.

ISO/IEC 17799, 2000, Information technology -- Code of practice for information security management.

Kolokotronis, N., Margaritis, C. and Papadopoulou, P., 2002, "An integrated approach for securing electronic transactions over the Web." Benchmarking 9(2):166-181.

Merriam-Webster Inc., 1996, Merriam-Webster's Dictionary of Law, Philippines, Merriam-Webster, Inc.

NIST, 2002, Risk Management Guide for Information Technology Systems. Washington, DC, National Institute of Standards and Technology: U.S. Department of Commerce, http://csrc.nist.gov/publications/nistpubs/800-30/sp800-30.pdf.

NIST, April 19, 2005, Practices & Checklists / Implementation Guides, National Institute of Standards and Technology: U.S. Department of Commerce, http://csrc.nist.gov/pcig/cig.html.

Pfleeger, C. P. and Pfleeger, S. L., 2003, Security in Computing. Upper Saddle River, NJ, Prentice Hall, pp. 462-475.

Siponen, M. T., 2000, "Critical analysis of different approaches to minimizing user-related faults in information systems security: implications for research and practice." Information Management & Computer Security 8(5):197-210.

Strang, R., 2001, "Recognizing and meeting Title III concerns in computer investigations." Computer Crimes and Intellectual Property 49(2):8-13.

Suh, B. and Han, I., 2003, "The IS risk analysis based on a business model." Information & Management 41(2): pp. 149-158.

Tan, D., 2003, Quanitative Risk Analysis Step-by-Step, SANS Institute, http://www.sans.org.

Wade, J., 2004, The weak link in IT security. Risk Management. 51:32-37.

Yazar, Z., 2002, A qualitative risk analysis and management tool - CRAMM, SANS Institute, http://www.sans.org.

SESSION 5 – SECURITY CULTURE

A RESPONSIBILITY FRAMEWORK FOR INFORMATION SECURITY

Shaun Posthumus[1] and Rossouw von Solms[2]
[1]*Nelson Mandela Metropolitan University, Shaun.Posthumus@nmmu.ac.za;* [2]*Nelson Mandela Metropolitan University, Rossouw.VonSolms@nmmu.ac.za*

Abstract: This paper demonstrates that information security is more than a technical issue, through the development of an information security responsibility framework that shows consideration for strategic and legal issues as well. It is important that information security be viewed as both a governance challenge and a management responsibility. In order to achieve this this paper addresses information security governance and the board's participation in directing and controlling security efforts. Furthermore information security management is addressed in order to demonstrate how information security should be implemented. Once a comprehensive picture of the information security function has been established, the roles of various individuals in terms of information security are discussed and mapped out in the responsibility framework in order to demonstrate the true scope of an organizations information security function.

Key words: Corporate Governance; Information Security Governance; Information Security Management; Responsibility; Accountability

1. INTRODUCTION

The storage, processing and transmission of business information has been greatly facilitated by the development of computers and computer networks and the widespread implementation of such information technology (IT) resources. These developments have enabled organizations to perform business transactions with their customers, suppliers and other business partners with greater efficiency and speed. However, Entrust (2004,

p. 3) states that "the very openness and accessibility that stimulated the adoption and growth of private networks and the Internet also threaten the privacy of individuals, the confidentiality of information and the accountability and integrity of transactions." For this reason information security, is a business priority and should be integrated into an organization's business processes, with responsibilities assigned to all concerned individuals (BS 7799, 1999). This involves more than merely addressing technical issues, at the department level that may generate information security risks, as information security is also a strategic and possibly a legal concern (Birman, 2000). Several sources, including Entrust (2004), Swindle and Conner (2004) and Posthumus and von Solms (2004) have asserted that information security efforts should include executive management and board-level participation through sound information security governance endeavors. These efforts should then be supported by a well planned information security management strategy that exemplifies the board's and executive management's guidance in terms of information security direction. In order for an organization to make a success out of its information security program, everyone in an organization should know their responsibilities in terms of information security.

It is the objective of this paper to highlight the information security responsibilities of various individuals within an organization, from both a governance and management perspective, through the development of an information security responsibility framework. Such a framework serves to draw attention to the fact that information security is in fact both a governance challenge and well as a management responsibility that involves more than merely an organization's operational or technical managers (IT Governance Institute, 2005). In order to successfully motivate the responsibility framework, this paper firstly discusses the importance of corporate governance and then information security governance, as an important responsibility of the board. Information security management is then discussed with the intention of demonstrating the significant role management plays in implementing information security based on the board's direction and guidance in this regard. Once a more comprehensive picture of the entire information security function has been established in this way, various information security roles and responsibilities are addressed. These roles and responsibilities are then mapped out to form the responsibility framework, highlighting where key personnel fit in, and thus demonstrate the true scope of the information security function.

2. CORPORATE GOVERNANCE

Corporate governance is the system that dictates how an organization is directed and controlled. It is most certainly a very important function in any organization. In order to clearly express the importance of corporate governance, it should be analyzed more closely.

2.1 What is Corporate Governance?

Sir Adrian Cadbury, in the foreword of Corporate Governance: A Framework for Implementation, asserted that "corporate governance is concerned with holding the balance between economic and social goals and between individual and communal goals ... the aim is to align as nearly as possible the interests of individuals, corporations and society." (World Bank Group, 1999). This definition clearly suggests that there are a wide variety of issues that organizations need to consider in order to operate effectively in such a dynamic business environment as that which is found to be the case today.

Corporate Governance is ultimately all about sound leadership efforts (King Report, 2001). Sound leadership and good corporate governance are exemplified by the expression of several essential characteristics. These characteristics include accountability, responsibility, discipline, transparency, independence, fairness and social responsibility (King Report, 2001). An organization's board of directors must practice fairness, transparency, accountability and responsibility in every action taken, as well as remain accountable to their organization but nonetheless act responsively and responsibly where the stakeholders are concerned (King Report, 2001).

Good corporate governance is an important function in an organization, but there is a need to further clarify this statement by exploring why.

2.2 Why is Corporate Governance Important?

The most reasonable motivation for why corporate governance is so important in all organizations today is that these organizations have to realize that they should not attempt to function autonomously from the social orders or environments in which they exist (King Report, 2001). This is because, according to Thompson and von Solms (2003), organizations are a more direct presence to the general public than government. Therefore organizations should be compelled to demonstrate those characteristics that constitute good governance endeavors if they hope to gain the trust and support of the community or markets that they service. If these organizations fail to demonstrate characteristics such as transparency, responsibility or accountability, for example, its executive leadership may be deemed untrustworthy, thus resulting in the financial demise of these organizations and therefore negatively effect the country's economy in some way (King Report, 2001).

Ultimately the quality of an organization's governance practices is really the only means of assurance its shareholders have that they will receive good returns on their investments in an organization (King Report, 2001). Corporate governance is therefore important because it is the mechanism that ensures that the best interests of an organization's shareholders are catered for. More specifically, corporate governance accomplishes this by regulating the use of an organization's resources in an appropriate manner, and placing accountability and responsibility onto those that govern the use of those resources (World Bank Group, 1999).

Good corporate governance can therefore be seen as the key to economic success and the stability of an organization. However, if corporate governance is not effectively implemented, some very negative consequences may transpire.

2.3 The Implications of Poor Corporate Governance

The poor corporate governance practices of the past have resulted in greater external scrutiny over the way companies operate today. As a result of such ineffective governance practices, boards of directors everywhere are now required to comply with a myriad of new laws and regulatory compliance mandates. The consequences of noncompliance with these stipulations involve swift legal action in the form of strict financial penalties or lengthy prison terms (Trillium Software, 2004). Thus regulatory intervention is obviously not the outcome of desire. Such intervention usually results in a tarnished corporate reputation and furthermore affects consumer and investor trust (Vericept Corporation, 2004).

Various legislative requirements aim to remind executives and boards of their corporate accountability and responsibility. However, there is a need to promote self governance, through an improved system of corporate governance, as an alternative to more legislation (Entrust, 2004). For this reason executive management and the board must ensure that they remain in complete control over their organization by understanding the full scope of their duties. This will ensure that their organization's valuable resources are not exploited in any way and the shareholders interests are preserved.

Since information is such an important asset to an organization it is the board's duty to ensure that this resource is also appropriately governed, the same as any resource. The Corporate Governance Task Force (2004), in the preface of Information Security Governance: A Call to Action, states that "the road to information security goes through corporate governance". Therefore the board needs to understand their role with regard to protecting information. Hence information security governance is a very important aspect of corporate governance.

3. INFORMATION SECURITY GOVERNANCE

Information security has become a business priority that demands the attention of corporate board's and executive management. Therefore there is a need to explore information security governance in order to demonstrate the role of the board in terms of protecting vital business information assets.

3.1 What is Information Security Governance?

The Corporate Governance Task Force (2004, p. 5) states that "corporate governance consists of the set of policies and internal controls, by which organizations, irrespective of size or form, are directed and managed. Information security governance is a subset of organizations' overall governance program." Therefore information security governance would include board-level involvement in terms of directing and controlling an organization's information security efforts through effective policies, beginning with the creation of the corporate information security policy, and internal controls that govern the use of their business information assets.

Business information is very important to an organization, because having the right information at the right time is essentially what gives an organization a competitive advantage over others (Gerber & von Solms, 2001). For this reason the board must ensure that the confidentiality, integrity and availability of business information are maintained, in order to protect the interests of the shareholders and generate business value. Information security governance, aims to achieve this by focusing on risk management efforts, reporting and accountability with regard to the use of business information assets (Corporate Governance Task Force, 2004). Moreover, the corporate information security policy is the means by which the importance of these activities is communicated to the organization by the board through the expression of information security goals and objectives for confidentiality, integrity and availability. This ensures that the risks affecting these characteristics of information are all adequately minimized to an acceptable level.

Information security governance is thus essential because it ensures that there is board-level involvement in terms of directing and controlling an organization's information security program, however there is a need to further clarify why this governance function is so important.

3.2 Why is Information Security Governance Important?

The vast implementation of computers and computer networks, which serve as a tool for service enablement and business value creation, also have the potential to significantly threaten the confidentiality, integrity and availability of business information. Due to the ease of accessibility to information and business services through the Internet and other networks, information is now primarily exposed to three fundamental elements that create potential risks. These three elements include firstly, the technology, which is used to store, process and transmit information; secondly, the people, i.e. customers and staff who access this information through various private networks and the Internet and thirdly, the business processes that deliver a particular business service that an organization provides (BS 7799, 1999). Information security governance is important because it brings accountability to each of these three elements, which are key components of corporate governance (Swindle & Conner, 2004). Promoting such accountability and responsibility for each of these elements of corporate governance is extremely important because of the many legal and regulatory pressures that boards of directors face today.

Once the board has understood the importance of information security governance as part of their corporate responsibilities and as a way to preserve the interests of their shareholders more fully, it would be necessary to explain how this function can be implemented further.

3.3 How can Information Security Governance be Implemented?

Information security can be said to be a priority of the board, and thus effective information security governance efforts are essential. Such efforts must enable the board to determine exactly what information security objectives their organization should fulfill in order to precisely define their information security direction and communicate such direction to the rest of the organization via the corporate information security policy. This would therefore serve to support the implementation of an accurate system of internal control. In order to ensure that the corporate information security policy communicates accurate information security objectives to the organization the board has to become aware of both internal and external security requirements and guidelines (Posthumus & von Solms, 2004). In other words they need to identify the security requirements that various sources outside of their organization have recommended, as well as identify internal security requirements based on the specific needs of their organization. These security requirements specifically include: firstly, the requirements to protect the IT infrastructure; secondly, the business requirements that preserve the confidentiality, integrity and availability of information; and thirdly, any legal, regulatory or statutory requirements (Humphreys, Moses, & Plate, 1998). These requirements together with the guidance of industry best practices and well-regarded security standards, like BS 7799 (1999), help the board to establish the foundation for an effective approach to information security (Posthumus & von Solms, 2004), beginning with the accurate definition of information security goals and objectives. Such an approach will most assuredly bring accountability to people, process and technology elements through a well planned information security policy that promotes effective risk management and reporting mechanisms.

Previous research conducted by Posthumus and von Solms (2004), entitled "A Framework for the Governance of Information Security", which has been published in Computers and Security, motivated the development of a framework for information security governance and the communication of an effective information security policy. Figure 1 illustrates this framework, as it was developed and discussed in the paper. The framework draws attention to several major security requirements and how they all contribute in order to guide the board in terms of accurate information security decision making and the development and communication of the corporate information security policy.

Once the board has expressed their support of information security through sound governance efforts, management must then implement information security in the organization through an effective information security management strategy.

4. INFORMATION SECURITY MANAGEMENT

Information security management is an important step toward fulfilling the stipulations of the board in terms of information security, based on various identified internal and external security requirements. Hence information security management should be explored in more detail.

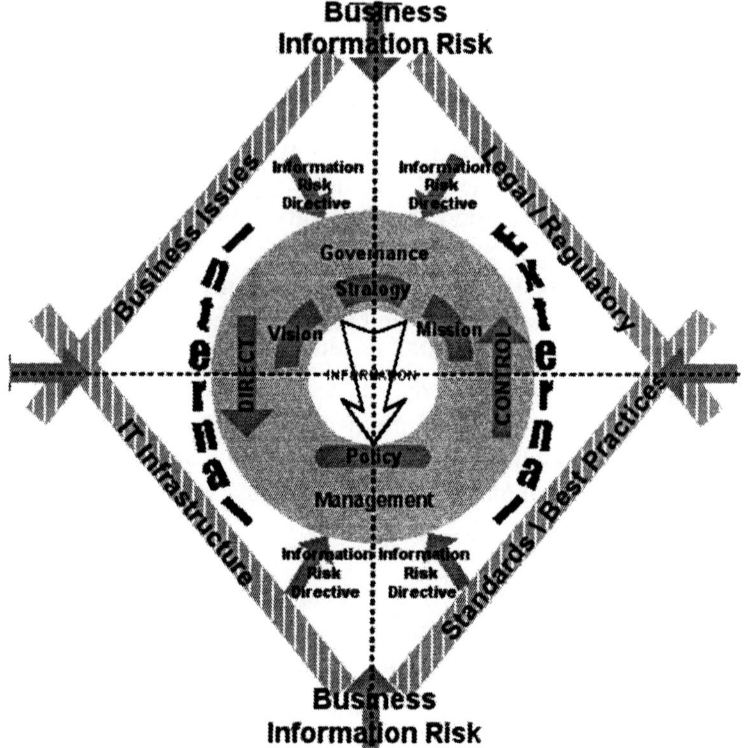

Figure 1. An Information Security Governance Framework

4.1 What Is Information Security Management?

Information security management is the process of carrying out various activities that facilitate the preservation of an organization's business information assets. This process is an expression of the information security objectives, which were stipulated by the board. Basically, information security management involves implementing security measures that exemplify the instructions of an organization's security policy, various security procedures and other security programs (Whitman & Mattord, 2003). Information security management aims to influence organizational culture (Whitman & Mattord, 2003), in order to create a secure information environment and mitigate business information risk.

Information security management is a continuous process, requiring constant review and adjustment in order to keep up with the latest technology developments and their associated risks (Whitman & Mattord, 2003) and to further ensure that the organizations information security goals and objectives remain fulfilled to the fullest extent. There are essentially six consecutive phases that constitute a successful information security management program. These phases include investigation, analysis, logical design, physical design, implementation and maintenance and change (Whitman & Mattord, 2003). The primary intention of an information security management program is to identify particular threats and create particular security controls that counteract those threats (Whitman & Mattord, 2003) and hence preserve confidentiality, integrity and availability of business information.

It is essential to differentiate between information security management and information security governance, in order to highlight why each of these functions are so important in terms of securing business information assets.

4.2 The Difference between Information Security Management and Information Security Governance

Information security governance and information security management together form the unified process that constitutes an organization's broader information security function. Each of these activities has a particular contribution to make in terms of information security and are thus both essential.

According to the King Report (2001) it is the responsibility of the board to effectively direct and control all aspects of their organization through sound governance efforts. This therefore includes directing and controlling information security efforts as this must become a part of an organization's key business operations (Entrust, 2004). Information security governance is thus a board-level responsibility and expresses the board's commitment to information security with the development of à corporate information security policy, also called a security program policy that outlines the organization's vision, mission and information security direction (Whitman & Mattord, 2003). The board further controls security efforts through reporting mechanisms. Frequent reports enable the board to review the effectiveness of their guidance with regard to information security and redirect such efforts as necessary. In addition to this various board-level committees make recommendations to the board so that they can make accurate decisions and effectively govern information security. Thus information security governance is all about strategy setting and the communication of information security objectives.

Information security management, on the other hand, is more concerned with how the stipulations of the board, expressed in the corporate information security policy, are implemented within an organization. Therefore activities such as identifying specific security controls and formulating procedures to counteract risks form the basis of the information security management function. Literature suggests that information security management usually does not include personnel beyond the ranks of an organization's chief information officer (CIO). Usually the chief information security officer (CISO), who is not in an executive level position, is responsible for managing an organization's information security program (Whitman & Mattord, 2003). Information security management is thus a management responsibility and does not include board-level participation. It is more concerned with how security will be implemented in the organization.

In order to gain a clearer understanding of what information security management actually entails, a more detailed discussion regarding this function is on order.

4.3 Information Security Management: The Process

Information security management begins with clear direction. This is achieved with the guidance of accepted security standards and codes of practice such as BS 7799 (1999). Additionally, the issuing of a corporate information security policy helps to express the commitment of the organization toward protecting the confidentiality, integrity and availability of business information. Hereafter a series of activities that aim to realize this commitment commence. Some of these activities include an initial assessment of various potential risks to information which is then followed by some form of risk management strategy. This enables an organization to identify and implement an assortment of physical, technical and operational security controls. Examples include burglar alarms, access control mechanisms and more specific security policies, procedures, standards and guidelines respectively. Some other activities that are carried out through an information security management program include staff training in security practices, testing the security infrastructure, detecting and responding to various security incidents and business continuity planning (Entrust, 2004). In addition to these activities auditing the security function and reporting to the board on its effectiveness are key elements that promote accountability and responsibility for the broader information security function.

However, in order to effectively enforce accountability and responsibility for information security throughout an organization, various individuals need to fully understand the roles they play in this regard.

5. INFORMATION SECURITY TASKS, ROLES AND RESPONSIBILITIES

Information security is a process that requires a commitment from many key individuals in an organization to ensure its effectiveness. Therefore there is a need to identify the key role players and examine their responsibilities more closely.

5.1 The Role of the Board of Directors

By this stage it should be clear that the primary role of the board is to oversee the interests of the shareholders by effectively directing and controlling an organization and ensuring that all resources are appropriately utilized. Therefore with regard to information as a business resource the board must understand its significance as well as the significance of protecting it through successful information security efforts (Corporate Governance Task Force, 2004). Additionally the board must support the establishment and implementation of a robust information security program by setting the information security direction and communicating this through the corporate information security policy. The board must also receive management reports on the utility and effectiveness of their security program (Corporate Governance Task Force, 2004). This enables the board to ensure that their organization's security efforts remain on track.

5.2 The Role of Board Committees

Board committees facilitate the board in carrying out their duties efficiently and show that the board's responsibilities are being appropriately accomplished (King Report, 2001). There are several board committees that can assist the board with their responsibility for information security. These committees specifically include: firstly, the IT oversight committee; secondly, the audit committee and lastly, the risk management committee. The role of the IT oversight committee is to advise the board on an appropriate IT strategy for an organization (IT Governance Institute, 2004). Thus the IT oversight committee must ensure that an organization's IT strategy supports information security, since IT is so closely linked to this resource (IT Governance Institute, 2004). The audit committee is responsible for conducting performance reviews of an organization's system of internal control and must also review all legal and regulatory compliance efforts (King Report, 2001), including that of information security. Lastly, the risk management committee advises the board regarding corporate accountability as well as management, reporting and assurance related risks (King Report, 2001). The risk management committee's terms of reference include technology risk, operational risk, disaster recovery risk, and compliance and control risks (King Report, 2001). Thus, generally speaking, the information provided to the board by these various board committees, regarding the effectiveness of current security efforts further facilitates the board in the review of the organization's security policy.

5.3 The Role of the CEO

The chief executive officer (CEO) is responsible for overseeing the entire information security program of the organization (Corporate Governance Task Force, 2004), and sign off the information security policy. Additionally he must oversee compliance efforts and enforce accountability for such efforts (Corporate Governance Task Force, 2004). Furthermore the CEO must also report compliance issues to the board, highlighting the level of acceptable risk, weaknesses in current information security practices and plans to strengthen these practices (Corporate Governance Task Force, 2004). The CEO must also allocate responsibility, accountability and authority for various security functions to the right personnel in an organization and appoint someone as the senior information security officer (Corporate Governance Task Force, 2004).

5.4 The Role of the CIO

An organization's CIO typically makes recommendations to the CEO on the strategic planning efforts affecting the administration of an organization's information resources (Whitman & Mattord, 2003). Furthermore the CIO converts an organization's strategic plans into strategic plans for information and information systems (Whitman & Mattord, 2003). Additionally, the CIO collaborates with other non executive managers in order to develop plans of a tactical and operational nature for the management of information and information systems. Such efforts would entail setting the policies and procedures for information security (Corporate Governance Task Force, 2004). Thus the CIO plays a major role in the drafting of the organization's information security policies.

5.5 The Role of the CISO

The CISO is responsible for the overall information security management function (Whitman & Mattord, 2003). Some of his responsibilities in terms of this include, collaborating with the CIO on strategic information security plans, establishing tactical plans and collaborating with other security managers on operational security plans (Whitman & Mattord, 2003). Additionally the CISO must plan the information security budget i.e. assign resources for executing information security and act as the representative for all other security personnel (Whitman & Mattord, 2003). The CISO thus plays a major role in implementing the specifications of the organization's information security policy at a management level.

5.6 The Role of Data Owners (The Business Unit Leaders)

One of the typical responsibilities of the business unit leaders includes implementing the specifications of more specific security policies and procedures (Corporate Governance Task Force, 2004). It is also their responsibility to audit and review the effectiveness of various security procedures as well as communicate the security policies and procedures to other subordinate personnel through various staff training initiatives (Corporate Governance Task Force, 2004). Additionally they must enforce compliance with the security policies (Corporate Governance Task Force, 2004).

These various security roles and responsibilities span the entire organization, involving personnel in both management and governance positions, including the board of directors. This helps to demonstrate that information security is in fact more than a technical issue, as Entrust (2004), the Corporate Governance Task Force (2004) and Posthumus and von Solms (2004) have motivated. Therefore in order to clearly elucidate how information security should be addressed as more than a technical issue, to include consideration for the legal and business issues as well, it should be shown how key individuals collaborate. This is best achieved through an information security responsibility framework.

6. AN INFORMATION SECURITY RESPONSIBILITY FRAMEWORK

An information security responsibility framework helps to demonstrate the true scope of the information security function in an organization as it involves both governance and management support in order to address the full spectrum of information risks and security requirements.

6.1 The Governance Side

The governance side of the framework involves actions by executive management and the board in order to address the strategic issues of information security from a business and legal perspective. In this regard, the CIO should consult with the IT oversight committee on the alignment of business and IT, which is part of this committee's duties (IT Governance Institute, 2004), and should also address information security, as this should be regarded as a business issue. The CIO should also consult with the audit committee regarding internal control and compliance efforts. Furthermore, the CIO advises the CEO on strategic plans regarding information management (Whitman & Mattord, 2003), and the information security efforts that are in place to preserve information. The CEO then reports all issues regarding the information security function to the board (Corporate Governance Task Force, 2004), along with the status of legal compliance efforts. The board must then direct and control the security function guided by the advice of the IT oversight committee and the audit committee to align the corporate information security policy with current business strategies and objectives.

6.2 The Management Side

The management side if information security involves actions by non executive management and the CIO in order to address the implementation issues of information security from an infrastructure and best practice point of view. It is important to note that the CIO plays a major role in the entire information security function, as this individual has contributions to make in terms of both the governance and the management of information security. In the context of information security management, the CIO works closely with the CISO to develop strategies for information security (Whitman & Mattord, 2003), that would involve activities such as risk management, risk monitoring, reporting and so forth. These strategies consider reports from the CISO concerning all issues regarding the status of the current information security management function. The status of the organization's information security management function is made clear to the CISO by reports from the business unit leaders concerning the effectiveness of the security function in various departments. The business unit leaders, or department heads, are also responsible for ensuring that all employees are trained in security awareness and comply with information security policies, practices and procedures so that they act responsibly with regard to the organization's information assets (Corporate Governance Task Force, 2004).

Figure 2 illustrates the responsibility framework for information security which involves the commitment of both the management and governance components in an organization in order to fulfill all of the necessary security requirements and effectively secure business information assets. An important point to note with respect to the framework is that it can be closely linked to the information security policy. More specifically, the corporate information security policy covers much similar ground to the framework. A key feature of the information security policy is the delegation of security responsibilities. Thus the framework can further facilitate the development of the information security policy as it can be viewed as a road map to better information security strategy development.

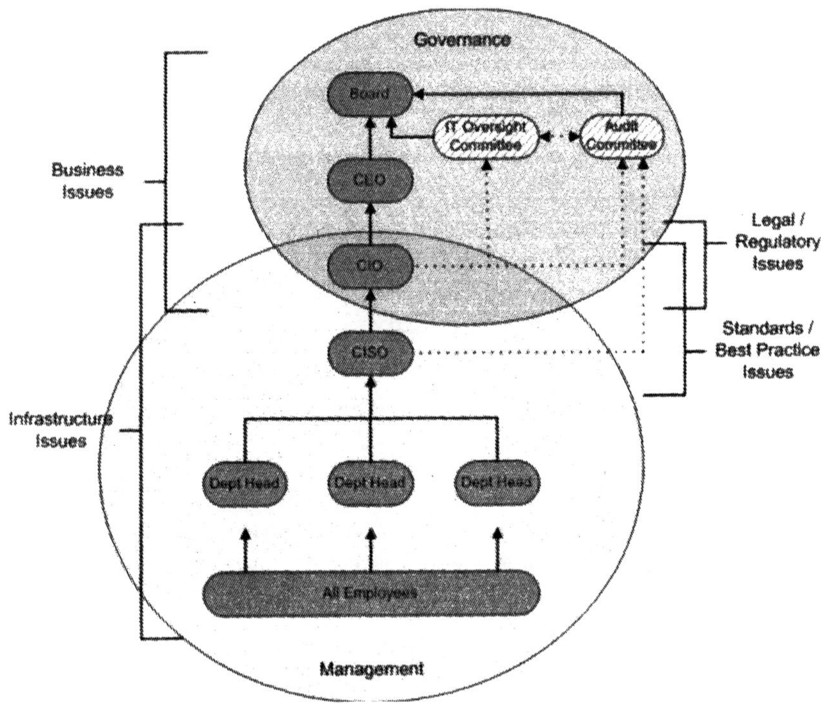

Figure 2. An Information Security Responsibility Framework

7. CONCLUSION

The development of an information security responsibility framework helps to show that both governance and management support are essential constituents of a comprehensive information security function. Both governance and management support enables an organization to satisfy the full spectrum of information security risks by addressing all information security requirements. Thus such a framework helps to illustrate that the true scope of the overall information security function involves a lot more than merely addressing technical issues (Entrust, 2004) but also includes consideration for strategic and legal issues as well (Birman, 2000). Consequently this enables the board to have complete control over an organization's resources, including information and in this way better preserve the shareholders interests and effectively govern their organization.

REFERENCES

Birman, K. P., 2000, The next generation internet: Unsafe at any speed. *IEEE Computer*, *33*(8), 54–60.

BS 7799, 1999, *BS 7799: Code of Practice for Information Security Management as a base for Certification.*

Corporate Governance Task Force, 2004, *Information Security Governance: A Call To Action.* Available from: http://www.cyberpartnership.org/InfoSecGov4_04.pdf.

Entrust, 2004, *Information Security Governance (ISG): An Essential Element of Corporate Governance.* Available from: http://itresearch.forbes.com/detail/RES/1082396487_702.html.

Gerber, M., & von Solms, R., 2001, From risk analysis to security requirements. *Computers and Security*, *20*(7), 577–584.

Humphreys, E. J., Moses, R. H., & Plate, E. A., 1998, *Guide to BS7799 Risk Assessment and Management.* British Standards Institution.

IT Governance Institute, 2004, *IT Strategy Committee.* Available from: http://www.ITgovernance.org/resources.htm.

IT Governance Institute, 2005, *Information Security Governance: Guidance for Boards of Directors and Executive Management.* Available from: http://www.isaca.org/ContentManagement/ContentDisplay.cfm?ContentID=15998.

King Report, 2001, *The King Report on Corporate Governance for South Africa.* Available from: http://www.iodsa.co.za/IoD%20Draft%20King% 20Report.pdf.

Posthumus, S., & von Solms, R., 2004, A framework for the governance of information security. *Computers and Security*, *23(8)*, 638–646.

Swindle, O., & Conner, B., 2004, *The Link between Information Security and Corporate Governance.* Available from: http://www.computerworld.com/securitytopics/security/story/0,10801,92915,00.html.

Thompson, K., & von Solms, R., 2003, *Integrating information security into corporate culture.* Masters dissertation, Nelson Mandela Metropolitan University, Port Elizabeth, South Africa.

Trillium Software, 2004, *Corporate Governance and Compliance: Could Data Quality Be Your Downfall?* Available from: http://www.trilliumsoftware.com/success/dqic.pdf.

Vericept Corporation, 2004, *Preventing Identity Theft and Loss of Intellectual Property: The Importance of Information Security in Internal Controls and Corporate governance.* Available from: http://www.vericept.com/Downloads/WhitePapers/Vericept_Fraud_IdentityTheft_WP.pdf.

Whitman, M. E., & Mattord, H. J., 2003, Principles of information security. In (pp. 153 – 190). Course Technology.

World Bank Group, 1999, *Corporate Governance: A Framework for Implementation.* Available from: http://www.worldbank.org/html/fpd/privatesector/cg/docs/gcgfbooklet.pdf.

INFORMATION SECURITY GOVERNANCE - A RE-DEFINITION

Rahul Rastogi[a] and Rossouw von Solms[b]
[a] *Nelson Mandela Metropolitan University, rahul.rastogi@eil.co.in,*

[b] *Nelson Mandela Metropolitan University, rossouw@petech.ac.za*

Abstract: Information is a fundamental asset of any organization and needs protection. Consequently, Information Security Governance has emerged as a new discipline, requiring the attention of Boards of Directors and Executive Management for effective information security. This paper investigates the literature on Corporate Governance, IT Governance and Information Security Governance to identify the components towards a definition of Information Security Governance. The paper concludes by defining Information Security Governance and discussing the definition, identifying and addressing all important issues that need to be taken into account to properly govern information security in an organization.

Key words: Corporate Governance, IT Governance, Information Security Governance, Information Security

1. INTRODUCTION

Much has been said in recent literature about bringing Information Security into the fold of Corporate Governance, thereby making it a crucial responsibility of the Board of Directors and Executive Management. Information Security Governance has, thus, emerged as a new discipline and responsibility for Board of Directors and Executive Management. But, before Board of Directors and Executive Management can discharge this new responsibility, the term Information Security Governance needs to be defined and understood.

Existing literature provides some guidance on Information Security Governance. However, in the opinion of the authors, this guidance is insufficient. The guidance is prescriptive and does not clearly bring out the meaning of Information Security Governance. In a recent article, the plight of Executive Management with respect to IT Governance is stated as most C-level executives responding to IT Governance with a "frustrated roll of their eyes" (Melnicoff, Shearer & Goyal, 2005, p. 1). We feel that the existing guidance on Information Security Governance will elicit similar reactions.

The objective of this paper is to propose a 'new' definition of Information Security Governance, identifying and addressing all important issues that need to be taken into account to properly govern information security in an organization. The definition answers the following questions:

- What is to be understood from Information Security Governance?
- Who formulates the framework to implement Information Security Governance in an organization?
- Where in the organization is Information Security Governance implemented?
- What are the benefits that Information Security Governance should deliver to the organization?

In proposing the definition of Information Security Governance, this paper first reviews how Information Security is evolving and how it is being brought under the purview of Corporate Governance. It then investigates the existing literature on Corporate Governance, IT Governance and Information Security Governance to identify the components of the proposed definition. The paper concludes by proposing the definition and discussing its various components.

2. THE EVOLUTION OF INFORMATION SECURITY AND THE EMERGENCE OF INFORMATION SECURITY GOVERNANCE

Over the years, IT has penetrated every aspect of modern business and today businesses are critically dependent on IT and information. This has led to the evolution of the role of Information Security. Further, because of the wide impact of information security breaches on organizations, Information Security is increasingly being brought under the fold of Corporate Governance. However, Board of Directors and executive management have very little guidance on what Information Security and Information Security Governance mean for their organization.

Regarding the evolution of Information Security and the emergence of Information Security Governance, two trends emerge from the current literature:

- The role of Information Security is changing – it is no longer about only protecting information assets, but also about assurance and trust (BSA, 2003, p. 3). Information Security is now a competitive weapon.
- Increasingly, Information Security is being linked to Corporate Governance. Many researchers in the field have motivated the need for integrating Corporate Governance and Information Security (von Solms and Thomson, 2003). Further, various regulations and legislation are formalizing this requirement (FISMA, 2002).

Information Security is thus evolving and leading to the emergence of Information Security Governance as a new discipline. Through this evolution and change, Boards of Directors and Executive Management need to understand the value that Information Security delivers for their organization and what they need to do to discharge their responsibility towards Information Security Governance.

This paper attempts to bring the required clarity and understanding by providing a definition of Information Security Governance for Boards of Directors and Executive Management. The following sections investigate the existing literature on Corporate Governance, IT Governance and Information Security Governance to identify the possible components of this definition.

3. CORPORATE GOVERNANCE

Corporate Governance emerged as a discipline when the ownership of an organization was separated from its management. Governance, then, means protection of owners' interests through oversight, direction and control of management by owners, the owners being represented by the Board of Directors. Thus one of the main aspects of governance is to assure the suppliers of finance that they would get a return on their investments (Shleifer and Vishny, 1996, p. 3). Corporate Governance provides this assurance by providing incentives to the board and management to "pursue objectives that are in the interests of the company and its shareholders" (OECD, 2004, p. 13).

Moving forward from these philosophical underpinnings, guidance is available on the operational and implementation aspects of Corporate Governance. Corporate Governance is implemented through structures such as an organization's management, board, shareholders and other stakeholders that are bound by relationships. These structures and relationships are then utilized to set objectives and to determine the means of attaining those objectives and monitoring performance (OECD, 2004, p. 13).

A recent trend in the literature on governance of corporations or enterprises is towards taking a wider view of governance, i.e. Enterprise Governance with Corporate Governance being a part of it, or being synonymous with it. Figure 1 shows the Enterprise Governance Framework consisting of the conformance and performance dimensions (CIMA, 2004, p. 2).

The conformance dimension consists of the organization using its "governance arrangements to ensure it meets the requirements of the law, regulations, published standards and community expectations of probity, accountability and openness" (ANAO, 2003, p. 13). The conformance dimension includes Corporate Governance (CIMA, 2004, p. 2).

The performance dimension consists of the organization using its "governance arrangements to contribute to its overall performance and the delivery of its goods, services or programs" (ANAO, 2003, p. 13).

Operationally, Governance is "basically concerned with structures and processes for decision-making and with the controls and behaviour that support effective accountability for performance outcomes" (ANAO, 2003, p. 13).

Together, the conformance and performance structures and processes implement governance through "providing strategic direction, ensuring that objectives are achieved, ascertaining that risks are managed appropriately and verifying that the organization's resources are used responsibly" (Hamaker, 2003, p. 1).

From the above discussion, Governance can be understood to consist of the following aspects:

- It involves the Board of Directors and Executive Management.
- It makes the Board of Directors and Executive Management responsible towards all stakeholders including shareholders and suppliers of finance.
- It involves the creation of an organizational structure specifying the distribution of rights and responsibilities among the various participants in the organization.
- Governance includes the specification of processes for directing, controlling and monitoring performance of the organization towards attaining its objectives.
- Governance has conformance and performance aspects.
- The conformance dimension of Governance involves the formation of decision-making guidelines and structures and the clear identification and articulation of responsibilities.

- The performance dimension of Governance involves performance measurement and accountability for performance.

This section has investigated the meaning of governance. The following section investigates the definitions of IT Governance. Since, today, information largely exists in the IT devices deployed in organizations, it is instructive to look at what Governance means to IT to understand how it can be applied to Information Security.

4. IT GOVERNANCE

Information today is largely manifest in the electronic form. Also, today Information Security is largely about controls applicable to IT. This section investigates some definitions of IT Governance to understand what governance means to IT, in an attempt to understand what it can mean to cover Information Security. This paper does not see Information Security Governance as a subset of IT Governance as the drivers for IT Governance are very different from those for Information Security Governance.

The IT Governance Institute (ITGI) defines IT Governance as follows :

"IT Governance is the responsibility of the board of directors and executive management. It is an integral part of enterprise governance and consists of the leadership and organizational structures and processes that ensure that the organization's IT sustains and extends the organization's strategies and objectives" (ITGI, 2003, p. 18).

Weill and Woodham (2002, p. 4) defines IT Governance as:

> "specifying the decision rights and accountability framework to encourage desirable behaviour in the use of IT".

Van Grembergen (2002, p. 1) defines IT Governance as:

> "the organizational capacity exercised by the Board, executive management and IT management to control the formulation and implementation of IT strategy and in this way ensuring the fusion of business and IT".

The key point of the above definitions of IT Governance is that they see governance as a mechanism for fusing or aligning business and IT and getting value out of IT implementation. The definitions focus on the 'performance' outcomes of value creation and resource utilization. Likewise, the proposed definition of Information Security Governance should focus on the 'performance' outcomes of Information Security Governance and the value delivered by Information Security to the organization. However, the 'performance' outcomes and value delivered by Information Security Governance would be different from that of IT Governance.

5. EXISTING GUIDANCE ON INFORMATION SECURITY GOVERNANCE

This section investigates the guidance on Information Security Governance provided in the existing literature. This will help put in perspective the definition proposed in this paper.

The existing guidance on Information Security Guidance has two main themes:

- Motivating that Information Security must be governed and
- Defining Information Security Governance and providing guidance for implementation of governance.

The motivation for Information Security Governance is derived from the fiduciary responsibility of Board of Directors and Executive Management towards corporate governance and protection of stakeholder interests. It is motivated that not only are the Board of Directors and Executive Management responsible for maintaining information security, but also that they are liable for legal action for breaches in information security at their organization (von Solms, 2001) (von Solms and Thomson, 2003).

Since Governance consists of structures, relationships and processes, the existing guidance (ISACF, 2001) (CGTF, 2004) (BSA, 2003) (FISMA, 2002) provides frameworks for implementing Information Security Governance. The implementation proceeds mainly by mapping Information Security Governance responsibilities to the organizational hierarchy. A summary is provided in Table 1 – Information Security Governance and Organizational Hierarchy.

The existing guidance represents the beginning of a trend towards providing frameworks for Information Security Governance. The frameworks are therefore not sufficiently detailed and, in our opinion, would lead to a 'frustrated roll of eyes', as stated earlier. Further, the frameworks do not explicate a model or definition of Information Security Governance and are prescriptive in nature.

We attempt to remedy this shortcoming partially by proposing a definition of Information Security Governance in the next section.

6. PROPOSED DEFINITION OF INFORMATION SECURITY GOVERNANCE

This section proposes the following definition of Information Security Governance:

"Information Security Governance consists of the frameworks for decision-making and performance measurement that Board of Directors and Executive Management implement to fulfill their responsibility of providing oversight, as part of their overall responsibility for protecting stakeholder value, for effective implementation of Information Security in their Organization, to ensure that:

a. The Organization practices due care and due diligence in its use of Information and IT Systems and that this care and diligence is extended to its partners and customers.
b. The Organization manages the risks associated with its use of Information and IT Systems and that the process for Information Security is effective, efficient and responsive to security incidents and existing or emerging vulnerabilities, threats and risks.
c. The Organization's Information and IT Systems can be trusted by all stakeholders, including, customers, partners and regulators.
d. There is alignment between the needs and strategies of Business, IT and Information Security.
e. The Organization complies with laws and regulations applicable to its use of Information and IT Systems.
f. There is visibility into the state of Information Security in the Organization, providing relevant details to concerned stakeholders."

Figure 2 depicts a model of Information Security Governance, based on this definition. The following sections provide a brief discussion of the various components and characteristics of this definition.

7. THE 'GOVERNANCE' ASPECT OF INFORMATION SECURITY GOVERNANCE

This section discusses the 'Governance' aspect of the definition of Information Security Governance, i.e., what is meant by Governance, as it is applied to Information Security.

The definition states that Information Security Governance is a part of Enterprise or Corporate Governance and that the responsibility of Boards of Directors and Executive Management for providing oversight for protecting stakeholder interests includes providing oversight for implementation of Information Security.

The mechanisms for providing governance include creating the decision-making and performance measurement frameworks. These frameworks are formulated by the Board of Directors and Executive Management, but they are to be applied across all the layers of the organization. For the purpose of this discussion, an organization is modeled as consisting of the following layers :

- Corporate Governance Layer
- Executive Management Layer
- Operational Management Layer
- Technical Execution Layer

Thus, according to the definition, the decision-making and performance measurement frameworks are formulated by the top two layers, whereas the frameworks are applied across all 4 layers i.e. throughout the organization. Each of the four layers will, however, have its own requirements for what decisions are to be taken and what performance measures are to be monitored and reported.

As stated earlier in section 3 on Corporate Governance, the two frameworks will indeed be implemented through organizational structures. These structures will be related by their decision rights, responsibilities and accountabilities and the structures will operate as per the defined processes. These details will form the two frameworks.

The formulation of the Decision-making framework will be guided by questions such as:

- What are the decisions to be taken?
- Who takes which decision?
- What process is to be followed?
- What are the standards, policies, guidelines etc. that are needed to guide decision-making?
- What are the checks, controls and balances for ensuring proper decision-making?

The formulation of the Performance-Measurement framework will be guided by questions such as:

- Who are the stakeholders and what value do they expect from Information Security?
- Are our decisions being implemented and to what extent?
- What metrics do we need to monitor and report?

The approach to applying governance to information security would then mean asking and answering the above questions, and many more such questions, as they apply to information security e.g.

- What does information security mean for us?
- How much security do we need ? What is our risk appetite?

- Who will decide information security project prioritization and budgeting?
- How do we ensure alignment between Business, IT and Information Security?
- What support do Information Security projects need from the organization?
- What is our security architecture?
- Etc.

In the next section, the value that governance will enable information security to deliver to the organization gets discussed.

8. THE 'PERFORMANCE' OUTCOMES ASPECT OF INFORMATION SECURITY GOVERNANCE

This section discusses the 'performance' outcomes aspect of the definition of Information Security Governance i.e., the value that governance allows Information Security to deliver to the organization. The value ranges from being an effective protective mechanism to strategic alignment between the needs of business and information security.

The first three 'performance' outcomes of Information Security Governance can be seen as a hierarchy:

a. Due care and due diligence in the use of Information and IT Systems i.e. a healthy control environment which is the base foundation,
b. An effective and efficient process with due commitment and allocation of resources which leads to … (the next higher layer mentioned below),
c. Internal and external trust in the organization's information and IT systems.

Information Security Governance has to ensure that appropriate entities are responsible for decision-making and accountable for performance measurement for delivering on the above objectives.

Another important aspect of information security implementation in organizations is the alignment that must be achieved between business, IT and information security. Information Security Governance has a crucial role in ensuring this alignment – not only must information security satisfy business and IT needs, but business and IT must conform to security guidelines. Information Security Governance delivers on alignment by ensuring that business, IT and information security participate in relevant decision-making and that appropriate performance metrics are defined.

Information Security is increasingly being regulated with many legislations and regulations being applicable. Information Security Governance has to ensure that the compliance posture of the organization is identified and that the appropriate regulations are complied with accordingly.

A major requirement for governance is to ensure reporting of relevant details to stakeholders. The purpose of this reporting is to ensure that stakeholders have visibility into the health of the organization. Information Security Governance has to ensure that the stakeholders are identified and their information needs are satisfied.

In this section, the elements of the value that information security delivers to the organization has been identified. Information Security Governance has a vital role in enabling this value delivery.

9. CONCLUSION

In this paper, a definition of Information Security Governance, based on a review of the current literature on Corporate Governance, IT Governance and Information Security Governance, was provided. This definition has two parts viz. the governance aspect and the value aspect. The definition links these two aspects together to show how governance can enable information security to deliver value to the organization.

The proposed definition is comparable to the definition of 'Internal Control' as proposed by (COSO, 1992) which defines 'Internal Control' as the responsibility of Board of Directors and Executive Management. The objectives of 'Internal Control' are effectiveness of operations, reliability of financial reporting and compliance with applicable laws and regulations (COSO, 1992). Likewise, the proposed definition is comparable to the 'Security Organization' control contained in ISO 17799 (ISO 17799). This control envisages a management framework consisting of allocation of responsibilities, co-ordination and approval processes. However, ISO 17799 does not provide any detailed framework for the implementation of this control.

The definition can serve as a foundation for developing a framework for Information Security Governance in organizations. This framework can then be used by Board of Directors and Executive Management to implement effective Information Security within their organization.

10. REFERENCES

ANAO (2003). Public Sector Governance Volume 1 Better Practice Guide Framework, Process and Practices. *Australian National Audit Office*. (online) (cited 05 May 2005). Available from Internet: URL http://www.anao.gov.au/WebSite.nsf/0/957e55a69b1050724a256d73001dfd1c/$FILE/Volume%201,%20Framework,%20Processes.pdf

BSA (2003). Information Security Governance: Toward a Framework for Action. *Business Software Alliance.* (online) (cited 05 May 2005). Available from Internet: URL http://www.bsa.org/resources/loader.cfm?url=/commonspot/security/getfile.cfm&pageid=5841&hitboxdone=yes

CGTF (2004). Information Security Governance: A Call To Action. *Corporate Governance Task Force.* (online) (cited 05 May 2005). Available from Internet: URL http://www.cyberpartnership.org/InfoSecGov4_04.pdf

CIMA (2004). Enterprise Governance Getting the Balance Right Executive Summary. *Chartered Institute of Management Accountants.* (online). (cited 05 May 2005). Available on Internet: URL http://www.cimaglobal.com/cps/rde/xbcr/SID-0AAAC564-30AB5F4F/live/enterprise_governance_summary_2004.pdf

COSO (1992). Internal Control - Integrated Framework Executive Summary. *The Committee of Sponsoring Organizations of the Treadway Commission.* (online). (cited 05 May 2005). Available from Internet: URL http://www.coso.org/publications/executive_summary_integrated_framework.htm

FISMA (2002). Federal Information Security Management Act of 2002. *U.S. Congress.* (online). (cited 05 May 2005). Available from Internet: URL http://csrc.nist.gov/policies/FISMA-final.pdf

Hamaker, S. (2003). Spotlight on Governance. *Information Systems Control Journal*, Volume 1, 2003. (online). (cited 05 May 2005). Available on Internet: URL http://www.shamrock-technologies.com/Journal_article2.pdf

ISACF (2001). Information Security Governance: Guidance for Boards of Directors and Executive Management. *Information Systems Audit and Control Foundation.* (online). (cited 05 May 2005). Available on Internet: URL http://www.isaca.org/Content/ContentGroups/ITGI3/Resources1/Information_Security_Governance_Guidance_for_Boards_of_Directors_and_Executive_Management/infosecurity.pdf

ISO 17799. ISO / IEC 17799:Code of Practice for Information Security Management. *International Standards Organisation, Geneva, Switzerland.*

IT Governance Institute (ITGI) (2003). Board Briefing on IT Governance, 2nd Edition. *IT Governance Institute.* (online). (cited 05 May 2005). Available on Internet: URL http://www.itgi.org/Template_ITGI.cfm?Section=ITGI&Template=/ContentManagement/ContentDisplay.cfm&ContentFileID=4667

Melnicoff, Richard M., Shearer, Sandy G. & Goyal, Deepak K. (2005). Is There a Smarter Way to Approach IT Governance ? (online). (cited 05 May 2005). Available from Internet: URL http://www.accenture.com/xdoc/en/ideas/outlook/1_2005/pdf/it_gov.pdf

OECD (2004). OECD Principles of Corporate Governance. *Organisation For Economic Co-operation and Development.* (online). (cited 05 May 2005). Available on Internet: URL http://www.oecd.org/dataoecd/32/18/31557724.pdf

Shleifer, Andrei and Vishny, Robert W. (1996). A Survey of Corporate Governance. *NBER Working Paper No. W5554.* (online). (cited 05 May 2005). Available on Internet: URL http://papers.nber.org/papers/w5554.pdf

Van Grembergen, W. (2002). Introduction to the Minitrack: IT governance and its mechanisms. *Proceedings of the 35th Hawaii International Conference on System Sciences (HICCS), IEEE.* (online). (cited 05 May 2005). Available on Internet: URL http://www.hicss.hawaii.edu/HICSS39/foscfp.htm

von Solms, Basie (2001). Corporate Governance and Information Security. *Computers & Security 20(3): 215-218 (2001).*

von Solms, R., & Thomson, Kerry-Lynn (2003). Integrating Information Security into Corporate Governance. *IFIP TC11, 18th International Conference on Information Security (SEC2003), Athens, Greece.* Kluwer Academic Publishers Group, Netherlands : pp. 169-180.

Weill, Peter & Woodham, Richard (2002). Don't Just Lead, Govern: Implementing Effective IT Governance. *MIT Sloan Working Paper No. 4237-02.* (online). (cited 05 May 2005). Available from Internet: URL http://ssrn.com/abstract=317319

Table 1. Information Security Governance and Organizational Hierarchy

(ISACF, 2001)	(CGTF, 2004)	(BSA, 2003)	(FISMA, 2002)
• Board • Management	• Board of Directors / Trustees • Senior Executive • Executive Team Members • Senior Managers • All Employees and Users	• Corporate Executives • Business Unit Heads • Senior Managers • CIOs / CISOs	• CEO • Business Unit Heads • Senior Managers • CIO / CISO

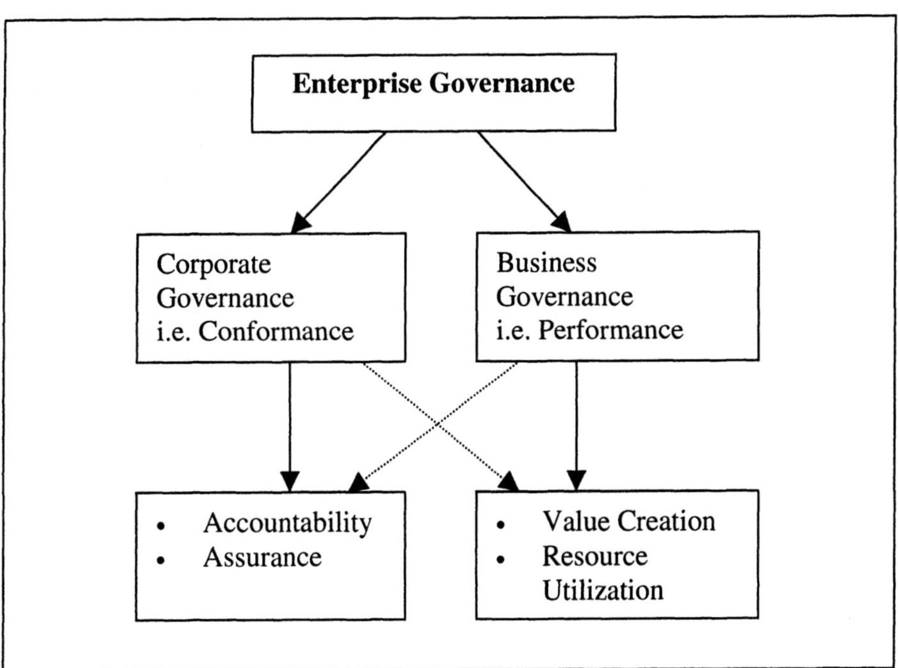

Figure 1. The enterprise governance framework (CIMA, 2004)

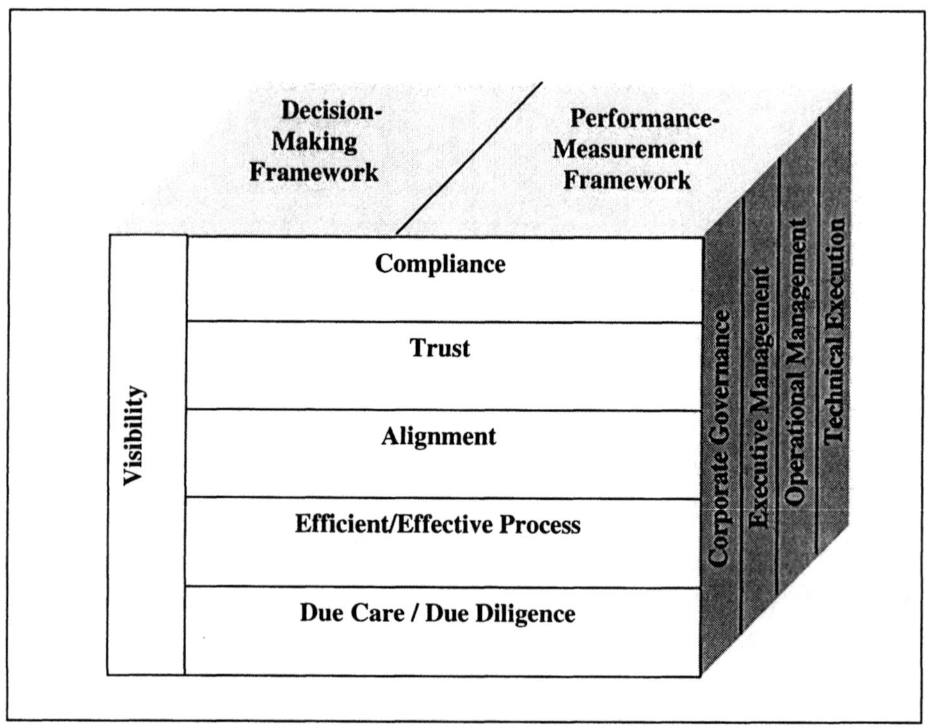

Figure 2. Information Security Governance Model

CAN WE TUNE INFORMATION SECURITY MANAGEMENT INTO MEETING CORPORATE GOVERNANCE NEEDS? (INVITED PAPER)

Louise Yngström
Department of Computer and Systems Sciences, Stockholm University/KTH

Abstract: This paper intends to stimulate discussion, research and new points-of-action for IS/IT security management from the background of corporate governance, contemporary debates of how to express observable consequences of IT and IT security, and of didactic issues. It is concluded that empirical research within IT security management is rare as compared to theoretical approaches but needed in order to have IS/IT security management on par with general management.

Key words: IS/IT Security Management, Corporate Governance, Holistic Approach.

1. BACKGROUND

Having been in the IS/IT security area for two decades following closely the development of thoughts, theories and practices from being seen and handled as a purely technical area into being seen and handled at least multidisciplinary the quest from von Solms&von Solms (2005) to start calling 'Information Security' 'Business Security' intensely focused my attention. The background to their quest is that in Corporate Governance Executive Management and Boards have started realizing their underlined responsibilities to asses how IT is providing added values and increased efficiency of IT to the organization. Governance does this by sets of policies and internal controls, of which information security policies and controls will be subsets (A Call to Action 2000). Also in the background are demands for compliances of controls to legal frameworks such as the Sarbanes-Oxley(SoX) Act and Basel II.

Would re-naming the core concept of the area make a difference? And in that case, does changing "information" to "business" make enough of a difference? How come management does not see that a lot of what is asked for is already there – or at least, that competences, insights and tools exist to be used given that IS security professionals are offered the opportunity to provide their services to the organizations? Have our proposals for communications and requests for funding through presenting elaborate risk analyses not been heard or understood? Have international efforts to develop standards and establish procedures of best practices passed unnoticed? Have current research on the need for users' awareness and abilities been neglected? The list of questions can be made much more exhaustive leaving most of us with a feeling of wading in a mesh of complex dependabilities between concepts where each piece of knowledge has infinite possible relations with other pieces of knowledge.

At the same time there is a feeling of being unjustifiably mistreated and misjudged as an area of proficiency; R&D including practices in IS/IT security has underlined, problematized, suggested, developed, used and evaluated working solutions for decades now. Schultz(2004) comments on these efforts in relation to the US SoX Act 2002; as the audit community studied the provisions of the Act it become clear to them that adequate controls sought for rest on well known and already existing IS/IT security control methodologies. His hopes are that even if it takes time for senior managers to understand the implications – that even financial /information/ systems have to show evidences of compliance originating from IS/IT security controls – their understanding will boost the practice of IS/IT security.

It is obvious that our understanding and conceptualization of the area 'Information Security Management' as compared to 'Corporate Governance' does not come through as equal/useful/sufficient/comparable/complementary to general management; changing 'information' to 'business' would hypothetically underline the similarities and usefulness.

This presentation intends to stimulate discussion in looking for aspects on IS/IT security management as viewed from inside and outside hoping to uncover points of action and research questions to further strengthen the IS/IT security management in relation to corporate management.

2. SOME OBSERVATIONS IN RELATION TO IS/IT SECURITY MANAGEMENT

In 2003 the Harvard Business Review published an article called "IT Doesn't Matter" by Nicholas Carr (2003) which excited a large part of the IT business community. Carr's main argument was that IT no longer gives competitive advantages to business – that is selectively adds value to business - but should be looked upon as any infrastructure similar to railroads or telegraphs. After all, everybody is using Internet – it does not add any values to the business just by the mere use. So IT is not a strategic resource but a part of the tactical cost structure of the business - and as such in need of being managed defensively watching costs and avoiding risks. Thus IT is seen primarily as vulnerabilities and only secondarily as opportunities. In classifying IT as an infrastructure the following traits were listed: governed by standards, not customized, scalable and replicable, one standardized delivery channel, and ubiquitous.

The counterarguments from the IT industry were active; even if IT partly can be viewed as an infrastructure that which matters is what you do with technology as such or the inherent information itself. IT has indirect effects such as creating new possibilities and options, new business models, use new information or old information in new ways, and use stable homogenized and standardized functionalities as platforms for new business (Sarup 2005). An example discussed was Amazon.com; using a common infrastructure as a stable platform created a new business model. However, since the concept as such could be copied the business model could not stay unique for very long thus successively degrading to tactical level. While tactics means efficiently and effectively controlling and protecting what you have, strategic means creating added value in such a way that the full procedure cannot easily be seen through from the outside. For Amazon.com, most of the value adding procedures built on being an early adapter of existing technology, while other examples build on value chains, where the full procedure cannot be mimicked. Dell was mentioned as such an example, where Dell through selling directly to customers got competitive advantaged through distributing goods more efficiently and obtaining information for managing inventories more efficiently, all in all leading to lower total costs as compared to competitors.

Value chains are structures and tools defining how to integrate and evaluate activities enabling a business to create unique over time lasting and not easily copied values. Typically a value chain model includes generic activities; in M Porter's model (Porter 1996) the generic activities are inbound logistics, operations, outbound logistics, marketing and service. The model helps organizing analyses and evaluations of values of strategic choices/activities for competitive advantages. There are unlimited choices possible – to use it efficiently an understanding of the economic levers existing within one's business area and how the strategy intends to exploit them is needed, together with knowledge about temporal interdependencies between value chain processes. There are examples in the literature of how value chains add value to IT (see for instance Burg and Singleton, 2005), but the same procedures for IS/IT security have hardly emerged.

Contrary, the IS/IT security area has a history of needs emerging – or rather mushrooming - from the technical area rather than from business. There were urgent operational needs along with developing control functionalities which later were divided between machines (technical) and humans (procedural). To balance results from using technical and procedural control structures the area was gradually understood as interdisciplinary – to meet demands of not only technical criteria but also human, organizational, and legal. How to define, construct, implement and evaluate these aspects of IS/IT security have been and is researched since long; in essence generally accepting that IS/IT security has to be viewed and handled holistically and inter- or multidisciplinary. Early on the need for management's support and interactions was identified using risk analysis as communication media to demonstrate in monetary units advantages reachable through efficient IS/IT security. Efficient and effective use of IS/IT security methodologies and functionalities were seen as facilitating competitive advantages apart from securing the assets of the organization. Especially all e-models in distributed environments were and are discussed from point of view as adding value to organizations and nations from the fact that without security functionality, e-applications hardly work. However, the value chain concept is not a generally used term in presenting claims.

Most often the communication device with general management is the risk analysis, intending to give a holistic picture of added values and cost/benefits to the organization. Repeatably costs are charged to IS/IT security while benefits and added values are accredited elsewhere in the organization. This seems to give general management the idea that security is only costs – thus of tactical rather than of strategic value to the company. Few studies underline these facts by figures and most models used do not provide such elaborations. I believe this has to do with that IS/IT security professionals hesitate to measure anything inexactly and risk estimates are in that aspect in the "grey zoon". However, two examples using system theory as scientific base come to my mind: one from Gothenburg City (Eriksson 1995, commented in Yngström 1996 p66-67) where costs for (new) security functionality made it possible to use e-invoices with the benefits of lowering costs of handling invoices by 20%. Expected outcomes were tactical as well as strategic which could not be seen solely in the ordinary charts. The second is a much more elaborate model, Business Requirements of Information Technology Security, BRITS, by Magnusson (1999) facilitating to balance IS/IT risks within and together with the ordinary corporate risk environment expressed by procedures and formulas familiar to corporate management. Contemporary research goes towards adapting the ROI (Return On Investment) for IS/IT security sector into ROSI, (Return On Security Investment). Similar discussions occur within the auditing community; Burg& Singelton(2005) claim neither ROI and TCO(Total Cost of Ownership) based methodologies nor the qualitative IE (Information Economics) methodologies avoid being subjective while stating the monetary value benefits. They suggest developing a balanced scorecard to map the intangible benefits identified in the value chain to observable consequences.

No doubt awareness and knowledge of consequences of IS/IT sec functionalities is difficult to grasp for non specialists, including corporate management. Research about usability aspects of security functionality is focused, for good reasons, on end-users. However, we stumbled over managers' understanding of business usefulness of a PGP resembling application while researching how non-linear teaching methods may facilitate users with learning and understanding of using an electronic ID-card as compared to contemporary linear teaching methods (Näckros 2005). While developing and testing the non-linear approach – a computer game – on a group of managers we had some very interesting informal feedback in their comments such as "now I know what's so good about the idea", "aha, this is how it works", "now I understand why everybody is talking about it". Unfortunately we could not go on experimenting with this group due to lack of time on their behalf, but general findings indicated that non-linear teaching methods within IS/IT security facilitate users to operate security functionalities safely – that is to understand the consequences of their actions - no matter which learning preferences or prior practical experiences they have. This exemplifies in one way the essence of holism, where subjective understanding of complex phenomena through some – often unknown – processes form a base for handling /defined parts of/ reality in such a way that the total outcome is acceptable as preferred/assessed by others. Whatever the definition of holism, it seems generally accepted that <complex phenomena> "have to be treated holistically".

During the curricula development of academic programs in information security in the 1990's the holistic aspect was much discussed. It was acknowledged that there were computer professionals lacking knowledge in security, and auditors and security managers lacking knowledge in computing. As an amalgamation of European universities' efforts to suggest a postgraduate academic program three tracks building on four mandatory courses were suggested; one track each for

- Information Systems Security,
- Distributed Systems Security and
- Dependable Systems.

Mandatory courses were

- Principles of information security, dependability and safety,
- Introduction to cryptography,
- Information systems security management and
- Computer systems security.

The course description for Information systems security management was:

"Management of information systems, models, frameworks and trends. The security manager within the organization: Roles and responsibilities. Implementing principles of management. Managing security policies. Fit of business with security strategy. Methodologies for the management of risks and for contingency management. Software for risk analysis reviews. Auditing for IS security. Management of physical security. Global model for information security management: Proactive and reactive approaches, predictable and unpredictable threats and opportunities. Disaster recovery. Business continuity planning. Awareness and incident reporting. Personnel management: selection, training, assessment. Developing and reviewing a security programme/policy of an organsation." (Katsikas and Gritzalis 1995, p17)

It was also identified that most information security professionals in those days were 'ex' something. In evaluations of the practical and academic backgrounds of students in the first Swedish academic bachelor program in Security Informatics 1985-88 7% had previous law studies, 47% previous studies in computer science and 33% previous studies in economics and management. In the same group previous experiences were from police and armed forces 16%, security 47%, IT industry 60% and various working experiences 11%. Amongst positions held by the same group (n=71 where 57 had distinct positions prior to the program) four years after the academic program were Corporate security and IT security manager and general management (14), IT security consultant and security coordinator (18), Project manager and programmer/system analyst (16), IT auditor (5), and teacher (4). (Yngström L 1996, table 4.1A p 105 and table 4-7 p 111). In the same survey it was evident that increasingly the academic backgrounds include law, economics and management, and computer science with a bias to computer science. And the percentage of students' practical backgrounds is decreasing as the average age of university students in the program is lowered; today most university students take the academic program prior to their career in IS/IT security.

Teemupekka Virtanen (2003) makes an interesting remark in a similar survey of Finnish academic and vocational IS/IT security education 1990-94. After various educational programs in IS/IT security people stay on in the same or a higher position within IS/IT security. The same phenomenon was also seen but not underlined in the Swedish study (Yngström 1996): of the 58 persons completing the Security Informatics program 1985-87 four years later 42 were professionally employed within the security/risk area in trade and industry, 22 returned to their former companies and positions while 20 changed positions leading to higher status and, to many of them, greatly raised salaries; however they all (but one) stayed in the IS/IT security area. Virtanen also found explicitly that the IS/IT security managers in 1994 expressed different educational needs than in 2002; even if they stayed in their old positions after the education, they had no longer need for deep specialization knowledge but rather for knowledge on business processes and managerial activities. IS/IT security management has become a managerial position - and a position difficult to be promoted from.

3. REFLECTIONS

In the IS/IT security area generally R&D has been more targeted towards theoretical than empirical issues (Bjorck 2005). This has many reasons, for instance: within the security area as such information about fabrics and details of the trade are usually viewed as sensitive, to collect and analyze such research material of relevance takes long time and large efforts, analyses need to be context and time dependant resulting in difficulties to generalize findings, etc. But it needs to be done, as Ross Anderson already 1993 underlined in "Why Cryptosystems Fail" (Anderson 1993), empirical research will facilitate the area with continuous learning mechanisms useful for adjusting or changing. For IS/IT security management obviously new knowledge and skills are needed to perform as expected – which are they and how can they be facilitated, learnt, planned? Currently two issues seem urgent, if not new: communicate the relevance of IS/IT security to business needs and formulate observable consequences useful to corporate management. One way to express this is to cite one of the Four Grand Research Challenges for IT security in the next decade as expressed by

(Grand Challenges 2003) "Develop quantitative information-systems risk management to be at least as good as quantitative financial risk management within the next decade." I hesitate to rename 'Information Security' 'Business Security', but maybe it will be part of the communication needed. Let's research that issue.

References

1. A Call to Action for Corporate Governance, IIA, AICPA, ISACA, NACD, <www.theiia.org/eSAC/pdf/BLG0331.pdf (March 2000)
2. Anderson, Ross: Why Cryptosystems Fail, 1st Conf.-Computer and Comm. Security '93 – 11/93 – VA, USA (1993)
3. Basel II at www.bis.org/publ/bcbsca.html
4. Bjorck, Frdrik J. Discovering Information Security Management, upcoming PhD thesis, Department of Computer and Systems Sciences, Stockholm University (2005)
5. Burg, William D., Singleton, Tommie W: Assessing the Value of IT: Understanding and measuring the link between IT and strategy. Information Systems Control Journal 3 (2005) 40-44
6. Carr, Nicholas G.: IT Doesn't Matter. Harvard Business Review. (May 2003)
7. Eriksson, Kjell: Electronic Highways in Sweden – Experiences from public sector. Safe EDI in the city of Gothenburg. In Yngström, L., (ed): Addendum to Proceedings of the IFIP TC11 eleventh international conference on information security, IFIP/Sec'95, South Africa, 9-12 May (1995) 6-10
8. Grand Challenges 2003 at http://www.cra.org/Activities/grand.challenges/security/home.html
9. Katsikas, S.,Gritzalis D. (eds): A Proposal for a postgraduate curriculum in Information Security, Dependability and Safety, European Commission, Erasmus ICP-94(&95)-G-4016/11, Report IS-CD-4a, Athens, (September 1995)
10. Magnusson, Christer: Hedging Shareholder Value in an IT dependent Business Society – the Framework BRITS. PhD thesis, Department of Computer and Systems Sciences, Stockholm University report No 99-015 (1999)
11. Näckros, Kjell: Visualising Security through Computer Games. Investigating Game-Based Instruction in ICT Security: an Experimental Approach. PhD thesis, Department of Computer and Systems Sciences, Stockholm University report No 05-014 (2005)
12. Porter, M.E., What is strategy? Harvard Business Review. 74 (1996) 61-78
13. Sarbanes-Oxley Act at www.sec.gov/spotlight/sarbanes-oxley.htm
14. Sarup Deepak. IT Does Not Matter ---Or, Does IT? Has IT moved from a strategic to a purely tactical function? Information Systems Control Journal 3 (2005) 28 – 31
15. Schultz, E. Eugene: Sabanes-Oxley – a huge boon to information security in the US, Computers & Security. 23 (2004) 353-354
16. Virtanen, Teemupekka: Changes in the profile of security managers. In Irvine, Cynthia, Armstrong, Helen (eds): Security Education and Critical Infrastructure, IFIP TC11/WG11.8 Third Annual World Conference on Information Security Education (WISE3), June 26-28, Monterey, California, USA, Kluwer Academic Publ, (2003) 41 - 49

17. Von Solms, Basie, von Solms, Rossow: From information security to ....business security? Computers & Security 24 (2005) 271 – 273
18. Yngström L A Systemic-Holistic Approach to Academic Programmes in IT Security, PhD thesis, Department of Computer and Systems Sciences, Stockholm University report 96-021(1996)

SESSION 6 – SECURITY MANAGEMENT

MEASUREMENT OF INFORMATION SECURITY IN PROCESSES AND PRODUCTS

Reijo Savola[1], Juhani Anttila[2], Anni Sademies[1], Jorma Kajava[3] and Jarkko Holappa[1]
[1]VTT Technical Research Centre of Finland, Oulu, Finland; [2]Quality Integration, Helsinki, Finland; [3]University of Oulu, Oulu, Finland

Abstract: In order to better understand the information security performance in products, processes, technical systems or organizations as a whole, and to plan, control, and improve it, security engineers, system developers and business managers must be able to get early feedback information from the achieved security situation. Systematic security metrics provides the means for managing security-related measurements comprehensively. We reflect on the use of information security metrics by presenting the results of an interview study carried out in Finnish industrial companies and State institutions. Furthermore, we discuss the application of security measurements from the business process and technical points of view. The role of technical security metrics is analyzed using mobile ad hoc networks as a case example.

Key words: security metrics; information security process; performance; security measurement; mobile ad hoc networks

1. INTRODUCTION

In today's information technology world, there is a growing need for information security (IS) solutions: information systems are more and more vulnerable because of the increased complexity. At the same time, information security demands increase due to emerging applications such as e-commerce and ubiquitous computing.

Despite advances in the field, the state-of-the-art solutions still lack clear and widely accepted mechanisms to manage information security in products and in organizations producing them. A major problem is that it is not easy to see the actual performance of the security achieved. In many cases, information security specialists in industry only get feedback from the market. There are no established practices for measuring information security performance for organizations' management purposes.

It is a widely accepted principle that an activity cannot be managed rationally if it cannot be measured. Information security metrics are needed to offer a means of assessing the security performance for business managers, information security specialists and system developers. Information security management has little value without measurements of the business processes and products produced.

The wide majority of the available security metrics approaches have been developed for evaluating the maturity of security engineering processes. Of these, the maturity model most widely used with some security metrics is the Systems Security Engineering Capability Maturity Model SSE-CMM ISO/IEC Standard 21827 (2002). Another well-known model, Trusted Computer Security Evaluation Criteria TCSEC, "The Orange Book" (1985), expresses the security engineering process using classes and divisions as evaluation levels. In the field of software engineering, practical measurement processes have already been standardized – for example – in ISO/IEC 15939 Software Engineering – Software Measurement Process (2002). The security metrics group in SSE-CMM model development is working towards standardization of the measurement processes within the scope of information security management.

According to Henning (2001), a security metrics model consists of three components: the *object* being measured, the *security objectives* (i.e. the "measuring rod" the object is being measured against, and the *method* of measurement. Jonsson (2003) sorts the methods of security measurement into the following topics:

- **Risk analysis** is an estimation of the probability of specific threats, and vulnerabilities, and their consequences and costs – it can be thought of as a trade-off to the corresponding costs for protection;
- **Certification** is the classification of the system in classes based on the design characteristics and security mechanisms;
- **Intrusion detection process** is a statistical measurement of a system based on the effort it takes to make an intrusion.

The main contribution of this work is an investigation of information security measurement practices in industrial and State institutions. Furthermore, the needs and possibilities of security metrics-based activities are studied from the process-thinking and technical points of view. The rest of the paper is organized in the following way: Section 2 discusses the needs for security metrics by analyzing the results of a recent interview study carried out in some Finnish industrial companies and State organizations.

Section 3 discusses information security and its measurements within business processes; Section 4 discusses technical information security metrics using mobile ad hoc networks as an illustrative example; and. finally, we present conclusions and discussion about future work.

2. SECURITY METRICS USED BY INDUSTRY – AN INTERVIEW STUDY

In order to resolve how different industrial companies and organizations define and use information security metrics, it is valuable to conduct surveys and interviews. Security metrics is an area that has not been studied very much. One reason for this can be that the information can reveal vulnerabilities in the organizations; thus it is desirable to keep such information hidden.

In early 2004, we conducted eight interviews in different types of major industrial companies and State institutions in Finland, and analyzed the results using the interpretative analysis method (Sademies, 2004; Sademies and Savola, 2004). The interviews encompassed seven interview themes and a total of 20 questions. The interview themes were:

1. Background
2. Security Objectives
3. Information Security Metrics
4. Metrics Implementation
5. Basis for the Metrics
6. Risk and Quality Management
7. Need for Metrics, Background and Development

2.1 Background

The interviewees mainly represented administrative personnel and product managers. Work experience and specialization areas were separating factors, but a common feature was that they were all somehow responsible for the organization's security. The interviewees were selected from organizations that have a history of co-operation with the research group, enabling a high level of trust in their answers.

2.2 Security Objectives

Defining security objectives is fundamental in security management as the objectives form the basis for the selection of the security requirements that are set in the security specifications. It is also an indication of how well security phenomena – i.e. the threats and security – are understood in the operation of the whole organization or technical system. According to the interviews, there are many types of security objectives with different points of view and qualities, even in one organization, but certain statements can describe the functioning of the whole organization. The most important security objectives for State institutions include:

- building and maintenance of customer trust,
- ensuring critical process functioning and backup of the main activities,
- ensuring congruence between the main tasks and the legislation, and
- backing up the change and keeping the policy optimized so that it is not too strict and thus adds to the user's ease of use.

Typical industrial organizations' security objectives are:

- to integrate information security work into business processes,
- to back up the business strategy, and
- to ensure product security.

According to the interviews, some reasons for using metrics are the need to raise the level of information security awareness and education, and to reduce the risk factors of human behavior and ensure availability, integrity and confidentiality.

2.3 Information Security Metrics

According to our interviews, information security metrics is usually understood as evaluation (auditing, vulnerability analysis, penetration testing) or as observation of system performance, mainly presented by technical means such as logs and firewalls. Also, it can mean measuring how the employees perform their work tasks.

We asked the interviewees what security objectives cause the need for security metrics in their organizations. The objectives are as diverse as the organizations, from raising personnel awareness about security matters to enabling business activities.

2.4 Metrics Implementation

A significant problem in metrics implementation is *the absence of relationship with processes*. There are a variety of different measurement technologies or methods applied, but they cannot be considered as useful as if they were applied in connection to with business processes.

The most hindering factors seem to be the lack of readiness or ignorance on the part of the top-level management to commit to information security issues, as well as an absence of documentation caused by unclear or inappropriate responsibilities. IS measurements should start from the organization's strategic planning. Metrics implementation strongly depends on the kind of decisions the responsible people in the organization are able to make about the information security resources and investments. Another problem, in addition to the lack of management information security awareness, is that some managers that do understand the significance of information security force the IS managers to take all the responsibility. This leads to a situation where top-level management does not commit to the decisions and there is a lack of strategic leadership concerning information security.

Technical metrics are used in all organizations and their implementation is more advanced than any other metrics. The technical means used are mainly PC and network monitoring, incident counting, auditing and risk management. The majority of the organizations use reactive rather than proactive methods.

2.5 Basis for Metrics

The need for security metrics is brought up in standards. Standards are used as guidance and applied according to an organization's own needs. The most common standards are the ISO/IEC 17799 (2001) or BS 7799 Code of Practice (BS 7799, 2002), VAHTI – Information Security Management Guidelines by the Finnish Government Information Security Management Board (Ministry of Finance of Finland, 2004). In addition, there is general related legislation.

2.6 Risk and Quality Management

Risk analysis is one type of security metrics application. In the interviewed organizations, risk assessment is mainly applied so that it is adjusted to the organization's own processes and purposes. The risks associated with the metrics themselves are, however, usually not well handled.

A progressive information security management is considered to be one domain of quality management. Some organizations explicitly recognize information security as a quality factor in itself, and aim to make the information security management a part of their process management.

Information security as a quality factor refers particularly to product quality in business because it is based on the customer requirements. In State institutions information security in the quality context mainly represents issues concerning personnel behavior and responsibilities. Audits are considered a practical methodology for assessing quality management.

2.7 Needs for Metrics, Background and Development

The interviews demonstrated that a need for the security metrics is that they naturally make it easier to analyze fault situations, and this requires systematic data collection and analysis. The metrics are found most useful when predicting or trying to understand future situations – i.e. when using metrics proactively. Often, there is too much information, making it difficult to find the *relevant data.* Data classification and rationalization is important in order to obtain better results, but it also helps to justify the need for effective information security methods. There is also a need for experience from history data collection and analysis, otherwise the situation usually remains purely reactive.

Security policies are sometimes difficult to keep up to date, and the situation very much depends on the personnel's information security skills and management's commitment. The documentation and structure of the security policies are not seen to be as significant as adjusting them to the organization's working culture.

The metrics are useful, not only for getting feedback on the information security level in the organization and products but also for proving it to the partners.

A standard objectively defining the information security performance would be useful. However, it is recognized that such a standard may be impossible to define so as to be applicable to every application field or case.

The most significant and challenging aspects in information security and measurement of information security are, without a doubt, the human factors. There is a need for education and maintenance of continuous awareness. The tool for that is developing the information security process with relevant policies and procedures.

Information security strategy can be difficult to define, and there are many factors that can rapidly cause changes in its direction. The situation will get more complicated as the technical systems become more complex, the threats more diverse and the attackers more skillful. It would be beneficial if the organization could adjust to changing situations by detecting its current state and studying its history, thus making predictions for the future.

Security requirements come from customers and legislation. This increases the value of the skill of being able to resolve customer needs as accurately as possible as well as being on top of legislation and market changes.

Fig. 1 describes some needs for IS metrics that were emphasized by the target organizations. The interviewees thought that those types of metrics would be relevant for the organizations to improve their functioning and security management. The metrics classification is according to Henning (2001), with certain modifications.

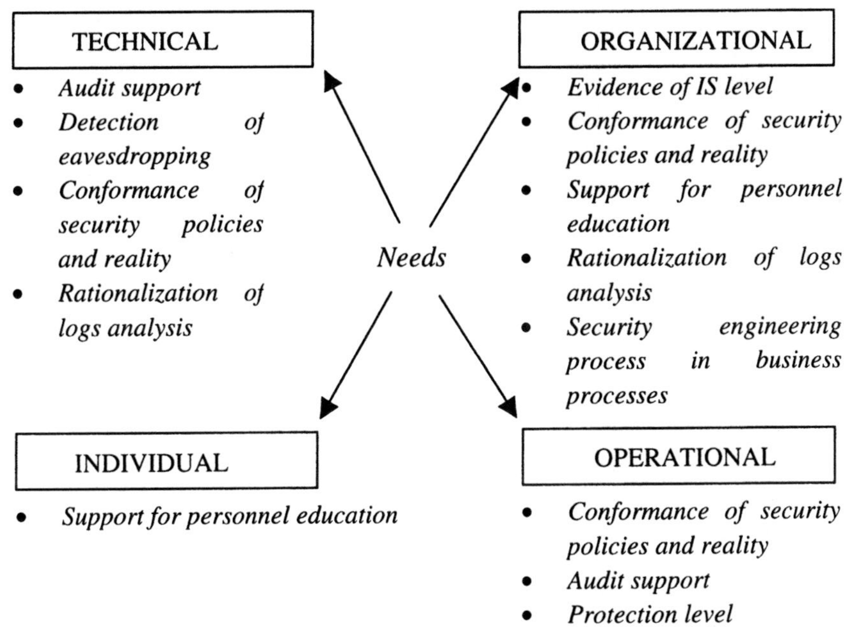

Figure 1. Some needs that are connected to security metrics according to the interviews

3. INTEGRATION OF INFORMATION SECURITY MANAGEMENT INTO BUSINESS MANAGEMENT SYSTEMS – A PROCESS VIEW OF SECURITY METRICS

The implementation of information security and its performance measurement forms an integral part of all business activities, and management activities in particular, both on the strategic and operational management level. Thus we may speak of integrated information security management.

As our interview study shows, security metrics are most efficient when they are used within business processes. In industrial companies and other organizations, business processes are just for carrying out the actual everyday business. The performance measurement process should be integrated into these natural organizational disciplines.

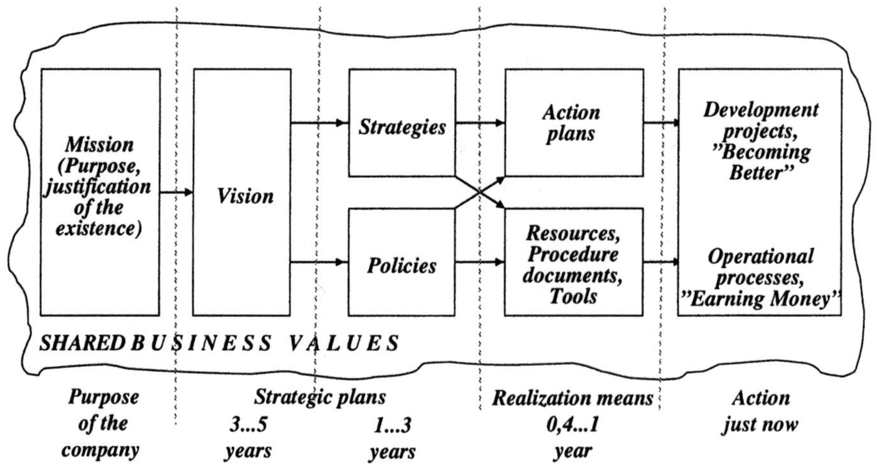

Figure 2. Elements of the business management system form the basis for integrating information security management. Each company must develop its own management practices incorporating the necessary skills for security solutions. Information security measurement and management should be embedded within this management system.

To achieve its aims, information security requires a professional approach and close co-operation between security experts and business executives. A company with superior information security knowledge has a great advantage over the competition, a lead that is difficult to close.

Neither technological solutions nor software-based security measures are sufficient as such. Even in principle, it is hardly likely that information security could be accomplished by means of separate information security systems; in fact, these might cause more harm than benefit. Business management systems (see Fig. 2) have no room for such systems; all business activities must be flavoured with professional information security measures.

According to the recognized international references (BS 7799, 2002; ISO/IEC 17799, 2000), information security comprises a variety of management-related issues, including:

- Security policy,
- Security organization,
- Asset classification and controls,
- Personal security,
- Physical and environmental security,
- Computer and network management,
- System access control,
- System development and maintenance,

- Business continuity planning,
- Compliance management,
- Data and information security, and
- Privacy protection.

Operationally, information security originates from process-related activities and information flows between these activities. Thus information security is affected directly in real time through process arrangements, tools and people which, in turn, are influenced by appropriate and systematic process management practices. As a consequence information security measurements should also be realized as a process management activity.

In today's world, E-Business is an existing reality and offers increasing opportunities to organizations in all sectors. It is important to realize that Internet-based E-Business is not merely a technological issue. The Internet provides a rapidly expanding worldwide communication infrastructure that covers all aspects of life. The net includes all people, organizations, cultures and communities, and it has already changed conditions for interaction as well as behaviors. E-Business is no longer concerned only with explicit data and information possessed by organizations but extends to *tacit knowledge*, which people rely on in communication. It follows that information security should also be adapted to these new business realities. And that is not the end of it – E-Business also creates new opportunities both for business management and operations and - consequently - for information security.

All these issues relate very strongly to the decisions and actions of the top management (the strategic viewpoint) and to the practices used in the management of business process (the operational viewpoint). In integrating information security practices and management, it is extremely important to understand information security issues within the context of business processes. This is because, in practice, information security is a cross-functional discipline, which requires close cooperation and multifarious expertise. Quality management has an established position in many organizations, along with an internationally recognized standardization basis. It has given rise to numerous practical principles and methodologies that are also useful in the field of information security (ISO 9000, 2000). Information security management is fully analogous to the management of many other areas of expertise important to a company. These include, for example:

- Finance,
- Quality,
- Business risks,
- Human resource development,
- Information management and communications,
- Occupational health and safety factors, and

- Environmental protection.

4. A TECHNICAL VIEW OF SECURITY METRICS

In the following we investigate security metrics from a technical system's perspective. A number of technical information security solutions – like Intrusion Detection Systems (IDS), firewalls, anti-virus software – use security metrics internally and as a basis for their reports.

Technical security metrics can be used to describe the security performance of technical objects. This includes algorithms, specifications, architectures and alternative designs, products, and as-implemented systems at different stages of the system lifecycle.

Using product-oriented technical security metrics, both *design vulnerabilities* and *implementation vulnerabilities* can be sought (Savola and Holappa, 2005). Design vulnerabilities can result from an insecure design, whereas implementation vulnerabilities are connected to poor implementation of a product. Thus the former term typically refers to lower technology maturity, see Fig. 3.

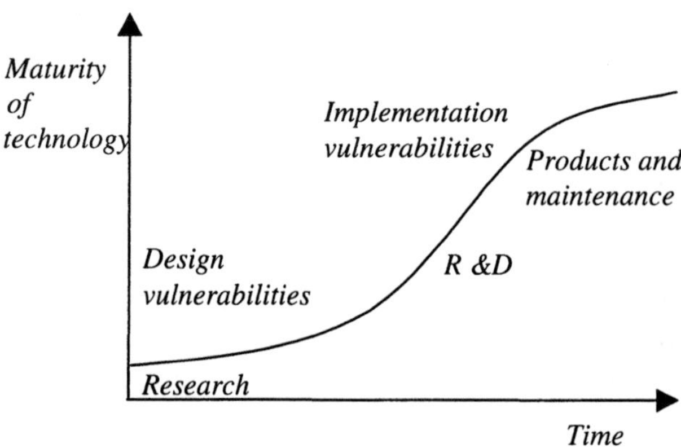

Figure 3. Design and implementation vulnerabilities

Traditionally, industrial-strength technical security metrics solutions mostly rely on the "*penetrate and patch*" or "*tiger team penetration*" approach. The technical systems are security tested by applying common security attacks and determining if such attacks are successful. If an attack results in an intrusion, an appropriate patch for the software is developed and applied to the system. Tiger teams often use dissimilar approaches, and their capabilities and experience vary a great deal. An essential problem is that the manual process of tiger team penetration testing easily results in statistically non-reproducible data.

Technical security metrics can be applied in many ways, including:

- **Goal establishment:** to establish goals and measure how well the object achieves those goals;
- **Prediction:** to predict security performance before implementation or in an implemented system, to predict possible intrusion using an Intrusion Prevention System (IPS);
- **Comparison:** to compare the security performance of objects;
- **Monitoring:** to monitor or scan the security performance of an object (e.g. Intrusion Detection System IDS); and
- **Fault analysis:** in the case of fault injection methods, metrics enable analysis.

The metrics are found most useful when they can be used *proactively* – predicting or trying to understand future situations. Security metrics can be used both for quantitative and qualitative analysis methods. Furthermore, metrics are more useful when they are meaningful for most of the object's lifecycle:

- **During research and development,** security metrics help researchers to develop more secure solutions and to find design vulnerabilities. Global-level security metrics are the most valuable metrics since they give the strongest feedback on security component solutions. Research-oriented security metrics can be constructed using analytical models that take account of factors contributing to security and the cross-relationships of components. Research-oriented metrics can concentrate on the critical parts, especially the technical challenges (e.g. routing and trust management in mobile ad hoc networks).
- **During system implementation,** technical security metrics can be used to find design and implementation vulnerabilities as a part of security engineering. These are also based on analytical models. If metrics are part of a security engineering process, they are more valuable.
- **During the system (product) maintenance phase,** technical security metrics can be used for preservation of the achieved security level during possible updates, integration or modifications, and to find implementation vulnerabilities. From the point of view of the security engineering process, a technical system can be constantly in the system maintenance phase. In addition to preservation of the security level, this level can be improved using feedback obtained from the application of security metrics.

4.1 Case: Security Metrics for Mobile Ad Hoc Networks

Mobile ad hoc networks – or MANETs – (IETF) have great potential for broad use in making ubiquitous computing possible and successful, enabling self-organization and dynamic operation. Applications vary from mobile entertainment to e-payments and all kinds of business services, often with high security demands. The ultimate goal of the security solutions for MANETs is to provide services for the desired security needs, mainly confidentiality, integrity, availability, authentication and non-repudiation, at the desired security level.

Table 1. Some component security metric areas for mobile ad hoc networks

Component metrics area	Sub-component metrics area
Trust and	Initial trust
key management	Operational trust
Routing	Routing information
Mobility	Identity information
	Packet forwarding information
Human factors	Usability
	Performance
	Security awareness of users
	Resistance to social engineering
	Freedom of application use
Cryptographic algorithms	Cryptographic strength
Wireless-ness	Listening
	Interference
Scale	Scale of size
	Scale of use
Physical protection	Tamper resistance of hardware
	Tamper resistance of software
	Location of node
Product quality	Functionality
	Reliability
	Usability
	Efficiency
	Maintainability
	Portability
Other factors	Privacy
	Legislation
	Commercial
	Cultural
	Force majeure scenarios

As an example, Table 1 lists some component security metrics areas (Savola and Holappa, 2005), a composition of which forms the basis for estimation of the overall security level in mobile ad hoc networks. The most critical component metrics emphasize *trusted information distribution* in a mobile ad hoc network. Trusted information includes key, routing, mobile entity identity and packet forwarding information. Technical challenges, such as the trusted information distribution, dominate the overall security level in the first stages of the technical evolution of MANETS. As the technology matures, aspects such as product quality become more emphasized. Please note that the framework presented in Table 1 does not offer an unambiguous view of the overall security assessment of mobile ad hoc networks since we do not know *a priori* the compositional hierarchy of causalities in such a concept as security.

Suitable mechanisms for information gathering from different classes of component security metrics are needed. This is a challenging task and requires a rigorous analysis of the metrics to be used.

4.2 Network Monitoring

Technical security metrics can also be used as a basis for security performance monitoring or scanning. In future security solutions, it might be possible to monitor the *security performance profile* of a network. Different networks operating at different security levels can be interconnected using more rigorous security protocols than networks operating at the same security levels.

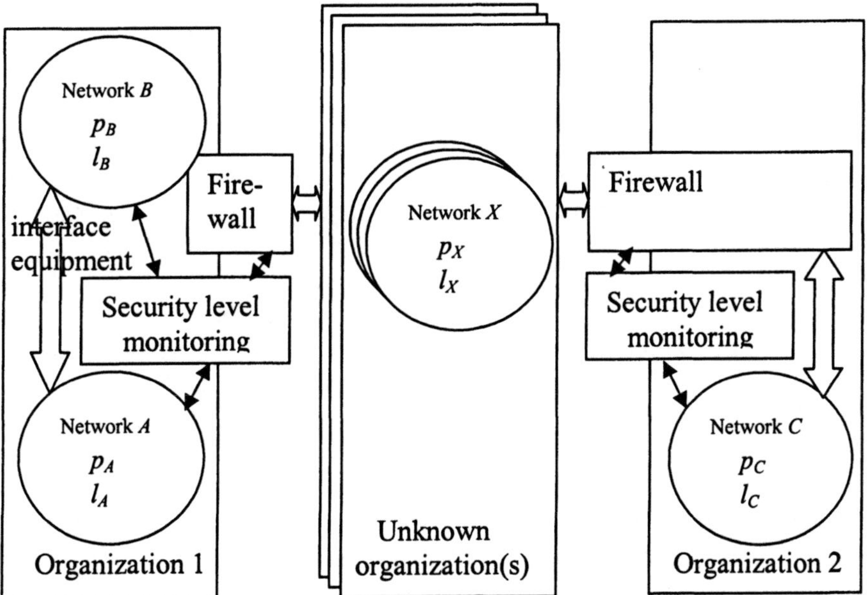

Figure 4. Security level monitoring used to support seamless interconnection of networks

Fig. 4 depicts an example of how security measurement could be arranged when connecting different networks together. Networks may have different security policies and different security levels, and they may be located in various organizations. While having different policies (p_A and p_B) within organization O_1, the networks security policy must be a subset of both organizations' policies – i.e. all policies must comply with those defined at the organization level:

$$p_1 = (p_A, p_B) \quad (1)$$

The organization's network security level is determined by the network that has the lowest security level:

$$l_1 = l_A \cap l_B \quad (2)$$

Administrative and organizational boundaries are usually protected with firewalls. This is to protect the organization's assets from threats that come from e.g. the public Internet without clearly defined security policies. A firewall is often combined with an intrusion detection function, which is one example of a technical security measurement tool.

5. CONCLUSIONS

Information security demands are growing due to the higher interconnection of networks and systems between individuals and organizations. The security performance of products, processes, technical systems, or a whole organization, can be managed if it is possible to measure it in a purposeful way, offering fast feedback to the organization's management. If the research community is able to develop intelligent and feasible mechanisms for the measurement and information gathering, in effective co-operation with the organization's responsible leaders, we might even learn more about the nature of security. In today's information technology world there is a lot of knowledge that has to be combined in a suitable way to assess the overall security performance – i.e. "find the forest from the trees." The current limited knowledge of the nature of security is hindering us from finding rigorous solutions to the aspects of overall security. Information security experts may also learn a lot from other areas of expertise, including general metrology science and quality management, as well as from the recognized measuring practices of business management.

The practice of measuring information security in Finnish industrial companies and in State institutions has not been well studied prior to this study. This study clearly demonstrates the unrefined state of the practical information security measurement practices in such organizations, the theoretical foundations of the issue, and the level of communication among experts and business people. The results of the interview study show that different organizations use different kinds of practices, and the measurements are not integrated with the business management disciplines. One reason for this is that the literature does not offer an unambiguous or consistent means of measuring information security performance. State-of-the-art approaches for security metrics do not include clear guidelines for their practical use in products, processes or organizations. Rigorous industrial-strength approaches for measuring information security components are certainly needed.

6. FUTURE WORK

Our intention is to develop an information security management and measurement methodology based on practices used in the field of quality management and measurement of products, processes and organizations. The quality management research community has gathered valuable knowledge and practical experience on approaches that, with suitable modifications, also have the potential to be applied in information security management.

In information security management, business processes and security policies and principles are used in combination with technological support. Together with business-integrated and process-based security metrics, technical security metrics are useful for overall measurement methodology.

Measurement of information security performance mainly serves an organization's internal business needs. Furthermore, collaborative organizations should be able to communicate with each other on the strengths and limitations of the information security management of their products and business processes.

REFERENCES

BS 7799-2., 2002, Information Security Management Systems – Specification with Guidance for Use. Part 2. British Standards Institution, London.

Henning, R. (ed.)., 2001, Workshop on Information Security Scoring and Ranking – Information System Security Attribute Quantification or Ordering (Commonly but Improperly Known as "Security Metrics"), Applied Computer Security Associates.

ISO 9000. 2000, Quality Management Standards. International Standardization Organization, Geneva, Switzerland.

ISO/IEC 15939. 2002, Software Engineering – Software Measurement Process, International Standardization Organization, Geneva, Switzerland.

ISO/IEC 17799., 2001, Information Technology – Code of Practice for Information Security Management, International Standardization Organization, Geneva, Switzerland.

ISO/IEC 21827., 2002, Information Technology – Systems Security Engineering -- Capability Maturity Model (SSE-CMM), International Standardization Organization, Geneva, Switzerland.

Jonsson, E., 2003, Dependability and Security Modelling and Metrics, Lecture Slides, Chalmers University of Technology, Sweden.

Internet Engineering Task Force (IETF) MANET Working Group; www.ietf.org/html.charters/manet-charter.html.

Ministry of Finance of Finland, 2004, Valtionhallinnon tietoturvallisuuden kehitysohjelma 2004-2006 (The Finnish Government Information Security Development Programme 2004-2006). In Finnish, English summary available.

Sademies, A., 2004, Process Approach to Information Security Metrics in Finnish Industry and State Institutions. VTT Publications 544, Technical Research Centre of Finland, Espoo.

Sademies A. and Savola R., 2004, Measuring the Information Security Level – A Survey of Practice in Finland. In: 5th Annual International Systems Security Engineering Association (ISSEA) Conference, Arlington, Virginia, October 13-15. 10 p.

Savola R. and Holappa J., 2005, Self-Measurement of the Information Security Level in a Monitoring System Based on Mobile Ad Hoc Networks. In: Proceedings of the 2005 IEEE Int. Workshop on Homeland Security, Contraband Detection and Personal Safety, Orlando, FL, 29-30 March, 8 p.

Trusted Computer System Evaluation Criteria (TCSEC) "Orange Book", 1985, U.S. Department of Defense Standard, DoD 5200.28-std.

A PROTECTION PROFILES APPROACH TO RISK ANALYSIS FOR SMALL AND MEDIUM ENTERPRISES

Vassilis Dimopoulos[1] and Steven Furnell[1,2]
[1]*Network Research Group, University of Plymouth, Plymouth, United Kingdom;* [2]*School of Computer and Information Science, Edith Cowan University, Perth, Australia*

Abstract: Performing a Risk Analysis has long been considered necessary security practice for organisations, however surveys indicate that Small and Medium Enterprises do not tend to undertake one. Some of the main reasons behind this have been found to be the lack of funds, expertise and awareness within such organisations, this paper describes a methodology that aims to assess these issues and be appropriate for the needs of this SMEs by utilising a protection profiles and threat trees approach to perform the assessment instead of lengthy questionnaires and incorporating other elements such as financial considerations and creation of a security policy.

Key words: protection profiles, risk analysis, threat trees, SMEs

1. INTRODUCTION

The growth of the Internet as a medium for business and commerce has caused information and systems security to be a growing problem. According to the 2004 survey findings from the UK Department of Trade and Industry (DTI, 2004), 74 % of the overall respondents had suffered a security incident during the previous year (as opposed to 44% in 2002, and 24% in 2000). Such incidents may result in financial losses to organisations, damage their reputation, disrupt the business continuity and sometimes may also have legal implications. Of these, a significant proportion is attributed to Small and Medium Enterprises (SMEs). Furthermore, according to the same survey, large businesses are more successful in repelling these attacks as less than one probe in a hundred resulted in a breach, whereas with smaller organisations the amount was one in fifty. There are several reasons for this apparent weakness of SMEs. Among others, the most important include certain characteristics that distinguish them and put them in a more vulnerable situation compared to large enterprises as far as their IT security is concerned. For example, SMEs have restricted budgets that reflect to their I.T. and I.S. investments; furthermore, as proved by various surveys including the author's own, there is a distinctive lack in personnel with specific IT security expertise being employed by SMEs (ISM, 2002; Dimopoulos et al., 2004b) and this reflects to their security practices, such as conforming with legislations, following industry standards and producing detailed and documented security policies and incident response procedures. These leave SMEs vulnerable to security threats and make them suffer incidents that are costly both to their budget as well as reputation and from which they are less likely to recover compared to well established large organisations. This lack of expertise usually means that security is left to the hands of the management or some general administrator which further raises an issue of lack of awareness on the methods available for securing critical IT assets and correct implementation of any selected countermeasures. Some of the characteristics of an SME that may contribute to a weaker stance on IT security have been gathered by Jennex and Addo (2003) and the main issues are summarised below:

- A relaxed culture and a lack of formal security policies (Blakely, 2002).
- A small IT staff with no security training (Blakely, 2002).
- Scarce investments in security technologies (Blakely, 2002).
- A lack of either business continuity or disaster plans (Blakely, 2002).
- Time, cost, and resource constraints restricting security efforts (Brake, 2003).
- Overly complex security solutions confusing SME staffs (Brake, 2003).
- Not knowing where to start (Brake, 2003).
- Security simply being put aside for more important things (Brake, 2003).
- Proliferation of 'always-on' connections increasing security risks (Suppiah-Shandre, 2002 and Donovan, 2003).
- Believing that they will not be targets of hackers or cyber terrorists and that anti-virus software is sufficient (Jones, 2002).
- Reliance on vendors and consultants for knowledge and expertise (Suppiah-Shandre, 2002) or on a single systems administrator (Donovan, 2003).

There are several practices that are available for SMEs wishing to ensure they are protected from such incidents. A key step in establishing appropriate security for a system is to assess properly the risks to which it is exposed. Without having done this, an organization cannot be sure to have an appropriate appreciation of the threats and vulnerabilities facing its assets, and questions could be raised over the suitability and sufficiency of security countermeasures that they may have introduced (e.g. are they actually providing the protection that the organization requires, and to an adequate level?). As a result, risk assessment, "A systematic and analytical process to consider the likelihood that a threat will endanger an asset, individual, or function and to identify actions to reduce the risk and mitigate the consequences of an attack" (Hamilton, 2004), is widely recognised as necessary procedure in order to assess organisational security properly. However, even though there are a number of relevant tools available in the market, surveys indicate that small and medium enterprises (SMEs) do not tend to undertake risk assessment. Recently, the author's SME security survey found that in the UK 60% of the SMEs questioned have never performed a risk analysis.

Even though the value and importance of a risk assessment is widely recognised, surveys still indicate that a significant proportion of companies do not perform any risk assessment at all, as well as suggesting that the likelihood of the issue being addressed is closely linked to organisation size. For example, the 2000 survey from the UK National Computing Centre (NCC, 2000) survey results indicated that approximately a third of respondents had never undertaken a risk assessment, with the problem again focusing primarily upon small enterprises. In organisations with 100 to 499 employees, the proportion that had not conducted risk assessment was a fairly respectable 16%. However, the figure increased to 31% in organisations employing 10 to 99 employees, and rose to 62% in those with fewer than 10 employees.

Figure 1 depicts the more recent findings arising from the authors' SME survey in the UK. These findings suggest a somewhat more worrying situation than the NCC findings, and further analysis reveals additional causes for concern. For example, of the respondents that perform a risk assessment, 15 of them (73%) claimed to do it in-house. However, only 2 respondents claimed to use a risk analysis tool, and none used any security baseline guideline like ISO 17799. This, considered together with the limited proportion of organisations that actually employ any security specialist, raises doubts about how thorough or effective their assessment may have been. Indeed, given that risk analysis is often "perceived as being complex, requiring specialist expertise" (Shaw, 2002), and that an evaluation of current commercially available risk analysis tools by Dimopoulos et al. (2004a) has shown that even they are not easy to use without appropriate expertise, it is apparent that many respondent SMEs are not well placed to assess risks for themselves.

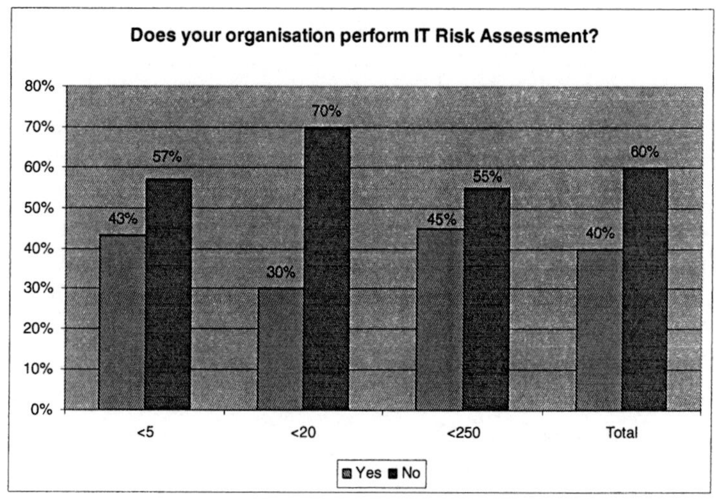

Figure 1. Organisations that perform risk analysis

The authors' survey further looked to establish the reasons why RA is not being performed and found that the main reason according to the respondents is the lack of in-house expertise as illustrated in Figure 2.

More recently, the author's SME security survey found that in the UK 60% of the SMEs questioned have never performed a risk analysis.

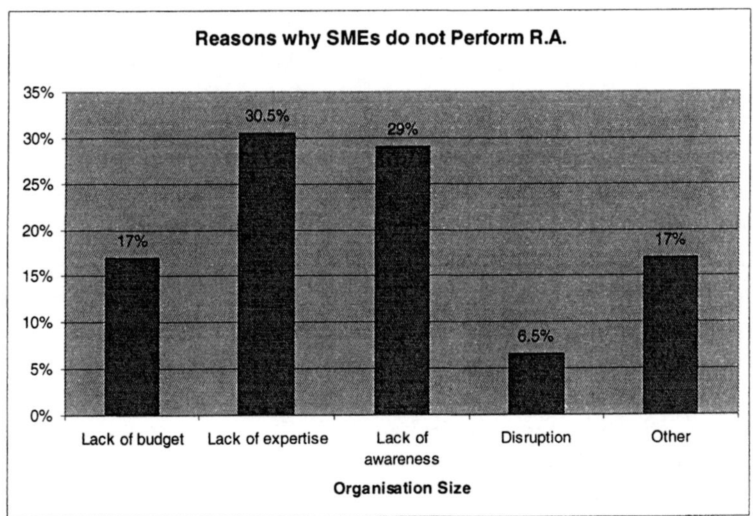

Figure 2. Reasons why some organisations do not assess risks

For organisations that are not capable of performing such an analysis due to the constraints described earlier there are theoretically several other solutions to follow. At present there are a number of approaches available to companies wishing to assess and strengthen their security, but two are often suggested as the best options for SMEs. These are the use of security checklists (Chong, 2003; Hurd, 2000) and baseline guidelines, or a combination of the two (Young, 2002). Security Checklists have the form of questions on common security issues, and can be used to raise awareness on security concerns and ascertain weaknesses (Heare, 2001). Guidelines are an alternative solution that can be followed in order to achieve security at a baseline level, but not as complete as the one accomplished after performing a risks assessment. A classic example of such documented security guidelines is ISO17799, the International Standard code of practice for information security management (British Standards Institution, 2000), unfortunately, only a small proportion of businesses are aware of the contents of such standards.

2. REQUIREMENTS

From what is discussed in the previous sections, it is clear that there is a need for a security methodology that addresses the problems associated with SMEs. In a previous paper, following is a summary of the requirements that have been established (Dimopoulos and Furnell, 2005) as necessary for this methodology that, if realised, will make it appropriate for this section of the industry.

- The awareness issue could also impede the new method, if not appropriately promoted.
- The methodology needs to be a progression of baseline, meaning that it would cover the security requirements of various types of organisations but without being too generic
- The methodology should be designed to enable anyone within the organisation who is aware of its requirements and assets to perform an analysis, resulting in a product which is user friendly, easy to use and produces comprehensive and easy to interpret results
- This investigation does not aim to produce a commercial product
- By incorporating economic elements such as the return on investment (ROI) and the annual loss expectancy (ALE) one of the aims is to make the management more aware of the impacts of a potential compromise (the other aim being to assist the management in selecting wisely which assets are worth protecting and how much should be spent on them)
- As part of the protection profile approach, at the outcome stage, the methodology should produce a profile of the organisations assets and implemented countermeasures which should be easily updateable.

3. ELEMENTS CONSTITUTING THE RESULTING METHODOLOGY

Generally, the resulting methodology will involve three major stages:

- The assessment stage, where information about the organisation and its network will be entered by the user
- The financial considerations stage, where the solutions that will appear as appropriate from the previous stage will be considered in terms of their cost-effectiveness for the organisation
- The output stage, where the user will be presented with the recommended solutions and further information that will be useful for the organisation

These stages are examined in the sub-sections that follow.

3.1 The risk assessment stage

Protection Profiles (PP) are used in this stage in order to simplify the assessment process. PPs are defined as "an implementation independent statement of security requirements that is shown to address threats that exist in a specified environment" (Commoncriteria, 2003). Therefore their function will be to identify what assets an organisation has, how important they are, what threats are associated with each asset and what countermeasures are relevant. In addition, the aim is to achieve this without requiring the user to fill lengthy and time-consuming questionnaires while at the same time enabling users with no security training to perform it. The structure for these profiles will have the form of simple threat trees which will commence from an asset and navigate the user through details for the asset, and conclude to a threat profile which is discussed later.

3.1.1 First profile stage (the initial profile stage)

To begin with, the person performing the analysis will be required to select from a basic set of options concerning the organisation being assessed, its size, function and other basic aspects that are described in this section. This will help build an initial organisational profile.

The type (i.e. which industry sector it is involved in) and size as well as the primary purpose of the organisation (e.g. research) will distinguish typical IT assets and personnel that are found in all organisations belonging in the same sector and rate their criticality to its operation. There are several types of organisations that need to be included, but the ones belonging to the same sector will typically have the same assets which will be of the same importance to them. According to the 2005 threat report from Symantec, even the organisations belonging to industry sectors that are very rarely targeted cannot neglect their security. On the contrary, by comparing the numbers in Figures 3 and 4, one can see that in proportion even though organisations such as manufacturing, transportation, entertainment and telecoms are rarely attacked, the impact of these attacks is the most severe. High tech, however, which is the most targeted industry hardly suffers any severe losses. Such results firstly highlight that organisations from all sectors should take security seriously but furthermore that for each type of organisation the impact of loss of one asset can be far more severe than for another. As an example the downtime of a high-tech organisation's IT network has far less impact, both financial as well as to its reputation, than if the network of a bank is compromised.

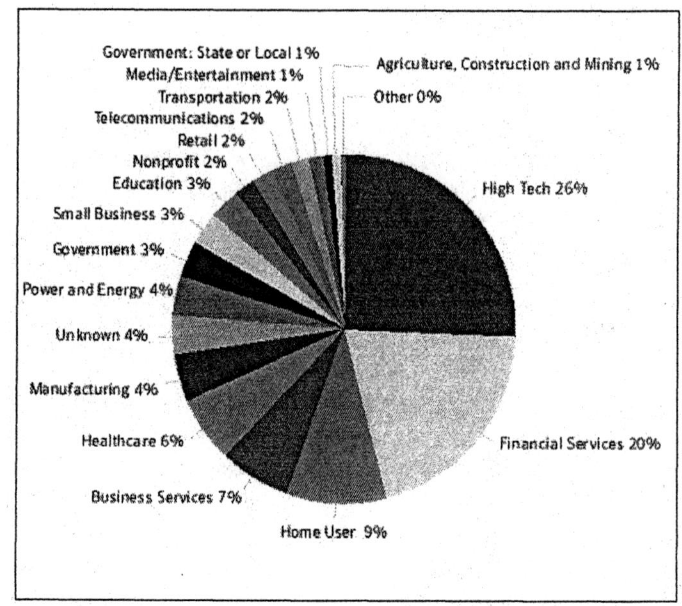

Figure 3. Percentage of attacks by industry sector (Symantec, 2005)

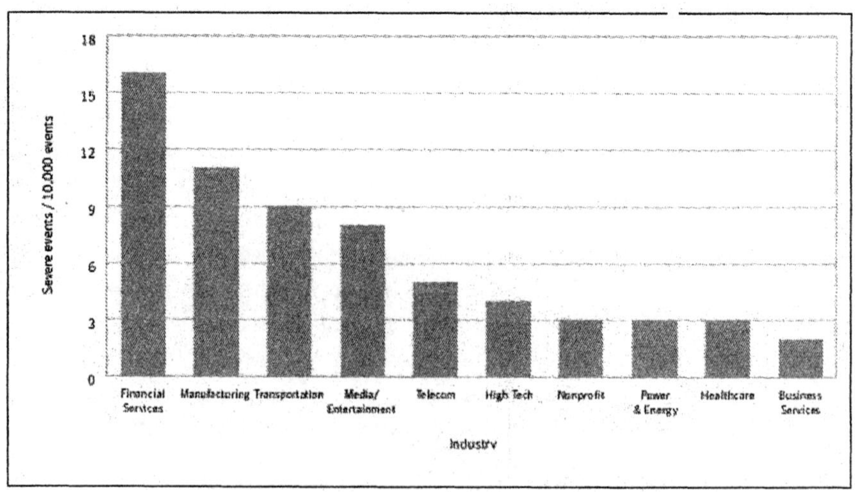

Figure 4. Attacks categorised by severity (Symantec, 2005)

A supplementary issue that needs to be investigated in this stage of the profiles is the geographical location of the organisation. This, in combination with the industry sector, will determine which legislations and standards an organisation needs to conform with. Hence there will be some knowledge in advance of which assets are the most critical and how to avoid their compromise as well as any resulting legal implications.

Another outcome that can be derived when selecting what industry sector the organisation being assessed belongs to and producing apart from producing a list of the typical assets found within such an organisation, will also produce a rating of how critical each of these assets is to the specific type of organisation, enabling this way the tool to set a threshold for the appropriate compromise between security and convenience (i.e. facilitating a decision on how much access and productivity can be compromised to tighten security as illustrated in Figure 5). For example, in a research/university institution it is normally essential that the employees have access to the Internet, while in a bank having an employee browsing web pages is often considered a misuse of resources.

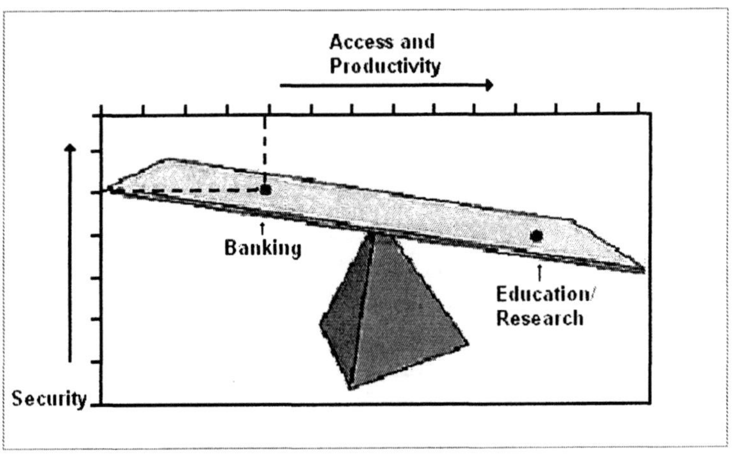

Figure 5. The essential balance between security and productivity (modified from Cisco, 1995)

In addition, producing a list of what type personnel is typically being employed will assist with configuration of the countermeasures issues and access rights to different assets and resources at the output stage of the methodology. Finally, what is further gained from weighing up the level of security instead of going for a "raw" tightening of security approach is that it will also assist in the effective operation of the organisation, in the sense that it will prevent excessive security from becoming a nuisance to employees that actually need quick access to certain organisational assets. As an example, however sensitive the confidentiality of patient records might be for hospitals, it would be almost completely impractical to deploy biometric access security to these resources to doctors that need emergency access to them and cannot afford false rejections when trying to access them in an emergency situation.

A further significant issue that will be evaluated in this stage is the position within the organisation and level of security expertise of the person performing the assessment. This will then determine how technical the particular assessment will be. As a result, if the user is aware of technical issues and (for example) is the one who has set up the network for the organisation, a straightforward analysis can be performed by identifying threats to the assets and what consequences they might cause, classifying the main threats with respect to the potential result towards an asset i.e. (Meyer, 1995):

- Disclosure: loss of confidentiality and privacy
- Modification: loss of integrity
- Fabrication: loss of authenticity
- Repudiation: loss of attribution

and how critical the effect of each would be to an organisation depending and on which industry sector it belongs to. The respondents can be distinguished to several levels in terms of their work function within an organisation, senior management, med and lower level management, supervisory and finally technical support staff. The advantages of making such a distinction within the methodology are that it enables even a person with no assumed technical IT knowledge at all (e.g. a manager) able to perform an assessment based on certain other aspects. Thus instead of asking technical issues, the assessment can be based on the business impact of breach of a specific asset and by considering the business functions of an organisation according to the type of the organisation and the sector thus identify the critical assets.

Moreover, making the methodology appropriate for anyone within an organisation who is involved at some level with the assets or the IT will help eliminate the significant issue of a tool becoming a disruption to company activities, since it will not require inputs from everyone but anyone involved with knowledge of the organisation will be able to perform at least some level of the analysis. This will be further complemented with the elimination of lengthy questionnaires by using profiles. In addition, the level of expertise of the user will not only affect the different types of approaches to the assessment that will follow, it will also affect the output of the methodology which will be tailored to match the expertise of the user. A final consideration that will be carried out in this section is that of security policy issues. The importance for an organisation to have a security policy is widely recognised therefore the aim is for the methodology to assist with creating one. This creates a need at this stage for the user to reply to questions related to the efficiency of any already existing policy if there is one.

All this initial information that is discussed in this section will lead to the tool producing a list of assets for an organisation which will then be used as an input to the next part of the methodology. Since these will include all the typical assets found within the type of organisation that is being assessed, the input of the user will again be required in order to review and discard any that are not appropriate to the specific organisation.

3.1.2 Second profile stage (main protection profiles)

Having established what assets can be found within the organisation and ranked them in terms of their importance (according to industry sector, legislations etc), the next step is to analyse the details for each asset and the possible threats and countermeasures. This will be achieved by creating threat trees, like the one in Figure 6, for each asset. The user will use threat trees to select appropriate solutions in a graphical mode describe these will be combined with a graphical interface aimed to illustrate to the person performing the analysis, the effects of the solutions

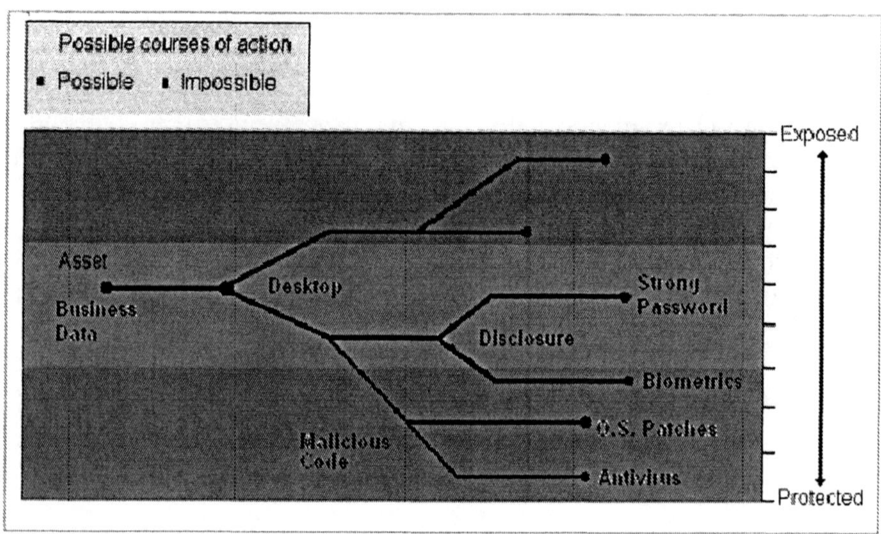

Figure 6. Graphical implementation using threat trees

At the end of each threat tree the tool will produce a threat profile for each asset being assessed.

Table 1. Example of a threat profile

Threat name :	Malicious Code			
Definition:	Software capable of performing an unauthorised function on a target system			
Example:	Virus	Trojan Horse	Worm	Spyware
Likelihood level:	High			
Damage Level:	High			
Countermeasure:	O.S. Patches	Antivirus Software	Firewall	Awareness Initiatives
Importance Rating:	5/5	5/5	5/5	4/5
Implementation Order:	1	2	3	4

Each profile at the final level would include a general statement of relevant threats along with suggestions for consequent countermeasures (including an indication of the level of protection that they would provide). Table 1 is an indication of how such a threat profile will be structured. This aims to increase managerial awareness about the various threats, and assist with the selection of countermeasures, while also suggesting the order in which the countermeasures need to be implemented in the case of an SME not being able to deploy all the solutions (e.g. due to budgetary constraints).

This part mainly concerns the selection of countermeasures and not their configuration, which is an issue that is assessed by another type of protection profiles later.

If this is done for each asset, at the end there needs to be a selection of only one countermeasure for each possibly by contrasting the importance of the asset with the probability of the risk it is exposed to and the resources required to protect it. All three of these factors will have a different value according to the type and the purpose of the organisation and also different weights. For example the probability of the risk will be a factor affecting the final selection of a countermeasure but will not have as much influence as the importance of the asset so that the security of the asset is not actually "left to luck".

3.2 The financial considerations stage

Once the tool will have constructed a list of possible security solutions relevant to the organisation being assessed and the threats it is exposed to there is a need for a financial consideration of the solutions. This is a general issue for all organisations since it is not good practice to invest more funds on securing an asset than what this asset will actually cost them if compromised. It is however an even bigger issue for SMEs that have a limited budget to start with. Evaluating the solutions from a financial perspective will also help raise managerial awareness since it will make clear to them how costly a loss of an asset will be. This stage will therefore estimate the Return on Investment offered by implementing security solutions, a fundamental step for the methodology to become this way a progression of baseline guidelines and standards but without requiring the level of knowledge RA requires from the user.

The basic aspects that need to be considered in the calculation of the ROI. are the frequency of occurrence of a certain threat multiplied by the damage that it will potentially cause if it occurs (in business terms the Annual Loss Expectancy - ALE) and then this will be compared with the cost of implementing a solution which would prevent this from happening.

$$\frac{A.L.E.}{C.m.C.} = R.O.I. \text{ (where C.m.C. is the Countermeasure Cost)}$$

If the ROI. factor in the result of the calculation is lesser than 1 (e.g. if the ALE is £1000 while the CmC. is £5000 this will give at the result an ROI. factor of 0.2) this will mean that securing the asset is not cost–effective for the organisation. The user will then be presented with certain other solutions. In general when investing in a security solution is not cost-effective the solution would be to either leave the asset unprotected which is not particularly wise or mitigate the risk for example insure the particular asset so the cost of a potential loss is actually transferred to an insurance company. In the case that the recommended solutions are cost-effective but due to budgeting issues the organisation cannot afford to implement all the required countermeasures, some other factors need to be taken in consideration and the solutions that have been proved to be necessary will need to be compared between them to determine which is more important in terms of cost in relation with the probability and frequency that a compromise of this asset will occur. The intention here is also to use the available budget as efficiently as possible. A main issue in this stage that requires future work is an investigation into A way to estimate the "weights" of assets, the costs of countermeasures and all the elements involved in this stage without needing to enter exact numerical values which would make it very time consuming.

3.3 The output stage

Finally the output stage which to be useful to an SME needs to be simple, updatable, produce policy and assist with the implementation (the updatable organisational profile).

It is essential for a tool with the specifications described earlier in this paper to have the flexibility to respond to new security concerns as they arise and to upgrade as new technologies become available (Cisco, 1995) but without the need to perform an analysis from scratch every time a new asset is introduced. Being updatable also makes the methodology more efficient from another perspective; since it will be designed to be performed by individuals with a variety of responsibilities within the organisation and accordingly produce results of a different format, what can happen is for example if it is initially performed by a manager and the output is of a more generic guidance form, a network administrator can then get back and perform it again producing more technical results that will compliment the initial ones.

Following the risk analysis, an organisation should develop a security plan to address those vulnerabilities, that present a high level of risk. The security plan should be implemented by a security policy, which defines how security will be handled. (Loukis et al., 2002). The importance of introducing a precise yet enforceable security policy is that it constitutes a first step towards enhancing a company's security by informing staff on the various aspects of their responsibilities, general use of company resources and explaining how sensitive information must be handled. The policy will also describe in detail the meaning of acceptable use, as well as listing prohibited activities (Danchev, 2003). This makes a security policy an important output of the tool and also of great use to an SME that does not employ a security specialist who would otherwise perform the task. This lack of expertise is the main reason why it is crucial that the methodology also produces a document assisting with the implementation of the countermeasures at the output stage. Figure 7 illustrates the complete block diagram representation of this methodology indicating where it will be necessary for the user to provide with inputs, as well as where there are outputs.

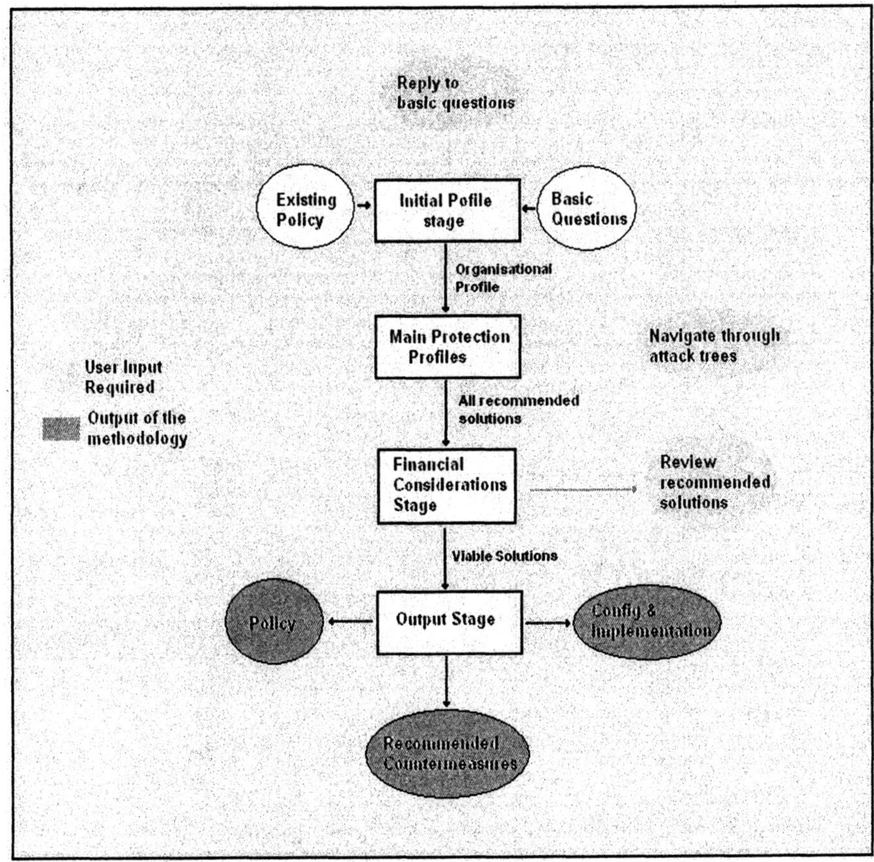

Figure 7. Resulting methodology

4. CONCLUSIONS

This paper has discussed a methodology can be derived that assesses the needs of SMEs. The need for, and requirements of, such a methodology were established from an evaluation of commercially available risk analysis tools for SMEs, as well as from a survey of SME attitudes towards risk analysis (details of which have been presented in previous papers). The discussion presented here was an initial consideration of all the elements that should constitute the methodology. Future work will include a detailed analysis of the components of each part of the methodology, its integration into a tool and subsequent evaluation of its effectiveness (the latter involving representative SME contexts, as well as feedback from security professionals).

5. REFERENCES

Blakely, B., 2002, Consultants can offer remedies to lax SME security, TechRepublic, 6 February 2002, http://techrepublic.com.com/5100-6329-1031090.html

Briney, A. and Prince, F., 2002, 2002 Information Security Magazine Survey, does size matter?, *Information Security Magazine*, September 2002, http://www.infosecuritymag.com/ 2002/sep/2002survey.pdf.

British Standards Institution, 2000, Information technology. Code of practice for information security management. BS ISO/IEC 17799:2000. 15 February 2001. ISBN 0 580 36958 7.

Brake, J., 2003, Small business security needs for the changing face of small business, Micro and Home Business Association, 14 August 2003, http://www.security.iia.net.au/downloads.

Chong, C. K., 2003, Managing Information Security for SMEs. May 2003, Information Technology Standards Committee, http://www.itsc.org.sg/standards_news/2002-05/kinchong-security.ppt.

Cisco Systems Inc., 2005, Cisco IOS Security Architecture, 5 May 1995, http://www.cisco.com/warp/public/614/9.html.

Commoncriteria, 2003, What is a Protection Profile (PP)?, http://www.commoncriteria.org/ protection_profiles/pp.html.

Danchev, D., 2003, Building and implementing a successful information security policy, http://www.windowsecurity.com.

Dimopoulos, V., Furnell, S., Barlow, I. and Lines, B., 2004a, Factors affecting the adoption of IT risk analysis, *Proceedings of the Third European Conference on Information Warfare and Security (ECIW 2004)*, Egham, UK, 28-29 June 2004.

Dimopoulos, V., Furnell, S., Jennex, M. and Kritharas, I., 2004b, Approaches to IT security in small and medium enterprises, *Proceedings of The 2nd Australian Information Security Management Conference 2004 (InfoSec04)*, Perth, Western Australia, 25 November 2004.

Dimopoulos, V. and Furnell, S.M., 2005, Effective IT security for small and medium enterprises, *Proceedings of the 4th Security Conference*, Las Vegas, USA, 30-31 March 2005.

DTI. (2004) Information Security Breaches Survey 2004. Department of Trade & Industry, April 2004. URN 04/617.

Hamilton, C., 2004, Are you at risk? How to assess threats & your ability to respond, Virgo Publishing, Inc., 2004, http://www.publicvenuesecurity.com/articles/3b1feat3.html.

Heare, S., 2001, Data center physical security checklist December 2001, SANS, http://www.sans.org/rr/paper.php?id=416.

Hurd, D., 2000, Security checklist for small business, http://www.itsecurity.com/papers/nai.htm.

Jennex, M.E. and Addo, T., 2004, SMEs and knowledge requirements for operating hacker and security tools. *IRMA 2004 Conference*, New Orleans, Louisiana, 23-26 May 2004.

Jones, H., 2002, Small firms warned over hackers, British Broadcasting Company, BBC News, 9 November 2002, http://news.bbc.co.uk/1/hi/technology/2428983.stm.

Loukis, E., and Spinellis, D., 2002, Information systems security in the Greek public sector, *Information Management and Computer Security*, 2002 http://www.dmst.aueb.gr/dds/pubs/jrnl/2000-IMCS-pubsec/html/ispa.html.

Meyer, K., Schaeffer, S., and Baker, D., 1995, Addressing threats in World Wide Web technology, *11th Annual Computer Security Applications Conference*, IEEE Computer Society Press, pp123–132

NCC, 2000, *Business Information Security Survey 2000*. National Computing Centre, http://www.ncc.co.uk/ncc/.

Shaw, G., 2002, Effective security risk analysis, April 2002, http://www.itsecurity.com/papers/insight2.htm.

Suppiah-Shandre, H., 2002, Security - top priority for all, SME IT Guide, International Data Group, Singapore, February 2002, http://smeit.com.sg.

Symantec, 2005, *Symantec Internet Security Threat Report Trends for July 04–December 04*, Volume VII, March 2005, http://www.symantec.com.

A UML APPROACH IN THE ISMS IMPLEMENTATION

Andrzej Białas
Institute of Control Systems, 41-506 Chorzów, Długa 1-3, Poland; e-mail: abialas@iss.pl

Abstract: The paper deals with the modelling of the Information Security Management System (ISMS). The ISMS, based on the PDCA (Plan-Do-Check-Act) model, was defined in the BS7799-2:2002 standard. The general model of the ISMS was presented. The paper focuses on the Plan stage elaboration only, basing on the previously identified ISMS business environment. The UML approach allows to achieve more consistent and efficient implementations of the ISMS, supported by the computer tools. The paper shows the possibility of the UML use in the information security domain.

Key words: Information Security Management System; ISMS; PDCA model; IT security framework; risk management; development; computer-aiding; security engineering; UML; modelling.

1. INTRODUCTION

The paper presents the concept of modelling the Information Security Management System (ISMS), using the Unified Modelling Language (UML)[1-2]. The ISMS was defined within the BS7799-2:2002[3] standard as "*the part of the overall management system, based on a business risk approach, to establish, implement, operate, monitor, review, maintain and improve information security*" in the organization. The ISMS, based on the PDCA (Plan-Do-Check-Act) management model, should be created and refined in accordance with other management systems (business, quality, environment, etc.) coexisting in the organization The ISMS implementation is unique for every organization and depends on its business needs, environment features, and related risk concerning the factors that disturb the achievement of business objectives by the organization. The standard[3] provides general directions how to establish and maintain the ISMS within the organization. Every organization needs more detailed implementation methodology, basing on a wider group of standards and know how.

The paper features the UML-based approach to the implementation of the ISMS to achieve more consistency and efficiency offered by this language. Using graphical symbols instead of textual descriptions, the UML language allows intuitive, semiformal presentation of ideas and concepts. The basic knowledge of the UML elements is usually sufficient. The modelling approach is growing and the UML approach is commonly used, not only by IT developers but also in such domains as business management, logistics, transportation and telecommunications, to solve their specific modelling problems. The paper presents how the UML can be used by security managers and developers. This will be exemplified by very basic elements of this language, i.e. class and activity diagrams. It will also be shown that a computer-aided tool supporting information security management processes within the organization can be developed on the basis of this ISMS model.

The works on UML extension, called UMLsec[4], provide a unified approach to security features description. These works deal with modelling the IT security features and behaviours within the system under development, but they do not focus on the IT security management process. Some works deal with modelling complex security-related products[5] which consist of other security-related products and require advanced composition methods based on the Common Criteria[6]. The composition problem was considered there a modelling problem with security as its subject domain. Other papers[7] focus on the UML-based development method, constraints languages and tools used for advanced Java smartcards designs that meet the highest evaluation assurance levels (i.e. EALs) defined by the standard[6].

Usually, implementation methodologies are the consultants' know-how and are seldom published in details. An example of the ISMS implementation methodology, including the simple risk analysis method, is presented in the SANS Institute publication[8] but it is not based on the UML approach.

The paper presents a new concept of using UML in ISMS modelling and development. It will be shown that the general UML specification of the ISMS is feasible and, due to its coherency, the ISMS:

- can be better understood by a wider group of its potential users, while ISMS deployment,
- enables more effective information security management,
- allows to create computer-aided tools, based on the UML specification.

By nature the ISMS systems are based on the risk approach. This requires proper risk analysis and management methodology implementation. The paper shows how to solve this problem using the UML modelling approach.

The paper refers to more extensive works on the UML-based ISMS implementation[9-11]. It focuses on the elaboration of the Plan stage processes, i.e. ISMS scope, policy and risk issues. The processes are exemplified by simple UML class or activity diagrams. Some of them have conceptual meaning only, for the ISMS idea presentation. Others were refined during the development of the computer-aided tool.

2. UML REPRESENTATION OF PDCA MODEL

The general model of the ISMS, defined in the standard[3] and based on the PDCA concept, was developed and presented in the Figure 1.

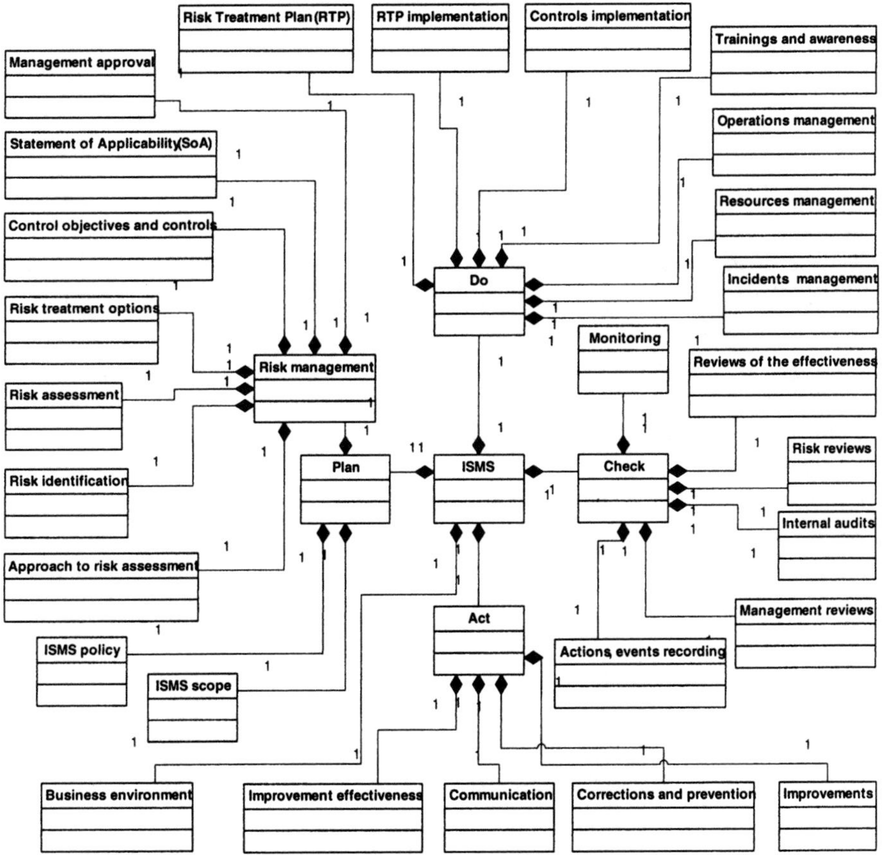

Figure 1. General structure of the ISMS.

There are four stages in the entire ISMS: Plan, Do, Check, and Act, each containing elements defined by the standard. Every class, concerning security management processes or their sub-processes, represents: ISMS documents, like ISMS policy, risk treatment plan; or ISMS operations, like tools for the risk analysis, monitoring or security management support. In reality, the classes shown in the Figure 1 represent a set of classes grouped in hierarchical complex structures that are not discussed in this paper.

Please note that there is one additional class in the Figure 1. It concerns high-level risk analysis and is called *Business environment.* This class represents ISMS entry into business processes and ensures appropriate positioning of all ISMS elements to meet business needs of the organization.

Starting from the *ISMS scope* and going clockwise to *Improvement effectiveness*, all ISMS elements specified in the standard[3] can be met. Please note aggregations linking classes on the class diagram.

3. BUSINESS ENVIRONMENT OF THE ISMS

The ISMS is a part of the overall management system of the organization and must reflect its business needs and existing risks. All relationships between information security and business processes should be identified. The standard[3] focuses on this topic but does not specify in details how this can be achieved.

To specify properly these relationships the *Business environment* class was defined (Figure 2). This class encompasses *Business domains*, where *Business objectives* are reached by means of processes (*Process description*), using *Underlying IT system*, with respect to the *Quality or Environment management requirements* (please note marked dependencies), if the latter exist. Discussions on business environment[11] show that the ISMS business environment will be viewed by the set of *Business level security objectives* expressing security needs. The identification of business environment concerns the high-level risk analysis. Information on risk issues is gathered and analyzed on the basis of interviews-workshops methodology. This information is represented by the set of attributes of the *Business domain* class. The derived global risk value is expressed by the *HighLevelRisk()* operation results. To assess these issues, some predefined quality measures[11] were defined. (please note these classes on the diagram).

All business processes providing business objectives should be analyzed and their importance for the organization should be assessed (attribute: *criticality4organization*). The other question is the level of participation of IT systems in the development of these processes, represented by the *ITDependencyDegree* attribute.

Protection needs regarding security attributes i.e. information integrity, availability and confidentiality are identified for each of the business processes. The business impact, caused by loss of these attributes, is analyzed with the use of predefined damage scenarios (e.g. from BSI[13], like those used by SANS[8]).

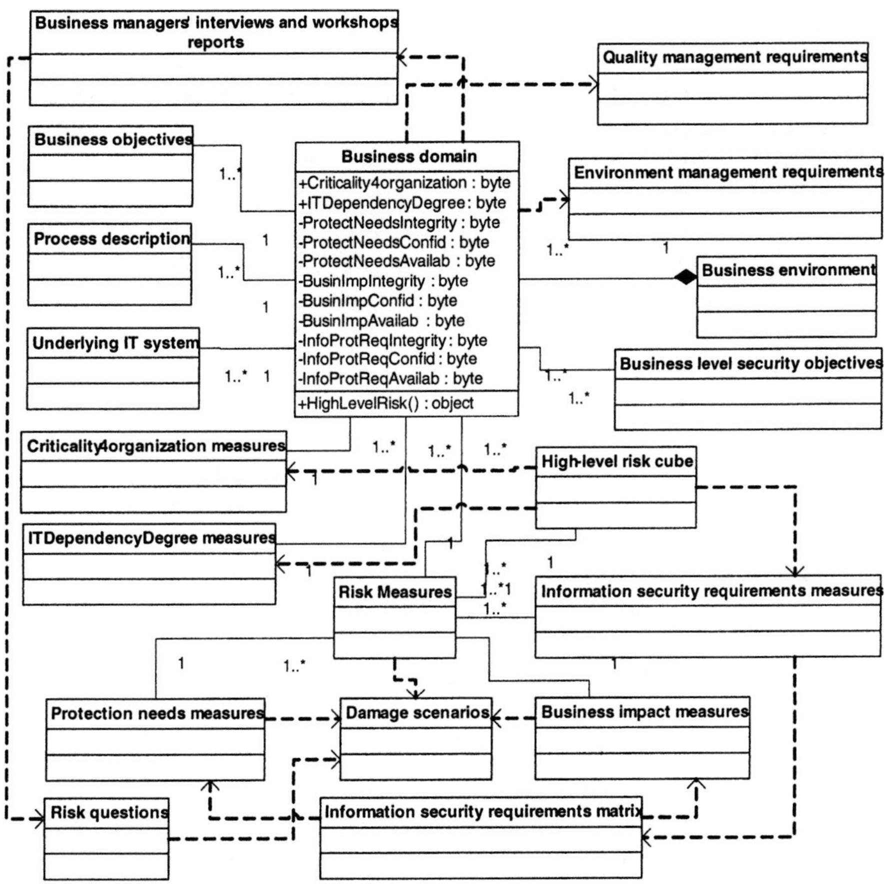

Figure 2. General structure of the ISMS business environment.

The information security protection requirements are derived from: protection needs regarding the security attributes, and business impacts caused by the loss of values of these attributes (please note all mentioned attributes). These requirements are based on the assumed matrix of predefined risk values.

The information security protection requirements, the criticality level, and the IT dependency degree – expressed in the assumed predefined scales – constitute a three dimensional measure of the high level risk within the business domain. This measure is represented by the "risk cube", by analogy with the risk matrices. On this basis, filters and risk views can be implemented, allowing the users to trace different risk factors.

Additionally, the information security requirements can be considered separately for every attribute, allowing to trace the risk within the integrity/confidentiality/availability cross-sections. They can also be considered globally, using a cumulated measure for all attributes.

Different aspects of the above mentioned high-level risk factors and their assessed values can be used for the following tasks, concerning Plan stage processes elaboration:

- to order business processes with respect to their criticality level, IT dependency degree, and information security requirements,
- to set business level security objectives for all business domains, expressing what should be done to meet the security needs,
- to choose adequate risk management options for the organization or its business domains,
- to formulate risk acceptance criteria for the organization.

All these collected data serve as input for a detailed risk analysis performed within the selected domains when appropriate. This approach is a type of a high-level risk analysis, compliant with the standard[12], refined by BSI[13] and used there for partitioning all IT systems of the organization into domains which can be covered by the base control, or safeguarded on the basis of risk analysis results.

4. PLAN STAGE ELABORATION – EXAMPLE

The Plan stage focuses on the information security policy and on planning the controls relevant to the assessed risk level. Before that, however, the area of the organization covered by the ISMS must be precisely defined, regarding different aspects. The basic elements of the Plan stage, concerning the ISMS scope and policy, are presented in the Figure 3. Others, concerning low-level risk management, will be discussed later.

This class diagram is another example of using the UML for the ISMS specification. Both the *ISMS scope* and the *ISMS policy* are expressed as classes, aggregating their subclasses. Their names, belonging to the information security management domain[3], suggest responsibility of each class. The *Plan* includes also the third class, *Risk management*, that groups all low-level risk management elements (Figure 1).

The elaboration process of the *ISMS scope* elements placed in the Figure 3, based on the *Business environment* (Figure 2), is shown in the Figure 4 as an example of the UML activity diagram. Any activity may use objects (please note underlined names) of given classes on input, producing or modifying other objects on its output. Some actions can be done concurrently. Generally, it is the simplest way to present an activity during the elaboration process, though sequence or collaboration diagrams can also be useful. The UML sequence diagrams are similar to well known block schemes of algorithms.

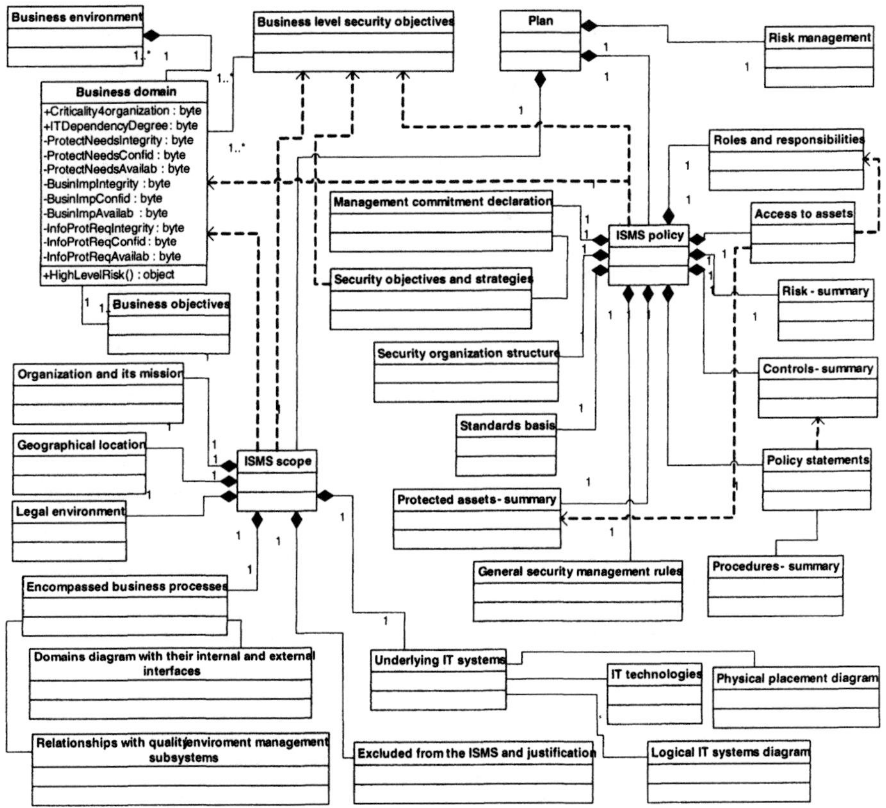

Figure 3. The Plan stage elements – the ISMS scope and policy.

Starting from a short presentation of the organization's mission (i.e. previously identified business objectives), geographical location, legal environment (acts and statutory regulations should be compliant), a business processes map is created with consideration of the underlying IT systems and their placement. For some areas of the organization excluded from the ISMS, justification is needed. Any organization ought to have assets inventory, encompassing different types of assets, including sensitive information. The presented approach assumes identification of assets based on the previously specified business domains. The assets may have different roles assigned, e.g. owner, administrator, responsible person, etc. For this reason the adequate security organization structure and roles should be established. Please note that most of the *ISMS scope* specification elements can be derived directly from the previously specified objects of classes belonging to the *Business environment* class.

For well defined management scope, the management rules can be assumed, described by the *ISMS policy* class. Its basic elements are presented in the Figure 3.

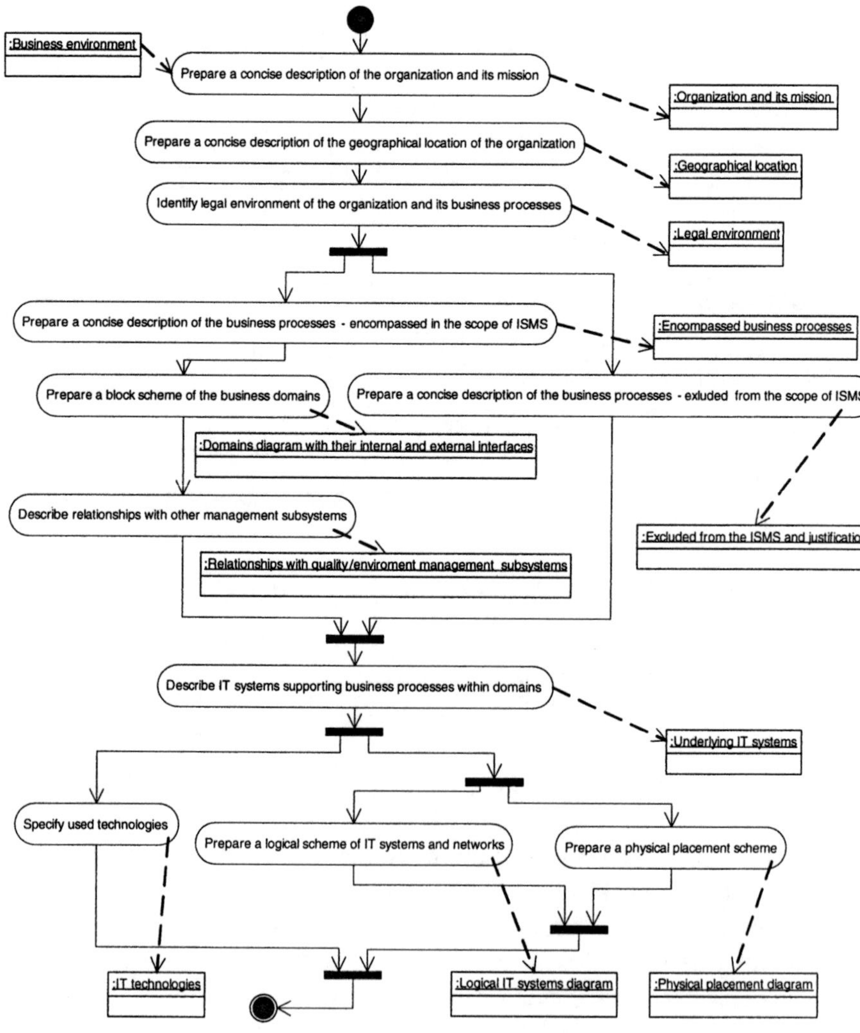

Figure 4. The ISMS scope elaboration.

The Figure 5 features another UML example, showing how to elaborate them.

Please note that the *ISMS policy* can be completed as a result of risk assessment and treatment.

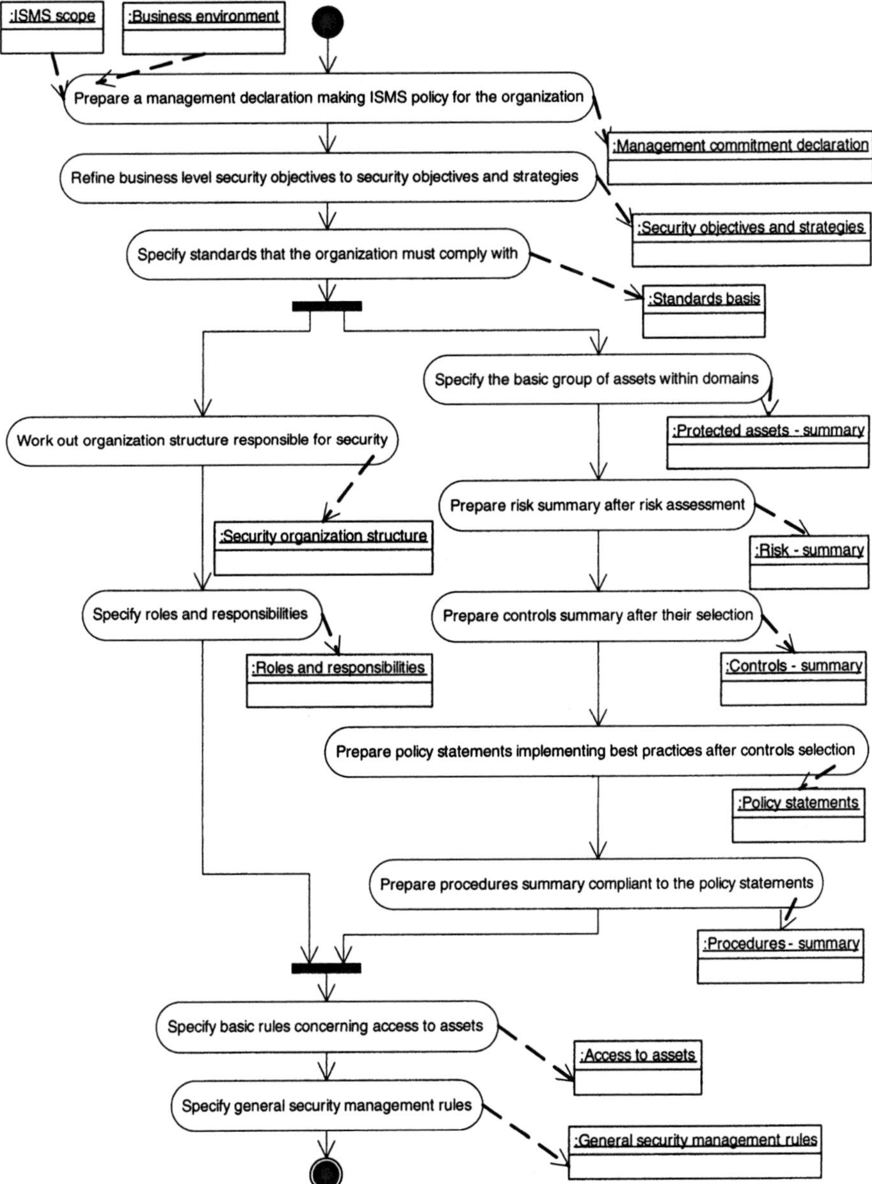

Figure 5. The ISMS policy elaboration.

The main *Risk management* elements belonging to the class *Plan*, and access control elements are presented in the Figure 6. The business domains usually differ from one another with respect to the following: high-level risk assessed, underlying IT systems and working environment. Thus, low-level risk management can be provided separately for every domain in accordance with the risk approach applied by the organization.

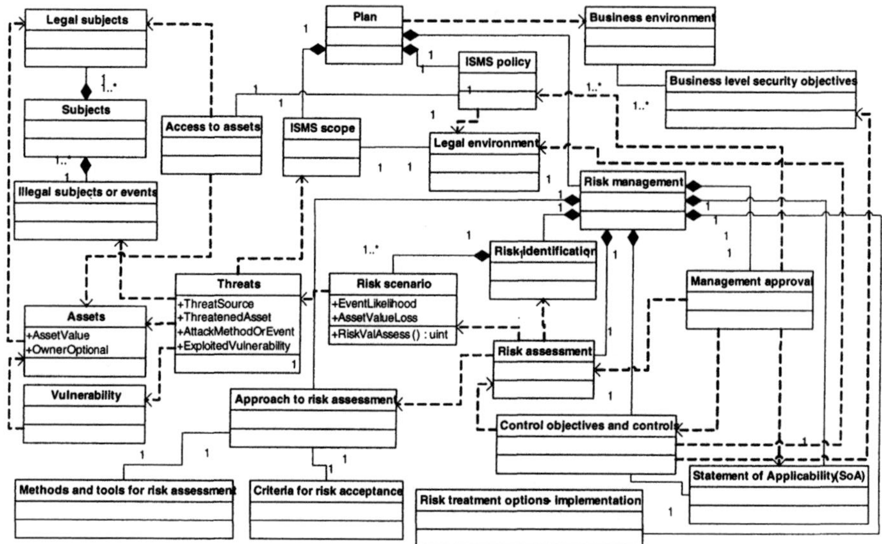

Figure 6. The Plan stage elements dealing with low-level risk management.

A detailed (low-level) risk analysis approach[12] was implemented. The elaboration of the *Risk management* elements is not discussed in detail but it is very similar to the actions previously presented on activity diagrams. The diagram also presents access control management to assets. Similarly to the concept presented in the author's paper[14], *Legal* and *Illegal subjects or events* classes were specified. The *Access to assets* class specifies access rules of any *Legal subject.*

The *Illegal subjects or events* class represents forces exploiting *Vulnerability* and initiating *Threats* for the *Assets*. Any of these undesirable events is described by the *Risk scenario*. The assessed risk value depends on the loss of the asset value and the event likelihood (please note appropriate class attributes). The presented detailed risk analysis can be qualitative, quantitative or mixed mode. Please note that some risk management issues, as summary information, can be added now to the *ISMS policy*.

The *Control objectives and controls* are derived from the *Business level security objectives*, *Risk assessment* and *Legal environment* classes, and will be used to obtain a set of recommended safeguards during control implementation (Do stage is not discussed). They need justification (why selected/rejected) represented by the *Statement of Applicability (SoA)* class. At the completion of the standard Plan stage efforts, all data needed for the risk treatment plan elaboration and deployment are prepared (Do stage). The elements presented in the Figure 6 provide a risk management framework for the ISMS, used and updated during the whole ISMS life cycle.

5. CONCLUSIONS

The paper deals with the ISMS specification based on the UML. It encompasses all PDCA stages including the introductory high-level risk analysis for appropriate positioning of the whole model within the organization. The UML-approach for the ISMS specification was exemplified on the Plan stage elaboration. Using Plan stage specification, all structures – Do, Check, and finally, Act, can be successively elaborated, but it is not discussed there. Only main class diagrams and activity diagrams were shown in the paper. Use-case models, the assumed 4-layer software architecture and its implementation were not discussed there either.

The presented concept was used for the development of the prototype of a computer-aided tool[15], supporting information security managers, shown in the Figure 7 as the example. The application window contains main Plan stage elements, developed on the basis of high-level risk analysis results presented in the business environment window.

All main PDCA elements are implemented in the current version of the prototype at the basic level, while some details and features are still under development. The first feedback from customers shows that the tool is useful during security management – all activities are coordinated, records are sampled, the integrated tools and documents can be quickly reached, and internal security audits/reviews can be performed. Aside from BS 7799 compatible checklists, the tool has many others built in, concerning different legal and technical issues.

The first developers' experiences show that:

- taking advantage of the UML approach is fully possible for the ISMS implementation, just like in many other areas of the UML deployment,
- thanks to the UML it is possible to specify the entire ISMS and its processes in a modular way – methods, measures, tools, document templates can be changed,
- this flexibility allows tailoring the ISMS according to the size and specific needs of the organization (document templates defined for the assumed organization profiles).

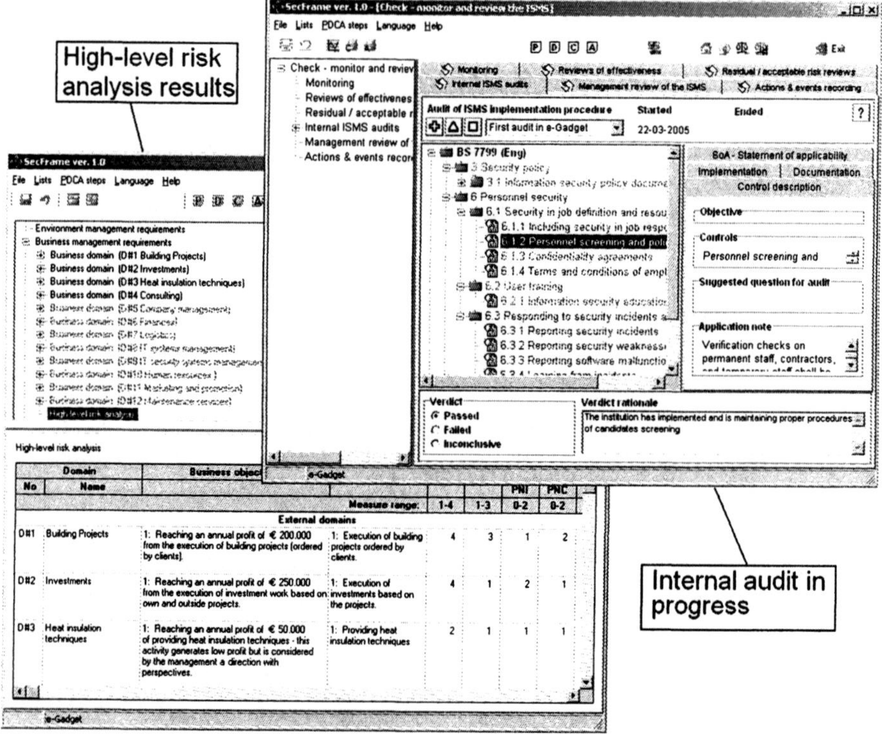

Figure 7. Information security management supporting tool[15].

In the same way it is possible to specify: business and its managing processes, security and its managing processes, IT systems and their managing processes and other assets – it is possible to create a unified information security management framework, well positioned within the business environment, basing on the UML approach. It can be assumed that the UML approach should be promising for the information security management as well, although this research area still needs further investigation.

REFERENCES

1. Booch G., Rumbaugh J., Jacobson I.: UML - Przewodnik użytkownika , Wyd. II, WNT, Warszawa 2002, (UML – User Guide).
2. UMLsite http://www.omg.org/uml/
3. BS-7799-2:2002 Information security management systems – Specification with guidance for use, British Standard Institution.
4. Jürjens J.: Secure Systems Development with UML, Springer-Verlag, 2004.

5. Galitzer S.: Introducing Engineered Composition (EC): An Approach for Extending the Common Criteria to Better Support Composing Systems, WAEPSD Proc., 2003.
6. Common Criteria for IT Security Evaluation, Part 1-3, ISO/IEC 15408.
7. Lavatelli C.: EDEN: A formal framework for high level security CC evaluations, e-Smart' 2004, Sophia Antipolis 2004.
8. Kadam Avinash: Implementation Methodology for Information Security Management System, v.1.4b, SANS Institute 2003.
9. Białas A.: IT security modelling, The 2005 International Conference on Security and Management, The World Congress In Applied Computing Las Vegas, June 20-23, 2005.
10. Białas A.: Designing and management framework for ICT Security, Joint Research Centre Cyber-security workshop, Gdansk, 9-11 September 2004.
11. Białas A.: The ISMS Business Environment Elaboration Using a UML Approach, KKIO (National Conference on Software Eng.), Cracow, 2005 (to be published by IOS Press).
12. ISO/IEC TR 13335-3:1998, Information technology – Guidelines for the management of IT Security, Part3: Techniques for the management of IT Security.
13. IT Grundschutz Handbuch, BSI – Bonn: http://www.bsi.de
14. Białas A.: IT security development – computer-aided tool supporting design and evaluation, In: Kowalik J, Górski J., Sachenko A. (editors): Cyberspace Security and Defense: Research Issues, NATO Science Series II, vol. 196, Springer 2005.
15. SecFrame: http://www.iss.pl

ACKNOWLEDGEMENT

The author wishes to thank the Director of the Institute of Control Systems for the permission to publish screenshots of the SecFrame application (Figure 7).

SESSION 7 – APPLICATIONS

ATTACK AWARE INTEGRITY CONTROL IN DATABASES (INVITED ABSTRACT)

Peng Liu
School of Information Sciences and Technology, The Pennsylvania State University, University Park, PA 16802, USA

Abstract: Traditional database integrity control is focused on handling integrity constraint violations caused by failures and operator mistakes. However, as there are more and more malicious attacks on database systems, the traditional integrity control concept becomes too *narrow* to handle data integrity degradation caused by malicious attacks. In this talk, we present a framework of attack-aware database integrity control, where the concept of *attack-aware integrity* is investigated, a set of new integrity control problems are identified and the corresponding solutions are explored.

Key words: Database integrity; attack-aware integrity.

CHARACTERISTICS AND MEASURES FOR MOBILE-MASQUERADER DETECTION

Oleksiy Mazhelis
Information Technology Research Institute
University of Jyväskylä
P.O. Box35, FIN-40014, Jyväskylä, Finland
mazhelis@titu.jyu.fi

Seppo Puuronen
Department of Computer Science and Information Systems
University of Jyväskylä
P.O. Box35, FIN-40014, Jyväskylä, Finland
sepi@it.jyu.fi

Abstract Personal mobile devices, as mobile phones, smartphones, and communicators can be easily lost or stolen. Due to the functional abilities of these devices, their use by an unintended person may result in a severe security incident concerning private or corporate data and services. Organizations develop their security policy and mobilize preventive techniques against unauthorized use. Current solutions, however, are still breakable and there still exists strong need for means to detect user substitution when it happens. A crucial issue in designing such means is to define what measures to monitor.

In this paper, an attempt is made to identify suitable characteristics and measures for mobile-user substitution detection. Our approach is based on the idea that aspects of user behavior and environment reflect user's personality in a recognizable way. The paper provides a tentative list of individual behavioral and environmental aspects, along with characteristics and measures to represent them.

Keywords: Mobile Terminal Security, User Profiling, Masquerader Detection

1. Introduction

Today, mobile devices have become a convenient and often essential component assisting us in our everyday life. These devices are becoming increasingly powerful, and the number of features and services available to their users is growing steadily. Some of the abilities of modern mobile devices are essential also from the security perspective. Among them are i) the ability to store (private and corporate) data, ii) the ability to perform mobile e-transactions, and iii) the ability to access a corporate intranet. These abilities pose security concerns, since only the legitimate user of the device should be permitted to access the private data and the corporate intranet, or to carry out mobile e-transactions allowed to the device. While these concerns are common for laptops and networked workstations, the problem is still more severe with mobile devices because they can be more easily lost or stolen – according to [16], 24% of PDA users experienced a loss or theft of at least one of their PDAs. Currently, in order to ensure the legitimacy of a user, an authentication procedure is performed, usually consisting in entering PIN/password by a claimant (a device user whose legitimacy is not verified yet). The authentication process is usually launched when the device is being turned on, or after idle time. However, many users find such protection mechanism inconvenient and do not use it [6]. Besides, sometimes a possibility exists to bypass the authentication procedure, or the authentication password can be compromised thus enabling illegal use of the device. Therefore, there is a strong need for further security means to resist the use of a mobile device by a non-legitimate person.

This paper is aimed at addressing the issue of detective security services in the context of mobile devices. We focus on the problem of *mobile-masquerader detection*, where masquerading can be defined as the use of the device's protected resources by an individual other than the legitimate user. In the context of a mobile device, the protected resources are the device itself along with the information stored on it, and allowed services.

The detective security means are based on the assumption that both normal and malicious activities are manifested in system audit traces, and that malicious activity can be detected through the analysis of these traces. A crucial issue in designing such means is to define what measures to monitor, and what models to assign to these measures [22, 10, 19]. However, the available frameworks, models, methods and approaches for detecting security breaches are often based on various heuristics and intuition of experts (as in [2, 9, 11, 20]), or are largely data-driven (as in [18, 8, 12]). As pointed out by McHugh, many works in intrusion detection have been based on "a combination of intuition and brute-force techniques" [15, p. 14]. Furthermore, these works are targeted at networked workstations and servers, and hence do not take into account the peculiarities of personal mobile devices.

In this paper, we consider the mobile-masquerader detection problem from *user identity verification* (UIV) point of view. The fact that cognitive processes of each human are individual is utilized in the paper. This part of psychological personality is a natural choice to verify one's identity. The difficulty is that the psychological personality cannot be directly observed and measured. To solve this problem, we relate the psychological personality to one's behavior and environment, by using Bandura's social cognitive theory [3] outlined in Section 3.2. Furthermore, the decomposition of human personality into multiple factors according to the multifactor theory of personality [17] as described in Section 3.1 is projected in individual aspects of behavior (considered in Section 4) and individual aspects of environment (considered in Section 5). Thereafter, some characteristics to describe these individual aspects are hypothesized, and the measures to represent these characteristics are proposed in Section 6. While the measures to be assigned to various characteristics are hypothesized in the paper, neither statistical nor other models to be assigned to these measures are considered.

2. Masquerader detection

Intrusion detection is aimed at revealing any deliberate unauthorized attempt to access information, manipulate information, or render a system unreliable or unusable [22]. Among the attacks, which intrusion detection techniques are supposed to detect is the masquerade attack, i.e. an attack performed by an impostor who masquerades as a user with legitimate access to sensitive data.

Intrusion detection approaches may be divided into those based on anomaly detection and those based on misuse detection. Approaches based on anomaly detection track user behavior and try to determine (on the basis of users' personal profiles) whether their current activities are consistent with an established norm. Contrary, misuse detection utilizes the knowledge about unacceptable behavior and directly searches for it.

In the context of masquerader detection, the above two approaches can be described as follows:

- *Masquerader detection via user identity verification.* The first approach involves continuous verification of user identity. In other words, it verifies whether the user is present and alarms if verification fails. This is therefore following the anomaly detection approach in the sense that deviations from an established norm are searched for.

- *Masquerader detection via impostor recognition.* The second approach is complementary to the first one and involves detecting predefined patterns associated with impostor activity or identity. Thus, it is aimed at detecting the presence of an impostor, and is following the misuse detection approach.

Most (if not all) of the masquerader detection techniques following anomaly detection approach, explicitly or implicitly assume the individuality of user behavior. For example, in the paper presenting neural network intrusion detection, the authors stated that they "believe that a user leaves a 'print' when using the system; a neural network can be used to learn this print and identify each user much like detectives use thumbprints to place people at crime scenes" [18, p. 943], and, later, "the set of commands used and their frequency, therefore, constitute a 'print' of the user, reflecting the task of the user and the choice of application programs, and it should be possible to identify the user based on this information" [18, p. 945].

Analysis of user behavior characteristics has proven fruitful in many approaches to anomaly intrusion detection, whose functioning involve detecting anomalies in user behavior. Probably the most often cited is the statistical approach used in NIDES [1]. More recently, many other approaches have been investigated as reported in [23], [19], [13], [11], [18], [24], and [20], to mention a few. In these approaches, different measures are monitored to model user behavior: frequencies and sequences of Unix shell commands or system calls, temporal parameters of user actions and temporal intervals between them, etc. The reported results indicate the feasibility of the use of these measures for masquerader detection. User behavior has not explicitly been considered. Rather, the choice of characteristics has been data and technology driven, i.e. governed by available data and processing techniques. The choice itself is based either on the intuition of researchers or other experts (as in [18]), or on the supporting knowledge discovery tools juxtaposing the data describing the behavior of different users (as in [12]).

Contemporary masquerader detection techniques may be enhanced. Namely, the set of measures currently employed in masquerader detection is limited and may be extended by taking into consideration individual behavioral and environmental aspects. Additional characteristics and measures may provide further information describing the user, and consequently, the detection accuracy may be improved. Besides, the reported techniques dealt with static hosts; i.e. masquerader detection techniques are rarely tailored to mobile computers or other mobile devices. The work of [25] and [21] taking into account mobility patterns of users for intrusion detection purposes are rather exceptional.

3. Employing personality factors for masquerader detection

Personality can be defined as "a dynamic organization, inside the person, of psychophysical systems that create a person's characteristic patterns of behavior, thoughts, and feelings" [5, p. 5]. From trait perspective, personality traits are considered as dimensions of individual differences that influence patterns of thoughts, feelings and actions [14]. According to [14], these traits represent individual difference variables. In this paper, an attempt is made to employ these individual differences for distinguishing between the user and a substitute, and personality is seen as a complex of relatively enduring aspects which make a person distinct from other individuals.

3.1 Multifactor-systems theory of individuality

Royce and Powell [17] present the theory of individuality and personality, which is "a comprehensive theory about how individuals differ from each other psychologically and how such differences give rise to differences in integrative personality, including world view, life style and self-image" [17, p. 5]. The theory hypothesizes that personality is composed of mutually interacting sensory, motor, cognition, affect, style, and value systems. The total psychological system is defined to be "a hierarchical organization of systems, subsystems, and traits that transduce, transform, and integrate psychological information" [17, p. 10].

According to the theory, personality is hierarchically organized. The six systems comprising personality can be divided into high-, middle- and low-level systems (Figure 1). The higher level systems in comparison with lower level systems "are concerned with longer units of time"; "have a higher priority of action", "are more closely related to the deeper (in the sense of significant) levels or aspects of personality" [17, p. 12]. Each system itself is further considered to include several subsystems. Moreover, each system is decomposed into a hierarchy of factors at several levels, from the lowest-level factors (first-order factors) to highest-level factors indicating the systems and subsystems of personality.

Factor values determine processes within various personality systems, e.g. values of the factors of the value system describe goal-seeking processes. At the same time, the goals established are not processes any more but rather "records in memory", i.e. storages. Such storages include goals established, the knowledge (operators, invariants) obtained, and the motor programs constructed. Due to individual differences and due to differences in learning environments, the content of the storages

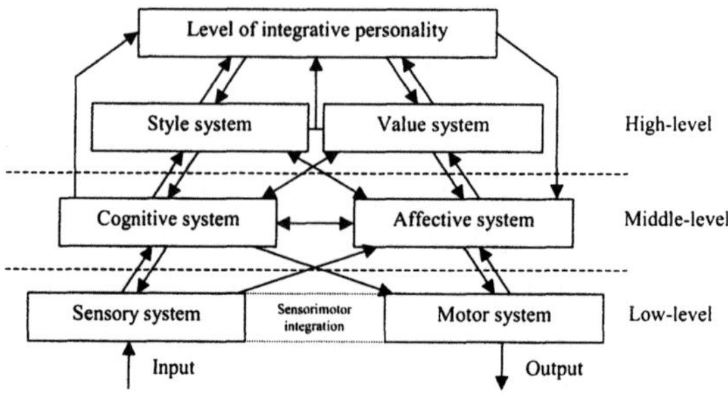

Figure 1. Integrative personality model [17, p. 12]

may also be individual. Thus, in addition to the variety of factors, the content of these storages comprise the personality of a human.

Taken together, the values of the personality factors along with the storage content can be thought of as an array of values describing, or encoding, one's identity. It is reasonable to assume that such identity description is peculiar for each human being. A superposition of the factor values is assumed to "identify a processor" [17, p. 47]. Therefore, an evident approach to the user identity verification would be to match a claimant's factor values against the previously acquired factor values of the legitimate user. The problem with such an approach is that it is highly difficult to obtain factor values automatically not to speak about user-friendliness. As referred by [7, p. 9], the traits "are not directly observable; they are inferred (as any kind of determining tendency is inferred)". The process of factor inference may involve for example answering specific questions or interview. In the context of UIV, such method would not be appropriate. Therefore, instead of inferring factor values, an alternative approach based on Social Cognitive Theory is adopted in this paper.

3.2 Social Cognitive Theory

Social Cognitive Theory considers psychological and biological personality of a human, his/her behavior, and environment as mutually interfered. According to the theory, a complex network of reciprocal influences between personality, behavior, and environment frames the being of human. The theory considers behavior of an individual being uniquely determined by personality, behavioral, and environmental factors, and largely regulated through cognitive processes. This suggests that the mind has an active role when an individual constructs his/her own reality [4].

In treating mobile-masquerader detection as user's identity verification, the fact that inherent constituents of human personality – cognitive structures and processes – are individual for each user can be employed. Due to the reciprocal determinism described in the Social Cognitive Theory, this individuality affects one's behavior and environment. Consequently, it is possible to assume that some aspects of behavior and environment are individual as well. The superposition of these individual behavioral and environmental aspects constitutes the reflection of one's personality, and thus it may be used to differentiate individuals. In two subsequent sections, some of these individual aspects of behavior and environment are hypothesized.

4. Individual behavioral aspects

While psychological personality is latent, it influences the individual's behavior and individual's environment, which can be observed more easily. The personality can be considered as reflected in some *aspects* of one's behavior and environment. In turn, the characteristics describing these behavioral and environmental aspects can be thought of as functions of multiple variables; some of these variables are personality factors. Since the superposition of factor values is individual, it is possible to hypothesize that the superposition of values of characteristics describing one's behavior and environment is also individual. Therefore, the behavioral and environmental characteristics reflecting personality can be used to verify the identity of a person.

To consider individual aspects of user behavior, we have categorized various behavioral aspects into three hierarchical levels: high, middle, and low levels corresponding to the division of personality systems into three levels (Section 3.1). The high-level aspects are hypothesized to reflect/manifest the peculiarities of high-level personality systems, i.e. the style and the value systems. Accordingly, these aspects are supposed to describe behavior that occurs over long time periods, involves selection of particular mode of action, requires high-level coordination, etc. In turn, middle- and low-level aspects of behavior manifest the peculiarities of respectively middle- and low-level personality systems.

For each of the three hierarchical levels, we consider the personality factors as well as the content of storages (goals, operators, invariants, and motor programs). As a result, a set of individual aspects of observed behavior have been recognized; these aspects are discussed below.

- High-level behavioral aspects reveal the peculiarities of values and styles of a user. The values determine what goals are selected, while styles determine how the stated goals are to be achieved. The following high-level aspects are recognized:
  - *Way of obtaining information (e.g. through communication with people, web-browsing, services).* This aspect is assumed to reflect the individuality of operators and goals, which in turn are influenced by factors of the value system, the affective system, etc.
  - *Way of communication with others (calls, email, SMS, etc.).* It is hypothesized that difference in operators is reflected in this aspect.
  - *Way of performing tasks.* It is assumed that sequences of actions employed, frequency of different sequences of actions, and other characteristics describing how the user carries out his/her tasks reflect the individuality of user operators and goals.
  - *Movements (routes, speed of movements, etc.).* As above, this aspect is assumed to manifest individuality of user operators and goals.
  - *Time/efforts devoted to work/businesses.* Need for endurance (a factor of the value system) is supposed to partly determine this aspect of behavior.
  - *Time/efforts devoted to entertainment.* Need for play (a factor of the value system) is supposed to be reflected in this aspect.
  - *Changes in behavior.* Need for change (a factor of the value system) is supposed to be reflected in this aspect. Behavioral changes implied here concern the behavior that is intentionally coordinated and regulated by a human, i.e. they concern high-level aspects of behavior.
- Middle-level behavior reflects the transformational processes within the cognitive system where the external information is processed in order to identify environmental invariants, and within the affective system where the cognitive information is processed in order to achieve the optimal internal arousal states. The peculiarity of these systems is manifested in the following behavioral aspects:
  - *Concepts used* are assumed to reflect individual differences in invariants.

  - *(Speed of) comprehension* is assumed individual as it is determined by multiple factors of the cognitive system (perceptual speed, verbal comprehension, memory span, associative memory, etc.).
  - *Decision making (e.g. time to respond).* Individuality of this aspect may be attributed to multiple factors of the cognitive system (perceptual speed, verbal comprehension, memory span, associative memory, memory for design, induction, deduction, spontaneous flexibility, etc.), but also to factors of the style system (e.g. reflection/impulsivity).
  - *Accuracy.* Personality factors of the cognitive system (deductive reasoning and spontaneous flexibility) and the affective system (surgency, autonomic balance, etc.) are hypothesized to influence this behavioral aspect.
  - *Disposition towards communication.* This aspect is assumed to be partly regulated by factors of the affective system (e.g. self-sufficiency, self-sentiment), but also by factors of the value system (e.g. need for exhibition).

- Low-level behavior is mainly regulated by the sensory and the motor personality systems responsible for transforming the environmental information into psychological information and back respectively. The individual behavioral aspects at this level are:
  - *Way of writing.* Individuality of this aspect may be explained by individuality of motor system factors (e.g. the dexterity and speed of small movements), motor programs (a dictionary of letters, rules to produce words, etc.), but also by the individuality of control-decision processes within the cognitive and the affective systems.
  - *Way of typing.* As above.
  - *Voice.* This aspect may be attributed to factors of the motor system (articulation, phonation, respiration), but also to factors of the cognitive and the affective system.

The above list of individual behavioral aspects does not pretend to be complete. These behavioral aspects were identified deductively by analyzing the factors suggested by [17]. While they recognize around 200 factors, for many of them we have not managed to reveal a linkage with observable behavioral aspects. Some aspects corresponding to other or the same factors may have been overlooked, and further analysis might reveal other aspects to be added to the list.

5. Individual environmental aspects

Above, it was hypothesized that due to the influence of personality on behavior, some aspects of human behavior are individual; furthermore, due to the influence of user personality through user behavior on his or her environment, some environmental aspects may also be individual (a person selects environment that fits his/her own personality). Individual aspects of behavior were considered in the previous section. In turn, this section is devoted to individual environmental aspects.

In the process of inferring individual environmental aspects, they are classified into high-, middle-, and low-level aspects. Similarly to the division of behavioral aspects, the division of environmental aspects is aimed at making the process of inference more structural. High-, middle-, and low-level environmental aspects are supposed to reflect respectively high-, middle-, and low-level personality systems. For each level, it is analyzed what aspects of environment could reflect the individuality of factors and storages of this level. As a result of this analysis, the following individual aspects of environment are hypothesized.[1]

- High-level environmental aspects are regulated by the factors and storages of the value and style systems determining the goals of a user and the ways to attain them. The individual environmental aspects of high level are:

  - *Choice of people to contact with.* This aspect is hypothesized to reflect the individuality of user goals and to a certain degree operators, but also the individuality of factors of the value system (e.g. need for affiliation, and need for nurturance).
  - *Choice of places to visit.* Individuality of places a user visits can be attributed to the individuality of goals, but also to the individuality of factors. Goals and operators partly determine the places a user has to visit, while needs and interests partly determine the places a user wants to visit.
  - *Choice of (software) tools.* Individual tools are supposed to be chosen according to individual goals, but also according to individual factors of the cognitive system (memory span, associative memory, etc.) and individual cognitive styles.
  - *Changes in the choice of environment.* Similarly to the above-mentioned aspect of changes in behavior, changes in the choice

[1] We limit the environmental aspects to those that may interact or otherwise contact with the device.

of environment are supposed to reflect the need for change (a factor of the value system). These changes correspond to changes in high-level environmental aspects, e.g. changes in places visited.

- Middle-level aspects of environment reveal the peculiarity of user's cognitive and affective systems involved in the processes of identifying invariants and attaining emotional activation needed. So far, only one aspect is recognized:
  - *Tendency of "being on-line"* is assumed to reveal the individuality of factors of the cognitive system (perceptual speed, verbal comprehension, extraversion, etc.), but also the need for exhibition (a factor of the value system).
- Low-level environmental aspects are determined by the factors from the low-level personality systems (sensory and motor) implementing the transformation between psychological information and physical energy. Among these aspects are:
  - *Choice of screen resolution.* It is hypothesized that the choice of screen resolution is partly determined by the visual acuity (a factor of the sensory system).
  - *Choice of volume level.* The choice of volume level is partly determined by the auditory acuity factor of the sensory system.

As well as the list of behavioral aspects proposed in previous section, the list of environmental aspects is unlikely to be complete. Further analysis may reveal other aspects reflecting personality factors and storages. The list therefore should be treated as initial and it should serve as a basis for further refinement.

6. Characteristics and measures

The personality factors and storages are latent and hence cannot be directly observed and measured. However, according to the Social Cognitive Theory (Section 3.2), they are reflected in different *aspects* of *behavior* and *environment*; some of these aspects are hypothesized in previous sections. Each of these behavioral and environmental aspects, in turn, may be described by one or several *characteristics*. For example, the accuracy in typing can be taken as a characteristic describing "accuracy" (middle level aspect of behavior). Tentative characteristics to describe various individual behavioral and environmental aspects hypothesized in previous sections are presented in Figure 2.

Personality reflected in behavior			Personality reflected in environment		
Level	Aspect	Characteristics	Level	Aspect	Characteristics
High	Way of communication with people, and performing other actions	• Device's facilities usage • Sequences of actions followed • Temporal lengths of actions • Temporal intervals between actions in a sequence • Use of shortcuts vs. use of menu	High	Choice of people to contact with	• People contacted with, conditioned on type of communication, time, etc.
High	Paths of movements	• Routes taken • Speed of move conditioned on route/time	High	Choice of places to visit	• Places visited, conditioned on time of day, week, etc.
High	Endurance	• Length of work day	High	Choice of tools	• Set of software installed
High	Changes	• Changes in behavior	High	Changes	• Changes in environment
Middle	Comprehension	• Time of reading a unit of textual information	Middle	"Being on-line"	• Time, when the user (or device) are online
Middle	Decision making	• Time between incoming event and response	Middle		
Middle	Concepts used	• Words or phrases used more often	Middle		
Middle	Accuracy	• Accuracy in typing, in menu item selection, etc.	Middle		
Middle	Disposition towards communication	• Time devoted to communication	Middle		
Low	Voice	• Statistical characteristics of voice	Low	Choice of screen resolution	• Current screen resolution
Low	Way of typing	• Temporal characteristics of keystrokes	Low	Choice of volume level	• Volume level
Low	Way of writing	• Pressure, direction, acceleration, and length of strokes	Low		

Figure 2. List of distinctive characteristics

For the purposes of automatically distinguishing the user and impostors, the behavior and environment, as reflecting the personality of a user, should be described by quantitative measurements. The model describing the regularities of these measurements should be created and stored for further reference during the verification process. Finally, the verification process is based on the comparison of current measurements against the information in the reference model. If the comparison reveals significant dissimilarity, it may indicate that a user substitution has taken place.

Table 1. Tentative measures to be employed in mobile-user masquerader detection

Characteristic	Measures (observable variables)
Device's facilities usage	Temporal interval between two consecutive evocations of a program or service of a same type
Device's facilities usage	Type of program or service evoked
Sequences of actions followed	Sequences of n actions
Temporal lengths of actions	Temporal lengths of actions
Temporal intervals between actions in a sequence	Temporal intervals between subsequent actions
Use of shortcuts vs. use of menu	For each menu command with shortcut, the chosen option
People contacted with, conditioned on type of communication, time, etc.	Phone number, e-mail address, or other address information of the contacted people
Routes taken	Sequence of cells traversed between two consecutive prolonged stops
Speed of move conditioned on route and time	Speed of move conditioned on route and time
Places visited, conditioned on time of day, day of week, etc.	Locations where prolonged stops were made
Length of work day	Time that the terminal is in the place affiliated with the user's workplace(s)
Changes in behaviour and environment	Changes in behavioural and environmental characteristics
Time of reading a unit of textual information	Time during which a document is open for reading
Time between an incoming event and response	Temporal interval between an incoming message (e.g. e-mail or SMS) is read and the response is written
Words or phrases used more often	Frequency of different words used in a piece of handwriting (with stylus) or typing
Accuracy in typing, in menu item selection, etc.	The ratio of errors (mistyped keystrokes, errors in menu item selection, etc.) to the overall number of actions
Time devoted to communication	Time during a day spent for communication (using terminal) including different types of communication (calls, e-mails, etc.)
Time, when the user is online	Time, during which the communication facilities of the terminal are not deliberately restricted
Statistical characteristics of voice	Cepstrum coefficients of the signal power
Temporal characteristics of keystrokes	Key duration time, inter-key latency time
Pressure, direction, acceleration, and length of stylus strokes	Pressure, direction, acceleration, and length of strokes
Set of installed software, current screen resolution, volume level	Changes of device configuration

In order to be able to measure quantitatively the characteristics of user behavior and environment, one or more appropriate *observable variables*, or *measures* should be assigned to each of them. These variables can be directly measured, and the results of the measurements can be stored as numerical or categorical values. Possible measures to be assigned to the distinctive characteristics are proposed in Table 1. For example, the ratio of mistyped keystrokes to the overall number of typed keystrokes may be employed as a measure to represent the characteristic of "accuracy in typing". Three characteristics – set of installed software, current screen resolution, and volume level – can be represented by a same measure indicating whether a change of configuration has been made. Therefore, these three characteristics were united in the table into a single characteristic.

7. Conclusions

Traditionally, the problem of deterring the use of lost or stolen mobile devices is addressed by the means of authentication at the preventive stage, and by the means of masquerader detection at the detective stage. The masquerader detection is usually approached through the detection of anomalous changes in user behavior and environment, or through the recognition of behavior and environment, which is common for impostors. The proposed solutions to the detection problem including frameworks, models, techniques, etc. are often based on heuristics, the experience or intuition of experts, or are data-driven. Such adhocness is likely to be one of the reasons making the development of new and improved solutions with high detection accuracy difficult.

Theories from the domain of psychology offer an opportunity to extend the viewpoint of a research dealing with masquerader detection. Using these theories, it is possible to explain the differences in human behavior and environment by differences of cognitive processes and psychological/biological factors. Applied in the security context, such theories shift the focus of research from the heavily technological aspects of the problem to the social and individual aspects concerning the human being interacting with the device. Such shift in focus may be useful for deepening the theoretical background of the masquerader detection, for determining the limitations of the contemporary research and thereafter for the development of improved solutions to the problem.

In this paper the mobile-masquerader detection problem is seen as a problem of verifying user identity. The behavior and environment are considered as reflecting the personality traits of a user. Accordingly, by analyzing certain aspects of behavior and environment, the user identity claim can be accepted or denied. A set of characteristics and measures potentially useful for mobile-masquerader detection has been proposed in the paper; however, further empirical research is needed in order to evaluate their suitability.

References

[1] D. Anderson, T. Lunt, H. Javitz, A. Tamaru, and A. Valdes. Detecting unusual program behavior using the statistical components of NIDES. SRI Technical Report SRI-CRL-95-06, Computer Science Laboratory, SRI International, Menlo Park, California, May 1995.

[2] Debra Anderson, Thane Frivold, and Alfonso Valdes. Next-generation intrusion detection expert system (NIDES): A summary. Technical Report SRI-CSL-95-07, Computer Science Laboratory, SRI International, Menlo Park, California, May 1995.

[3] A. Bandura. *Social Foundations of Thought and Action: A Social Cognitive Theory.* Englewood Cliffs, NJ: Prentice Hall, 1986.

[4] Albert Bandura. Social cognitive theory. *Annals of Child Development*, 6:1–60, 1989.

[5] C.S. Carver and M.F. Scheier. *Perspectives on personality.* Allyn and Bacon, Boston, 4 edition, 2000.

[6] Nathan L. Clarke, Steven M. Furnell, Philip M. Rodwell, and Paul L. Reynolds. Acceptance of subscriber authentication methods for mobile telephony devices. *Computers & Security*, 21(3):220–228, 2002.

[7] H. J. Eysenck. *The structure of human personality.* Methuen, London, 3 edition, 1970.

[8] Anup K. Ghosh, Aaron Schwartzbard, and Michael Schatz. Learning program behavior profiles for intrusion detection. In *1 st USENIX Workshop on Intrusion Detection and Network Monitoring*, pages 51–62, Berkeley, CA, USA, April 1999. USENIX Association.

[9] Steven A. Hofmeyr, Stephanie Forrest, and Anil Somayaji. Intrusion detection using sequences of system calls. *Journal of Computer Security*, 6(3):151–180, 1998.

[10] Terran Lane. *Machine Learning Techniques for the Computer Security Domain of Anomaly Detection.* Ph.D. thesis, Purdue University, W. Lafayette, IN, 2000.

[11] Terran Lane and Carla E. Brodley. Temporal sequence learning and data reduction for anomaly detection. *ACM Transactions on Information and System Security*, 2(3):295–331, 1999.

[12] Wenke Lee and Salvatore Stolfo. A framework for constructing features and models for intrusion detection systems. *ACM Transactions on Information and System Security (TISSEC)*, 3(4):227–261, 2000.

[13] Roy A. Maxion and Tahlia N. Townsend. Masquerade detection using truncated command lines. In *Proceedings of the International Conference on Dependable Systems and Networks*, pages 219–228, Los Alamitos, California, June 2002. IEEE Computer Society Press.

[14] R. R. McCrae and Jr. Costa, P. T. *Handbook of personality: Theory and research*, chapter A five-factor theory of personality, pages 139–154. Guilford, New York, 2nd edition, 1999.

[15] John McHugh. Intrusion and intrusion detection. *International Journal of Information Security*, 1(1):14–35, 2001.

[16] Pointsec Mobile Technologies. Half of all corporate PDAs unprotected despite employer risk. Pointsec News Letter 2, Available from http://www.pointsec.com/news/news_pressroom.asp (read 25.04.2005), June 2004.

[17] Joseph R. Royce and Arnold Powell. *Theory of personality and individual differences: factors, systems and processes.* Englewood Cliffs, NJ: Prentice Hall, 1983.

[18] Jake Ryan, Meng-Jang Lin, and Risto Miikkulainen. Intrusion detection with neural networks. In Michael I. Jordan, Michael J. Kearns, and Sara A. Solla, editors, *Advances in Neural Information Processing Systems*, pages 943–949, Cambridge, MA, USA, 1998. The MIT Press.

[19] Karlton Sequeira and Mohammed Zaki. ADMIT: anomaly-based data mining for intrusions. In David Hand, Daniel Keim, and Raymond Ng, editors, *Proceedings of the eighth ACM SIGKDD international conference on Knowledge discovery and data mining*, pages 386–395, Edmonton, Alberta, Canada, 2002. ACM Press.

[20] Jude Shavlik and Mark Shavlik. Selection, combination, and evaluation of effective software sensors for detecting abnormal computer usage. In *Proceedings of the 2004 ACM SIGKDD international conference on Knowledge discovery and data mining*, pages 276–285. ACM Press, 2004.

[21] Bo Sun, Fei Yu, Kui Wu, and Victor C. M. Leung. Mobility-based anomaly detection in cellular mobile networks. In Markus Jakobsson and Adrian Perrig, editors, *Proceedings of the 2004 ACM workshop on Wireless security*, pages 61–69. ACM Press, 2004.

[22] A. Sundaram. An introduction to intrusion detection. *ACM Crossroads*, 2(4):3–7, 1996.

[23] S. Upadhyaya, R. Chinchani, and K. Kwiat. An analytical framework for reasoning about intrusions. In *20th IEEE Symposium on Reliable Distributed Systems*, pages 99–108, New Orleans, LA, October 2001.

[24] Dit-Yan Yeung and Yuxin Ding. Host-based intrusion detection using dynamic and static behavioral models. *Pattern Recognition*, 36(1):229–243, 2003.

[25] Yongguang Zhang and Wenke Lee. Intrusion detection techniques for mobile wireless networks. *Wireless Networks*, 9(5):545–556, 2003.

A DISTRIBUTED SERVICE REGISTRY FOR RESOURCE SHARING AMONG AD-HOC DYNAMIC COALITIONS

Ravi Mukkamala,[1] Vijayalakshmi Atluri*,[2] and Janice Warner[2]

[1] *Department of Computer Science*
Old Dominion University
Norfolk, VA 23529
mukka@cs.odu.edu

[2] *MSIS Department and CIMIC*
Rutgers University
Newark, NJ 07012
{janice,atluri} @cimic.rutgers.edu

Abstract In a dynamic coalition environment, it is essential to allow automatic sharing of resources among coalition members. The challenge is to facilitate such sharing while adhering to the security policies of each coalition. To accomplish this, a *dynamic coalition-based access control* (DCBAC) has been proposed earlier, where security policies enforced by each coalition member are published in a centralized *coalition service registry* (CSR). In this paper, we propose a *distributed coalition service registry* (DCSR) system. In the DCSR system, several service registry agents cooperate to provide controlled access to resources. Distribution of the registries results in improved availability, higher concurrency, better response times to user queries, and enhanced flexibility. We employ secure group multicasting to communicate among the DCSR agents. The paper outlines the DCSR system, the supported functionalities and its underlying infrastructure.

1. Introduction

It is often necessary for organizations to come together to share resources without prior planning to accomplish a certain task at hand. This is driven by a number of applications including emergency and disaster management, peace keeping, humanitarian operations, or simply virtual enterprises. As an

*The work of Atluri and Warner is supported in part by the National Science Foundation under grant IIS-0306838.

example, in a natural disaster scenario, such as the earth quake in Turkey on May 1, 2003 and the Tsunami in Asia on December 26, 2004, government agencies (e.g., FEMA, local police and fire departments), non-government organizations (e.g., Red Cross) and private organizations (e.g., Doctors without Borders, suppliers of emergency provisions) needed to share information about victims, supplies and logistics [14]. Similar examples include homeland security applications where sharing of information across different organizations is needed for identifying criminal and terrorist behaviors, illegal shipments, and the like. In a commercial setting, organizations may share resources and information in order to cater to their clients by providing comprehensive services by drawing complementary services and skills from participating organizations.

Typically, resource sharing is done by establishing alliances and collaborations, also known as *coalitions*. Secure sharing often incurs significant administrative overhead since it may be required to provide access identification for each user who will have rights to the resources. Such a process does not suit the needs of a dynamic coalition where entities may join or leave the coalition in an ad-hoc manner.

Moreover, when coalition entities agree to share their information resources, the access control policies are agreed upon at the coalition level. These coalition level agreements are not at the level of fine-grained policies, in the sense that they do not specify which subjects are allowed to access specific resources. For example, an agreement between entities A and B is not an access control policy stating "a user Alice of entity A can access the *immigration* file of entity B." However, secure sharing of data requires enforcing fine-grained access control governed by each organization's security policies over the shared resources. Therefore, enforcing the coalition-level security policies requires transforming the high-level policies to implementation level. Likewise, it is necessary to ensure that local implementation level policies are not violated by coalition level policies.

In an earlier work [19], we have proposed a *dynamic coalition-based access control* (DCBAC) model that is specified based on the credentials possessed by coalitions as well as subjects. The DCBAC system comprises of four layers – (i) *coalition level*, which interacts with other coalition entities and is responsible for ensuring the authenticity of the coalition entity requesting access to its resources, (ii) *credential filter*, which is responsible for examining incoming credentials, and attaching appropriate credentials to outgoing requests, (iii) *credential* $\Longleftrightarrow$ *local access control mapper*, which converts local access control rules to policies concerning credentials for outgoing requests, and vice versa for incoming requests, and (iv) *local access control* layer, responsible for uniformly serving the access requests independent of whether it is a local access request or an external access request. Essentially, a request originating at a coalition entity, is transformed into a coalition level request as it percolates through the four layers at its end. Similarly, the incoming coalition level request is translated into a local access request as it flows down through the different layers. The information appended at each layer at one coalition entity is understood and dealt with the corresponding layer at the other coalition entity, much like the TCP/IP network protocol.

To accommodate sharing among true dynamic and ad-hoc coalitions, DCBAC employs a centralized *coalition service registry* (CSR) for coalition entities to publish their coalition level access policies. Any coalition entity wishing to access a specific resource of another coalition entity can obtain a *ticket* by submitting its entity credentials which are subsequently evaluated by the CSR. However, CSR suffers from the same limitations of any centralized system, such as limited availability and poor response time. In this paper, we extend the DCBAC model through a decentralized CSR (DCSR). Essentially, the coalition service registry is distributed among several coalition members. As we show in this paper, the distribution of the CSR functions enhances DCBAC's availability as there are multiple registries. Of course, the actual realized availability depends on the amount of replication of registry services and data among the DCSR functions. For example, in a fully-replicated scheme a service is registered at all agents resulting in high availability. However, the availability (for a particular service) with a non-replicated DCSR may be no different from that of a CSR. A partially-replicated scheme where a service is registered at one or more registries enhances the availability, with the degree of enhancement depending on the degree of replication. Of course, the cost of maintaining the replicas also increases with the degree of replication. The replication and distribution of CSR also increase concurrency of query execution, improve response times to user queries, and enhance flexibility. The benefits are achieved at the cost of additional communication cost. We propose the use of secure multicasting to maintain distributed registries.

This paper is organized as follows. Section 2 describes the DCBAC system on which the current system is based. Section 3 provides details of the proposed distributed registry system, the functionalities it supports, and details on the underlying infrastructure. Section 4 discusses the additional desirable functionalities supported by our DCSR system. Finally, section 5 summarizes our conclusions and outlines future research in this area.

2. Distributed Coalition-based Access Control (DCBAC)

In this section, we briefly review the DCBAC system proposed in [19], which is comprised of a four-layered architecture at the coalition entities and an independent component, the Coalition Service Registry (CSR). (The four layers are shown in Figure 1 but it has DCSR instead of CSR).

The CSR is the key to facilitating dynamic and ad-hoc collaboration as it allows any entity to describe the resources it is willing to share and its coalition level policies associated with the resources. Essentially, CSR is used to define the set of resources that coalition entities wish make available and to describe the interfaces and credentials used to access those resources. It mitigates the need to negotiate and establish collaboration policies among coalition entities.

To gain access to a desired resource, a user (or an organization on behalf of its user) submits the requested organizational level credentials to the CSR. CSR verifies these organization-level credentials and issues a *ticket* which can be submitted by individuals in the organization when sending an access request for the advertised resources. This *ticket* is a SAML assertion that asserts that the requester's organizational credentials match described policy requirements. Any user from the authenticated coalition entity must present to attempt to access the resources of another coalition entity would append this *ticket* to his request. Note that receipt of the ticket is not sufficient for access to the resources. Instead, the ticket merely confirms that the user is from an organization that matches the organizational level policy of the organization offering the resources.

We describe the functionalities of each layer in the following. The top layer is the coalition level. It interacts with the coalition level at other coalition entities and with the CSR. For outgoing requests, it is responsible for consulting the CSR to find the source of requested resources and for submitting organizational level credential to the CSR to obtain a "ticket" that indicates that it is allowed to make the request. On receiving an external service request, this layer validates the requesting coalition entity by validating the "ticket" received with the request. It checks if the coalition policy has changed since the ticket was issued. If so, the request is rejected by this level. The ticket is stripped off and the request is then forwarded to the credential filter.

The credential filter layer is responsible for filtering outgoing requests and their associated credentials. It filters out those credentials that the coalition entity does not want to reveal for privacy reasons. If it knows the full credential requirements for accessing the requested resource (because the requested resource has been previously accessed), it also filters out any unneeded credentials.

The credential⟺LAC mapper takes the local access control rules and converts them into a policy based on credential attributes and resource attributes. For incoming requests, it is responsible for mapping the requester's credentials to the local access control terminology and vice versa. When a request is received, it looks at the rights that can be associated with the submitted credentials and sees if they match the credential requirements for the requested resource. If the requested resource is a cluster, it identifies the specific resources that can be accessed.

The local access control layer enforces control on local services for both local and non-local requests. Local requests are received through the Local-user-Interface (LUI). The non-local requests are received through the Mapper layer. The LAC retrieves the requested resources and makes them available to the external requesting user. For outgoing requests, it submits the requests to the Mapper level.

3. Distributed Coalition Service Registry (DCSR)

In this paper, the centralized CSR component of the DCBAC architecture is distributed (using multiple agents), referred to as distributed coalition service registry (DCSR). In this section, we first describe the functionalities of the DCSR and then show how the proposed DCSR system satisfies these requirements.

DCSR Functionalities

1 *Register:* Maintain a registry of all shared services available: register, cancel, and update services

2 *Authenticate:* Authenticate the service requester's credentials

3 *Check conditions:* Check for any preconditions necessary to offer the requested service

4 *Generate ticket:* On successful checking, generate a ticket (token) asserting the requester's claim to use the service

In [19], we have shown how the above functionalities can be supported when a single centralized service registry (CSR) is employed. In the following, we discuss the additional challenges involved when a DCSR is employed. Our proposed DCSR system is illustrated in Figure 2. In particular, we present the details of the communication and computation infrastructure needed to implement the proposed DCSR system. The CSR agents are shown to be logically connected using a secure multicast group. The agents together implement DCSR.

3.1 Secure Communication Infrastructure

In a dynamic coalition environment, members join and leave in an ad-hoc manner. Accordingly, new registries (CSR) may join and leave the DCSR. In addition, new registries may be created to improve performance or some removed when the load is reduced. One way to achieve secure communication within such an ad-hoc group is to have a group key used by the sending agents to encrypt data, and the receiving agent to decrypt. Such a key is known as

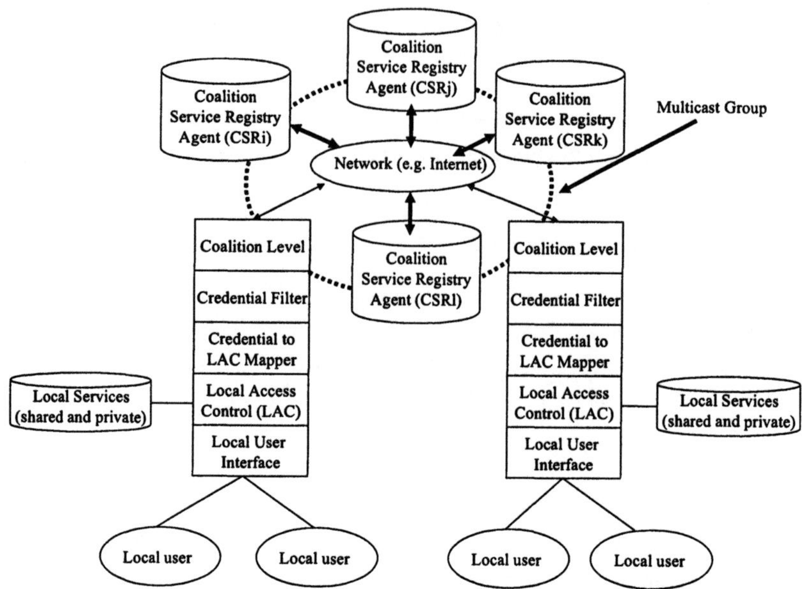

Figure 1. Distributed Coalition-based Access Control: Architecture

Traffic Encryption Key (TEK). The group key can be used as well in different security services such as authentication and maintenance of message integrity among the agents [22].

To facilitate the dynamic, distributed and secure nature of the registries, and to make the development of the registries independent of the communication infrastructure, we propose the use of an underlying secure communication infrastructure (SCI).

SCI supports the distributed CSR functions and DCBAC applications that are built on top of it in two ways. First, it facilitates the application development by separating the underlying communication and security functions from the CSR functionality. Second, since SCI communication primitives are generic, they can also be used to develop other DCBAC applications on top of the proposed services. Examples of SCI's communication primitives include secure propagation of update messages to support full or partial replication, a transparent fault tolerance mechanism to mitigate the effects of failures, support for confidentiality (current, forward, and backward secrecy), key management (key generation, assignment and distribution), etc [12].

Developing SCI involves designing group communication services and a key management scheme. The design and implementation of such components will vary based on the type of network connecting the CSR agents (e.g., the Internet, a wired or wireless LAN, a Mobile Ad-hoc Network (MANET), etc), as well as the number of CSR agents in DCSR. In the following, we describe some possible design options to fit different environments.

- **Wired-network** In case the coalition services are implemented on a wired network, (e.g., the Internet or a LAN), designing SCI will involve selecting a suitable group communication service as well as a key management scheme. Since most wired networks are IP-based, a network-level group communication scheme (such as IP-multicast) might be used [20]. Selecting a key management protocol will depend basically on the number of parties (agents) involved as well as the dynamic nature of the coalition membership. For small to medium sized coalitions (e.g., 10 to 50 members), a simple protocol such as GKMP [7] may be used. If the coalition size is large (e.g., more than 50) or if the frequency of membership changes (joins and leaves) is high, a more efficient protocol such as LKH [18] or EBS [5] may be used. It is worth noting that all of protocols involve a centralized key manager to perform rekeying. Such centralized entity may be replicated for reliability.

- **Wireless network** In some applications such as military or disaster management, a coalition may be formed on the spot by co-located agents that communicate via wireless radio. In such a case, group communication might be provided through broadcast and/or on-demand multicast. Broadcast may be appropriate for a small number of stationary agents colocated in a limited area that may be easily covered by short wave radio. In case of mobile agents and/or large coverage area, the service is considered as deployed in Mobile Ad-hoc Network (MANET) environment. Here, group communication may be provided through an on-demand multicast protocol (e.g., MAODV [17], ODMRP [21], etc). Key management can be performed through either GKMP or LKH based on the number of agents.

- **Ad-hoc network** Some applications may involve an ad-hoc coalition that interacts with base station agents on a wired network. In such case, group communication may be provided through Application-Level Multicast (ALM). The basic idea is to have end systems (agents) to establish an overlay network composed of their unicast links to distribute multicast traffic. Different topologies of ALM overlays were used in the literature including Single Tree [6, 8], Mesh Graphs [2, 3] or Logical Coordinate System [10, 16]. ALM provides the flexibility of delivering messages via unicast or multicast independent of the underlying network. Key management may be provided through any standard scheme (e.g., GKMP or LKH). However, ALM can assist in key distribution through selective unicast/multicast message delivery. An example of an architecture that utilizes this idea can be found in [13].

Algorithm 1 New Service Registration

```
INPUT: newsvc, User_credentials, replication_degree, registry_set
OUTPUT: exception_code
/* Check the user credentials */
if The registry can verify User_credentials then
    verify_credentials (User_credentails)
else
    Invoke verify_credentials (User_credentials) at another registry or authenticator
end if
if The credentials are invalid then
    return (1); /* Return exception code 1 */
end if
/* Check if the new service is already available */
if find(newsvc) then
    return (2); /* Return exception code 2*/
end if
/* Register the new service */
if registry_set = {} then
    agent_set = Select replication_degree registries from the DCSR agent list based on
    current load
else
    agent_set = registry_set
end if
Multicast (or Unicast) new_svc_reg request to agent_set
return (0); /* Return normal code 0 */
```

3.2 Computational infrastructure

Assuming the availability of a secure communication infrastructure (as described above), we now discuss ways to implement the basic functionality of DCSR on top of this infrastructure.

Registration Phase: First, consider the registration of a service (also shown in Algorithm 1). When a coalition member intends to register its local service for use by the coalition members, it uses this operation (new-svc-reg). This requires the user to specify the service details such as the service API, the required user credentials to use the service, details of authentication, the location of service, etc (embedded in *newvc* parameter). In addition, to provide fault-tolerance at the DCSR level, the requester has the option of specifying the degree of fault-tolerance (*replication_degree*). Finally, a member may wish to register the service with any set of DCSR agents. Alternately, he may specify a given set of agents, the (*registry_set*), where it needs to be registered . Since DCSR offers location transparency and replication transparency, the registering user may submit this request to any agent. The receiving DCSR agent validates the request and the requester (using *User_credentials*), and then starts implementing the request. Suppose the service is to be registered at a small number of agents, then the receiving agent may select these sites based on their current load and send the registration requests to them in a secure unicast fashion. If the set is large, the secure multicast could be used. To ensure that the registering user gets a prompt reply, the receiving agent immediately, without waiting for replies from the related agents, sends a reply. This is similar to the gossip protocol [1].

Algorithm 2 Query for a Service

```
INPUT: svc, User_credentials
OUTPUT: return_code, ticket
/* Check the user credentials */
if The local registry can verify User_credentials then
   verify_credentials (User_credentails)
else
   Invoke verify_credentials (User_credentials) at another registry or authenticator
end if
if Credentials are Invalid then
   return (3,{}); /* Return exception code 3 */
end if
/* Check if the service is available */
if svc is registered locally then
   generate_ticket (svc, User_credentails, ticket)
else
   Multicast (or unicast) generate_ticket (svc, User_credentails, ticket) to a chosen
   set of registries
   Await response from at least one registry
   if No response within the timeout period then
      Repeat the above step by choosing a different set of registries
   end if
   if No reply after repeated attempts then
      return (4,{}); /* Service unavailable */
   end if
end if
if ticket={} then
   return (5,{}); /*Return exception code 5*/
else
   return(0, ticket);
end if
```

Querying Phase: Second, consider the query service (also shown in Algorithm 2). Here, a coalition member intends to search for a service registered with DCSR. It sends the requested service details (included in *svc*) and its credentials (*User_credentials*). It has several options. It can unicast the request to a specific DCSR agent or multicast it to DCSR agents (with multicast address). In case of unicast, the receiving agent has two options. If the requested service is registered with it, it responds to the user and then interacts with it for authentication and then generating the token. In case the service is not registered with it, the agent multicasts the request to other DCSR agents. The agents that have the request service registered with them respond to to the original agent who then forwards it to the requester. While this offers complete location and replication transparency, there is a performance penalty due to several redirections. The performance may be improved by reducing the redirection in several ways. For example, the agent with the registration can directly respond to the user and then on directly interact with the user. Other performance penalty is due to a possibility of multiple agents (in case of replication) responding to the request. This may be minimized using several options. For example, the DCSR could internally maintain a directory service with information about all the agents. The original agent could first communicate with this directory service and then unicast the user's request to one of the agents with the registered service. The second option of a user multicasting its request to DCSR, the request may be handled by any agent that has the service registered with it. In this case, the performance penalties discussed are relevant here also. The same solutions suggested above are equally applicable.

Modification Phase: Third, consider changes to a registered service. Suppose a coalition member intends to withdraw a prior registered service. Once again, if the service has been registered with a known agent, the member could use unicast. Otherwise, multicast could be used. In this case, an agent that has the service registered with it would take the necessary action. However, there are several options to authenticate the coalition member. For example, one of the agents carries the authentication and then multicasts it to all others. Alternately, depending on the underlying infrastructure, the withdrawal message could be propagated using gossip messages.

4. Additional Functionalities

In addition to the functionalities in the earlier section, the proposed DCSR is expected to provide the following functionalities associated with distributed services.

Supporting transparency Since one of the primary requirements of any distributed system is transparency, we need to ensure that the distributed service registry system satisfies this requirement. Here, due to space limitation, we discuss a few types of transparencies, and show how the proposed system supports them.

1 **Location transparency**: This refers to the feature that enables service registries to be accessed without knowledge of their location. Our sys-

tem implements transparency to the user as well as the credential filter layer that interacts with the rest of the service registries at other locations.

Our system supports this transparency through redirection and secure multicasting among the service registries. We illustrate this concept using an example. Suppose a user at coalition C_i wants to register a service S_{i1} with a service registry, the request is sent to his coalition gateway. The request, after appropriate checks, is forwarded by the gateway to one of the service registries that it is aware of. In case, it is not aware of any or the one it is aware is not available, it could send the request to the DCSR multicast address. In either case, the request is received by one or more of the service registries and using a protocol (based on factors such as load balancing, type of service being registered, the coalition that is registering the service, etc.), the service is registered at one or more registries. Any authentication needed prior to the registration may be carried out by an assigned member of the DCSR. The authenticator is not necessarily the one where the service will be registered with. On successful registration, the coalition gateway is informed.

Similarly, if a user from C_i were to request for a service from other coalitions, the request is first forwarded to the coalition gateway which in turn forwards it to either the registry that it is aware of or to the DCSR multicast address. The request is received and processed by the relevant member. After appropriate authentication, the generated token is sent back to the gateway.

2 **Replication transparency:** A service may be registered at one or more service registries. But this aspect of replication is transparent to the user as well as the coalition gateway. The degree of replication may depend on several factors such as the desired availability of the service, the demand of the service among the coalition members, and the desired response time from the registry for that service.

In DCSR, the service registries, in coordination with a QoS server, decide on the number of registries that a service should be registered at. While the registering user gets a response immediately after one of the registries authenticates and registers it, the other copies are updated via secure multicast. The details of selection of the agents is omitted here.

Similarly, in case a user queries an agent for a service, either the agent directly handles it (if it has the entry), or send it over the multicast for other agents with information to reply. Finally, the reply is sent to the user by the original agent only.

3 **Failure transparency:** Failure or unavailability of registries should be concealed from a user of a coalition gateway. This is achieved by having replication as well as the multicasting feature to access the DCSR (as discussed above).

Supporting Failure handling In a distributed registry, with multiple service registries, the registries are likely to fail and later recover. In addition, new registries may be added and some of the current ones may disappear. The DCSR system handles these dynamic changes. This requires that the system detect failures, mask failures, and recover from failures.

First, consider the case of detecting registry failures. Clearly, the multicast membership protocol that maintains the service registry group is responsible for this function. Some of the standard techniques used for failure detection are timeouts, periodic message exchange, and primary-secondary associations. Typically, these functions are implemented either with a dynamic master controller or in a purely distributed manner [1]. Since there are several standard means to achieve this, we do not describe it any further [1].

Supporting Scalability In most cases, a coalition may start out with one or two members, and grow over time to several members. As the coalition grows, the load on the service registry is also likely to grow. In such cases, the DCSR system should scale itself accordingly. In our system, scalability is facilitated by the creation of new registries and making them members of the registry multicast group. The level of automation of the creation of new registries depends on the coalition policies. For example, to create a new registry on a node, if manual permission of its administrator is needed, then the system can only detect the need for a new registry and send messages to the coalition administrators. The rest of the process will be manual. On the other hand, if DCSR is permitted to create additional registries on certain nodes, it could carry this task automatically.

Determining the number of registries needed depends on the QoS expected from DCSR, load on the system, and current availability of the registries. Several heuristic solutions are available to solve this problem [9, 11]. The QoS server determines this factor.

Support for Currency Since a service could be registered at multiple registries in DCSR, there is a potential problem of currency or up-to-datedness of the registries. For example, if a new service were to be registered by a user, and from its QoS requirements it is determined that it should be registered at two specific registries, then the registration may take place either in an atomic manner or asynchronously. In order to place minimal overhead on the system, we have adopted the latter approach. So the service will be *eventually* registered at all the selected registries but there could be a period where it is registered at some but not so at others. This inconsistency does not pose much of a problem.

What is more serious is deregistration or removal of services at user's request. Since a service is potentially registered at multiple registries, when it is rescinded (or revoked), it should be revoked at all registries. The proposed secure multicast supports the propagation of the updates. In addition, DCSR could impose a limited time registration (as in Jini [4] and .Net [15]) of services and require periodic renewals when a coalition demands higher level of currency or consistency for a service.

Support for Concurrency DCSR operates in a concurrent an distributed environment where multiple users could register services, revoke services, or query for services. The requests may be either received at individual registries or via the multicast address. In the case of queries, the individual registry may handle the request or send it on the multicast group. The case of registration/revocation are handled differently. In this case, in situations where a request is received at individual registry, it multicasts the same and awaits treats it as any other multicast request. In any case, the user is unaware of the concurrent operations.

Supporting Placement Flexibility Since we are dealing with a coalition with heterogeneous members, the proposed system allows flexibility in the selection of registries for registering services and executing queries. For example, a coalition may require that its services be registered at its own registries or a set of coalition sites. In addition, there could be certain sites designated to act as registries while others could be implemented along with other coalition functions. In fact, some coalitions may not have the capability to hold any registries and hence all its services may be registered elsewhere. The DCSR registry system affords this flexibility once again with the help of the multicast group of CSRs. When a coalition member requests for service registration, it may request for a particular CSR (or CSRs) or any CSR. The default is assumed to be any, and hence the selection left to the QoS server.

Supporting Functional Flexibility Due to the heterogeneous capabilities of the coalition members stated above, all members may not be capable of installing registries that are fully functional. For example, if one of the members is not capable of performing authentication functions for a service requester, it should be possible to offload this function to another registry at another member. Our DCSR allows this flexibility. For example, it may be possible to have sites which specialize in authentication while some specialize in answering the queries, once they have been authenticated. Similarly, some sites may insist that they themselves issue tokens for their members while others want the registries to issue tokens. These flexibilities are allowed by the system through multicast. For example, if a CSR does not have the capability to authenticate the requester, it could pass the credentials to another server (or a specialized authentication server) that could carry it out. Subsequently, it would send a reply to the requesting CSR. The user is unaware of these functional distributions.

5. Conclusions and Future Work

In this paper, we have presented a distributed service registry system for a dynamic coalition. This is an extension of our previous work (DCBAC) on a coalition-based access control system to automatically translate coalition level policies into subject-resource level policies by employing an attribute-based approach. DCBAC considers the attributes associated with user credentials and those associated with resources, making the formation of specific groups of subjects and resources unnecessary. While DCBAC employed a centralized registry service for coalition members, the current work employs a distributed registry service (DCSR). The proposed system employs secure multicasting to securely communicate among the CSRs. We have described the several features of a distributed service such as different types of transparency, fault handling, scalability, placement flexibility, and functional flexibility that it offers. In addition, we provided details on how the system supports these features. We intend to carry out a performance analysis of the proposed system in small, medium, and large-scale coalition environments. In addition, we plan to determine the off-the-shelf products that could be used to prototype the system and measure its performance.

References

[1] K. Birman. *Reliable distributed systems: Technologies, web services, and applications*. Springer, 2005.

[2] Y. Chawathe, S. McCanne, and E. A. Brewer. RMX: Reliable multicast for heterogeneous networks. *IEEE Infocom*, pp. 795-804, 2000.

[3] Y. Chu, S.G. Rao, and H. Zhang. A case for end system multicast. *ACM SIGMETRICS 2000*, Santa Clara, California, USA, 2000.

[4] W.K. Edwards. *Core Jini*, Prentice-Hall, 1999.

[5] M. Eltoweissy, H. Heydari, L. Morales, and H. Sudbourough. Combinatorial optimization of key management in group communications. *Journal of Network and Systems Management: Special Issue on Network Security*, March 2004.

[6] P. Francis. Yoid: Extending the Internet multicast architecture. April 2000, http://www.aciri.org/yoid/docs/index.html.

[7] H. Harney, and C. Muckenhirn. Group Key Management Protocol (GKMP) Specification. *RFC 2093*, 1997.

[8] J. Jannotti, D. K. Gifford, K. L. Johnson, M. F. Kaashoek, and J. O'Toole. Overcast: Reliable multicasting with an overlay network. *Fourth Symposium on Operating Systems Design and implementation.* pp. 197-212, San Diego, CA, October 2000. USENIX Association.

[9] V. Kalogeraki, L.E. Moser, P.M. Melliar-Smith. Dynamic modeling of replicated objects for dependable softreal-time distributed object systems. *Proceedings Fourth International Workshop on Object-Oriented Real-Time Dependable Systems*, pp. 48-55, January 1999.

[10] J. Liebeherr, T. Beam. HyperCast: A Protocol for maintaining multicast group members in a logical hypercube topology. *First International Workshop on Networked Group Communication (NGC '99)*, Lecture Notes in Computer Science, Vol. 1736, pp. 72-89, 1999.

[11] Y. Lin, B. Kemme, M. Patino-Martinez, and R. Jimenez-Peris. Consistent data replication: Is it feasible in WANs? *Europar Conf.*, Lisbon (Portugal), 2005.

[12] M. Moharrum, R. Mukkamala, and M. Eltoweissy, Efficient secure multicast with well-populated multicast key trees. *Tenth Int. Conf. Parallel and Distributed Systems (ICPADS'04)*, pp. 215-224, 2004.

[13] M. Moharrum, R. Mukkamala, and M. Eltoweissy. A novel collusion-resilient architecture for secure group communication in wireless ad-hoc networks. *Journal of High Speed Networks*, 2005 (to appear).

[14] C. Philips, T.C. Ting, , and S. Demurjian. Information sharing and security in dynamic coalitions. *SACMAT*, 2002.

[15] J. Prosise. *Programming Microsoft .Net,* Microsoft Press, 2002.

[16] S. Ratnasamy, M. Handley, R. Karp, and S. Shenker. Application-level multicast using content-addressable networks. *Third International Workshop on Networked Group Communication (NGC '01)*, London, England, 2001.

[17] E. Royer and C. Perkins. Multicast operation of the ad-hoc on-demand distance vector routing protocol. *5th Annual ACM/IEEE International Conference on Mobile Computing and Networking (MOBICOM'99)*, Seattle, WA, USA, August 1999, pp. 207-218.

[18] D. Wallner, E. Harder, and R. Agee. Key management for multicast: Issues and architectures. *RFC 2627*, 1999.

[19] J. Warner, V. Atluri, and R. Mukkamala. A credential-based approach for facilitating automatic resource sharing among ad-hoc dynamic coalitions. *19th Annual IFIP WG 11.3 Conference on Data and Application Security,* Storrs, CT, August 2005, Springer LNCS 3654,pp. 252-266.

[20] R. Yavatkar, J. Friffioen, and M. Sudan. A Reliable dissemination protocol for interactive collaborative applications. *ACM Multimedia 1995*, pp. 333-343. November 1995.

[21] Y. Yi, S. Lee, W. Su, and M. Gerla. On-demand multicast routing protocol (ODMRP) for ad hoc networks. *IETF MANET Working Group Internet Draft*, Feb. 2003.

[22] M. Younis, M. Youssef, and K. Arisha. Energy-aware management in cluster-based sensor networks. *Computer Networks*, Vol. 43, No. 5, pp. 649-668, December 2003.

SESSION 8 – ACCESS MANAGEMENT

A TRUST-BASED MODEL FOR INFORMATION INTEGRITY IN OPEN SYSTEMS[!]

Yanjun Zuo[1] and Brajendra Panda[2]

[1]*Department of Information Systems and Business Education, University of North Dakota, Grand Forks, ND, USA;* [2]*Department of Computer Science and Computer Engineering, University of Arkansas, Fayetteville, AR, USA*

Abstract: While it is difficult to apply conventional security services to a system without a central authority, trust management offers a solution for information assurance in such a system. In this paper, we have developed a policy-oriented decision model based on object trust management to assist users in selecting reliable and secure information in an open system. In the proposed model, an object represents a topic or issue under discussion, and it may have multiple versions, each of which represents a subject's opinion towards the characteristics of that object. The developed trust-based decision model assists a user to select one object version with desired level of quality and security features from available versions of a given object. The model balances both positive and negative aspects of an object version, and an evaluator can explicitly specify, in form of a policy specification, which features of an object version are not acceptable and which features are favorable. A high-level policy language, called *Selector*, expresses the policy specification in an unambiguous way. *Selector* consists of primary and residual policy statements. It supports recursive function calls, and the invoked external functions are defined separately from the language itself. The proposed decision model doesn't guarantee to select the "best" version for a given object. Rather it ensures that the selected version meets a user's requirement for information integrity.

Key words: trust decision model; information integrity; information security policies; policy language; trustworthy computation

[!] This work was supported in part by US AFOSR under grant FA9550-04-1-0429 and was performed when the first author was with the University of Arkansas.

1. INTRODUCTION

Information integrity has a wide scope and it primarily used to refer to a set of mechanisms to protect information from unauthorized modifications during the information transmission or in storage. In this paper, information integrity focuses on evaluating the quality and security features of a given piece of information. It contains a set of methods for an evaluator to select external information with the required level of quality and security in an open environment. An open system is a general term and, in this paper, it represents a decentralized system organized by a set of loosely coupled computer systems without a single administrative authority. Examples of open systems include various virtual organizations such as Grid systems, Peer-to-peer systems, and virtual communities. Ensuring the security and quality features of external information is crucial for the participants of an open system to confidently share information. But the conventional security and information assurance mechanisms don't scale well while being applied to those open systems. They have been developed based on a closed-world assumption where the users are known in advance. This assumption is no longer valid for an open system. Rather, trust management helps eliminate the scalability limitation of traditional security models. Existing research on trust management focuses on subject trust, however, e.g., how the trustworthiness of a subject is evaluated and how access control is granted to a subject based on its attributes and/or properties. Research on object trust has not received much attention.

In our discussion, a *subject* represents an independent entity in an open system, which produces and consumes information. A piece of information expresses a topic or issue in discussion. The term *object* is used to denote such a topic or issue. This notation (object) is chosen because it is frequently used together with the term, subject. An object has a value or a set of values, called object value(s), representing the inherent features(s) of the object. For instance, if the current economic growth is considered as an object, then its object value is a real number representing how fast the economy is growing. The object values expressed by different subjects for a given object could be different. It is very likely that different subjects have different views on a given issue or topic. For example, different groups of economists may have used different analytical tools and collected different sets of data to calculate the economic growth rate. Hence, they have different opinions on this value.

The term *object version* is used to represent such an opinion that a subject has on the object value(s) for the given object. In addition, the owner of an object version also supplies its confidence in the proposed object value(s), which is expressed as the trust that the owner places on the proposed object value(s).

Information processing is accumulative and recursive, e.g., some information is formed by using others as its components. For instance, a public key encryption algorithm (e.g., RSA) uses those methods for large primary number generation and testing, key distribution, and one-way function (e.g., modular operation) as its building blocks. In component-based software development, e.g., Java Beans and Microsoft COM, a software program is constructed by using various pre-developed modules, library functions, and methods. In business world, the Dow Jones Industrial Average summarizes 30 stock prices in average and divides it by a constant, called "divisor". Information derivation is a major form of information processing in a data intensive system for science and commerce. In domains as diverse as global climate change, high-energy physics, and computational genomics, science is becoming increasingly dependent on the generation and reuse of massive amounts of data, a trend sometimes known as data-intensive science.

Our model is applied to an open system, where information derivation enables the system to keep track of the components of an object version, i.e., how the object version has been formed and which components are used. Then that information is helpful for a user to evaluate the trustworthiness of the object version in term of its quality and security.

In [1] the authors proposed a standard format to represent different versions of a given object and the component information for each version. Furthermore, they developed a method to allow an evaluator to measure the trustworthiness of an object version based on the trust values of its components and the composing functions used to form the object version. For simplicity, an object version is specified in the following format:

owner → *{object, object value(s), trust value, components, composing functions}*

An object can have multiple versions as provided by different subjects. To distinguish among available versions of an object, say O, the symbol $V^{(O)}_i$ is used to denote the ith version of O. O is called the target of object of $V^{(O)}_i$. Given multiple versions of an object, a user may want to select one version, if any, which satisfies its requirements for quality and/or security. This process is called "trust decision", which is an important part of object trust management. Existing virtual organizations provide only preliminary approaches for selecting trusted information in term of its quality and security. For instance, in Peer-to-peer systems, a peer assesses a given piece of information based on the reputation and trustworthiness of the owner of the information. But that is not a reliable way to evaluate the quality and security features of the information itself. In this paper, a trust-based decision model has been developed. The selection criteria are defined based on both the intrinsic and extrinsic features of the given information, and those features provide an evaluator more insights into the inherent trust characteristics of the information. A policy specification can then be defined based on this trust model, and a high-level policy language is applied to formally express the policy specification.

2. RELATED WORK

Existing research on trust management includes trust modeling [2, 3, and 4], automatic trust negotiation [5, 6, and 7], reputation based trust management [8, 9, and 10], among others. Examples of trust management systems include PGP [11], X.509 [12], PolicyMaker [13], KeyNote [14], Referee [15], etc. Our model is different from the previous work in that our approach concentrates on evaluating the trustworthiness of a given object version (or a piece of information), while the existing models focus on trust at subject level. Studying the information quality and security at object level gives a user higher confidence to use a piece of information since that information has been directly assessed instead of relying on the information's extrinsic attributes such as its owner's reputation. Making a decision merely based on a subject's trustworthiness is not always reliable. We know that even the most honest people make mistakes. It is advantageous to assess the intrinsic features of external information and perform trust evaluation at object level. Then the information can be consequently selected based on its trust features.

Related work on policy languages includes [16, 17, and 18] (to cite a few). In [16] McDaniel has discussed in detail execution conditions in order to determine if a policy should be applied. *Ponder*, a policy language as proposed in [17], consists of a set of statements that define a choice in the behavior of a system. The language itself is declarative and object oriented. In [18], *Rei*, another policy language, was introduced. The core of that policy language is policy objects, which describe the concepts of rights, prohibitions, obligations, and dispensations. The "*has*" construct as defined in *Rei* represents the possession of a policy object by a subject.

Selector, the high-level policy language presented in this paper, is simple and flexible. An instance of *Selector* is composed of a set of policy statements. A *select* or *deny* primary statement immediately selects or denies an object version, which offers some features that the user has strong likeness for or can't tolerate, respectively. A *warning* or *rewarding* policy statement allows the accumulations of negative or positive effects of a given object version. Then the implied statements are applied to test if the accumulated effects are significant enough to make a decision.

Like *Ponder* and *Rei*, *Selector* supports positive and negative rules as well as recursive external function calls. But *Selector* is designed specifically for expressing a policy specification to select external information by evaluating the intrinsic and extrinsic feature of the information. This feature makes it different from both *Ponder* and *Rei*, which focus on user aspect and specify policies for management and security of distribute systems. For instance, *Ponder* includes authorization, filter, refrain and delegation polices for specifying access control and obligation policies to specify management actions, and supports a common means of specifying enterprise-wide security policy [17]. Key concepts of *Ponder* include domains, roles, and relationships, which support it as an object-oriented policy language. *Rei* handles authorizations, prohibitions, obligations and dispensation policy rules and allows policies to be split into actions, constraints and policy objects. Hence both languages specify rules to describe allowed actions for subjects and *Selector* specifies favorable and prohibitive features of objects. In addition, *Rei* defines actions and policy objects separately and allows them to be linked dynamically to subjects. *Selector* uses domain dependent function blocks in rule expressions. The feature of domain dependency increases implementation efficiency, as compared with *Rei*, at the expense of extensibility and portability.

3. THE TRUST-BASED DECISION MODEL AND POLICY SPECIFICATION

3.1 Methodologies

The goal of the trust decision process is to select one version, if any found appropriate, from available versions of a given object. Making a trust selection relies on evaluating trust features of those available object versions. The trust features of an object version are quantitatively expressed by its values for a set of trust-related attributes of the target object. The concept of trust-related attribute is defined as below.

Definition 1: A *trust-related attribute* of an object refers to the object's intrinsic or extrinsic attribute, whose value, given a version of the object, describes the quality and/or security features of the object version and hence can help an evaluator assess the trustworthiness of that object version.

Figure 1 describes object O, its three trust-related attributes, and the values of those attributes given O's three versions. The attribute, "possibility of viral infection", describes one security feature of O's versions. Given a version of O, its value for this attribute helps an evaluator measure how much to trust this object version in term of its safety to execute, i.e., free of viral infection. Another attribute, "correctness of the algorithms", concerns the quality feature of a version of O. The value for this attribute, given an object version, helps the evaluator decide how much the quality (correctness) of the object version should be trusted in term of the algorithms it used to solve a problem. The third attribute, "the owner's reputation", indicates the reputation of the object version's owner in supplying information. An object version's value for this attribute, i.e., its owner's reputation, provides the evaluator important information in measuring the quality and/or security feature of the object version.

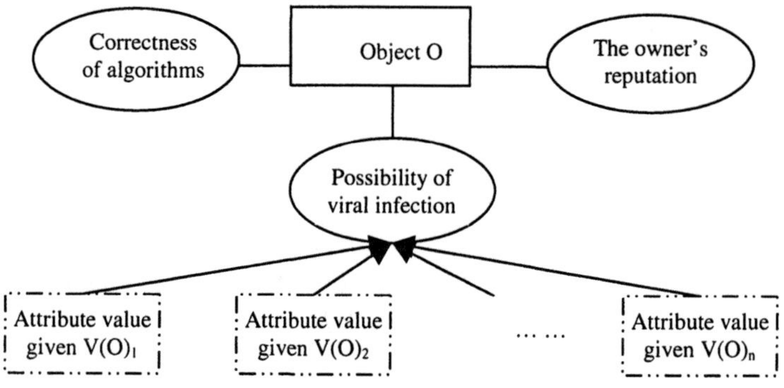

*Figure 1.*Object O, its Attributes, and the attributes' values given O's three Versions

Some trust-related attributes are considered as positive semantically in the sense that users want to see higher values for them. For instance, the reputation of the owner of a given object version is a positive trust attribute. In contrast, some attributes are considered negative, and users want to see lower values for those attributes. For instance, the possibility of virus infection for an object version describes a negative feature for that version. Users want to see this possibility as very low. When an object version has a high value for a negative attribute, and a user can't tolerate that feature expressed by this negative attribute value, then the object version must be rejected.

Definition 2: A *dominating negative attribute value* of an object version refers to such a value of the object version for a negative attribute that the feature represented by this value is so "negative" that a system can not accept the object version based on this feature.

The corresponding attribute is called a *dominating negative attribute* of the target object.

In a trust selection process, a user first identifies a set of *dominating negative attributes* and specifies a set of testing conditions such that if any object version possesses a value for one of the dominating attributes and that value is beyond a threshold (i.e., the object version has a very negative feature and can't be accepted by the user), the object version must be denied.

On the other hand, an object may have a positive attribute which is so attractive. If a version of that object has a value for such a favorable attribute, and that value is good enough (or beyond a threshold), then the object version can be selected.

Definition 3: A *desired positive attribute value* of an object version is such a value of the object version for a positive attribute that the feature represented by the value is highly "favorable." Moreover, the object version can be accepted by a system if the object version does not possess any dominating negative attribute values.

The corresponding favorable attribute is called a *desired positive attribute* of the target object.

As an object version can have complicated features, it is difficult to draw a clear line between a "good" version and a "bad" version. An object version may have some positive trust features; but these merits are not good enough for a user to make a "select" decision. On the other hand, a version may have some negative aspects but those unfavorable features are not severe enough for the user to make a "deny" decision. Hence the proposed trust selection process uses a scoring system to allow the values for those negative and positive features to be quantitatively accumulated. Then a decision may be made based on those accumulated negative or positive features. A policy specification can then be developed for selecting an object version, if any found appropriate, which satisfies the user's requirements for information quality and security.

Definition 4: A *policy specification* consists of a set of trust based security rules, called *policy rules*, expressed in a natural language specifying high-level descriptions of what features of an object version can not be tolerated and thus that object version must be denied as well as what features are favorable and thus that object version can be accepted.

There are four types of policy rules in a policy specification as discussed below:

(1) The first type is to specify dominating negative attribute(s) of an external object and the corresponding testing conditions.
(2) The second type is to specify desired positive attribute(s) of an external object and the corresponding testing conditions.
(3) The third type is to specify either positive or negative attribute(s), for which one object version has a value for that attribute but that value is not significant enough (for an evaluator to make a "select" or "deny" decision). However, those positive or negative features should be accumulated accordingly for the object version. Two variables, *Number of Rewards* and *Number of Warnings*, are

introduced to maintain the accumulated utilities for the positive and negative features of an object version respectively.

(4) The fourth type is to verify whether the accumulated positive and negative utilities for an object version under evaluation enable the system to make a decision after balancing their overall effects.

A policy rule of type (1), (2), or (3) is also called a *primary rule*. More specifically, a rule of type (1) is called a *primary negative rule*, and a rule of type (2) is called a *primary positive rule*. A rule of type (3) is called an *accumulating rule*. A rule of type (4) is called an *implied rule*. An implied rule takes the pair of accumulated positive and negative features of a given object version as input and produces one value from set {*deny, select, indecisive*}.

All the primary policy rules are evaluated and enforced in a pre-defined order. Primary negative rules, if any, can not appear after any other types of primary rules. In other words, a policy specification must start with a set of primary negative rules, if any. Those primary negative rules specify dominating negative attributes of an object and their testing conditions. If an object version has one of those values as tested true by such a condition (i.e., it has a negative feature that can not be accepted by the system), that object version must be denied. If an object version does not possess any of the negative features as specified by a primary negative rule, it is tested based on other primary positive rules and accumulating rules. Finally, if all the versions of the given object have been evaluated and no version has been selected, then a *residual rule* (as will be discussed in Section 4.3) is applied and a version may be selected for that object.

3.2 An Example

A policy specification example has been given in Figure 2, where system S evaluates object version $V^{(O)}_i$ to determine if $V^{(O)}_i$ satisfies its requirements for information quality and security. The policy specification starts with a primary negative rule, which indicates that if $V^{(O)}_i$ is detected as infected by viruses, then S rejects $V^{(O)}_i$ immediately and the following rules of the policy specification will not be evaluated. For this rule, the dominating negative attribute is "infection by viruses", and the corresponding testing function is "verify if a given object version has been affected by viruses". If $V^{(O)}_i$ is tested as "false", i.e., $V^{(O)}_i$ has not been detected as affected by a virus, then the evaluation continues and the second policy rule is evaluated for $V^{(O)}_i$. The second policy rule is a primary positive rule. According to this rule, S can select $V^{(O)}_i$ if (1) $V^{(O)}_i$'s components are publicly known as "recommended object versions" (hence publicly known as trustworthy). It is assumed that all recommended object versions based on user evaluations are maintained in a list, called *RecommendedObjectVersionList* and this list is accessible to all participant in a virtual organization, and (2) the composing functions used to form $V^{(O)}_i$ have been verified as correct and appropriate. For this rule, "component correctness" and "composing logic correctness" are two desired positive attributes. The first is checked by its corresponding testing condition to determine if $V^{(O)}_i$'s components are members of *RecommendedOjbectVersionList*. The second is to determine (by site domain experts or external service providers) if the composing functions are correct and appropriately used. If the answers to both of the two testing conditions are "yes", then $V^{(O)}_i$ can be selected and the decision process for the target object, O, is completed. If the answer to at least one of the testing conditions is "no", the evaluation process continues and the next rule in the policy specification is evaluated for $V^{(O)}_i$. The third rule is also a primary positive rule and can be interpreted in a similar way. The fourth rule is an accumulating rule. It indicates that for a positive attribute, "membership of the owner of a given object version to *GoodContactList*", if $V^{(O)}_i$ satisfies the corresponding testing condition, two units of rewards can be accumulated for $V^{(O)}_i$, i.e., *Number of Rewards* is incremented by two. *Good ContactList* is maintained locally by the evaluator and contains all other subjects, which the evaluator has contacted before and whose performance were satisfied. Similar explanations can be applied to the remaining rules.

After all the primary rules have been evaluated, the accumulated *Number of Rewards* and *Number of Warnings* for $V^{(O)}_i$ are used to determine if $V^{(O)}_i$ should be selected, denied, or indecisive based on the two implied rules.

The policy specification (to evaluate object version $V^{(O)}_i$):

(Primary rules):

1. Deny $V^{(O)}_i$ if it has been affected by viruses;
2. Select $V^{(O)}_i$ if $V^{(O)}_i$'s components are publicly known as trustworthy and the composing functions used to form $V^{(O)}_i$ are verified as correct;
3. Select $V^{(O)}_i$ if the overall trust value of $V^{(O)}_i$ (the combination of its primary and secondary trust values) is greater than 0.95;
4. Give $V^{(O)}_i$ two unit of rewards if the owner of $V^{(O)}_i$ had been in transaction with S and its performance was satisfied;
5. Give $V^{(O)}_i$ two units of warnings if the owner of any component of $V^{(O)}_i$ has reputation value less than 0.4;
6. Give $V^{(O)}_i$ two unit of rewards if the owner of any component of $V^{(O)}_i$ is S's business partner.
7. Give $V^{(O)}_i$ three units of warnings if the program expressed by $V^{(O)}_i$ has been tested with memory leakage while being executed.

Figure 2. Example of a Policy Specification

In the evaluation process of an object version, if a "select" decision for that version is made, the process of evaluating the target object is completed. If a "deny" decision for an object version is made, the evaluation process only for that version is completed. In both cases, the remaining policy rules for that version are not evaluated or applied.

4. *SELECTOR* – THE POLICY LANGUAGE

A policy specification is defined in a natural language, e.g., English. Rules expressed in a natural language could be ambiguous. In computer science literature, a policy language with well-formatted syntax is often used to express a policy specification. In this paper, a policy language, called *Selector*, has been developed to express a policy specification.

Selector is a high-level policy language. According to Bishop [20], a high-level policy language expresses policy constraints on entities using abstractions without specifying the implementation issues. Translating a policy specification to an instance of a policy language is conducted manually.

Selector consists of a set of policy statements to express the corresponding policy specification rules. The term "statement" is used for *Selector* in order to distinguish it from the term "rule" for a policy specification. More specifically, *Selector* is composed of a "primary statement list" and a "residual statement list". The residual statements help an evaluator select a version if all the primary statements have been evaluated based on the available versions of a given object and no version has been selected.

```
Selector            ::= primary_statements  implied_statements residual statements
primary_statements ::= primary_statement primary_statements | ε
 primary_statement ::=  select_statement | deny_statement |
```

Figure 3. High Level Structure of Syntax of *Selector*

The high-level structure of *Selector* is expressed in Figure 3. The syntax of both primary statements and implied statements of *Selector* is introduced in the following sections.

4.1 Primary Statements

A primary policy statement has the following format:

$$Action \leftarrow (LoopControl:)?\ Fc(C_1, C_2, \ldots, C_n)$$

The terms for the above statement are explained below:

(1) *Action* ∈ {Select, Deny, [Warnings *x*], [Rewards *y*]} and each element is a self-explanatory function identifier. There are four types of primary statements: (a) *Select statement*: the *Action* is *Select*. Such a statement expresses a primary positive rule in the corresponding policy specification; (b) *Deny statement*: the *Action* is *Deny*. Such a statement expresses a primary negative rule in the policy specification; (c) *Warning statement*: the *Action* is [Warnings *x*]. Such a statement expresses an accumulating rule in the policy specification to accumulate the "points" for the negative features of the object version under evaluation; and (d) *Rewarding statement*: the *Action* is [Rewards *y*]. Such a statement expresses an accumulating rule in the policy specification to accumulate the "points" for the positive features of the object version.

(2) *(LoopControl:)?Fc*$(C_1, C_2, \ldots, C_n)$, the right hand side of a primary policy statement, consists of two parts, each of which is explained below.

(2.1)The first part, *(LoopControl:)?* is an optional loop control structure as indicated by the question mark (?). It controls recursive executions of the second part. More specifically, a loop control structure is in one of the following formats:

forAll variable; ST, Function(variable, other arguments)

forSome variable; ST, Function(variable, other arguments)

The terms, *forAll*, *forSome*, and *ST* (shorthand for *Such That*) are key words in *Selector*. *Variable* is called a control variable. *Function(variable, other arguments)* is called a control function and it specifies the allowed possible values for the control variable.

The semantic meaning of control structure is determined by the *forAll* and *forSome* loop control qualifiers. As implied by its name, *forAll* requires that every value of *variable* as specified by *Function(variable, other arguments)* satisfy $Fc(C_1, C_2, \ldots, C_n)$, i.e., $Fc(C_1, C_2, \ldots, C_n)$ is evaluated as true for this *variable* value, in order to evaluate the right hand of the primary policy statement as true. *forSome* requires only one value of *variable* as specified by

Function(variable) make $Fc(C_1, C_2, \ldots, C_n)$ true in order to evaluate the right hand side of the primary policy statement as true.

(2.2) The second part of the right hand of a policy statement, $Fc(C_1, C_2, \ldots, C_n)$, is an Boolean expression. Each argument, C_i, called a *conditional statement*, can be evaluated as either true or false. Conditional statements are combined by logical operators such as AND, and OR with the following format:

*Function(Arguments) (AND || OR Function(Arguments))**

The symbol "*" specifies that the term preceding "*" can appear multiple times.

Figure 4 shows the policy language statements (an instance of *Selector*) corresponding to the policy specification given in Figure 2.

(Primary statements)

1. Deny ← AffectedByVirus($V^{(O)}_i$)
2. Select ← (forAll *Variable*; ST, Component($V^{(O)}_i$, *Variable*)):
   Member(*Variable*, RecommendedObjectVersionList) AND
   FunctionCorrect(ComposingFunctions($V^{(O)}_i$));
3. Select ← Greater(T(S, $V^{(O)}_i)_{Overall}$, 0.95);
4. [Rewards 2] ← Member(Owner($V^{(O)}_i$), GoodContactList)
5. [Warnings 2] ← (forSome *Variable;* ST, Component($V^{(O)}_i$, *Variable*)):
   Less(Reputation(Owner(*Variable*)), 0.4)
6. [Rewards 2] ← (forSome *Variable*; ST, Component($V^{(O)}_i$, *Variable*)):
   Partner(Owner(*Variable*), S)
7. [Rewards 3] ← MemoryLeak($V^{(O)}_i$)

(Implied statements)

Deny ← Greater(*Number of Warnings*, 4)

Select ← Greater(*Number of Rewards*, 4)

Figure 4. The Set of Policy Statements Expressing the Policy Specification Rules Given in Figure 2. *AffectedByVirus, Component, Member, FunctionCorrect, ComposingFunctions, FunctionCorrect, Greater, Less, Partner, Owner,and MemoryLeak* are names of external library functions.

4.2 Implied Statements

Two implied statements are defined below

Select ← GreaterThan (Number of Rewards, Threshold $_1$*)*

Deny ← GreaterThan (Number of Warnings, Threshold $_2$*)*

Threadhold$_1$ and *Threshold*$_2$ are supplied by the system administrators. The implied statements are applied to a given object version after all the primary statements have been evaluated towards the object version. If the implied statements still don't make a decision regarding that object version, it is added to a set, *Candidate*, which keeps the residual object versions for the target object.

4.3 The Residual Statements

Applying the primary policy statements to all the versions of object O leads to two possible results:

(1) A "*select*" decision has been made and the trust decision for O is completed; or

(2) No decision has been made and some versions have been added to *Candidate*.

The *residual statements* select a version from *Candidate*. One way is to select the version with the highest trustworthiness. In this case, the residual statement has the format:

$$V^{(O)} \leftarrow select\ V^{(O)}_i\ with\ Max(T(S,\ V^{(O)}_i)_{overall})$$

where $V^{(O)}$ represents the version selected by *S* for O, *select* and *with* are two key words, *Max* represents a function to select the maximum value of an input set, $V^{(O)}_i$ is an element of *Candidate*, and $T(S, V^{(O)}_i)_{overall}$ represents the overall trust value of $V^{(O)}_i$ for S, which can be calculated as the weighted average of the primary trust and secondary trust values of $V^{(O)}_i$ as below:

$$T(S,\ V^{(O)}_i)_{overall} = \lambda * T(S,\ V^{(O)}_i)_{primary} + \gamma * Trust(S,\ V^{(O)}_i)_{secondary}$$

where λ and γ are weights assigned to the primary and secondary trust values of $V^{(O)}_i$ for *S*. Those two trust values are explained next.

Definition 5: The *primary trust value* of an object version $V^{(O)}_i$ for an evaluator, such as a subject S, denoted as $T(S, V^{(O)}_i)_{primary}$, is the trustworthiness of $V^{(O)}_i$ for S in term of its quality and/or security, which is calculated based on S's direct experiences of studying the closely related information about $V^{(O)}_i$, e.g., the trustworthiness of the components of $V^{(O)}_i$ and the appropriation of composing functions used to form $V^{(O)}_i$.

Definition 6: The *secondary trust value* of $V^{(O)}_i$ for S, denoted as $T(S,V^{(O)}_i)_{secondary}$, is the trustworthiness of $V^{(O)}_i$ obtained through secondary experiences of S, e.g., the information S has on the trustworthiness of $V^{(O)}_i$ from other parties such as the owner of $V^{(O)}_i$, a recommender, or user evaluations.

$Trust(S,V^{(O)}_i)_{secondary}$ can be calculated, in its simplest form, as the mathematical product of the trust level of the object version for its owner, S' and the trust level of S' for S. The trust level of S' for *S* is called *subject trust* since it measures the trustworthiness of one subject for another. Several trust models have been proposed to evaluate the subject trust values (see [3] and [4] for more information). Other methods exist to calculate secondary trust value of an object based on transitive and discounted recommendations from third parties (see [2]). We will not discuss them here due to space constraints.

In order to calculate Trust(S, $V^{(O)}_i)_{primary}$, *S* studies the component information of $V^{(O)}_i$, i.e., how it has been integrated, to what degree those components should be trusted, which set of composing functions have been used to form $V^{(O)}_i$, etc. Let elements in the set $\{C_1, C_2, ..., C_n\}$ denote the components of $V^{(O)}_i$ and elements in the set $\{S_1, S_2, ..., S_n\}$ represent the owners of those components with S_i being the owner of C_i for $0 < i \leq n$ respectively. T(S, $V^{(O)}_i)_{primary}$ can be calculated by the following formula (see [1] for more information):

$$T(S, V^{(O)}_i)_{primary} = \Gamma_{(S, V(O)i)}(F, T(S, C_1), T(S, C_2), ..., T(S, C_n))$$

where $\Gamma_{(S, V(O)i)}$ represents the trust function to evaluate Trust(S,$V^{(O)}_i)_{primary}$ based on the trust values of the components of $V^{(O)}_i$, and $T(S, C_i)$ represents the trust value of component C_i for S, where $1 \leq i \leq n$; Trust function $\Gamma_{(S, V(O)i}$ takes composing functions represented by F and a set of component trust values as input. A trust function can provide answer to the question "how much should a compound object version be trusted given the trust values of its components and the composing functions used to form that compound object version?" Developing a general format for a trust function is both domain and user dependent. Two common cases are discussed below.

Case 1: For a weighted average composing function $F = (w_1 * C_1) + (w_2 * C_2) + ... + (w_n * C_n)$, the corresponding trust function is

$$T(S, V^{(O)}_i)_{primary} = \Gamma_{(S, V(O)i)}(F, T(S, C_1), T(S, C_2), ..., T(S, C_n)) = w_1 * T(S,C_1) + w_2 * T(S,C_2) + ... + w_n * T(S, C_n)$$

where $w_1, w_2, ..., w_n$ are real numbers in the range [0, 1] and they add up to 1. Intuitively, if a composing function has the format as a weighted average, then the same parameters in the composing function are used to integrate the trust value of each component in order to calculate the trust value of the compound object version.

Case 2: For the composing function $F = c * A$, where c is a constant parameter, the corresponding trust function is

$$\Gamma_{(S, V(O)i)}(F, c, T(S, V^{(O)}_i)) = T(S, V^{(O)}_i)$$

5. OBJECT VERSION ATTRIBUTE VALUE DISCOVERY

The attribute values of a given object version are important for an evaluator to assess the trustworthiness of the object version in term of its quality and security. Attribute value discovery is to collect (calculate, test, analyze, or verify) the values of a set of attributes given an object version. Some trust attribute values of an object version can be calculated such as a owner's reputation and trustworthiness. Others can be dynamically tested, statically analyzed, or verified from the owner or a trusted authority.

The quality and security features of an object version can be tested by internal experts or external service providers. In either case, testing can be conducted statically or dynamically (see [21, 22, 23, 24, and 25] for more information about software feature testing). The former requires systematic analysis of the object version in term of its structures, algorithms, functions, etc. The source code of the object version is required for static analysis. Traditional methods for detecting security flaws include penetration analysis and formal verification of security kernels. Other general testing techniques include path testing, data-flow testing, and syntax testing. Dynamic analysis is to test the security and/or quality features of the object version in a controlled environment through a series of well-planned experiments.

Different from the above scenario, where the evaluator is responsible for verifying the quality and security features of a given object version, the ConCert project [19] requires that the producer of a code supply proofs for the security of the code. The project uses certificates to verify the security features of external programs and files. Certifiable policies cover type and memory safety (including system call or device access), control-flow safety, resource usage (CPU, Memory), abstraction boundaries, privacy and information-flow properties, and much more. Certifications are based on intrinsic properties of code, not the code producer's reputation. The proofs provided by those certificates are written in a specific machine-checkable form. There are several certified code systems: (1) Proof carrying code. Compiler produces a safety proof in logic and certification consists of proof checking; (2) Typed Assembly Language. Compiler produces type annotations for the machine code that imply safety and verification is type-checking. Both techniques work with native code and no expensive/complicated JIT compilation step is required. According to [88], the code developers follow the following procedure to supply certificated code: (1) start with program in safe language such as Java, SML, Safe C, (2) transform the code and simultaneously the reason that it is safe, and (3) finish with machine code, checkable certificate.

There are other forms of information certifications. For instance, information users can utilize redundancy check (or reworking) to verify the correctness of a given piece of information. For an active code, the provider can run the code on a given set of inputs and then the execution trace is used as a proof of the correctness of the code. For other types of information, native certifications may be used: theorem proof and facts or experiments. Those methods can be used in the proposed decision model.

6. CONCLUSIONS

This paper introduces a policy-oriented trust-based decision model for subjects to select reliable and secure information in an open system. It is a crucial step for achieving security and quality of service in such an open system where there is no single authority and where traditional security models do not work effectively. The proposed model allows a user to specify what features of external information it can't accept and what features are favorable to it. Based on this model, an example of a policy specification has been defined. *Selector*, a high-level policy language, has been developed to express the user-defined policy specification that allows automatic evaluation of the trustworthiness of available object versions of a given object and select one that meets the user's requirements for information quality and security. The paper also introduces object trustworthy calculations, which are important for users to make trust decisions. Compared with other decision-making approaches, our trust selection model is easy to understand and can be applied in computing systems. The model allows users to specify their customized policies to address their concerns for information integrity.

ACKNOWLEDGMENT

We are thankful to Dr. Robert L. Herklotz for his support, which made this work possible.

REFERENCES

1. Y. Zuo and B. Panda, "Component Based Trust Management in the Context of a Virtual Organization," In Proceedings of the 2005 ACM Symposium on Applied Computing, New Mexico, USA, March 2005

2. A. Josang, "An Algebra for Assessing Trust in Certification Chains," In Proceedings of the Internet Society 1999 Network and Distributed System Security Symposium, San Diego, USA, 1999

3. A. Rahaman, S. Hales, "Supporting Trust in Virtual Communities," In Proceedings of the 33rd Hawaii International Conference on System Sciences, Hawaii, USA, 2000

4. I. Ray, S. Chakraborty, "A Vector Model of Trust for Developing Trustworthiness Systems," In Proceedings of the 9th European Symposium on Research in Computer Security, Sophia Antipolis, French Riviera, France, 2004

5. T. Yu, X. Ma, M. Winslett, "PRUNES: An Efficient and Complete Strategy for Automated Trust Negotiation over the Internet," In Proceedings of the Conference on Computer and Communication Security, Athens, Greece, 2000

6. T. Yu, and M. Winslett, "Interoperable Strategies in Automated Trust Negotiation," In Proceedings of the Conference on Computer and Communication Security, Philadelphia, USA, 2001
7. W. Winsborough, N. Li, "Towards Practical Automated Trust Negotiation," In Proceedings of the IEEE 3rd International Workshop on Policies for Distributed Systems and Networks, IEEE Press, Monterey, USA, June 2002
8. L. Xiong, L. Liu, "A Reputation-based Trust Model for Peer-to-Peer E-Commerce Communities," In Proceedings of the IEEE Conference on E-Commerce, Newport Beach, California, USA, 2003
9. B .Yu, M. P. Singh, "Towards a Probabilistic Model of Distributed Reputation Management," In Proceedings of the 4th Workshop on Deception, Fraud and Trust in Agent Societies, Montreal, Canada, 2001
10. L. Mui, M. Mohtashemi, A. Halberstadt, "A Computational Model for Trust and Reputation," In Proceedings of the 35th Hawaii International Conference on System Science, Hawaii, USA, 2002
11. "An Introduction to Cryptography, in PGP 6.5.1 User's Guide," Network Associates Inc., p.11-36, http://fi.pgpi.org/doc/pgpintro/
12. Adams, C. and S. Farrell, "RFC2510 – Internet X.509 Public Key Infrastructure Certificate Management Protocols" http://www.cis.ohio-state.edu/htbin/rfc/rfc2510.html, 1999
13. Feigenbaum, J., "Overview of the AT&T Labs Trust Management Project: Position Paper," In Proceedings of the 1998 Cambridge University Workshop on Trust and Delegation, UK, 1998
14. Blaz, M., "Using the KeyNote Trust Management System," AT&T Research Labs, http://www.crypto.com/trustmgt/kn.html, 1999
15. Chu, Y.-H., J. Feigenbaum, B. LaMacchia, P. Resnick and M. Strauss, "REFEREE: Trust Management for Web Applications," AT&T Research Labs, http://www.farcaster.com/papers/www6-referee, 1997
16. P. McDaniel, "On Context in Authorization Policy," In *Proceedings of the Eighth ACM Symposium on Access Control Models and Technologies*, Como, Italy,June 2003

17. N. Damianou, N. Dulay, E. Lupu, and M. Sloman, "The Ponder Policy Specification Language," In Proceedings of the Policy Workshop 2001, Bristol, UK, January 2001

18. L. Kagal, "Rei: A Policy Language for the Me-Centric Project," HP Labs Technology Report, 2002

19. Chang, B., Crary, K., DeLap, M., Harper, R. and Liszka, J., "Trustless Grid Computing in ConCert" http://www.cs.cmu/~concert/talks/Murphy2002Trustless/trustless.ppt#1
20. M. Bishop, "Computer Security – Art and Science," Addison-Wesley, 2003

21. C. E. Landwehr, A. R. Bull, J. P. McDermott, and W. S. Choi, "A Taxonomy of Computer Program Security Flaws," *Computing Surveys*, 26(3): pp. 211-255, 1994

22.K. Ashcraft and D. Engler, "Using programmer-written Compiler Extension to Catch Security Holes," In *Proceedings of 2002 IEEE Symposium on Security and Privacy*, pp. 143-159, Berkeley, CA, USA, 2002

23.M. Bishop and M. Dilger, "Checking for Race Conditions in File Accesses," *Computing Systems*, 9(2), 1996

24.H. Chen, H. and D. Wagner, "An Infrastructure of Examining Security Properties of Software," In *Proceedings of ACM Conference on Computer and Communications Security (CCS)*, Washington DC, USA, 2002

25. B .V. Chess, "Improving Computer Security Using Extending Static Checking," In *Proceedings of 2002 IEEE Symposium on Security and Privacy*, pp. 160-173, Berkeley, CA, USA, 2002

SCALABLE ACCESS POLICY ADMINISTRATION (INVITED PAPER)

Opinions and a Research Agenda

Arnon Rosenthal
The MITRE Corporation

Abstract: The emerging world of large, loosely coupled information systems requires major changes to the way we approach security research. For many years, we have proposed construct after construct to enhance the power and scope of policy languages. Unfortunately, this focus has led to models whose complexity is unmanageable, to reinventing technologies that other subdisciplines have done better, and to assumptions that large enterprises simply do not satisfy. We argue that it is time to emphasize a different challenge: radical scale-up. To achieve this, it will be crucial to emphasize simplicity, integration with (non-security) enterprise knowledge, and modularity for both models and administration. This position paper will illustrate the problems, and describe possible ways to achieve the desired capabilities.

Key words: Policy administration; access policy; scale; role based access control; semantic web; simplicity; security; privacy.

1. INTRODUCTION

We can no longer rely on inaccessibility to protect data integrity or confidentiality. In ancient times (i.e., the 1980s), only a few users could reach each data object, due to barriers of system connectivity, protocols, and data format standards. These barriers have diminished, due to cheaper storage and communication, standards, software advances (e.g., service oriented architectures, data integration environments), and new practices (e.g., cross-domain guards examine traffic to protect networks previously isolated for security). In today's interconnected world, we need appropriately selective access control policies.

There are daunting challenges in administering such access control policies at enterprise scale (including virtual enterprises, such as supply chains and military coalitions). A grand challenge for our field (IFIP 11.3's name, *Data and Application Security* seems appropriate) is to create a foundation for specifying, changing, reasoning about, and enforcing such policies.

The enterprise problem seems to have two fundamentally different sorts of challenges –specific policy needs, and scale.

For accommodating the many specific real world policy needs, our field has developed a rich base of "point" techniques. These include privilege limitation (e.g., negative policies, predicates, revocation), result filtering, separation of duty, inference control, temporal and spatial conditions, audit log mining, chains of trust, and so on – infinitely. The *scale* picture is less encouraging, due both to sheer volume (of enterprise knowledge and of policy specification), and to the problem of integrating the different techniques (from above) into commercially viable, extensible tools.

***Our Thesis:* Our research community should treat scale as the *central* unmet requirement for an enterprise security system.**

Large scale data and application security is challenging both for enterprises and for the vendors who build tool suites to simplify administration. In our opinion, progress has been very slow, and one reason is the lack of research results that are worthwhile and ready to transfer. Many researchers' models contain good insights, but are neither simple enough nor robust enough to have attractive cost/benefit. Enterprises and tool vendors therefore choose to invest in other areas (such as GUIs to existing engines).

Most current research (in our unscientific sampling) concerns new specific capabilities. We pose the questions: Will we improve most by creating new features which will then be difficult to integrate? Or will techniques that promote scalability (both policy and integration) have a higher payoff?

1.1 Paper Goals and Roadmap

This is a very informal position paper, intended to stimulate discussion of the "big picture". We ask throughout whether conventional data security research (e.g., at ACM SACMAT, VLDB TDM, or IFIP 11.3 Data and Application Security conferences) is on track to produce a foundation for scalable security administration. Our goal is to provoke debate, and to provide useful questions and metaphors. To that end, we make broad claims about (painfully) vague notions like "simplicity". We hope our claims are

80% true; we welcome feedback and refinements. We leave it to the reader to determine whether our diagnoses apply to their own research.

Our aim is to encourage researchers to produce results that will be useful for enterprise problems. Elegant results are always good research; even if the original motivation is weak, they provide insight into other problems. Intricate techniques for minor challenges are not. Assemblages of incomplete and conceptually overlapping capabilities are suitable for initial exploration, but they add little clarity to techniques or architectures, and their immaturity makes them poor investments for implementers. We focus on being more *scalable* in proposed features, models and system designs. We hope the criteria remind researchers of interesting questions, and reviewers of under-emphasized evaluation criteria.

To be clear, we believe that a result can be valuable without being enterprise-ready. In fact, we point at a paper as problematic for scalability only if we felt it had other significant research contributions. But it is a serious problem for the field when perhaps 80% of results violate scalability tenets. An enterprise wants to build its initial systems on ideas that extend to large scale, not to require a wrenching transition and separate skill base.

Three important prerequisites for scalability seem absent from the majority of access control research papers:

- *Simplicity*: We should not needlessly sacrifice the power to capture enterprise complexities. Yet if our formalisms are too expressive or too complex, we will lose two critical capabilities: the leverage of automated reasoning-based assistants, and ability to widely share the administrative load (e.g., with domain experts and less technical security personnel). Section 2 proposes a principle – ruthless simplicity -- for avoiding both dangers.
- *Reaching out*: Access policies involve organization and domain knowledge, and express conditions on all sorts of data (e.g., Time and Space). Unfortunately, we often treat access control as a self-contained subsystem, both for formalisms (e.g., role based access controls, spatial data types) and for enterprise descriptions (e.g., the enterprise's organization chart as part of a role hierarchy). As a result, access control systems have limited access to external tools and to enterprise knowledge.
- *Modularity*. Few research papers componentize their models to export well-defined services. Fewer still define interfaces that reach out for services beyond the paper's core idea. Research ideas would be much easier to use in large systems if they fit with other peoples' partial solutions, instead of specifying how to handle the peripheral issues.

Section 1.2 reviews general requirements for access controls, and explains what we mean by Scalability. Sections 2 and 3 respectively discuss

Simplicity and the need to reach out, rather than "do it yourself" just for the security system.

1.2 Requirements Discussion

The enterprise's tasks include integrating the tools from multiple vendors, training administrators, and especially administering the policies. Tasks involved in administering the policies include:

- *State policy from business viewpoint.* For example, a hospital upper management committee might state a governing policy, in English, over broad classes of information such as Patient Treatment, Patient Outcomes, Hospital Cost data, and so forth, for release to appropriate medical personnel, researchers, and regulators.
- *Based on the governing policies, derive a "concrete" policy on implemented objects.* Upper management does not specify a policy for every object in the automated system (e.g., table, message, or service). Instead, one must implement the intent of the business policy by deriving a suitable policy to be evaluated upon access to each concrete object, e.g., for Read privileges on a Toxin_Screen message type.
- *Translate the derived policy down to the physical enforcers.* These are likely to use a variety of languages (e.g., DBMS and middleware, with vendor variants.) The forces for heterogeneity (e.g., mergers, decades of legacy, decentralized acquisition decisions, distinct needs; virtual organizations that must interoperate with many constituent companies) are not disappearing. Diversity will continue.
- *Understand the net effect of all the policies that the system is actually enforcing.*
- *Change policy, and understand the consequences.* To help manage change, some models propose ways to edit policy sets, e.g., temporarily enabling or disabling. We are unsure if these belong in a security model or just in an editor. Automated reasoning is needed to help administrators understand how a change affects an object of concern to them.

Today, most of the above tasks are done manually. Many of the techniques scale poorly in terms of policy specification, administrator training and creating tool environments. Enterprises therefore compromise, to reduce specification labor and required skills. For policy, they can manage only coarse distinctions, e.g., based on what organization a person belongs to, or what data the network is on. The resulting policies are not really appropriate.

Tools are also inadequate. Vendors find that access control tool suites involve many parts, often more than one company can provide. Standards (e.g., XACML) are currently weakly supported. An enterprise faces a substantial consulting cost to integrate or migrate the various products used within it.

2. SIMPLICITY

Enterprises' policy management involves many people, and a huge number of policies. Tools need to provide numerous services (e.g., specification, analysis, enforcement) for a large number of constructs. To scale, the central foundations need to be *very* simple. A complex initial model when compounded by implementation needs, will render the whole confusing, opaque, and inextensible. In addition, formalism expressiveness (which enables richer input to reasoning and tools) needs to balance with the computational cost or undecidability of complex formalisms. Finally, administrators will reject features or environments that seem too difficult. We need models usable by administrators may who are unskilled or unmotivated – think Homer Simpson rather than CS graduate student.

We fear that in our data security research community, most proposed models are already too complicated, and thus, we believe, an unsuitable conceptual foundation. We speculate that researchers are motivated to seek a model that will meet all real requirements. The usual response to an unmet requirement is to add constructs to the model. Complexity is the consequence.

Many of the challenges faced by enterprise policies were previously faced by data management, and we find the parallels provocative and informative. For example, both data management and access control policies touch all the enterprise's structured data and many of its services. Both areas need to empower domain experts rather than rely on technical experts. Both have employed declarative formalisms (e.g., SQL, role hierarchies) that enable automated reasoning. Below, Section 2.1 gives a whirlwind tour of database history and its relevance to access control. Section 2.2 focuses on simplicity.

2.1 Parallels with the History of Data Management

Research has played a major role in creating the DBMS industry, which is large (according to Gartner, >$10B [PM]) and furnishes the base tier of enterprise architectures. Somewhat surprisingly (to this researcher), the contribution may not be primarily from innovation. The head of Microsoft's database research observes that developers (who outnumber researchers 60:1) are quite smart enough to innovate. Rather, the crucial and unique contribution of researchers was in clarification and formalization, i.e., *simplification.* [Lo]. This seems a key role for access control researchers, too.

Looking at databases in enterprises, we note that the main cost of database ownership is now salaries for administration, rather than hardware or software purchase. That is, increasingly, administration cost and responsiveness often determine if an application is cost effective. Today, access control activities at MITRE's sponsors (typically, large US government organizations) are mainly at an earlier stage. They are now deploying mechanisms that controls rely on (e.g., authentication, trust, policy engines, role and attribute based access control). There is also concern about efficient evaluation. Within a few years, however, we expect that policy administration will be recognized as a major roadblock, in cost, project delays, and guaranteeing adequate assurance.

Another lesson is that database tools were able to greatly reduce the skill requirements. As design methodologies were originally created, there was discussion of how to teach their ideas to the mass of business experts who were suddenly designing data schemas. This never happened. Instead, the subtleties (e.g., dependency theory) were built into the tools, and most administrators learned just enough to supply the required inputs. Where the inputs to a technique were too hard to supply (e.g., multi-valued dependencies), the technique withered. So rather than rely on better trained administrators (perhaps Lisa Simpson?), access control also should resolve subtleties *inside* the tools.

Having even an imperfectly-observed standard DBMS language was tremendously valuable, in an unanticipated way. The original goal – enabling enterprises to port from one product to another—was rarely cost effective. However, vendors of application development and end user query tools could (at bearable cost) make their products work with any of the ~5 major DBMS products. The result was the development of the "front end" application development industry, distinct from DBMS vendors. A similar split might be beneficial for security tools. In fact, the standard for Role Based Access Control appears to have been highly beneficial [NIST]. We can also learn from mistakes of DBMS standardization. As the SQL standard expanded, there was too little investment in abstraction to "factor" common portions out of the new pieces. Partly as a result, the detailed standard is huge, has minor inconsistencies in treatments of similar situations (e.g., access controls for procedures versus views), and is understandable only to a small priesthood. It is not too soon to seek a more elegant, more formal basis for XACML (e.g., to move difficult-to-scale conflict resolution to relevance predicates).

SQL security is not the principle means by which enterprises protect data; most protections are in middleware or in application code. Still, the number of systems using it is still very large. Extrapolating to all vendors the estimate that 30% of Oracle installations make nontrivial use of SQL security (W. Maimone, personal communication), we have 30% of >1 million installed systems. Oracle has offered both roles and delegation (grant option) since the 1980s, and recently Microsoft SQL Server implemented some negative privileges.

SQL *industrial* experiences deserve more attention than they get from security researchers – even if one (reasonably) believes that SQL's strengths (e.g., grant option) deserve less attention than the general predicates of XACML. For example, the very useful survey [BS] focuses only on the academic literature. Roles are indeed recent – in the research literature. Also, it describes time-sensitive Revoke semantics from early research papers, rather than the easier-to-administer time-insensitive operations from DBMS products and the SQL standard. Researchers could use SQL security as a source of experience with various constructs (e.g., how much is delegation used?) and as prior art when proposing new constructs. Perhaps more important, researchers could help abstract and extend SQL. Specific needs, especially those suitable for graduate student projects, are discussed in [RW]

In the 1980s, demands arose to add many new datatypes to DBMSs, e.g., for temporal, spatial, and textual data. SQL now includes low-end constructs such as a DATE datatype and simple text matches with wildcards. But the community rejected adding a *particular* form of each rich domain. Needs were simply too varied, e.g., should spatial locations use flat or spherical geometry, and the specialized expertise was outside the database community. Instead, the major vendors have provided general mechanisms for adding new data types (e.g., to specify language operators, storage, indexing, etc.), and then partnered with other organizations to meet the wide variety of specific needs.

Finally, we learned that to get administrators to supply accurate, current metadata, one must have the right incentives. Data files and queries are generated from database schemas, so these are current. In contrast, database conceptual models (e.g., entity relationship) almost invariably become obsolete shelfware after a system is deployed. Mandates to keep it up to date are ignored, or else errors creep in. As a result, quality problems soon make the conceptual models unusable. Similarly, we will find it difficult to keep policies or role hierarchies up to date if the burden is entirely on security administrators. Where possible, one wants to exploit information that users have other reasons to keep current.

2.2 Getting a Simpler Model

Access control models in the research literature have become quite complex. They involve a wide variety of features, often with unscalable assumptions (e.g., "all metadata is public") and restrictions on applicability (e.g., not applying to views or services). In the world of policy engines, some proposed languages (e.g., Ponder) are so powerful that they can be used only by professional programmers, and tools cannot effectively analyze their behavior. Even the simpler OASIS standard language XACML has a wide variety of features that seem difficult to mesh with policies that apply to different granules of the database (table, row-set, or "all data with personally identifiable information").

We have a dilemma: All these complications were motivated by real requirements, but the whole will not scale. To escape it, we propose a two-model (or perhaps n-model) approach. We would not design the same vehicle to act as both a bicycle and a fuel truck. Analogously, proposals [KKKR] that we create a unified formalism for all our work may be suboptimal.

We base our thinking on database (and pre-database) history. In the early 1970s, many practitioners recognized the need to scale data sharing beyond the files managed by a single business application. Two lines of work ensued. Some researchers looked at the full spectrum of data management requirements, and observed the need for additional operators. They therefore added richer datatypes and persistence to COBOL, PL/1, and other popular general purpose programming languages. The result was to make the languages more complex and skill intensive. Also, since the languages were already Turing complete, there was only limited ability to provide analysis, synthesis, query optimization, and automated GUI generation tools.

At the same time, IBM researchers took a radical step – they divided business data processing into two portions. The new portion provided a clean, rigorous abstraction of manipulations of tables (relations). The "old" portion consisted of applications coded in general purpose programming languages, plus requests to the relational database. The researchers also took on the difficult task of interfacing the two portions.

The relational model they created was ultra-simple, insufficient on its own even for routine tasks such as generating hierarchically structured reports. Yet this is the approach that succeeded.

The relational researchers ruthlessly exiled all tasks they could not (at that time) handle cleanly. But within their chosen arena, they could support a simple abstraction with very powerful services. SQL was able to insulate users from details of iteration, access strategy, and file and index structures. Virtual tables were definable, and were useful for both convenience and security. The implementations were strengthened gradually, until they could handle huge loads. As discussed in Section 2.1, an industry of application development tools developed, evolving more quickly than the performance-optimized database engines. Later decades added additional capabilities, sometimes as separate models, without (excessively) compromising tractability. For the 1990s, the great extensions were triggers, distribution, and objects (including the ability to plug in numerous managers for temporal and spatial data). In our decade, DBMSs are supporting irregular and hierarchical data (i.e., XML). The (relatively) simple models have enabled great progress and became the foundation layer of enterprises' data architectures.

Of course, there are many aspects of database history that access control researchers and tool developers ought not to emulate. First, the interface to the residue capabilities is awkward. (M. Stonebraker memorably referred to the interface between databases and application code as "like gluing an apple to a pancake".) The conceptual and run-time costs of this interface must be included in assessing SQL cost/benefit. Also, databases lack a clean model of sequential execution, and this has complicated both the programming language interface and event-based features (triggers, handling constraint violations). Researchers need to continue extending the abstract foundation, rather than leave all extensions to ordinary programmers. Finally, as we will discuss in Section 3.2, we should keep closely aligned with abstract models of enterprise knowledge.

Much security research today resembles adding operators to create persistent COBOL. To change this, we make a radical proposal"

Proposal 1: Take "simplicity" as an absolute constraint on for the "foundation" model

That is, access control research should emulate the database field by pursuing a two-model (or n model) approach. The foundational models should *rigorously* exclude anything that is not tractable for knowledge capture, visualization, and reasoning.

This foundational model should only include treatments that are suitable for *all* uses. It might include services to create or delegate administrative rights. It should not hardwire choices that depend on semantics of the particular enterprise, e.g., whether Deny always overrides Allow. As an example of such a model, one might start with positive policies with predicates (e.g., provisions) and on object sets of different granularities. It may recognize that there are a variety of relationships among objects (e.g., IS-A, Part-Of, predicate-based restrictions as an alternative to negatives) and that each will have its own security semantics. (Section 3.2 suggests supporting just the relationships present in the OWL-DL language.)

One other line of research is badly needed – simplicity metrics. To achieve simplicity, then both researchers and acquisition contracts need to measure it, at least comparatively. Most new proposals make no attempt at the issue, and we know of no general approach. Even in our experience, we have too often conversed about model constructs, with each party claiming (to the other's puzzlement) to have a clearly simpler model. We applaud recent research that gives practitioners' insight into models' relative *logical* expressiveness [TL]. However, logical expressiveness gives little insight into scalability; it is central only to logicians. We hope the spirit of comparison might move on to formalizing and comparing criteria that *are* central -- simplicity and administrator workload.

3. THE TENDENCY TO "DO IT YOURSELF"

Rich access control policies involve substantial knowledge about the enterprise and its environment, e.g., relationships among users, and natural groupings of privileges. This security-*relevant* knowledge is then captured in security-*specific* formalisms, to be managed using security-*specific* tools. We contend that this approach will not be suitable for the long term. There is a rich tradition, and growing industry, of knowledge management capabilities outside the security industry, and enterprises have many other uses for such structural knowledge. The redundancy increases cost and promotes inconsistency, with neither side getting full information. We need to reuse outside resources, not reinvent them in the security system.

We now look at three examples of reinventing rather than reusing. Section 3.1 discusses specialized datatypes, e.g., for Time and Space. Section 3.2 contains the bulk of the discussion. It looks at capturing organizational descriptions within the security systems, e.g., the organization of users, privileges, data, and operations.

3.1 Specialized Datatypes

Policies need to be sensitive to temporal or spatial conditions, so researchers have proposed corresponding extensions to access control models, e.g., [BJBG, AC]. This practice seems appropriate for prototypes, but if one takes it as a proposed model, we have two serious concerns:

- *Each proposal supports just one out of many viable treatments.* For example, should a spatial extension to access control models offer 2-D or 3-D, flat or spherical or ovoid geometry for the earth? Each is needed by a large community; each requires a complex implementation, including distance computations search indexes, and displays.

- *Lack of expertise.* We have expertise in security. The spatial and temporal research communities are far more expert in their domains. Do we intend for reviewers at security conferences to judge the novelty of a proposed spatial model?

It would be *far* better to allow applications and enterprises to reach out. Applications employ dozens of spatial and temporal facilities, to meet their own needs. Services are also available for text, imagery, audio, and video. We should not settle for one treatment in each domain, and then keep up with progress. An attempt to implement our own best try will leave us with a few obsolescent functions.

Since access controls do need to cope with data from these rich worlds, what should the responsibilities of security researchers? First, we should describe policy needs involving these multimedia types. Second, provide design guidance in being able to plug such datatypes into a security model. Is any change needed in security policies and tools when query language is extended with new datatypes? Will policies require very fast checks of certain predicates, and hence suitable indexes? There may also be architectural guidance, e.g., about whether the extensions are better made part of the query system or the security system, and whether there are special vulnerabilities (e.g., to resetting a workstation clock, or the need to evaluate security-sensitive predicates before transferring control to user-defined functions). Finally, researchers could identify *general security capabilities* one needs in order to plug in such predicates well. For example, a *general* (non-spatial) security feature that understands "contained in" might be useful when administrators grant access to large spatial regions, but each user requests ask for a tiny rectangle.

3.2 Describing the Organization

Access control decisions need to examine a myriad of considerations about the user, the request, the object accessed, and the world context. One major complication is that the policy-maker's terminology probably differs from that used in the automated system's requests, databases, and messages. For example, the policy may refer to "Product Planning", "Customer-Related Information" and "Massachusetts customers" while the request comes from a Yield-Analyst, asking about Deliveries to Zipcode 02138.

Many organizations use role based access control (*RBAC*) to begin to organize such knowledge. The textbook [FMC] provides excellent descriptions of many RBAC approaches, which for our purposes includes both pure roles (NIST) and also role+group approaches. We believe that RBAC designers found a sweet spot for the 1980s and 90s, offering the following strengths:

- An easily-grasped means of organizing knowledge, with an intuitive visualization (acyclic digraph) and editing operations.
- A standard, which enables products to interoperate. (For example one vendor can provide a management interface, and another an enforcer).
- A formal and computationally efficient inference theory. (RBAC infers authorization, based on role activations and reachability).

Unfortunately, RBAC is painful to apply to large enterprises [KKKR], for the reasons listed below. Section 3.2.1 will elaborate and discuss the limitations of access control researchers' proposed ameliorations.

- The administration team needs to convert the enterprise's complex structure to a single graph (or perhaps a role and a group graph). Having one graph for enterprise structure is analogous to defining an enterprise database using one table.
- RBAC formalisms are confined to the access control community. One cannot expect a rich base of tools, or of trained people, compared to the resources for knowledge management in general.
- Enterprise knowledge is split into roles versus ordinary data. Such barriers have very predictable effects, reducing the information available on each side. Yet role information may be useful for budgeting (e.g., how many people are in Medical roles) and ordinary management information (e.g., what customer is Joe assigned to today) is useful for security. Attempts to import data across the barrier tend to be expensive and incomplete.

A decade ago, general knowledge management formalisms could not compete with RBAC. For example, Datalog offered more representational and inference power, but lacks an interface standard, a convenient typing mechanism, and a graph visualization. Other formalisms had tiny user communities and inefficient inference (e.g., the AI community's Knowledge Interface Format). Despite the above limitations, RBAC was the right choice then. But times are changing.

We believe that the "general knowledge" approach is on the verge of being industrially viable. OWL (the web ontology language) is a standard endorsed by the World Wide Web Consortium (*W3C*). A significant experimenter and early adopter community uses OWL for knowledge capture and as a basis for data integration. Inference is complete and reasonably efficient at the first two compliance levels, OWL Lite and OWL DL.

Proposal 2: It is time to move access control research and tools to general knowledge base formalisms (perhaps using OWL) rather than by adding features to RBAC.

It is time to apply the principle "Don't do it all alone! Access policies need to reflect the structure of the enterprise and its environment. We need to exploit both knowledge management expertise, and to share knowledge with the rest of the enterprise. RBAC was a fine idea for its time, and its core functionalities (aggregating users and privileges, activation for authorization) will always be needed. But it is time to reorganize to separate its security aspects (role activation as precursor to authorization, policies on which groups can exercise which roles, under what circumstances) from its enterprise knowledge. By using OWL, we can get:

- *Better expressive power and structuring, while (mostly) preserving simplicity.* GUIs can hide the complexity from administrators with simple tasks. The system architecture is simplified by removing the dichotomy and the extra formalism.
- *Larger user and tool communities.* The semantic web community is already beginning to provide skilled users and tools (including freeware) for OWL, including interfaces, reasoning engines, and import/export wrappers to exchange data to other formalisms (relations, XML, etc.)

3.2.1 RBAC and its proposed extensions

RBAC (especially the "only roles" form from NIST) makes enforcement easy (no doubt a factor in adoption by vendors), but is impoverished as a means of describing an enterprise. We now discuss limitations both of RBAC and of attempts at extensions.

RBAC offers just only a small, fixed set of types, essentially only Role and perhaps Group. (To a first approximation, User and Privilege are just singleton Groups and Roles). When administrators map their understanding of the enterprise to a role hierarchy, the mapping resides in human heads -- notoriously low capacity, unreliable storage devices. This mapping is not explicitly stored, hard to edit, not backed up, hard to share among the different heads, and inaccessible to display or reasoning tools.

A first step beyond NIST RBAC is to add a second fundamental node type – group. (This step has been well described by Sandhu and by Osborn [FKC]). Next, [KKKR] proposes a third primary type, representing processes (i.e., operations). These fixed extensions help administration, but are not sufficient. For example, for grouping people in an organization, one aggregates along many dimensions – rank, organization, project they work on, skills, and so forth. Oracle Label Security offers an extensible grouping capability, but it is proprietary and limited to access control uses. It is best to let enterprises define their own descriptive categories. They need a general mechanism to define new types.

The need to express conditionals is well known, e.g., that Gold_Frequent_Fliers are Passengers with Mileage > 50000, or that certain privileges require mileage >75000. To augment User with attributes like Mileage, several researchers allow roles to have parameters [LMW, KKKR]. However, we now have two differently-behaved categories, first class (roles, groups) and second class (parameters that cannot aggregate into graphs). We also need to support a parameter mechanism (which OWL natively supports as properties) as well as a predicate language.

Attribute Based Access Control (ABAC) seems simultaneously more elegant and more powerful for enterprise modeling. As a security model, it provides an authorization rule. The bulk of it, though, is concerned with defining attributes and their structuring operators. For example, [WWJ] provides a technically powerful and elegant logic for the KM aspect of security. It seems to have roughly the power of OWL, perhaps a bit more.

Yet while the research contribution is real, vendors are unlikely to flock to it. Despite its technical merits, this logic is supported only by its authors. Even if one looks at the underlying technology, Datalog, there is no standard software interface that would enable tool interoperability. More ambitiously, one wants a rich variety of services for reasoning, explanation, and exchanging data with outside. To obtain these, access control should plan to adopt whatever standard becomes widely used in the knowledge management community.

Clustering around a standard can even improve research quality. When each paper defines its own formalism, we reduce the opportunities for synergy -- among access control researchers, among our prototypes, with researchers in other subdisciplines (e.g., heterogeneous databases), and with industry. Also, with a self-defined model one may completely ignore many necessary features (e.g., metadata and views in SQL security). If instead one starts with a fuller model and explicitly defers some features, one will probably avoid unnecessary incompatibility, and junior researchers will see the gaps and fill them.

From the other side, semantic web researchers [IJITM, KF+, QA, AS] are interested in using OWL in access controls. Many of the semantic web researchers' insights apply to our problem, but there may be difficulties. First, some models seem complex; e.g., the override rules in [QA] look plausible but lack theoretical justification and will be difficult for administrators to apply. More fundamentally, they aim at data that is already in OWL, which includes little of today's data.

Our formulation is subtly different. We define access controls' target as all enterprise data (e.g., files and relational and XML objects), but do not require that the target data be modeled semantically in OWL. Semantically-aware access controls need enriched semantic descriptions (e.g., in OWL) only for structures that policies will exploit. Roughly speaking, this is structure that would be expressed in a role hierarchy. No OWL wrapping is needed for target data, even if that data is referenced in simple predicates. Creation of OWL models can proceed incrementally, only when applications (including access policies) need it.

To summarize, we believe security research would have more influence if, instead of exploiting obscure formalisms, it built on a more popular technology that gives an 80% solution. The researchers could then identify requirements and techniques for the extensions that security needs.

4. SUMMARY

As a researcher from a database rather than security background, we have observed that concern with *administrative* scalability have not been principal drivers in the security community. Many proposals seem, unnecessarily, to omit simplicity, reaching out, and modularity. We have described several important aspects of scalability, and given our impressions of which currents in data security research seem to promote it.

REFERENCES

[AC] V. Atluri, S. Chun, An Access Control Model for Geo-spatial Data, *IEEE Transactions on Dependable and Secure Systems*, October-December, 2004

[AS] S. Agrawal, B. Sprick Access Control for Semantic Web Services, *IEEE ICSW*, 2004

[BJBG] R. Bhatti, J. Joshi, E. Bertino, A. Ghafoor, X-GTRBAC Admin: A Decentralized Administration Model for Enterprise Wide Access Control, *ACM SACMAT Conference*, Yorktown Heights, 2004

[BS] E. Bertino, R. Sandhu, Database Security—Concepts, Approaches, and Challenges, *IEEE Transactions On Dependable And Secure Computing*, January-March 2005

[CCF] S. Castano, S. De Capitani di Vimercati, M.G. Fugini, Automated Derivation of Global Authorizations for Database Federations, *Journal of Computer Security*, 1997

[FKC] D Ferraiolo, R. Kuhn, R. Chandramouli, *Role Based Access Control*, Artech House, 2004

[GO] E Gudes and M. Olivier, Security Policies in Replicated and Autonomous Databases, IFIP11.3 Database Security 1998

[IJITM] Call For papers Special Issue on: Access Control and Inference Control for the Semantic Web, International Journal of Information Technology and Management (IJITM) http://www.inderscience.com/browse/callpaper.php?callID=189

[KF+] L. Kagal, T. Finin, M. Paolucci, N. Srinivasan, and K. Sycara, G. Denker, Authorization and Privacy for Semantic Web Services, *IEEE Intelligent Systems*, 2004

[KKKR] A. Kern, M. Kuhlmann, R. Kuropka, A. Ruthert, A Meta Model for Authorisations in Application Security Systems and their Integration into RBAC Administration, *ACM SACMAT Conf.* Yorktown Heights, NY 2004.

[LMW] N. Li, J. Mitchell, W. Winsborough: Design of a Role-Based Trust-Management Framework. *IEEE Symposium on Security and Privacy 2002*

[Lo] D. Lomet, *A Role for Research in the Database Industry, ACM Computing Surveys 28(4es), Dec. 1996,*

[NIST] National Institute of Science and Technology (website) Role Based Access Control http://csrc.nist.gov/rbac/

[Oasis] Oasis Consortium, eXtensible Access Control Markup Language (XACML) and Security Application Markup Language (SAML), http://www.oasis-open.org/

[PM] T. Prickett-Morgan, Gartner Says Database Market Continued Its Recovery in 2004, UNIX Guardian, June 9, 2005

[QA] L. Qin, V. Atluri, Concept-level Access Control for the Semantic Web, *ACM Workshop on XML Security,* 2003

[RW] A. Rosenthal, M. Winslett Security of Shared Data in Large Systems: State of the Art and Research Directions, Tutorial, *ACM SIGMOD Conf,* 2004, and *VLDB.* 2004

[TL] M. Tripunitara, N. Li, Comparing the power of access control models, *ACM conference on Computer and communications security,* 2004

[WWJ] L. Wang, D. Wijesekera, S. Jajodia, A Logic-based Framework for Attribute based Access Control, *ACM FMSE* 2004

ACKNOWLEDGEMENTS

This work was supported by the technology program at the MITRE Corporation. The author benefited greatly from Frank Manola's insights about the semantic web.

SEMANTIC INFORMATION INFRASTRUCTURE PROTECTION (INVITED ABSTRACT)

Paul Thompson
Dartmouth College, Hanover, New Hampshire 03755, Paul.Thompson@dartmouth.edu

Abstract: The information infrastructure, consisting of the Internet and numerous intranets, extranets, and other networks, is a key national critical infrastructure, interwoven with other critical infrastructures. Protecting the information infrastructure is important in its own right, and also because of the steadily increasing interdependence of other critical infrastructures on the information infrastructure. This paper describes an approach to information infrastructure protection that was developed as part of the semantic hacking project. Attacks on computer and other networked systems can be categorized as physical, syntactic and semantic. Autonomous agents being fed misinformation in the battlespace is a primary example of a semantic attack. Physical attacks seek to destroy hardware, while syntactic attacks, such as worms and viruses target the network infrastructure. Attacks specifically against a human user of system are also referred to as cognitive attacks. Because misinformation and deception play a much more significant role in intelligence and security informatics than in other informatics disciplines, such as science, medicine, and the law, such an emerging discipline must concern itself with semantic attacks and countermeasures.

Key words: Infrastructure Protection; Network Security; Semantic Attacks.

Author Index

Erratum

The Publisher regrets that the following figures on pages 86 and 90 were obscured during the printing of the title: *Security Management, Integrity, and Internal Control in Information Systems*, edited by P. Dowland (Eds.), Springer, ISBN: 0-387-29826-6.

The publisher wishes to correct the following text on page 172 in the title: *Security Management, Integrity, and Internal Control in Information Systems*, edited by P. Dowland (Eds.), Springer, ISBN: 0-387-29826-6. The sentence "...;ISO 17799 is mainly used to address HOW issues…" should read "...;ISO 17799 is mainly used to address WHAT issues...".

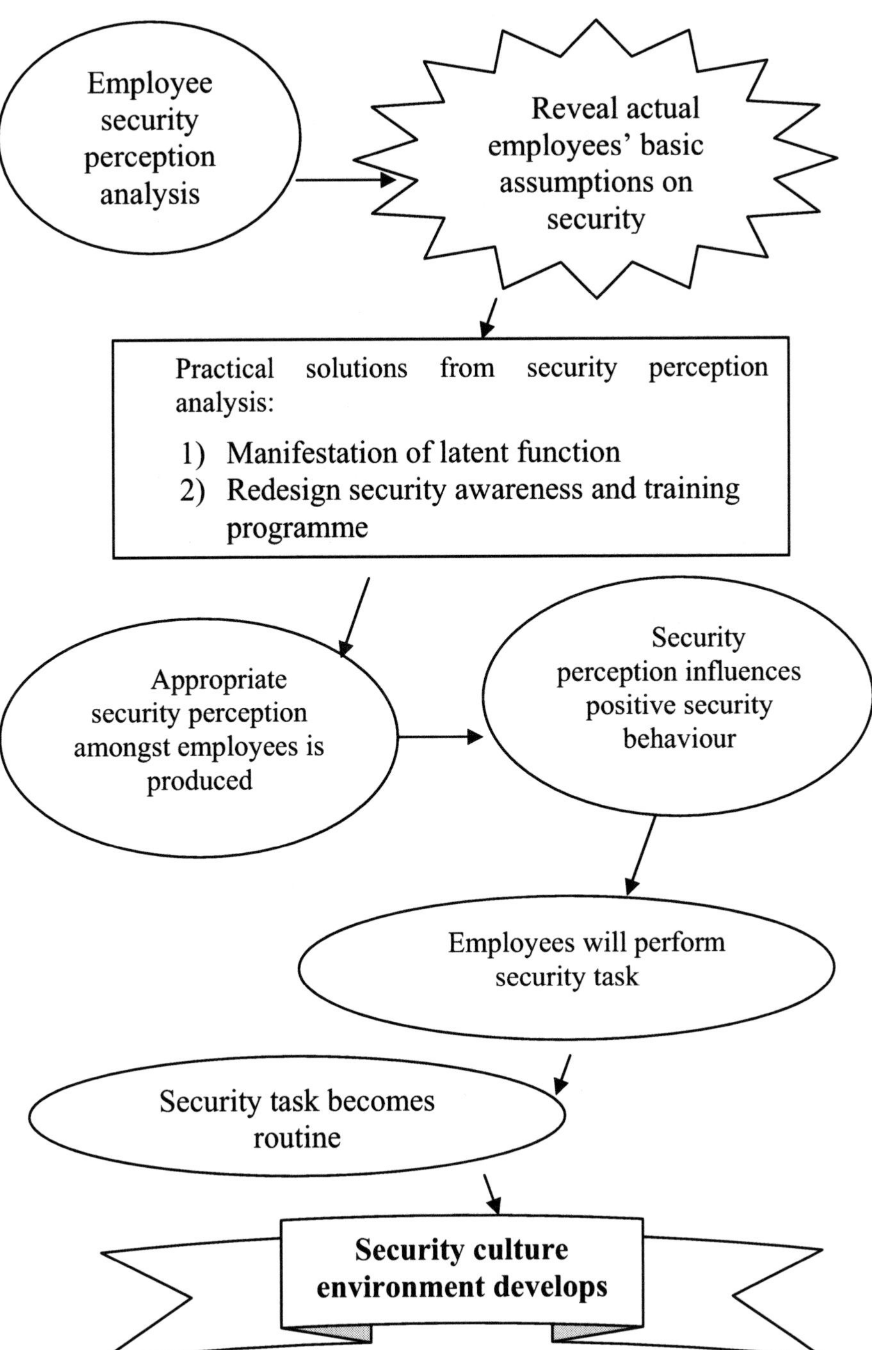

Figure 1: Employee security perception solutions for cultivation of information security culture

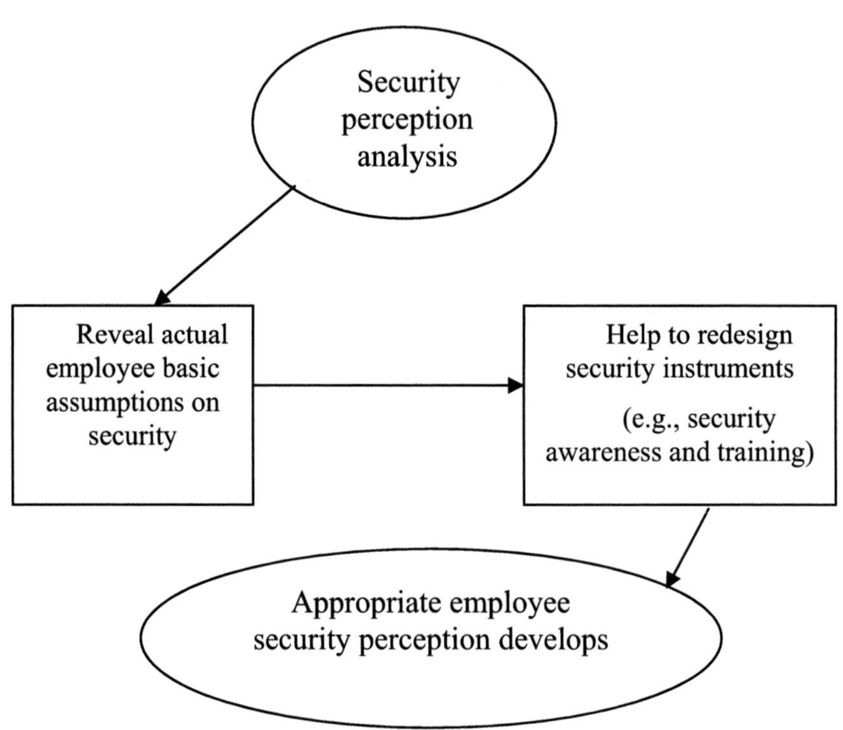

Figure 1: The Practical ways for establishing appropriate employee security perception

CPSIA information can be obtained at www.ICGtesting.com
Printed in the USA
LVOW072129071011

249658LV00006B/16/P

9 780387 298269